20.75

THE TRIBES OF THE
ASHANTI HINTERLAND

A *Ten'dana*

THE TRIBES OF THE
ASHANTI HINTERLAND

BY

Capt. R. S. RATTRAY

WITH A CHAPTER BY
Professor D. WESTERMANN

VOL. I

OXFORD
AT THE CLARENDON PRESS

Oxford University Press, Ely House, London W. 1

GLASGOW NEW YORK TORONTO MELBOURNE WELLINGTON
CAPE TOWN SALISBURY IBADAN NAIROBI LUSAKA ADDIS ABABA
BOMBAY CALCUTTA MADRAS KARACHI LAHORE DACCA
KUALA LUMPUR SINGAPORE HONG KONG TOKYO

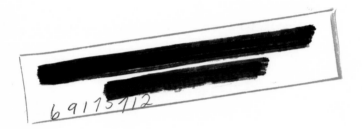

FIRST PUBLISHED 1932

REPRINTED LITHOGRAPHICALLY IN GREAT BRITAIN
AT THE UNIVERSITY PRESS, OXFORD
BY VIVIAN RIDLER
PRINTER TO THE UNIVERSITY
1969

I DEDICATE
THESE VOLUMES TO
Sir RANSFORD SLATER
AS AN EXPRESSION OF MY ADMIRATION FOR
HIS WORK AS A COLONIAL ADMINISTRATOR
AND AS A TOKEN OF MY GRATITUDE FOR
HIS ENCOURAGEMENT AND ASSISTANCE
WITHOUT WHICH THEY WOULD NOT
HAVE BEEN WRITTEN

PREFACE

THE Northern Territories of the Gold Coast comprise an area of approximately 30,600 square miles, with a population, according to the census report of 1921, of 530,355. It is bounded on the south by Ashanti; on the west by the French Ivory Coast; on the north by the Haut–Sénégal–Niger, this boundary running approximately along the 11th parallel; and on the east by the late German colony of Togoland, now known as the Mandated Area, which is divided into two parts and administered by the British and French Governments respectively.

In contrast to Ashanti with its tropical forests, the Northern Territories consist for the most part of open orchard country or treeless plains where an occasional baobab-tree breaks the otherwise flat monotony. The climate is hotter and less humid than the coastal region. The inhabitants are for the most part farmers and hunters, and the majority of them still go about naked or dressed only in skins and leaves. They may, without fear of contradiction, be described as a 'primitive people'.

The position, when an anthropological survey was first undertaken in this area among the tribes which form its half-million inhabitants, was briefly as follows—what is about to be stated can best be followed by reference to the atlas.

Across the map of the Gold Coast we find, stretching from about the 5th to the 8th parallel, the word 'Akan', postulating, and in fact correctly designating, a single linguistic and ethnic group. Turning to north of the Black Volta, we find a veritable mosaic, where, in the more remote hinterland, the patterns become smaller and more numerous. Each of these pieces represents a tribal group about which it is hardly an exaggeration to state that little (in many cases, nothing) was known as to its linguistic and ethnological affinities with regard to its neighbours,[1] very little about its religion, customs, and social organization, and 'nothing as to the constitution of the native courts or tribunals'.[2]

The following list comprises most of the important 'pieces' in our

[1] Almost our only source of information about this region is a small book entitled *Natives of the Northern Territories of the Gold Coast*, by A. W. Cardinall.

[2] Memorandum compiled by the Governor of the Gold Coast on *Native Administration in the Gold Coast and its Dependencies*.

kaleidoscopic picture. (I give the names as spelt on our maps, which are sometimes, however, not the correct local designations.) Mo, Nchumuru, Kratchi, Nanumba, Gonja, Dagomba, Konkomba, Chokosi, Bimoba, Mamprusi, Kusasi, Nabdam, Talansi, Nankanni, Kassena, Builsa, Isala, Dagati, Wala, Lobi.

Here was apparently a rather difficult problem for a single individual to undertake to unravel in a somewhat limited time,[1] but the task did not prove quite so difficult as at first sight it appeared. Clearly, the first thing to do was to try to establish what linguistic affinities—if any—existed between the languages spoken by the various tribes. With this aim in view, a preliminary language survey was undertaken and extensive vocabularies were collected, including *inter alia*, the classificatory nomenclature employed by the various tribes and also some notes on the grammar and syntax of those languages which were examined.

The first four chapters of this volume contain the results of this linguistic survey. Any value these data may have has been greatly enhanced by the monograph contributed by Professor Westermann, based on the material thus collected, and also upon his own individual researches.

One important fact immediately emerged from these preliminary investigations. The majority of the population which inhabit this territory were found to speak a language which has a common root or basis, i.e. Dagomba, Mamprusi, Nanumba, Kusasi, Nabdam, Talansi, Nankanni, Builsa, Dagati, Wala, Lobi (and possibly a few others). When I state that, according to our last (1921) census reports, the above tribes, all speaking dialects of a common language, comprise over 80 per cent.[2] of the whole population of the Northern Territories, the importance of this statement will be seen to be considerable, and this fact should go a long way to assist in solving the language problem in these parts.

In addition to this main language group, which I have named the 'Mole group' after that (suggested) parent language, there were found two other main linguistic groups which have been classified by me under the purely arbitrary headings of the 'Gbanya' (*Anglice* Gonja)

---

[1] About two years.

[2] The Nankanse (*Anglice* Nankanni) whose customs are dealt with in the early portion of this volume, are by far the largest tribe, numbering as they do almost double any other tribe. Hence the prominence given to their particular culture in this volume.

and the 'Kasen'-Isal' group respectively. Gbanya will be found on the map marking an area which extends right across the southern portion of the Northern Territories. It would be entirely erroneous, however, to assume that this title designates a single linguistic or even a single tribal area. The Gbanya language is undoubtedly akin to that of Kratchi and Nchumuru and is related to Brong, which in turn links it with the Akan stock. It is the language of the upper ruling class who supply 'Chiefs' in the territorial area which has been named by us after the language which these 'strangers' speak. The majority of the people who inhabit 'Western Gonja' do not, however, talk that language, but speak a tongue which is akin to Isal (*Anglice* Isala), and call themselves Vagala. This name does not even appear on our maps or in any official publication. This language in turn has been found to be very similar to another hitherto unrecorded language, i.e. Tampolem', which is spoken around Daboya and again in N.E. Mampruse. Thus, Vagale, Tampolem', and Isal form a single linguistic, and, as will be seen later, a single ethnic group which had a common origin. The tribes speaking Vagale and Tampolem' (like the Lobi) appear to be among the last survivors in this northern area of those tribes which still trace inheritance through the sister's son—like the Akan. Evidence, indeed, is not lacking, that in the not very remote past—and contrary to all our preconceived ideas on this subject— the whole of the Northern Territories was inhabited by peoples inheriting through the female line, the change-over to a patrilineal way of reckoning among other of the tribes being due to the invasion of those outsiders who, in so many localities, to-day form the ruling class. This is a discovery of some interest, both from the anthropological and the purely practical point of view.

Along with the Vagala, Isala, and Tampolense may possibly be classed (from a language standpoint) the Kasena-speaking tribes, which include the Awuna and Fĕra. Of the few remaining tribes, the Chokosi in the north-eastern corner are Akan, being descendants of Ashanti fighting men—an interesting page of Gold-Coast history to which further reference will be made elsewhere in these volumes. Thus far, then, the outstanding result of this preliminary language survey has been to reveal the fact, that instead of consisting of a veritable babel of unrelated tongues, the Northern Territories of the Gold Coast comprises a fairly homogeneous linguistic area, comparing not unfavourably in this respect with the conditions to be found in the South.

Another misconception has also been finally removed, namely that Hausa ever was a *lingua franca* of these parts. Although it is true, that, just as all over the Gold Coast, especially in the larger towns, we find groups of these aliens, i.e. settlers from Northern Nigeria, the Hausa language is unknown to the masses, and even the so-called Mohammedan elements in the population, are, with very few exceptions, such only in name. These independent researches thus confirm that conditions in this respect were accurately summarized in the last census report, in which it is stated that 'no statistics are supplied of the number of professing Mohammedans, as those obtained were considered to be unreliable. The number of true Mohammedans must be relatively small, as the inhabitants of the *Zongos* mostly belong to the Northern Territories and for the most part are really pagans.'[1]

It may in fact be stated with assurance, that alien (i.e. Northern Nigerian) influences are practically negligible in the Northern Territories, although abortive attempts are sometimes made by these Natives to assert claims to important positions in the Administration. A simple solution of this alien problem, which might arise in large cosmopolitan towns like Salaga, is that these communities should be run on their own lines, which would possibly follow the Nigerian model, as being more suited to their pseudo-Islamic characteristics. These alien Hausa settlers are an asset to the Gold Coast—and form a most desirable and stable element in the community. It would, in my opinion, be as unfair not to make special provision for them in any ordinance conferring Native Jurisdiction on the *soi-disant* 'Pagan' courts, as it would be a mistake slavishly to model the general administrative machinery of the 'Pagan' courts on Lord Lugard's great conception of 'Indirect Rule', as put successfully into practice under wholly different conditions in the Nigerian Emirates. I shall allude to this point again later on in my preface.

This linguistic survey served a threefold purpose: to clarify my ideas concerning local language groupings; to help to familiarize myself with the local dialects and languages; and thirdly, and not the least important, the personal contacts thus made assisted me in getting to know and in becoming known by the old men and women with whose intimate everyday life I was about to seek permission to mingle.

Turning now from the consideration of linguistics, I next proceeded to an examination of the ethnological and historical relationships between the tribes which have been enumerated. In this field

[1] Census report for 1921, p. 123.

it was found that our own and their distinctive appellations and designations fell even more completely away than in the case of language. Over the whole area, and embracing all three language groups, we had, it was found, a people who possessed a practically uniform religion, a uniform tribal and totemic organization, and an identical political constitution or system of tribal government. The outstanding feature of the last named was the *Ten'dana* or *Tegatu* or *Tinteintina* (or whatever was the local dialectal form) or Priest-King. 'In the past, in the Northern Territories, there were no Chiefs, only *Ten'dama*',[1] is a statement which I have frequently heard made. Such a statement is the result of confused thinking and shows complete lack of knowledge of the local social organizations under which these tribes formerly lived, and in many cases still live. The case should rather be stated thus: 'In the past the *Ten'dama* were the only Chiefs known.' Had a series of events (which will be briefly described presently and dealt with more fully later on in these volumes) not greatly affected the local constitutional system, these *Ten'dama* or Priest-Kings would undoubtedly have evolved into the type of Native ruler with whom we are familiar among the Akan; that is a ruler who was not only high-priest and custodian of the land of his tribe and of the ancestral spirits, but one who was a Chief or King on a territorial basis whose sanctions were secular and physical rather than spiritual; in other words, what the average European implies when he uses the word 'King' or 'Chief'. Here in the North, this natural process of evolution, from the Priest-King to the Territorial ruler, was interrupted by external influences which produced a really remarkable state of affairs. These it is well we should understand before embarking on schemes for Indirect Rule or a new Native Administration.

The student who approaches the study of the history and constitution of the tribes who inhabit the Northern Territories of the Gold Coast, comes to his task with certain well-known stock facts at his disposal, which have been so long and so unhesitatingly accepted that he does not think at first of questioning their authenticity. Confirmation of these facts is, moreover, apparently to be had on every hand when he turns for it to certain Native authorities. For a considerable time, therefore, I accepted without question the shop-worn story of the origin of the Mampruse, Dagomba, and Moshi peoples as having migrated from the east, and thence to Gambaga, from whence they

[1] Singular *Ten'dana* (or alt. *Ten'dan'*, *Tenedan'*, &c.).

radiated all over the country, and also the somewhat similar tradition of the so-called Gonja nation in the south-west. Were the anthropologist to confine his researches to the doings and sayings of those Natives whom he finds vested with minor authority under the local Government, real anthropological history would never be written. In my dealings with the plain folk, from whom most of the anthropologist's really valuable information is ultimately derived, facts were soon disclosed which were irreconcilable with the commonly accepted and current accounts hitherto credited by us and substantiated by the Chiefs or their agents.

When we speak and think of Dagomba and Mampruse as compact tribes who reached their present homes by some mass migration from the eastward, and talk of a Gonja 'nation' as having hailed from Mande, we are obscuring and confusing an issue which it is necessary we should understand, if we wish to avoid possible mistakes and injustices in our Administration.

These facts are as follows: the majority of the tribes who inhabit the Northern Territories were, I am convinced, residents in or near the localities where we now find them, centuries before the ancestors of those whose names many of the divisions now bear had arrived in this part of Africa. Upon these more or less autochthonous peoples, with their very primitive institutions, descended small bands of strangers within comparatively recent historical times. They were better armed, better clothed, familiar with the idea of kingship or chieftainship in our modern sense, in some cases conversant with the rudiments of Mohammedanism and accustomed (even if circumstances had not later compelled it) to a patrilineal manner of reckoning descent. These strangers superimposed upon the primitive tribes, among whom they settled, a new and unheard-of political conception, namely the idea of territorial and secular leadership in place of the immemorial institution of a ruler, who was the high priest of a totemic clan and dealt only in spiritual sanctions. These warrior bands—possibly refugees or off-shoots from one or other of the Negro kingdoms of the interior—were composed of males alone. The result was that in a few generations their descendants were speaking the language of the tribes among whom they settled, from among whom they were compelled to find wives, and whose manners and customs they came largely to adopt. While always endeavouring to keep for direct descendants all posts of secular authority based on the principles with which they were familiar, the tendency was nevertheless for them to become merged more and more with the people among whom they had settled, to whom, in course of time, they gave the name by which they called themselves formerly or which they had adopted. Thus it came about that when the European (who in these parts comes in contact chiefly with the ruling class) inquires the origin of the tribe, he is given that of the rulers. It would be as logical to infer that all inhabitants of England had come from Normandy in A.D. 1066 because Duke William and his followers hailed from France. When this influx of foreign fighting men took place, whose descendants were to become the dominant race, the position was somewhat as follows: there was an indigenous population, possibly originally of not more than two linguistic stocks; these peoples, even where their language differed considerably, had an almost identical social and political organization; the outstanding feature of this was a grouping of totemic clans under Priest-Kings whose influence and authority were considerable, although both depended upon moral and spiritual and not physical punishments; these indigenous peoples inherited through the sister's son. It will come as a surprise to many to be informed that several of these Northern-Territory tribes still practise the Akan system of tracing inheritance through the sister's son, while those who do not, show clear traces of a change over to a patrilineal system within comparatively recent historical times.

If my hypothesis is correct, namely, that rulers and ruled in the Northern Territories of the Gold Coast were for the most part not so very long ago of different races; that they possessed social systems which in the one case traced the inheritance of property through the male, in the other through the female; which in one case relied on physical, in the other on spiritual, sanctions to deter the wrongdoer; in the one case grouped peoples under a territorial classification, while in the other it took cognizance only of totemic clans—then clearly it must be of importance to discover as many details as possible concerning the old order of things, before later and comparatively new forms of government had been thrust upon the people. It appears to me indisputable, that where the latter had taken little or no consideration of the former, then an exotic type of rule must have been imposed on the mass of the people, which could not be exactly racy of the soil.

Two distinct lines of research were thus indicated: (a) what was the machinery of government which the foreign rulers introduced among the people who became nominally subject to them, which had been superimposed upon an earlier type of political organization that now lay like the lower writing of a palimpsest beneath this later impress? (*b*) secondly, what was the nature of this old régime, of its customs and religion, which had in some measure been adopted by the strangers? To the local authorities, working more or less in the dark, and contemplating changes in the Native Administration, a knowledge of these subjects is indispensable.

In these volumes I have dealt with the second line of inquiry first, because it is in one sense the more important. It really forms the foundation upon which all our present conceptions of modern conditions must be based. Throughout I have followed more or less the lines adopted in my previous study of the Ashanti. The subjects of my inquiry have been allowed to speak, in a large measure, for themselves. They have permitted me to mingle with them and attend their most intimate rites. My rôle has been for the most part to stand aside and record what I saw and what I heard. A slight departure from these methods is to be found in the inclusion of Aboya's narrative of events in his native village. This I have placed immediately following the chapters dealing with linguistics. It gives us, more clearly than anything I could write, the local colour which we should carry in our mind's eye onward throughout these pages.

I have already stated that when these invading bands (travelling as wandering soldiers of fortune, and never, I believe, as the migration of a tribe) came down upon the inhabitants of the Northern Territories, the latter were (as indeed they still are) living in very primitive conditions. Each group was ruled, or rather guided, by a Chief, i.e. a *Ten'dana* assisted by the heads of kindred groups. The authority of all the *Ten'dama* lay, as will be seen, in their supposed control of the supernatural, whose power they could invoke to punish wrongdoers.

Wealth in our modern sense was unknown; the people went about naked; their property consisted only in bows and arrows, pots, calabashes, and live stock. Disputes were settled by the Elders of each family group. The priestly ruler was appealed to only in cases affecting a breach of the tribal taboos, or in matters of wider than family import. Fear of the anger of the ancestral or other spirits moulded every action to a degree far surpassing anything found even among the ancestor-worshipping Ashanti—ancestral spirits moved between God and man and man and God—a link which is missing or less obvious in the South; men and women spent a considerable part of their lives at the soothsayers' shrines. These and many other aspects of their everyday life will be found described in these pages. This

life to-day is almost exactly what it was when these invaders swooped
down upon them. The foreigners who came among this people had
long since passed from the primitive to the barbaric state. They
settled down among these so-called savages. What was the result?
I am convinced that in most cases this innovation, or invasion if we
like to call it so, after the first upheaval, made very little difference
to these communities as a whole. The new rulers were readily
accorded at least an outward form of respect, which the African, up
to a point, is always willing to pay to any one more powerful than
himself. Extortion by Chiefs in those days was almost out of the
question—every one was so poor. Family ties, too, were quickly
woven, and family property was secure, as is always the case in
Africa, unless under actual war conditions—and these invaders in
most cases came to settle down and not to loot.[1] They were shrewd
enough to realize that, if they were to maintain even a titular leadership, they must insist on descent and inheritance through the male
line as alone conferring title to the office of territorial ruler, yet even
so they sometimes allocated lesser administrative posts to the *ma-bisi*
(mother's children). What then became of the old-time Chiefs, the
Priest-Kings, under these new conditions? The answer to this
question is, that in the majority of cases the *Ten'dana* at first continued
to function almost exactly as heretofore. The secular territorial ruler
was too superstitious to interfere with his work, which was almost
wholly of a spiritual nature. The result was that among many of
these tribes, before our advent, there had been evolved a kind of
dual mandate. There was the secular ruler descended from the leader
of the early warrior bands. He was recognized by every one as a kind
of titular head, he had a red fez and wore clothes, but really inter-
fered hardly at all with the life or private affairs of the masses. All
religious or magico-religious concerns continued to be managed and
conducted by the former priestly rulers, who now, however, functioned nominally under the territorial Chief. The former continued
to assert his original title to be custodian and trustee of the land of
his people, a claim which few, even of the most arrogant secular
Chiefs, ever dared to dispute, even at the present day. 'The people
belong to me, the land belongs to the *Ten'dana*', is a statement I have
repeatedly heard made. The new foreign Chief and the old tribal
Ten'dana thus came to work hand in hand. All matters pertaining to

---

[1] An exception to this was the invasion of what is now Eastern Dagomba by the
Mampruse Chief, Na Nyagesa, when many *Ten'dama* were put to death.

the religious welfare of the tribe were handed over by the secular ruler to the *Ten'dana*, while in administrative and secular matters the former took the lead, but in conference with the former tribal Elders, who thus became his counsellors when any matter cropped up which affected more than the Chief's immediate following. Quite a workable and satisfactory Native administration was thus evolved by a blending of the old and the new. To-day, in some parts of the North, there are still a few Chiefs functioning exactly as described, with very happy results.

The sphere of influence of these foreign soldiers of fortune who became Chiefs did not, however, effectively embrace the whole of the Northern Territories. It was mainly confined to the north-east, west, south-east, and south-west. Down the centre, and radiating from it, lay an area where their influence did not reach to any great extent. In these areas the old Priest-Kings continued to rule undisturbed until a far ruder and more revolutionary invasion than that I have described broke upon them. This was the advent of the white man. The results which followed this event can only be briefly summarized. When the first Englishman arrived on the scene, with the usual following of detribalized Africans, after our custom he demanded to see 'the King', who was required to produce water, firewood, and carriers. Now, the tribal rulers, the *Ten'dama*, who were old aristocrats in their own way, and had moreover seen what had generally been the fate of their fraternity, who had appeared before the officials of other Continental powers in these parts, kept aloof and in the background. Some wholly unimportant, and often worthless individual (from the local standpoint), was thrust forward to confront the strangers. Often he was a slave or descendant of a slave, sometimes he was the village bastard, sometimes the only man in the village with a loin-cloth. Each and all of the above have actually figured from time to time among our European-made African aristocracy in these parts. This emissary was told the white man's demands and hastened off to inform the real Chief, i.e. the *Ten'dana*, who saw to it that the order was carried out. At first, this individual acted as a kind of intermediary between the *Ten'dana* and the white man, and was merely regarded with faint contempt by all the villagers, who were well aware of his real status, and in their hearts considered him a fool to act thus as a figure-head who might sooner or later have to bear the brunt of the white man's anger. In course of time, however, many of these individuals came to dig themselves in and became more assured and confident of their positions. Their brothers and sons came to form a little coterie backed up by the European. The real ruler, almost before he realized it, often to his wonder and indignation, found himself becoming of less and less account even in the eyes of his people, until at length there made its appearance in this part of Africa something which every one, African and European alike, who understands anything about the real Africa, knows to be an anomaly—a local despotic ruler. There are many of these petty unconstitutional European-made Chiefs in the Northern Territories. Some of them are fine men, and all are most careful to function satisfactorily before the European Official. From a Commissioner's point of view they are often the most efficient and hard-working Chiefs. They realize very fully that they would not hold their position for a day without Government backing, so take good care to please the local Government representative. I myself have seen this type of Chief stand up and declare that the land of the tribe was his and that no *Ten'dana* existed or ever had existed in his division. This extreme type is happily somewhat rare, but he exists and is a real menace. His very efficiency *vis-à-vis* the white man makes him all the more so, and tends to hide the underlying current of discontent which everywhere exists among the subjects of such a ruler. The example he thus affords often also tends to confirm the ignorant assumption of certain Europeans, who would find in such really unnatural conditions what they consider proof of the fact that democracy did not exist in this part of Africa. This is a great mistake. These local upstarts would not survive long were we to leave the country. I have dealt at some length with this subject, a consideration of which is commended to those in authority. A remedy is simple and need cause no great upheaval. All that is necessary is to insist that every rightful *Ten'dana* who is not actually a Chief, and the *Ten'dana*'s hereditary Elders should act with the Chief as his councillors. Commissioners can do a great deal towards this end by merely insisting, when interviewing Chiefs, on seeing and greeting these Elders.[1] Again, when any one of these Chiefs dies or is removed from his post, every effort should be made to reinstate the rightful ruler in his place.

Native Rulers in the Northern Territories. It will be apparent from what has now been recorded, that the Chiefs in this region do not all fall into one category. There are at least three well-defined groups

---

[1] As is always done in Ashanti. Compare the present semi-official recognition of Queen-Mothers in Ashanti as compared with their position some ten years ago, when they were unrecognized by us.

into one or other of which each Native ruler falls. Each class of ruler also in practice represents a distinct type of Native Administration, though in theory all are supposed to be identical. These three types may be classified as follows:

(*a*) A few rare cases where the old traditonal ruler—the Priest-King—still functions, but now in the dual rôle of secular and spiritual leader, i.e. as a Chief in the modern sense.

(*b*) Those Chiefs, originally aliens, whose title to that office dates from long before the advent of the European in these parts. Such rulers are, for example, those of Mampruse, Dagomba, and Gonja.

(*c*) Chiefs whose title dates only from the time of European intervention and was created by us. These are often Natives without a vestige of any traditional qualifications to hold such office. Such Chiefs, I have termed Government-made Chiefs.

Those rulers who fall into the first class, the descendants of the old rulers of the people with whom they are one, are possibly the ideal, but except where we find them already functioning, this ideal is difficult of attainment. Much, as I have already suggested, may, however, be done, by filling vacancies when they occur in the ranks of Government-made Chiefs, by installing the former and rightful holders of the office in that position. A consideration of those Chiefs who fall into the second category has shown us that many of them had, before our advent, evolved quite an equitable system of administration by working hand in hand with the former leaders of the tribe. The tendency to-day is unfortunately for them more and more to ignore their councillors, which formerly they dared not do, and to act as autocratic rulers. In this attempt they are sometimes encouraged consciously or unconsciously by European officials who fail to understand the fundamental democratic principles, which always really underlay even what on the surface appears to be savage absolutism and autocracy.[1]

The first portions of these volumes, dealing with the original inhabitants, as distinct from their foreign rulers, will show how truly democratic was the political structure upon which the invaders had to build. In later chapters the system of government is examined, on a territorial basis—and often to outward appearances autocratic—which the new rulers tried to introduce. The study of the latter subjects resulted in some very interesting disclosures.

[1] See *Ashanti Law and Constitution*, chapter XXXVIII: 'Some Basic Principles in the Ashanti Constitution'.

As a close student of the Akan, and in particular of the Ashanti, I had, needless to state, been constantly on the alert for origins or traces of this stock in the land from which popular tradition reported it to have come. During the time in which my investigations were confined to the primitive tribes in the north and elsewhere, who had not been affected by the foreign influences which I have here briefly outlined, I could not find any direct trace in language, traditions, or other records to link up these tribes with the people in the Colony. It was true, one could everywhere see in their primitive organization and customs, either the germs of more developed institutions among the Akan, or, clear-cut, sharply focused, and in full operation, customs and beliefs which in the southern state had become blurred or nearly atrophied. For example, the *Ten'dana*, in all his religious and spiritual activities, was the exact prototype of an Ashanti Chief in his capacity of *Asase wura* (owner of the land)[1] and custodian of the ancestral spirits of the clan. He would have, and in some cases, as we have already seen, actually had, developed into our modern conception of a Native ruler. Such evidence was, however, hardly convincing enough even from a diffusionist standpoint, and might possibly be due to what anthropologists have come to call 'convergent evolution'. In any case the evidence was not enough to prove any direct historical contact between the Ashanti and these particular tribes. It was not until I turned my attention to the more civilized elements in the community, as represented by the upper ruling class, and visited the head-quarters of the Native Administration at Naleregu and Yendi, that an unexpected and most interesting disclosure was made. A fairly elaborate and comparatively organized system of Native Administration was found to have been in existence, comprising a 'palace' (i.e. Chief's household), territorial, political, and military organization which were mainly—and in some cases even down to minute details including the terms used to designate them—those of the Akan (Ashanti). The old familiar titles of offices again appeared under names either identical or so slightly altered as to be easily recognizable as corruptions of the Akan language. All the highly elaborated Ashanti organization, with its wonderful system of decentralization, and the secret and solemn enstoolment ceremonies practised by Ashanti Kings, were again found to be in existence here. One of the *Na* (Chiefs) had even a Golden Stool, and the symbol of office and chieftainship was the Stool.

[1] It is just possible, however, that he had arrogated this title to himself from some original holder of the office such as a *Ten'dana*.

It seems hardly necessary to stress the importance of this discovery at the present time, when the Gold Coast Government is contemplating the introduction of 'Indirect Rule' among these tribes. A knowledge of the facts which are now disclosed for the first time in these volumes should help to simplify matters for us considerably and afford us a working formula upon which to base an Administration ordinance suited to local conditions. I do not wish to be misunderstood: that system should not slavishly follow the Akan model on which indeed it is based, but should be what many of the old-time Chiefs had themselves evolved, i.e. a combination of what was in existence when their first ancestors came here, and what they borrowed from elsewhere and built upon that underlying structure.

The question now naturally suggests itself: Where did these strangers who invaded the Northern Territories centuries ago obtain the idea of an elaborate system of decentralized administration on an exact parallel to that found in Ashanti, and a terminology for various offices which is also derived from that language? There are, I think, two alternative answers to this question. I have for some time past been inclining more and more to the opinion that we were on the wrong lines in talking of, and seeking for, origins and lines of migrations for the people whom to-day we call the Ashanti, in terms of a compact or composite tribe. My late experience in the North has greatly strengthened this opinion and clarified much that was hitherto obscure. I am of the opinion that, in the South, we had originally a pure Negro people with a civilization and a culture very similar to what we now find in the North. Traditions of a time when they (the Ashanti) went about naked or in a leaf-covering and used bows and arrows, and had stone hoes, have been noted by me in previous volumes. The forest belt had probably been their habitat from time immemorial. Their later barbaric civilization and the more striking features of their constitution, the reshuffling of tribal units and the formation of territorial groupings, these are the origins we have to trace. We have been confusing, I believe, the migration of a few families of a higher and more civilized type, who produced these changes, with the migration of a people.

I have stated above that an almost identical form of administrative machinery, including in many cases a terminology which is clearly Akan, has been discovered in the most remote area of the Northern Territories, among a people who without a doubt are composed of the two distinct elements which I suggest have also gone to form the

Ashanti nation, i.e. an indigenous and very primitive population, and a thin upper stratum of a superior ruling class. Were the strangers who in the North founded the great states of Mampruse and Dagomba, on lines which no one who reads these volumes can deny are those found in Ashanti to-day, of the same stock and origin as those who, wandering on farther south, developed what are now the great Akan-speaking states ? If that were so, then we should have gone a long step farther in tracing the origin of at least those who formed the backbone of the Ashanti people. It must be confessed that it is a plausible and even a possible explanation. But it is not the only one, and until further evidence is forthcoming, it would be premature to assume that it is the correct one.

It has been noted that, in the far north-east of what is now the Mandated Territory, we have a compact little state whose inhabitants are, and still speak, Akan. I have shown, however, that this tribe is not a residue of that stock which had been left behind in some far distant coastward migration, but that the Chokosi are, in fact, an offshoot of the Akan, who reached their present habitat coming from the South. There is clearly a possibility, therefore, that the striking similarity between Dagomba, Mampruse, and Gonja constitutional machinery and nomenclature, and that of the Akan, may be due to the former group having modelled their political organization upon the latter. We now know, from a history of the Chokosi, that the Mampruse employed Akan gun-men (*Kanbonse*) to help them in their wars, and the intimate association between Ashanti and Dagomba is well known. There has thus apparently been ample opportunity for these northern kingdoms to have learned from, and modelled their administrative and political machinery on, that of the southern kingdom. It would be possible to adduce arguments in support of both theories, but such a discussion would be going beyond the scope and intentions of the present volumes. These have been written in order to furnish data which will assist those in authority to build up a sound Native Administration. We have a fine chance here in the Northern Territories of the Gold Coast, with its really first-class human material and interesting existing constitution, to produce a Native Administration which will be a model to other territories.

Twenty-two years' experience of the Gold Coast has shown me that there is sometimes a tendency to plan out and elaborate schemes for local projects upon lines which have been evolved, perfected, and introduced with success—elsewhere. Such a scissors-and-paste policy may produce quite satisfactory results—on paper. What is required here, however, in view of the present scanty state of our knowledge, is for us to examine those human records which alone can supply us with the information which we require.

I therefore pass on to those who come after me my contribution to this end, in the certainty that they will continue this important task upon which will largely depend the future progress and well-being of those for whom and with whom we of the Gold Coast Political Service have laboured.

R. S. R.

28 January 1931.

CONTENTS

VOLUME I

LIST OF ILLUSTRATIONS

VOLUME I

I

CLASSIFICATORY SYSTEMS

AS in a previous work on the Ashanti, it is proposed in the present volume to begin with an examination of the terminology employed by certain tribes (whose general culture is about to be investigated) to express their relationship terms. In this chapter will be found, drawn up in tabular form, the names used in the classificatory systems of fourteen tribes.

From these tables may be gathered, not only much of their social organization, but their perusal will also enable us to observe, more or less at a glance, how closely related in language the majority of these peoples are to each other. We have been over-ready, I think, in the past, to regard these Northern-Territory tribes as more or less separate groups, each with a culture and language of its own. A large part of my thesis will be devoted to showing that this is not the case. The notes in the present chapter are somewhat brief, as the many ramifications of the subject with which it deals will be re-examined later in that portion of these researches which treats of social anthropology, as distinct from what is to be regarded as a preliminary linguistic survey. This latter has been undertaken in order to bear out and prove a hypothesis on which this entire work is based. This I have already outlined in the Preface, namely, that it should be possible to regard the Northern Territories of the Gold Coast as a more or less homogeneous cultural, and—to a lesser extent—linguistic area, rather than as a mosaic comprising a welter of tongues and divergent customs.

For my present purpose I have split up the the data contained in these tables into several heads, grouping, under one or another of these, those languages—really, it will be seen, dialects of a common basic language—under which each would appear to fall. My classifications into these categories are arbitrary, and are only such as those at which the ordinary student could arrive by an examination of the tables. Professor Westermann will later deal with this and all other linguistic material and classify it under headings which his great experience and knowledge will render philologically accurate.

I propose, therefore, to group the first ten 'languages' under one head. This I will call the 'Mole group'.[1] Such a title is chosen only

---

[1] From an historical point of view it would be more accurate to take Mampelle

for want of a better heading. Nine of these 'languages' have obviously a great deal in common with the tenth, i.e. with Mole, and this language alone, among all the rest, has had any considerable literature written upon it.[1]

Gbanya (Anglice *Gonja*) seems here to fall into a group of its own, while *Kasene* and *Awuna* (*Fĕra*) (obviously but dialects of a common tongue) appear to have remote affinities with Isal.[2] This last language, again, as I shall endeavour to prove presently, is closely allied to Tampolem' and Vagale. These do not appear at all in these tabular representations, but they will be examined later, when brief vocabularies will prove—by comparison with Isal—their undoubted affinity with that language.

I now propose to take each generation of the tables in turn, and to draw attention to particular points which will assist the student, who is without a knowledge of these languages, the better to understand them and the particular significance of each term.

I. The Mole Language Group

This group includes, besides the language after which it is named, the following:

(*a*) *Mampelle*: The language spoken by the people called Mampruse.

(*b*) *Dagbane*: The language spoken by the Dagbwandaba (*Anglice*, Dagomba).

(*c*) *Kusal*: The language of the Kusase.

(*d*) *Nankane*: The language of the Nankanse (*Anglice* Nankanni).

(*e*) *Dagare*: The language of the Dagaba (*Anglice*, Dagati).

(*f*) *Nabte*: The language of the Namnam (*Anglice*, Nabdam).

(*g*) *Bulea*: The language of the Bulse (*Anglice*, Kanjaga).

(*h*) *Wale*: The language of the Wala.

(*i*) *Loberu*: The language of the Lobe.

The First Generation, that of the Speaker.

The word for 'husband' in Dagbane appears to be irregular, but this is only because the wife addresses her husband as 'master of the home' (*Yidana*) instead of as 'husband'. A similar idiom, it will be noted, is used elsewhere to express 'husband's elder brother', 'husband's mother's brother's son', 'husband's father's sister's son', &c.

as the parent stock, but the linguistic prominence attained by Mole more than balances this claim of Mampelle to be recognized from the historical standpoint.

[1] Works by F. Froger, *Étude sur la Langue des Mossi*, &c., &c.; and by R. S. Rattray, *An Elementary Mole Grammar*.   [2] Also heard, 'Isalen'.

Among the Mampruse, after a wife has borne a son to her husband, she will address him as 'father of So-and-so'. Among the majority of these tribes a junior may not call a senior by what we would term his or her 'Christian name', but a husband may address his wife thus. Among the Nankanse, however, a wife is generally addressed by her husband by the name of her village, the final vowel in the name of which is changed to *a*, e.g., the village is Winkoŋo, the name is Winkoŋa.

In Kusal, instead of the usual word for wife (*Paya*,[1] or one of its variations) we find a totally different word, i.e. *Coro*. This word also appears in the Gbanya language, but with a different meaning.

Brothers and Sisters: The word for 'brother' and 'sister' will be seen to vary in some of the 'languages' according to the sex of the speaker. In cases where there is not any special word, the sex is indicated by the addition of an adjective meaning 'female'; 'sister' being then designated by a term which means literally 'female brother'.

In-laws: In-laws in this generation are generally designated by *Dakyia* (*Daki, Dakya, Dakyiɛ, Kye*, &c.), but 'brother's wives' also often become just 'wives' to the speaker, or in some cases 'lovers' (*Zaba* in Nankane, *Nɔʮ* in Bulea). The latter word does not appear to be of Mole stock. The converse too holds good, 'husband's brothers' becoming just 'husbands' or 'lovers'.

Father's brother's children: These are just either (*a*) 'brothers' or 'sisters' or (*b*) 'father's children',[2] my informants sometimes giving the first, sometimes the second term, or even occasionally varying these by saying, 'little father's child' or 'big father's child'. ('Father' in all such cases is of course the term by which the speaker's own father's brother is known.) 'Little father' implies that the person spoken of is younger than the speaker's own father, and 'big father' that he is older.

Africans generally have a dislike for or are incapable of thinking in the abstract. Often, therefore, my informants, on being asked for a relationship term, would visualize a concrete case, with the result, that when I asked for example, for 'brother's child' they would give me the words for 'younger' or 'elder brother's child', drawing their example from their own family circle. I mention the fact thus early,

[1] The orthography here used is that recommended by the International Institute of African Languages and Cultures.

[2] Compare the Ashanti; *vide Ashanti*, p. 29.

because this peculiarity is often the cause of certain irregularities in the text of these tables, which it will be seen are thus more apparent than real.

Father's sister's children, and *Mother's brother's children*: I hope to show later that cross-cousin marriages, which, with rare exceptions, are no longer permitted by tribal custom, were once the common form of union in these parts. It is of interest therefore to note that most of these dialects have a special name for the above relationships, e.g., *Pɔgodoba-biga*, &c., &c., with reciprocal *Yasib'-biga*, &c., &c. Besides these special names we also find these relations addressed simply as 'brothers' or 'sisters', 'younger' or 'older' as the case may be. It seems possible that these alternatives may be of later origin, and that they may have arisen after cross-cousin marriages came to be discouraged. Nabte, for example, appears only to have the latter terms for these relationships, although the absence of the special names may very possibly be due to an omission on my part to inquire if they existed.

Mother's sister's children: They, like 'father's brother's children', are designated by names which mean literally (*a*) 'mother's' children, or alternatively, (*b*) 'brothers' or 'sisters' (younger or older as the case may be). Sometimes, too, the 'mother's' age is more particularly given, and she is described as 'small mother'. This denotes that she is younger than the speaker's own real mother. The above variants in terminology, coupled with the fact that the sex of the children may be given in some cases, while in others the common gender is employed, will explain most of the apparent discrepancies in the tables. Also, as already noted, some of the dialects do not have a special word for 'brothers' or 'sisters' when the opposite sex is speaking.

This concludes the speaker's generation.

GENERATION (I) OF ASCENDANTS.

The word for 'father' is derived from a common root, *ba* or *sa*, with, in case of Nankane and Nabte, the addition of a word, the root of which is *dɔge* (to beget), the meaning of *Sa dɔgere* thus being 'father the begettor'.

Bulea is an exception; it borrows the word *Ko* from the Kasene language.

Father's brothers: As already noted, they are simply 'fathers', 'little' or 'big', according to whether they are younger or older than the speaker's own father. The wives of father's brothers are simply 'mothers' to the speaker. Loberu has a name for such which, however, only means 'father's wife' (*sa pɔy*).

Father's sisters and Mother's sisters:[1] These have already been dealt with under the heading of 'father's sister's children' and 'mother's sister's children'. It has been noted that 'father's sister' has a distinct and separate name in the classificatory vocabulary, instead of being merged in a whole group, as is the case, for example, with a father's brother.

Father's sister's husband: This relationship is variously expressed by terms, which when translated, mean:

(*a*) *Father's sister's husband.*
(*b*) *Father.*
(*c*) *In-law.*
(*d*) *Father-in-law* (Nankane).
(*e*) *Father's husband.*

In the last, 'father's sister' has simply (like father's brother) merged with 'father', the sex being wholly ignored. This is not uncommon. The Nankane terminology is here of particular interest. A marriage with a father's sister's child is now absolutely forbidden, yet here we have the term 'father-in-law' applied to the father of a child who is no longer even a potential spouse for the speaker.

Mother: Note that in Nankane there is a parallel to the *sɔ dɔgere* already mentioned, the mother being sometimes called 'Mother-the-bearer'.

Mother's brother's wife: This, in most of the different dialects, is rendered alternatively by:

(*a*) *Mother.*
(*b*) *Mother's brother's wife.*
(*c*) *Mother-in-law* (Mampelle).

Now, a Mampurug (singular of Mampruse) may not marry his mother's brother's daughter unless his mother and the girl's father were half-brother and -sister. The nomenclature is thus suggestive of a time when such unions were permissible.

Mother's sister's husband: He may either be so described, or he may be called simply 'father'.

GENERATION (2) OF ASCENDANTS.

Father's father: In Wale, the alternative name given is derived from the Kasen'-Isal group. Dagare, Bulea, Wale, and Loberu,

---

[1] Note in Nankane the word *bi'a*, which occurs in *Ma bi'a*, means 'little', and should not be confused with *bia* (child) in the same language.

instead of the word derived from the common root *Υab*, employ a circumlocution meaning literally 'great-father' (compare also 'great-mother').

Son's sons: The only departure from the use of a word with a root common to all, is in Bulea, which has *na-bik* (compare *nane-bi* in Gbanya). The rest of this generation do not call for any special comment.

FIRST GENERATION OF DESCENDANTS.

Son: This is generally rendered simply by the word for 'child', the gender being understood as masculine. The adjective for 'male' is, however, occasionally added.

Daughter: Rendered by 'female child', the sex being always clearly shown by the suffixing of *pugela*, *pugena puya*, &c., to the word for 'child'.

Son's wife: She may be designated variously as:

(*a*) *Son's wife*.

(*b*) *Child* (as in Mampelle).

(*c*) *In-law* (*Diemba*).

(*d*) *Mother*.

(*e*) *San-poy* (with variations in Nankane, Nabte, Bulea, meaning obscure).

(*f*) *Grand-mother* (*na-pɔyɔ*) in Wale.

Some of these terms are rather unusual and call for special notice. There is, among all these tribes, a peculiar horror of a father ever having sexual intercourse with a son's wife. This idea is seen reflected in the terminology employed to designate the latter's relationship to her father-in-law, and vice versa. *Buke ta loge woo nyebe san-pɔya* ('He is such a rascal (or so weak-minded) as to have sexual intercourse with his son's wife') is a well-known Nankanse saying. 'She is not your wife; she is not your lover; you may not even sit together on the same mat; she is the same as your daughter; you would be killed by the Spirits if you had sexual intercourse with her; if you even ever dream you do so, you must give a sheep or goat to the Spirits and confess.'

Your son's daughter thus becomes your 'daughter', and you her 'father', or she is your 'mother' (but here the reciprocal would be too familiar). This brings us to the terms '*San-pɔy*', and '*Na-pɔyɔ*'. I am still doubtful as to the exact meaning of the former expression. The Natives themselves cannot say what it is, but I think it may possibly be derived from *Sa, Sam*, or *Samba*, i.e. father, and thus mean 'father's wife'. This would be in conformity with the derivation of the Wale term, *Na-pɔyɔ* (with reciprocal *Nabale*). These words mean literally, 'grandmother' and 'grandfather', respectively. *Pɔyɔ* is here an adjective, not a noun, as is more clearly seen in other dialects of Wale, where this word becomes *Na-paya*, i.e. female *Na* (as opposed to *Nabale*, male *Na*). This curious terminology would therefore appear to be employed in order to convey and enforce the impression of the aloofness (in sexual matters) which social custom demands.

The derivation of *Danyama* (Nankane) and *Denyam* (Mampelle), I have not been able to trace. *Danyama* is also used in Nankane for 'father's sister's son's wife', 'wife's mother's mother's sister's son', and 'husband's mother's father's sister's son'.

Brother's son's and daughters: These are either so designated in full, or become simply the speaker's own 'sons' and 'daughters.'

Sister's sons and daughters: These are called (*a*) 'son' and 'daughter' or 'child' (*b*) 'sister's son' or 'daughter', or (*c*) *Yaseya* (or one of its variants). This last term is significant in view of a fact which I shall try to prove later on in these volumes, namely that, matrilineal descent, with inheritance through the sister's child, was once the vogue all over the Northern Territories. These researches have indeed disclosed the interesting truth that, contrary to all our preconceived ideas on this subject, there are several tribes which still practise this manner of tracing descent, while many others show distinct traces of a change over to a patrilineal way of reckoning within comparatively recent times.

Mother's sister's daughter's children: These are either: (*a*) described in full as above, or become, (*b*) speaker's own 'children' ('sons' or 'daughters'), or, (*c*) the same term is used as in describing the speaker's own sister's son or daughter, i.e. *Yaseya* (or variants), and *bi-pugela* (or variants) respectively.

Mother's brother's son's children: They are described alternatively, (*a*) in full, as above, or (*b*) as the speaker's own 'sons' or 'daughters'.

In-laws: In this generation they are commonly *demba* or its dialectal equivalents, but the males are also in some cases 'fathers' to the speaker.

THIRD GENERATION OF DESCENDANTS.

In this generation, we have a form of terminology which is strikingly reminiscent of that found in the Ashanti Classificatory system. Great-grand-children in Ashanti, it will be recollected, are called *Nana nka' so* (don't touch-the-ear-grandchild). Here again, in the north, it is taboo among many of the tribes for a great-grandchild to touch or look into his great-grand-parent's ear. He is called 'grand-child-cut-ear', the exact meaning of the expression is, however, obscure.

GENERATION OF THE SPEAKER'S WIFE.

Wife's brothers: They are uniformly called *Dakyea, Dakyia, Daki,* &c. (with reciprocal *Dakyea,* &c.). 'You may abuse your wife's brother and say anything you like to him, because he cannot take your wife from you', said a Wala informant to me. *Ti tu tab* ('We can curse each other'), say the Kusase. The same idea is found among the Lobe, Dagare, &c. I shall deal with this privileged familiarity in full elsewhere.

Wife's brother's wife: *Zoa-poa* (Mampelle) means lit. 'friend's wife'.

Wife's sister: It will be noted that in Mole, Mampelle, Dagbane, Kusal, Nankane, Dagare, and Wale, she is called by a word which means 'wife'. Among the Northern Territory tribes, a considerable variation in custom exists with regard to the position of a man's wife's sister in the matrimonial market. Among the Kusase, a man may marry his wife's sister, during the lifetime of his wife, but he may not make a 'lover' of her, nor may he marry two sisters, one of whom is *nyere* to the other. *Nyere* is a term applied to two children born consecutively of the same parents, i.e. no other brother or sister intervening between them.

Among the Moshi, who, it will be observed, still call a wife's sister 'wife', it is forbidden to marry a wife's sister while the first wife (her sister) is still alive. The same rule applies to the Wala. Among the Dagaba, on the other hand, a man has right of access to his wife's sister, if she is not already married to another. (So, too, among the Isala.) Among Nankanse, a man has a right to a wife's sister if not *nyere* (see above) and this is also the case among the Lobe, even if a *nyere* sister (*Ture* in Loberu), such a marriage generally being arranged by the married sister herself. Among the Dagbwandaba (*Anglice* Dagomba) a man may not marry his wife's sister while the wife is still alive. The reciprocal of 'wife's sister', i.e. 'sister's husband', is, as one would expect after reading the above, generally rendered by the word commonly applied to 'husband'.

FIRST GENERATION OF A WIFE'S ASCENDANTS.

All are *dema* (with its variations) except in Bulea, which appears to borrow a word from another language group. Much of the respect or avoidance of parents-in-law among all these tribes is, I believe, due to a fact which one hears constantly reiterated, i.e. parents-in-law may, and often do, influence their daughters to leave their husbands. I shall have more to write on this subject later on in these volumes.

FIRST GENERATION OF WIFE'S DESCENDANTS.

Wife's brother's and Wife's sister's children: They are generally so designated, but are also sometimes spoken of as 'children' of the speaker, i.e. 'son' or 'daughter' as the case may be. The 'in-laws' in this generation are usually *demba* (or one of its variants).

II. THE GBANYA CLASSIFICATORY SYSTEM

To any one familiar with the Ashanti language, it at once becomes apparent that several of the terms used in the Gbanya classificatory system are either identical with, or bear a very striking resemblance to, those employed in the Southern State. This resemblance to Ashanti becomes even more striking when we come to compare the Gbanya and Ashanti systems of numeration and their vocabularies.

The Ngbanya (Gonja) themselves explain these similarities by stating that: 'When we first settled here [i.e. in the Northern Territories], we found the Ashanti in the country and married their women. Our language thus became like Ashanti.' Whether this is the real or merely an aetiological explanation, Professor Westermann will doubtless be able to state, and I will leave the philological or historical discussion of the subject until later on in this volume to pass on to a brief examination of the tables themselves.

THE SPEAKER'S GENERATION.

Husband: *Kul*, compare Ashanti, *Kunu* or *Ku*.

Elder Brother: *Da*, this is possibly the same root as in Mole, *dawa* (pl. *dapa*), seen again in Isal, *De*, meaning male; *Da-pekye* thus would mean 'female *da*', i.e. 'sister'.

Father's brother's children: These are 'brothers' and 'sisters'.

Father's sister's children and Mother's brother's children: Marriage with cross-cousins is still enjoined among this tribe. Note the special names for these relationships, i.e. *Tana-pibi*, and *Wɔpa-pibi*, besides the usual description of 'brother' or 'sister'. *Wɔpa* for maternal uncle is *Wɔfa* in Ashanti.

Mother's sister's children: These are the speaker's 'brothers' or 'sisters'.

In-laws: The in-laws in this generation are generally *coro* (this word we have already seen used in Bulea for 'husband') or they are designated in full as 'So-and-so's wife' or 'husband'. There is an interesting exception where we find 'the father's brother's son's wife,' called *Ni*, i.e. 'mother' (Akan *o-ni* 'mother'). Compare the similar term used for 'son's wife' among the Nankanse and Nabte and the term 'grandmother' in Wale, already noted.

GENERATION (1) OF ASCENDANTS.

Father: *Toto*, while not the word used in Ashanti for 'father', is a common personal name for males in that language.

Father's brothers: They are 'fathers', 'big' or 'little' to the speaker, and their 'wives' are his 'mothers'.

Father's sisters and Mother's sisters: These are *Tana* and *Ni* (mother) respectively, as already noted.

Father's sister's husband: This is *Toto*, i.e. 'father'.

Mother: *Ni*, compare Ashanti, where '*Ni* is one of the variants of '*no*,' *na*.

Mother's sister's husband: He is 'father' to the speaker.

GENERATION (2) OF ASCENDANTS:

Throughout we have a terminology which is almost identical with that of Ashanti. *Nana-kye*, is 'female *nana*'.

FIRST GENERATION OF DESCENDANTS.

Son: Rendered by 'child' or 'male-child'.

Daughter: 'Female-child'.

Son's wife: This relationship, with other in-laws in the above generation, are expressed by *sea*, compare Ashanti *ase*.

Brother's children: They become the speaker's 'children'.

Sister's children: A sister's child is designated by a special name, *wɔpa-bi* (compare Ashanti *wofase*).

Mother's sister's daughter's children: See above. The in-laws in this generation are *sea*.

THIRD GENERATION OF DESCENDANTS.

The reciprocal of 'son's son's son', besides the common form, is *da*. This means literally 'elder brother'. When I inquired why a great-grandson should thus address his great-grandfather, I was informed that it was because of the familiarity existing between them. Privileged familiarity between certain relatives will be discussed later.

GENERATION OF THE SPEAKER'S WIFE.

The terminology employed does not call for any special comment except to note that marriage with a wife's sister is forbidden during the lifetime of the wife.

FIRST GENERATION OF WIFE'S ASCENDANTS.

All in this generation are *sea*. The customary respect for, and avoidance of parents-in-law, is found among this tribe, the reason ascribed being that 'If you do not give them great respect, they will take your wife away, and leave your stick (penis) on a stone.' 'You may not sit on the same mat as your mother-in-law.'

FIRST GENERATION OF WIFE'S DESCENDANTS.

These do not call for any special notice.

III. THE KASEN'-ISAL GROUP

Under this head, which, as I have already made clear, is purely arbitrary, has been grouped the classificatory system of the *Kasene* (*Kasem*),[1] *Awuna* (or *Fĕra*), and *Isal*. As indicated elsewhere, two other 'languages' have also been found with very distinct affinities to *Isal*, namely *Tampoleme* and *Vagale*. They will later be dealt with briefly in an appendix.

FIRST GENERATION, THAT OF THE SPEAKER.

Husband: *Bala* in Isal, the word used for 'husband', means in Kasene and Awuna 'male' and is the same word, I think. It is also found in the form *balo*.

Brothers and Sisters: It will be noted that Kasene and Awuna have special terms for these relationships when the opposite sex is speaking while Isal has not.

In-laws: In this generation, the term used in Isal does not appear to have any relation philologically to the word used in Kasene and Awuna. As was noted in the Mole group, 'brother's wives' (and the reciprocals) here also may be classified as 'lovers' *Bolo* (Kasene), *Nandoŋ* (Isal), with *Nandoŋ mie* (or 'small lover') as the term for the wife of the father's sister's son.

Father's brother's children: The terms used for these follow the customary classificatory nomenclature; such persons are 'sons', 'daughters', or 'children' of the speaker.

[1] There is an excellent little treatise on this language entitled, *Grammaire de la Langue Kasséna ou Kassené*. See footnote on p. 59.

Father's sister's children and Mother's brother's children: These are: (*a*) 'brothers' or 'sisters', or: (*b*) In Awuna there appear to be special names for the relationship, i.e. *Nakana-bu*, recip. *Nabira-bu*. My Kasena informants declared that they did not know the word *Nakana*, but they gave me later its reciprocal *Nabira*; it therefore seems probable that the other term also exists in their language. *Na-bira* is possibly derived from *Na* or *Nu* (mother) and *bira* (male), 'male mother', i.e. 'mother's brother'. Isal has also the special word *Nyelma-bi* for 'father's sister's child', with the reciprocal, *Nera-bi*.

Mother's sister's children: They are 'brothers' or 'sisters' of the speaker, 'younger' or 'older' as the case may be. *De-vala* (Isala) is a variation of *De-bala* (*bala*, male).

Generation (1) of Ascendants.

Father: In Kasene, the name for 'father' (*ko*), appears to be more akin to the word used in Gbanya (and Ashanti). Bulea, it will be seen, also uses the word *ko*.

Father's brothers: As in all the other classificatory systems, these are grouped simply as 'brothers', 'small' or 'big' as the case may be.

Father's sisters and Mother's sisters: These have been noted under the heading, 'father's sister's children' and 'mother's sister's children'. The remainder of this generation do not call for any special comment.

Generation (2) of Ascendants.

In this generation the Isal has separate terms for 'father's mother' and 'mother's mother', i.e. *Nahama* and *Naha* respectively, as an alternative for the usual form, *Nabalma*, while Awuna has an alternative *naha* for *nunu* (mother's mother).

First Generation of Descendants:

Son: Expressed by the word meaning 'male child' or simply by 'child'.

Daughter: *Tɔlɔ*, in Isal seems to depart from the usual form.

Son's wife: She is so termed, and there are apparently none of the curious names for this relationship found in the Mole group. (See p. 6).

Brother's children: These, besides being so described, are also the speaker's own 'children'.

Sister's children: These are either so described (the seniority of the sister sometimes being given) or become the 'children' of the speaker.

Mother's sister's daughter's children: These are either as designated, or become the speaker's own 'children'.

Mother's brother's son's children: They are so described or alternatively become the speaker's own 'children'.

In-laws: There is a marked absence of any special word to designate in-laws, such as exists in the previous groups which have been investigated. The females-in-law are simply designated as the wives of So and so, while the males seem to become, as it were, honorary 'fathers' to the speaker. This peculiarity, however, also exists in the classificatory systems previously examined.

THIRD GENERATION OF DESCENDANTS.

The terminology employed does not present any new features.

GENERATION OF THE SPEAKER'S WIFE.

The males in this generation are sometimes *dɔɔ* which probably means just 'male', but Isal has also a special term '*bagyeŋ*'. The wife's sister again, as is so generally the case, is 'wife' to the speaker.

FIRST GENERATION OF WIFE'S ASCENDANTS.

Wife's father: Kasene and Awuna each have a term which means 'male' with a prefix, '*Tin*', which I am informed indicates respect. The Isal *Hel-bal*, means literally 'wife's-male'; the reciprocal which means 'child' is also normal.

FIRST GENERATION OF DESCENDANTS.

The terms used are all such as have already been dealt with. *Nabalma* as reciprocal of *Bi-hal*, seems unusual, and it is possibly a mistake for *Nymea*.

SPEAKER'S GENERATION

English.	Mole.	Mampelle.	Dagbane.	Kusal.	Nankane.	Dagare.
Husband	Sida	Sira	Yidana	Sid	Sera	Sere
Wife	Paɣa	Poa	Paɣa	Poa	Pɔɣa	Pɔgɔ
Elder brother	Kyɛma	Bere	Biele	Ber	Kyɛma	Bere, Kpɛma
Younger bro.	Yawa (pl. Yapa)	Sozoa-bila	Tuzɔ	Pito	Yebega	Yɔ
Elder sister	Tawa ka-seŋa (m.s.)	Bere poa	Biele-paɣa	Tɔ kpɛm	Ta kyɛma	Kpɛma
Younger bro.	Tawa (w.s.)	Sozoa do bila	Tuzɔdo	Tɔ bil	Ta bila or Ta bil	Yɔ
Elder brother's wife	Kyɛma paɣa	Bere poa or poa	Paɣa	Ber poa	Zaba	Bere pɔgɔ
Husband's younger bro.	Sida yawa	Sira-pira	Yidana-bila	Sid pito	,,	Sere-bile
Younger bro.'s wife	Yaw' paɣa	Sozo'-bil'-poa or Poa	Tuzɔ-paɣa or Paɣa	Pito poa	Zaba	Yɔ pɔgɔ
Husband's elder brother	Sid' kyɛma	Sir' kpɛma	Yidana-kpɛma	Sid kpɛm	,,	Sera-kpɔŋ
Elder sister's husband	Dakyia	Dakyia	Dakyia	Daki	Dekya	Dakyiɛ
Wife's younger brother	,,	,,	,,	,,	,,	,,
Younger sister's husband	Dakyia	Dakyia	Dakyia	Daki	Dekya	Dakyiɛ
Wife's elder brother	,,	,,	,,	,,	,,	,,
Father' bro.'s son	Ba biga	Ba bia	Ba-pir'-bia or Biele or Tuzɔ	Ba pit' bi or Ba-ber-bi	Kyɛma (Yebega)	Sa bie
Father's bro.'s son	,,	,,	Ba-kpem-bia or Biele	Ba-ber-bi or Ba-pit bi	Yebega (Kyɛma)	,,
Father's bro.'s son's wife	Ba bi' paɣa or Paɣa	Sozoa poa	Ba-pir'-bia or Biele or Tuzɔ	Ba pit (or ber) bi-poa or Pɔgɔ	Pɔɣa or Zaba	Pɔgɔ
Husband's fa-ther's bro.'s son	Sida	Sire-bere or Sire Kpɛm	Ba-kpem' bia or Biele	Sid	Sira or Zaba	Sera

SYSTEMS

N bte.	Bulea.	Wale.	Loberu.	Gbanya.	Kasene.	Awuna (Fĕra).	Isal.
Ser	Coro	Sera	Sere or Sire	Kul	Biro	Bira	Bala
Pɔɣ	Pɔg	Pɔɣɔ	Pɔɣ	Kye	Kane	Kan	Hal
Kpwɛm	Toa-kpaɣe	Biɛrɛ	Kpɛ̃	Da	Zon-baro	Zono	Mala
Yebeg	Toa-ba	Yao	Ye-bile	Sepo	Nyane	Nyan	Dana
Tɔ kpɛm	Toa-kpaɣe	Yao-pɔɣa-kpɔŋ	Ye'-pugle-kpɛ̃	Da-kye	Nakɔ	Nakɔ	Mala or De-hala
Tɔ bil or Tɔ yebeg	Toa-ba	Yao	Ye'-dible	Sepo	Nabɔ	Nabɔ	Dana
Zaba or Pɔɣ	Nɔn	Biɛrɛ-pɔɣɔ	Kpɛ̃-pɔɣ	Da-pekye	Kane or Bolɔ	Kan	Hal
Zaba or Ser	,,	Sera-yao	Sire-bile	Kul-sepo	Biro	Bira	Nandɔŋ or Bala
Zaba or Pɔɣ	Pɔg	Yao-pɔɣɔ	Ye-bile-pɔɣ	Sepo-bekye	Kane or Bolɔ	Kan	Hal
Zaba or Ser	Coro	Sera-kpɔŋ	Sire kpɛ	Kul gbɔmso	Biro	Bira	Nandɔŋ or Bala
Daki	Kye	Dakyea	Dakyie	Coro	Dɔɔ	Dɔɔ	Bagyene
,,	,,	,,	,,	,,	,,	,,	,,
Daki	Kye	Dakyea	Dakyie	Coro	Dɔɔ	Dɔɔ	Bagyene ＼
,,	,,	,,	,,	,,	,,	,,	,,
Kpɛm (Yebeg)	Yoa	Yao	Ye'-bile	Da	Ko-bu or Nyane	Ko-bu or Nyan	Dana
Yebeg (Kpɛm)	Moa	Biɛrɛ	Kpɛ̄	Sepo	Ko-bu or Zon-baro	Ko-bu or Zono	Mala
Pɔɣ or Zaba	Pɔg or Nɔŋ	Yao-pɔɣɔ	Ye'-bile-pɔɣ	Ni	Nyan-kan	Nyan-kan	Nandɔŋ or Hal
Ser or Zaba	Coro or Nɔŋ	Sera	Sere	Pibi	Biro-zon-baro	Bira-zono	Bala or Nandɔŋ

SPEAKER'S GENERATION (*cont.*)

English.	Mole.	Mampelle.	Dagbane.	Kusal.	Nankane.	Dagare.
Father's bro.'s daughter	Tawa	Ba pira-bi-pugena *or* Sozo'-poa-bila	Ba-pira-bi-puŋa *or* Tuzɔ-paɣa	Tɔ	Ta	Yɔ pule
Father's bro.'s son	,,	Ba-kpɛm-bia	Ba-kpɛm-bia *or* Biele-dɔɔ	,,	,,	Bere
Father's bro.'s daughter's husband	Dakyia	Dakyia	Dakyia	Daki	Dekya	Dakyiɛ
Wife's father's bro.'s son	,,	,,	,,	,,	,,	,,
Father's sister's son	Pɔgodaba-biga, Yaseŋa	Porobia *or* Bere	Pirib-'bia	Pugudu'bi *or* Pito	Pugra bia *or* Sɔta bia *or* Ta (*w.s.*) Yebega	Puro bie *or* Yɔ
Mother's bro.'s son	Yesiba-biribla	Nyes'bia *or* Sozoa-bila	Ɖahab-bia	Asib'bi *or* Ber	Aseba dayoa *or* Ta (*w.s.*)	Ariba bie *or* Bere
Father's sister's son's wife	Pɔgodaba bi-paɣa	Poa *or* Porobia-poa	Paɣa *or* Pirib'-bi-paɣa	Pugudu'bi poa	Zaba *or* Pɔɣa *or* San poɣa	Puro bie pɔyɔ
Husband's mother's bro.'s son	Sida-yesi-ba biga	Sira *or* Sira nye-siba-bia	Yidana *or* Yidaŋa-ŋahab'-bia	Sid asib'bi	Zaba *or* Danya-ma *or* Sira	Sere ariba bie
Father's sister daughter	Pɔgodoba-bi-pugela	Poro-bi-pugena *or* Sozoa-poa	Pirib'-bi-' puŋa	Pugudu'bi	Ta *or* Pu-gra-bia	Yɔ pule
Mother's bro.'s son	Yasiba-biribla	Nyes'-bia *or* Bere doo	Ɖahab'-bia	Asib' bi	Ta *or* Aseba dayoa	Bere
Father's sister's daughter's husband	Dakyia	Dakyia	Dakyia	Daki	Dema *or* Dekya	Dakyiɛ
Wife's mother's bro.'s son	,,	,,	,,	,,	,,	,,
Mother's bro.'s son	Yasib'-biga	Nyes'-bia *or* Bere	Ɖahab'-bia	Asib' bi *or* Ber	Aseba dayoa (bia) *or* Ma ta dayoa *or* Kyɛma	Ariba-bie *or* Bere

Nabte.	Bulea.	Wale.	Loberu.	Gbanya.	Kasene.	Awuna (Fẽra).	Isal.
Tɔ	Toa	Yao-pɔyɔ	Ye'-pu-gule	Da-kye	Nakɔ	Nakɔ	De-hala
„	„	Yao-dao	Ye-deb	Sepo-nyen	Nabɔ	Nabɔ	Mala (or Dana)
Daki	Kye	Dakyea	Dakyie	Coro	Nakɔ-biro or Dɔɔ	Nakɔ-bira or Dɔɔ	Bagyeŋ
„	„	„	„	„	Kan-nabɔ or Dɔɔ	Kan-nabɔ or Dɔɔ	„
Yebeg	Moa (Yoa)	Pure-bie or Biɛrɛ	Sa-arbile	Da or Ta-na-pibi	Ko-nakɔ-bu	Nyina-nakɔ-bu or Na-kana-bu	Dana or Nyelma-bi
Kpwɛm	Disuɔ-bik	Aheba-bie or Yao	Ma-deb-bie	Sepo or Wɔ-pa-pibi	Zon-baro or Dy-ane or Na-bira	Na-bira bu or Zono	Mala or Nera-bi
Zaba	Pɔk or Nɔŋ	Pure-bie-pɔyɔ	Sa-arbile-pɔy	Da-bekye or Bekye	Ko-nakɔ-bu-kane	Nyina-nakɔ-bu-kan	Hal or Nandɔŋ mie
„	Coro or Nɔŋ	Sera-abe-ba-bie	Sera-ma-deb-bie	Kul-sepo or Kul	Biro-na-bira-bu	Bira-na-bira-bu	Bala or Nandɔŋ-mie
Tɔ	Toa	Pure-bie or Biɛrɛ	Sa-arbile-bie	Da, &c.	Ko-nakɔ-bu	Nyina-nakɔ-bu	De-hal
„	„	Aheba-bie or Yao	Ma-deb-bie	Sepo, &c.	Nu-nabɔ-bu	Nu-nabɔ-bu	De-bala
Daki	Kye	Dakyie	Dakyie	Coro	Ko-nakɔ-bu-biro	Nyina-nakɔ-bu-bira	Bagyeŋ
„	„	„	„	„	Kan-na-bira-bu	Kan-na-bira-bu	„
Ahab dayɔ or Kpwɛm	Disɔ-bik	Aheba-bie or Yao	Ma-deb-bie	Da or Wɔpa pibi	Nu-nabɔ-bu, or Nabira-bu	Nu-nabɔ-bu	Dana

SPEAKER'S GENERATION (*cont.*)

English.	*Mole.*	*Mampelle.*	*Dagbane.*	*Kusal.*	*Nankane.*	*Dagare.*
Father's sister's son	Pɔgodoba biga	Poro-bia *or* Sozoa	Pirib-bia	Pugudu bi *or* Pito	Pugra bia *or* Sɔ ta-dayoa (bia) *or* Yebega	Puro bie *or* Yɔ
Mother's bro.'s son's wife	Yasib'-bi-paɣa	Poa *or* Nyes'-bi-poa	Paɣa *or* Dahab'-bi'-paɣa	Asib' bi poa *or* Poa	Zaba *or* Pɔɣa *or* Ma	Ariba-bi-pɔgɔ- *or* Pɔgɔ
Husband's father's sister's son	Sid'-pɔgodo-ba-bi-ribla	Sira-kpɛm *or* Sira-pira *or* Sira-puro-bia.	Yidana *or* Yidana-pirib-bia	Sid pugudu bi *or* Sid	Zaba *or* Sida *or* Dayoa	Sera
Mother's bro.'s daughter	Yasib'-bi-pugela	Sozo'-poa, *or* Nyes'-bi-pugena	Dahab'-bi-puŋa	Asib' bi pugle *or* Tɔ	Ta *or* Aseba pɔyoa *or* Ma ta pɔyoa	Araba pɔyo *or* Yɔ-pule
Father's sister's son	Pɔgodoba-biribla	Bere-doa *or* Poro-bia	Pirib-bi-debega	Pugudu bi *or* Tɔ	Ta *or* Pugra-bia *or* Sɔ-ta-pɔyoa	Yɔ-dɔ *or* Bere
Mother's bro.'s daughter's husband	Yes'-bi-pugela-sida	Dakyia	Dakyia	Asib' bi pugle sid *or* Daki	Aseb'-pɔyoa-sida *or* Sɔ	Araba-pɔyo-sera *or* Dakyiɛ
Wife's father's sister's son	Paɣa-pɔgodo-ba-biga	,,	,,	Poa pugudu bi *or* Daki	Dekya *or* Dayoa *or* Dema-dayoa	Pɔgɔ poro-bie *or* Dakyiɛ
Mother's sister's son	Ma-bil-' biga *or* *simply* Kyɛm *or* Yawa	Ma-bi-ta-doa *or* Bɛre	Ma-pir'-bia	Ma bi, Pito *or* Ber	Ma-bia-dayoa *or* Yebega	Ma-bile-bie *or* Bere
Mother's sister's son	Ma-kaseŋ-biga *or* Ma-kyɛm-sɔba-biga	Ma-bi-ta-doa *or* Sozoa	Ma pir'-bia	Ma bi *or* Ber *or* Pito	Ma-bia-dayoa *or* Kyɛma	Ma-kpɛm-bie *or* Yɔ

Nabte.	Bulea.	Wale.	Loberu.	Gbanya.	Kasene.	Awuna (Fĕra).	Isal.
Pugla bi or Yebeg	Ko-ŋisin	Puro-bie or Biɛre	Sa-arbile	Sepo or Tana pibi	Ko-nakɔ-bu	Nyina-nakɔ-bu	Mala
Zaba or Pɔɣ	Disɔ-bik-pɔg	Aheba-bie-pɔɣɔ or Pɔɣɔ	Ma-deb-bie-pɔɣ	Da-bekye	Nu-nabɔ-bu-kan	Nu-nabɔ-bu-kan	Hal, or Nandɔŋ mie
Zaba or Ser	Coro-ko-ŋisin	Sera or Sera-puro-bie	Sire-sa-arbile	Kul-sepo	Biro-zono or Bir-nyane or Biro-ko-nakɔ-bu	Bira-zono (or Nyan) or Bira-nyina-nakɔ-bu	Bala or Nandɔŋ mie
Tɔ or Ahab' pɔɣoyɔ	Toa	Aheba-bie or Yao-pɔɣɔ	Ma-deb-pɔɣya or Pɔɣ	Da-kye	Nu-nabɔ-bu, or Nabira-bu-kɔ	Nu-nabɔ-bu-ko	De-hal
Tɔ or Pugla bi	„	Puro-bie or Yao dao	Sa-arbile or Sire	Sepo-nyen	Nabo or Ko-nakɔ-bu-baro	Nabɔ or Nyina-nakɔ-bu-bala	De-bala
Daki or Pɔɣoyɔ ser	Kye	Aheba-bie-pɔɣɔ-sera or Dakyea	Ma-deb-pɔɣya-sire	Coro	Nu-nabɔ-bu-biro or Na-bira-bukɔ-biro	Nu-nabɔ-bu-bira	Bagyeŋ
Daki or Dem bi	„	Diema-aheba or Dakyea	Diem arbile	„	Kane-nabɔ or Kane-ko-nakɔ-bu	Kan-nabɔ or Kan-nyina-nakɔ-bu	„
Ma-pir-bi (or dayɔ) or Kpwɛm	Yoa	Yao	Ye-bile	Da	Nyane or Zon-baro	Nyan or Zono	Mala or Dana
Ma Kpɛm dayɔ or Yebeg	Moa	Biɛrɛ	Ye-kpẽ	Sepo	Zon-baro or Nyane	Zono or Nyan	Dana or Mala

SPEAKER'S GENERATION (*cont.*)

English.	Mole.	Mampelle.	Dagbane.	Kusal	Nankane.	Dagare.
Mother's sister's son's wife	Paɣa	Poa, *or* Ma-bi-ta-doa-poa	Paɣa	Poa	Zaba *or* Pɔɣa *or* Mabia-dayoa-pɔɣa	Pɔgɔ
Husband's mother's sister's son	Sida	Sira, *or* Sira-bi-ta	Yidana	Sid	Zaba *or* Sida *or* Sida-ma-kyema-dayoa	Sera
Mother's sister's daughter	Ma-bil'-bi-pugela *or* Tawa	Ma-bi-ta-pugeŋa	Ma-pir'-bi-puŋa	Ma-bi-pugle *or* Tɔ	Ta *or* Ma-bia-pɔyoa	Yɔ pule
Mother's sister's son	Ma-kaseŋ (*or* kyɛm-sɔba)-biga *or* Tawa	Ma-bi-ta-doa	Ma-pir'-bi-debega	Ma-bi-dao *or* Tɔ	Ta *or* Ma-kyɛma-dayoa	Berɛ
Mother's sister's daughter's husband	Dakyia	Dakyia	Dakyia	Daki	Dekya *or* Ma-bia-pɔyoa sida	Dakyea
Wife's mother's sister's son	,,	,,	,,	,,	Dekya *or* dema-dayoa	,,

GENERATION (1) OF ASCENDANTS

English.	Mole.	Mampelle.	Dagbane.	Kusal	Nankane.	Dagare.
Father	Ba *or* Samba	Ba	Ba	Ba	Sɔ *or* Sɔ-dogere *or* Dogera	Sa
Son	Biga	Bia	Bia	Bi	Dayoa *or* Bia	Bie
Father's elder brother	Ba-kaseŋa *or* Ba-kyɛm-sɔba	Ba-kpɛma	Ba-kpɛma	Ba Kpɛm	Sɔ-kyɛma	Sam-kpɛme
Younger bro.'s son	Biga	Sozoa	Ba-pir'-bia	Bi	Yebega doyoa	Bie
Father's younger brother	Ba-bila	Ba-pira	Ba-pira	Ba pito	Sɔ bi'a	Sam bile
Elder bro.'s son	Biga	Bere bia	Biele-bia	Bi	Kyɛma dayoa	Bie
Father's bro.'s wife	Ma	Ma	Ma	Ma	Ma	Ma
Husband's bro.'s son	Biga	Bie	Bia	Bi	Bia *or* Dayoa	Bie

Nable.	Bulea.	Wale.	Loberu.	Gbanya.	Kasene.	Awuna (Fĕra).	Isal.
Zaba or Pɔɣ	Pɔk or Nɔŋ	Yao-bile-pɔyɔ	Ye-bile-pɔɣ or Pɔɣ	Be-kye	Nyane-kane	Nyan-kan or Zono	Hal, or Nandɔŋ
Zaba or Ser	Coro or Nɔŋ	Sera-biɛrɛ	Sire-kpẽ or Sire	Kul	Biro-zon-baro	Bira-nyan (zono)	Bala or Nandɔŋ
Tɔ	Toa	Yao-pɔyɔ	Ye-pugule	Da-kye	Nakɔ	Nakɔ	De-hal
,,	,,	Yao-dao or Biɛrɛ	Ye-dible	Sepo-nyen	Nabɔ	Nabɔ	De-vala
Daki	Kye	Dakyia	Dakyie	Coro	Nakɔ-biro or Dɔɔ	Nakɔ-bira or Dɔɔ	Bagyene
,,	,,	,,	,,	,,	Kane-nabɔ or Dɔɔ	Kan' nabɔ or Dɔɔ	,,
Ba or Ba dogodo	Ko	Ba	Sa	Toto	Ko	Nyina	Nyema
Dayɔ or Bi	Bik	Bie	Bie	Pibi	Bu-baro	Bu-balo	Bi
Ba Kpwɛm	Ko-moa	Ba-kpɔŋ	Sa-kpẽ	Toto-gbom or Gbɔmso	Ko-zono or Ko-zimbaro	Nyina-zono	Nyema-kohean
Dayɔ or Bi	Yoa-bik	Bie	Bie	Pibi	Bu	Bu	Bi
Ba pit	Ko-yoa	Ba-bile	Sa-bile	Toto-Kar	Ko-nyane	Nyina-nya	Nyema kuwie
Bi or Dayɔ	Moa-bik	Bie	Bie	Pibi	Bu	Bu-balo	Bi
Ma	Ma	Ma	Sa pɔɣ	Ni	Nu	Nu	Naŋ
Bi or Dayɔ	Bik	Bie	Bie	Pibi	Bu	Bu	Bi

GENERATION (1) OF ASCENDANTS (*cont.*)

English.	Mole.	Mampelle.	Dagbane.	Kusal.	Nankane.	Dagare.
Father's sister	Pɔgodoba *or* Ba	Poroba	Piri-ba	Pugudu	Pugera *or* Sɔ	Puro *or* Ba
Brother's son	Biga	Sozoa-do-bi' *or* Bere-kpɛm-bia	Bia	Bi	Ta dayoa	Bie
Father's sister's husband	Pɔgodoba-sida	Poroba-sira *or* Ba *or* Dakyia	Ba	Ba *or* pugudu sid	Pugera-sera *or* Dakya *or* Sɔ *or* Dema	Puro sera
Wife's bro.'s son	Paɣa-biga	Bia *or* Ba-dakyia	Bia	Bi	Dakya *or* Dema *or* Dayoa	Bie
Mother	Ma	Ma	Ma	Ma	Ma, Ma-dogerɛ *or* Dogera	Ma
Son	Biga	Bia	Bia	Bi	Bia, Dayoa	Bie
Mother's brother	Yasiba	Nyesiba	Dahaba	Asib	Aseba, sɔ, ma-ta	Araba
Sister's son (*m.s.*)	Yaseŋa	Nyesiŋa	Dahaŋa	Asiŋa	Ta bia (*m.s.*) Dayoa	Araba *or* Bie
Mother's bro.'s wife	Yasiba-paɣa	Dema	Ma	Asib-poa *or* Ma	Ma *or* Aseba-pɔɣa	Araba pɔyɔ
Husband's sister's son	Sida-yaseŋa	Dema	Bia	Sid-asiŋa *or* Bi	Zaba bia *or* Pɔkya-bia	Sera araba
Mother's sister	Ma-bila *or* Ma-kyɛ-ma	Ma-pira *or* Ma-kyɛ-ma	Ma-pira	Ma bil (*or* Kpɛm)	Ma bi'a (*or* Kyɛ-ma)	Ma bile (*or* Kpɛme)
Sister's son	Biga	Bia	Biele-bia	Bi	Dayoa *or* Bia	Bie
Mother's sister's husband	Ma-bil' *or* Ma kyɛm-sida	Ma-pira *or* Ma-kpɛm'-sira	Ma-pira-yidana	Ma pit (*or* Kpɛm)-sid	Ma bi'a sera *or* Sɔ	Ma bile-sera
Wife's sister's son	Paɣa-biga	Poa-bia *or* Dakyia-bia *or* Bia	Paɣa-biele-bia	Daki-bi	Dakya-bia *or* Dayoa	Pogɔ bie *or* Da-kyiɛ-bie

Nabte.	Bulea.	Wale.	Loberu.	Gbanya.	Kasene.	Awuna (Fĕra).	Isal.
Ba	Ko	Pure or Nyana	Pure or Sa	Tana	Ko-nakɔ	Nyina-nako, or Nakana	Nyelma
Bi	Bik	Bie	Bie	Pibi	Bu	Bu	Bi or Nera
Ba	Ko-coro	Ba-or Pure-sera	Pure-sire	Toto	Ko-nakɔ-biro or Ko-tim-baro	Nakan-bira	Nyelma-bala
Bi	Pɔgɔ-bik	Bie	Po-ye-deb-bie	Pibi	Bu or Kane-nabɔ-bu	Bu or Kan-nabɔ-bu	Bi
Ma	Ma	Ma	Ma	Ni	Nu	Nu	Naŋ
Bi	Bik	Bie	Bie	Pibi	Bu (baro)	Bu (balo)	Bi
Ahab or Sog	Ɖyiso	Aheba or Aseba	Araba or Ma-dib	Wɔpa	Nabira	Nabira	Nera
Bi or sog	Ɖyisiŋ	Aheba or Bie	Arbile or Ye-pɔy-bie	Wɔpa-bi or Pibi	Nakɔ-bu or Bu	Nakɔ-bu	Bi
Ma or Ahab-pɔy	Ma	Ma or Aseba-pɔyɔ	Ma-deb-pɔy or Pɔy	Wɔpa-bekye	Nabira-kane or Nu	Nabira-kan	Nera-hal
Zaba bi	Bik	Bie or Sera-aseba	Sire-ar-bile or Sire	Pibi	Bu	Bu	Bi
Ma pit	Ma	Ma-bile (or Kpɛma)	Ma-bile or Ma-kpɛ̃-Bie	Ni-gbom (or Kar)	Nu (ny-ane or Zimbaro)	Nunya	Naŋ
Bi	Bik	Bie	Bie	Pibi	Bu	Bu	Bi
Ba	Ma-coro	Ba or Ma-bile-sera	Ma-bile or Kpem-sire	Toto	Nu zim-bar-biro	Nunya-bira	Naŋ-bala or Nyema
Daki-bi or Dayo	Pɔg-bik	Dakyea-bie or Bie or Pɔyɔ-bie	Pɔy-bie or Dakyie-bie	Pibi	Kane-bu or Bu	Bu	Bi

GENERATION (2) OF ASCENDANTS

English.	Mole.	Mampelle.	Dagbane.	Kusal.	Nankane.	Dagare.
Father's father	Yaba	Yaba	Yaba	Yaba	Yaba	Sankuma
Son's son	Yageŋa	Yaŋa	Yaŋa	Yaŋa	Yiŋa	Yaŋa
Father's father's brother	Yaba	Yaba	Yaba	Yaba	Yaba	Sankuma
Brother's son's son	Yageŋa	Yaŋa	Yaŋa	Yaŋa	Yiŋa	Yaŋa
Father's mother	Yaba	Yab'poa	Yab'paγa or Paγa	Yaba	Yab pɔka	Makuma
Son's son	Yageŋa	Yaŋa	Yaŋa	Yaŋa	Yiŋa	Yaŋa
Father's father's bro.'s wife	Yab'paγa	Yab'poa	Yab'paγa	Yab-poa	Yab-pɔka	Makuma
Husband's bro.'s son's son	Yageŋa	Yaŋa	Yaŋa	Yaŋa	Yiŋa	Yaŋa
Father's father's sister	Yaba	Yab'poa	Yab paγa	Yaba	Yaba-poγera	Makuma
Bro.'s son's son	Yageŋa	Yaŋa	Yaŋa	Yaŋa	Yiŋa	Yaŋa
Father's father's sister's husband	Yab'-pɔksida	Yaba	Yaba	Yab-poksid	Yab-poγera sera	Makuma-sera
Wife's bro.'s son's son	Yageŋa	Yaŋa	Yaŋa	Yaŋa	Yiŋa	Poγɔ-yaŋa
Mother's mother	Yaba	Yab'poa	Yab'paγa	Yaba	Ya-pɔka	Makuma
Daughter's son	Yageŋa	Yaŋa	Yaŋa	Yaŋa	Yiŋa	Yaŋa
Mother's father	Yaba	Yaba	Yaba	Yaba	Yaba	Sakuma
Daughter's son	Yageŋa	Yaŋa	Yaŋa	Yaŋa	Yiŋa	Yaŋa
Mother's mother's bro.	Yaba	Yaba	Yaba	Yaba	Yaba	Sakuma
Sister's daughter's son	Yageŋa	Yaŋa	Yaŋa	Yaŋa	Yiŋa	Yaŋa
Mother's mother's bro.'s wife	Yab' paγa	Yab' poa	Yaba-paγa	Yab poa	Yaba	Sankuma-pɔγɔ
Husband's sister's daughter's child	Yageŋa	Yaŋa	Yaŋa	Yaŋa	Yiŋa	Yaŋa

Nabte.	Bulea.	Wale.	Loberu.	Gbanya.	Kasene.	Awuna (Fĕra).	Isal.
Yab	Ko-kpweŋ	Sankuma or Nabale	Sakum	Nana	Nabaro	Nabalo	Nabalma
Yaŋ	Da-bik	Yaŋa	Yaŋ	Nanebi	Nao	Nao	Nihi
Yab	Ko-kpweŋ	Nabale	Sakum	Nana	Nabaro-nyane (or Zimbaro)	Nabal-nya (or Zono)	Nabalma
Yaŋ	Da-bik	Yaŋa	Yaŋ	Nanebi	Nao	Nao	Nihi
Ya-pok	Ma-kpweŋ	Na	Makum	Nana-kye	Ko-nu	Na	Nahama
Yaŋ	Da-bik	Yaŋa	Yaŋ	Nanebi	Nao	Nao	Nihi
Ya-pok	Ma-kpweŋ	Na	Makum	Nana-kye	Nabaro-kan	Nabal-kan	Nabalma-hal or Hal or Nandoŋ
Yaŋ	Da-bik	Yaŋa	Yaŋ	Nanebi	Nao	Nao	Bala or Nandoŋ
Ya-pok	Ko-kpweŋ	Na	Makum	Nana-kye	Nabaro-nako	Nabalo-nako	Nabalma
Yaŋ	Da-bik	Yaŋa	Yaŋ	Nanebi	Nao	Nao	Nihi
Yab	Ko-kpweŋ-coro	Nabale	Makum-sire	Nana	Nabaro-nako-biro	Nabalo-nako-bira	Nabalma-bala
Yaŋ	Pog-ŋa-bik	Yaŋa	Poy-yaŋ	Nanebi	Nao	Kan-nao	Nihi (or Bi?)
As above	Ma-kpweŋ	Na	Makum	Nana-kye	Nu-nu	Nu-nu or Na	Naha
,,	Da-bik	Yaŋa	Yaŋ	Nanebi	Nao.	Nao	Nihi
,,	Ko-kpweŋ	Nabale	Sakum	Nanebi	Na-bira	Nu-nyina	Nabalma
,,	Da-ŋisiŋ	Yaŋa	Yaŋ	Nana	Nao	Nao	Nihi
Yab	Ko-kpweŋ	Nabale	Sakum	Nanebi	Nu-nu-nabo	Na-nabo	Nabalma
Yaŋ	Da-bik	Yaŋa	Yaŋ	Nana	Nao	Nao	Nihi
Yab-pok	Ma	Na	Sakum-poy	Nana-kye	Nu-nu-nabo-kane	Na-nabo-kan	-Nabalma-hal
Yaŋ	Bik	Yaŋa	Sire-yaŋ	Nanebi	Nao	Nao	Nihi

GENERATION (2) OF ASCENDANTS (*cont.*)

English.	Mole.	Mampelle.	Dagbane.	Kusal.	Nankane.	Dagare.
Mother's mother's sister	Yaba	Yab'poa	Yab'-paɣa	Yaba	Yaba	Makuma
Sister's daughter's child	Yageŋa	Yaŋa	Yaŋa	Yaŋa	Yiŋa	Yaŋa
Mother's mother's sister's husband	Yab'-pɔk-sida	Yab-doa *or* Yaba	Yab-dɔɔ	Yaba	Yaba	Makuma-sere-pɔɣɔ
Wife's sister's daughter's son	Yageŋa	Yaŋa	Yaŋa	Yaŋa	Yiŋa	Yaŋa

FIRST GENERATION OF DESCENDANTS

English.	Mole.	Mampelle.	Dagbane.	Kusal.	Nankane.	Dagare.
Son	Biga *or* Bi'ribla	Bia	Bia *or* Bi'debega	Bi	Bia *or* Dayoa	Bi, Bi dɔ
Father	Ba *or* Samba	Ba	Ba	Ba	Sɔ	Sa
Daughter	Bi'-pugela	Bi'-pugeŋa	Bi-puŋa	Bi-pugle	Pɔ'yoa	Pɔyɔ-ya
Father	Ba *or* Samba	Ba	Ba	Ba	Sɔ	Sa
Son's wife	Bi' paɣa	Bi'-poa *or* Bia	Bi'paɣa *or* Diemba	Bi-poa	San-pɔya *or* Dayoa-pɔya *or* Pɔ'yoa *or* Ma	Bie-pɔyɔ *or* Pɔyɔ-ya
Husband's father	Samba	Denyam'-dɔɔ *or* Ba	Ba *or* Diemba	Ba	Danyam dɔ or Sɔ	Sa
Daughter's husband	Demba	Dema	Diemba	Diema	Dema	Diema
Wife's father	Demba *or* Samba	,,	,,	,,	,,	Diema *or* Sa
Elder bro.'s son	Biga	Bia *or* Bere-bia	Bia *or* Biele-bia	Bi	Dayoa *or* Kyema-dayoa *or* Bia	Bie
Father's younger brother	Ba-bila	Ba	Ba	Ba-pito *or* Ba-bila	Sɔ-bia *or* Sɔ	Sanbile
Elder's bro.'s son's wife	Bi'paɣa	Bi'poa *or* Bia	Biele-bi'-paɣa	Bi-poa	San-pɔya *or* Pɔyoa *or* Ma *or* Dayoa-pɔya	Bie-pɔyɔ

Nabte.	Bulea.	Wale.	Loberu.	Gbanya.	Kasene.	Awuna (Fĕra).	Isal.
Yab	Ma-kpweŋ-baŋ (or Kwage)	Na	Makum	Nana-kye	Nu-nu-nyane (or Zimbaro)	Nanya	Naha
Yaŋ	Bik	Yaŋa	Yaŋ	Nanebi	Nao	Nao	Nihi
Yab	Ma-kpweŋ-coro	Na-sera	Makum-sire	Nana	Nu-nu-nyane-biro	Nanya-bira	Naha-bala
Yaŋ	Po-ŋa-bik	Yaŋa	Pɔy-yaŋ	Nanebi	Nao	Nao	Nihi
Bi or Dayɔ	Bik-nu'-dɔ	Bie	Bie	Pibi-nyen	Bu-baro	Bu-balo	Bi-(bala)
Ba	Ko	Ba	Sa	Toto	Ko	Nyina	Nyema
Pɔyɔ yɔ	Bik-nu-pɔ	Bi-pɔyɔ	Pɔy-ya, or Bi-pɔy	Pibi-kye	Bu-ko	Bu-ko	Tɔlɔ or Bi
Ba	Ko	Ba	Sa	Toto	Ko	Nyina	Nyéma
San-pɔy or Ma or Pɔyɔ-yɔ	San-pɔg	Na-pɔyɔ or Ma	Bie-pɔy	Sea	Bu-kane	Bu-kan	Bi-hal
Ba	Doa	Nabale	Sire-sa	„	Ko	Nyina	Nyema
Dem	Kye-kyem-bik	Diema	Diem	Sea	Bu-ko-biro	Bu-ko-bira	Hel-bala or Tɔlɔ-bala or Bi
„	Ko or Da-chɔp	„	Diem or Pɔy-sa	Sea	Ko	Nyina	Hel-bala or Nyema
Bi or Kpwɛm-dayɔ	Moa-bik	Bie	Bie	Pibi	Bu	Zono-bu-balo or Bu	Bi
Ba	Ko-ba or Ko-yoa	Ba-bile	Sa-bile	Toto-kar	Ko	Nyina	Nyema
San-pɔy or Ma or Dayɔ-pɔy	San-pɔg	Na-pɔyɔ	Bie-pɔy	Sea	Bu-kane	Zono-bu-kan	Bi-hal

FIRST GENERATION OF DESCENDANTS (*cont.*)

English.	Mole.	Mampelle.	Dagbane.	Kusal.	Nankane.	Dagare.
Husband's father's younger brother	Samba	Ba *or* Denyama	Ba	Danyama	Danyam *or* Sɔ	Sa
Elder brother's daughter	Bi'pugela	Bere-bi-pugeŋa	Biele-bi-' puŋa	Bi-pugle	Pɔyoa *or* Kyema-pɔyoa	Pɔya
Father's younger brother	Ba-bila	Ba-pira	Ba-pira	Ba-bil	Sɔ *or* Sɔ-bia	Sanbile
Elder bro.'s daughter's husband	Demba	Dema	Diemba	Diema	Dema	Diema
Wife's father's younger bro.	,,	,,	,,	,,	,,	,,
Younger bro.'s son	Bi'(ribla)	Bia	Bia	Bi	Yebega-dayoa	Bi-dɔ
Father's elder brother	Ba *or* Sam'-kyema	Ba-kpem	Ba-kpɛma	Ba	Sɔ-kyema *or* Sɔ	Sankpeme
Younger bro.'s son's wife	Bi'paɣa	Bi'poa	Bi'paɣa	Bi-poa	San-pɔɣa *or* Ye-bega-dayoa-pɔɣa	Bie-pɔɣɔ
Husband's father's elder brother	Ba	Ba *or* Danyam-doo	Ba *or* Diemba	Danyam	Danyama *or* Sɔ	Sa
Younger bro.'s daughter	Bi'pugela	Bi'pugeŋa	Bi'puŋa	Bi-puŋa *or* Bi-pugle	Yebega-pɔyoa *or* Pɔyoa	Pɔya
Father's elder brother	Sam'kyema *or* Ba-kyem-sɔba	Ba	Ba	Ba	Sɔ *or* Sɔ-kpema	Sankpeme
Younger bro.'s daughter's husband	Demba (Remba)	Dema	Diemba	Diema	Dema	Diema
Wife's father's elder brother	,,	,,	,,	,,	,,	,,
Younger sister's son	Yaseŋa	Nyeseŋa *or* Bia	Dahaŋa *or* Bia *or* Tuzɔ-paɣa-bia	Aseŋa	Dayoa *or* Ta-bia	Araba

Nabte.	Bulea.	Wale.	Loberu.	Gbanya.	Kasene.	Awuna (Fĕra).	Isal.
Dayɔ-pɔɣ	Doa	Nabale	Sire-sa	Sea	Ko	Nyina	Nyema
Pɔɣ-yɔ or Kpwɛm-pɔɣ-yɔ	Le	Bie	Bi-pɔɣ or Pɔɣ-ya	Pibi	Bu-kɔ	Zono-bu-kɔ	Tɔlɔ
Ba-pit	Ko	Ba-bile	Sa-bile (or Sanbile)	Toto	Ko	Nyina	Nyema
Dem	Kye-kyem-bik	Diema	Diem	Sea	Bu-kɔ-biro	Zono-bu-kɔ-bira	Hel-bala or Tɔlɔ-bala or Bi
Dem	Na-cɔp-ba or Kpwake	„	„	„	Ko	Nyina	Hel-bala or Nyema
Pit-dayɔ	Bik	Bie	Bie	Pibi	Nyane-bu-baro	Nyan-bu-balo	Bi
Ba	Ko-kpwake	Ba-Kpɔŋ	Sa-kpẽ	Toto gbom	Ko	Nyina	Nyema
Pit-dayɔ-pɔɣ	San-pɔk	Na-pɔyɔ (or Paɣa)	Bie-pɔɣ	Sea	Nyane-bu-baro kane	Nyan-bu-balo-kan	Bi-hal
Ba	Doa	Nabale	Sire sa	„	Ko	Nyina	Nyema
Pɔɣ-yɔ	Le	Bie	Bi-pɔɣ	Pibi	Nyane-bu-kɔ	Nyan-bu-kɔ	Tɔlɔ
Ba	Ko	Ba-kpɔŋ	Sa-kpẽ	Toto	Ko	Nyina	Nyema
Dem	Kye-kyem-bik	Diema	Diem	Sea	Nyane-bu-kɔ-biro	Nyan-bu-kɔ-bira	Tɔlɔ- or Hel-bala
„	Ɖa-cɔp	„	„	„	Ko	Nyina	Hel-bala or Nyema
Bi or Tɔ bi	Toa-bik	Aseba	Arbile	Wɔpa-bi	Nyane-nakɔ-bu-baro	Nya'-nakɔ-bu-balo	Bi

FIRST GENERATION OF DESCENDANTS (*cont.*)

English.	Mole.	Mampelle.	Dagbane.	Kusal.	Nankane.	Dagare.
Mother's elder brother	Yasiba	Nyes'ba or Ba	Dahaba or Ba	Asib	Aseba or Ma-ta	Araba
Younger sister's daughter	Yaseŋa	Nyeseŋa or Bia	Dahaŋa or Bia or Tuzo-paɣa-bia	Aseŋa	Ta-bia or Ta bia-poyoa or Pɔyoa	Araba
Mother's elder bro.	Yasiba	Nyes'ba or Ba	Dahaba or Ba	Asib	Aseba or Ma-ta	Araba
Sister's son's wife	Yaseŋa pagha	Bi'-poa or Nyeseŋ-poa	Bi'-paɣa	Aseŋ-poa	Sanpoya or Poyoa	Araba-poyɔ
Husband's mother's brother	Sida yasiba	Ba or Danyama	Da or Diemba	Sid-asib	Danyama or Sɔ	Sere-araba
Sister's daughter's husband	Demba	Dema	Diemba	Diema	Dema or Denyama	Diema
Wife's mother's brother	,,	,,	,,	,,	Dema or Pɔɣa-aseba	,,
Mother's sister's daughter's son	Bi'-ribela	Ma-bi-ta-bi-dibiga or Nyeseŋa	Dahaŋa	Aseŋa	Dayoa, or Ta-bia or Ma-bi'a-poyoa-dayoa	Araba or Bi-dɔ
Mother's mother's sister's son	Samba or Ba	Nyeseba	Dahaba	Asib	Sɔ or Ma-ta	Araba or Sa
Mother's sister's daughter's daughter	Bi'-pug'la	Ma-bi-ta-ti-pugeŋa	Dahaŋa	Aseŋa	Poyoa or Ta bia	Araba or Pɔya
Mother's mother's sister's son	Samba or Ba	Nyeseba	Dahaba	Asib	Sɔ or Ma-ta	Araba or Sa
Mother's sister's daughter's son's wife	Bi-paɣa or Bi-pug'la	Nyeseŋ-poa	Dahaŋa paɣa	Aseŋ-poa or Bi-poa	Sanpoya or Poyoa or Ma-bi'-a-poyoa-dayoa-pɔɣa	Pɔya or Bie-poyɔ
Husband's mother's mother's sister's son	Samba	Danyama	Yidan'-ma-tuzɔ-dɔɔ	Sid-asib or Ba	Sɔ or Danyama or Sera ma-ma-dayoa	Sa

Nabte.	Bulea.	Wale.	Loberu.	Gbanya.	Kasene.	Awuna (Fĕra).	Isal.
Ahab or Ba	Ma-toa	Aseba	Ma-deb	Wɔpa	Ko	Nyina	Nyema or Nera
Tɔ-bie or Pɔy-yɔ	Toa-le	Aseba	Arbile	Wɔpa-bi	Nyane-nakɔ-bukɔ	Nya-nakɔ-bubɔ	Tɔlɔ
Ahab or Ba, or Ma-tɔ	Ma-toa	Aseba	Ma-deb	Wɔpa	Ko	Nyina	Nyema or Nera
Sanpɔy or Pɔy-yɔ	San-pɔk	Na-paya or Ma	Pɔy	Sea	Nakɔ-bu-baro-kane	Nakɔ-bu-balo-kan	Bi-hal
Ba	Doa	Nabale	Sira	„	Ko	Nyina	Nyema
Dem	Kye-kyem-bik	Diema	Diem	Sea	Nakɔ-bukɔ-biro	Nakɔ-bu-bo-bila	Hel-bal or Tɔlɔ-bala
Dem or Pɔy-ahab	Da-cɔp	„	„	Sea	Ko	Nyina	Hel-bal or Nyema
Bi or Tɔ-bi or Ma-pit-pɔy-yɔ-dayɔ	Toa-bik	Aseba or Bi-dao	Arbile	Wɔpa-bi	Nu-bukɔ-bu-baro	Nu-nyan-bu-kɔ-bu-balo	De-hal-bi or Bi
Ba or Ma-tɔ	Ma-toa	Aseba or Ba	Ma-deb	Wɔpa	Ko	Nyina	Nyema or Nera
Pɔy-yɔ or Tɔ-bi	Le	Aseba or Bi-paya	Arbile	Wɔpa-bi	Nu-bukɔ buko	Nu-nyan-bu-kɔ-bu-ko	Tɔlɔ
Ba	Ko	Aseba or Ba	Ma-deb	Wɔpa	Ko	Nyina	Nyema
Sanpɔy or Pɔy-yɔ or Ma-pit-pɔy-yɔ-dayɔ-pɔy	Kye-kyem-bik	Na-paya	Arbile pɔy	Sea	Nu-nyane-bukɔ-bu-baro-kane	Nu-nyan-bukɔ-bu-balo kan	Bi-hal
Ba or Danyam or Ser-ma-ma-dayɔ	Da-cɔp	Nabale	Sire-ma-deb	„	Ko	Nyina	Nyema

FIRST GENERATION OF DESCENDANTS (*cont.*)

English.	Mole.	Mampelle.	Dagbane.	Kusal.	Nankane.	Dagare.
Mother's sister's daughter's daughter's husband	Demba	Dema *or* Nyeseŋa-sira	Diemba	Diema	Dema *or* Dem-nyina	Diema
Wife's mother's mother's sister's son	,,	Dema *or* Poa-nyeseba	,,	,,	Denyama	,,
Mother's bro.'s son's son	Bi'-ribla	Bia *or* Nyeseba-bi-bia	Bia	Bi-ribiŋ	Bia-dayoa *or* Aseba-dayoa-dayoa, *or* Ma-ta-dayoa-dayoa	Bi-dɔ
Father's father's sister's son	Samba	Ba *or* Ba-pora bia	Ba	Ba	Poɣere-yaba-dayoa	Sa
Mother's bro.'s son's daughter	Bi'-pug'la	Bi'-pu-geŋa *or* Nyeseba-bi-bi-pugeŋa	Bi-puŋa	Bi-puŋa	Pɔyoa *or* Aseba-dayoa-pɔyoa *or* Ma-ta-dayoa-pɔyoa	Pɔya
Father's father's sister's son	Samba	Ba *or* Ba-poro-bia	Ba	Ba	Poɣere-yaba-dayoa	Sa
Mother's bro.'s daughter's son	Bi'-ribla	Bia *or* Nyeseba-bi-pu-geŋa-bia	Bia	Bi-ribiŋ	Dayoa *or* Aseba-pɔyoa-dayoa *or* Ma-ta-pɔyoa-dayoa	Bi-dɔ
Mother's father's sister's son	Samba	Ba *or* Ma-poro-bia	Ba	Ba	Sɔ *or* Ma-sɔ-ta-bia *or* Ma-pugera-dayoa	Sa
Mother's bro.'s daughter's daughter	Bi-pug'la	Bia *or* Nyeseba-bi-pu-geŋa-bia	Bia	Bi-puŋa	Pɔyoa *or* Aseba-pɔyoa-pɔyoa *or* Ta-bia	Pɔya
Mother's father's sister's son	Samba	Ba *or* Ma-poro-bia	Ba	Ba	Sɔ &c. as above	Sa

Nabte.	Bulea.	Wale.	Loberu.	Gbanya.	Kasene.	Awuna (Fĕra).	Isal.
Dem	Bik coro	Diema	Diem	Sea	Nu-nyane-buko-buko-baro	Nu-nyan-buko-buko-bira	Tolo-Bala
Demnyan	Da-cop	„	„	„	Ko	Nyina	Nyema
Bi or Dayo or Ahab-dayo-dayo or Ma-to-dayo-dayo	Da-bik	Bi-dao	Ma-deb-bie-bie or Yaŋ	Pibi	Nabira-bu-baro-bu-baro	Nabira-bu-balo-bu-balo	Mala or Nana
Pugda-yab-dayo	Ko	Ba	Sa-arbile or San-kum	Toto	Ko	Nyina	Mala or Nana
Poyo or Ahab-dayo-poyoyo or Ma-to-dayo-poyyo	Le	Bi-paya	Ma-deb-bie-bie or Yaŋ	Pibi	Nabira-bu-baro-buko	Nabira-bu-balo-bu-ko	Tolo
Pugda-yab-dayo	Ko	Ba	Sa-arbile or San-kum	Toto	Ko	Nyina	Nyema
Dayo or Ahab-poyuo-dayo	Bik	Bi-dao	Ma-deb-bie-bie or Yaŋ	Pibi	Nabira-buko-bu-baro	Nabira-buko-bu-balo	Bi
Ba or Ma-ba-to-bi	Ko	Ba	Sa-arbile or San-kum	Toto	Ko	Nyina	Nyema
Poyo or Ahab-poyyo-poyyo	Le	Bi-paya	Ma-deb-bie-bie or Yaŋ	Pibi	Nabiro-buko-buko	Nabira-buko-buko	Tolo
Ba, &c. as above	Ko	Ba	Sa-arbile or San-kum	Toto	Ko	Nyina	Nyema

FIRST GENERATION OF DESCENDANTS (*cont.*)

English.	Mole.	Mampelle.	Dagbane.	Kusal.	Nankane.	Dagare.
Mother's bro.'s son's son's wife	Bi'-paɣa or Bi'-pugla	Bi'-poa	Bi-paɣa or Diemba	Bi-poa	San-pɔɣa or Ma or Pɔyoa or Aseba-dayoa-dayoa-pɔɣa	Pɔya or Bi-pɔɣa
Husband's father's father's sister's son	Samba	Denyama	Ba or Diemba	Ba	Sɔ or Sera-sɔ-puɣe-ra-dayoa	Sa
Mother's bro.'s son's daughter's husband	Demba	Dema or Nyeseba-bi-puge-ŋa-sira	Diemba	Diema	Dema	Diema
Wife's father's father's sister's son	,,	Dema or Poa-ba-puro-bia	,,	,,	Dema or Pɔyo sɔ-puɣera-dayoa	,,
Mother's bro.'s daughter's son's wife	Bi'-paɣa or Bi-pugla	Bi-poa	Bi'-paɣa	Bi-poa	Sanpɔya or Ma-ta-pɔyoa-dayoa-pɔɣa	Pɔya or Bi-pɔyɔ
Husband's mother's father's sister's son	Samba	Denyama	Ba	Ba	Sɔ or Danyama	Sa
Mother's bro.'s daughter's daughter's husband	Demba	Dema	Diemba	Diema	Dema	Diema
Wife's mother's father's sister's son	,,	,,	,,	,,	Dema or Pɔy-ma-sɔ-ta-bia or Pɔya-ma-pu-ɣera	,,

THIRD GENERATION OF DESCENDANTS

Son's son's son	Yageŋa-tuble-kyega	Yan-tob-kyea	Yan-teb-kyie	Yaŋ-yit	Yina	Yan-tuloma
Father's father's father	Yab'-ka-seŋa	Yaba	Yaba	Yab-yit	Yaba	Sankuma

Nabte.	Bulea.	Wale.	Loberu.	Gbanya.	Kasene.	Awuna (Fĕra).	Isal.
Sanpɔy or Ma or Pɔy-yɔ or Ahab- dayɔ- dayɔ- pɔy	San-pok	Na-paga or Ma	Yan pɔy	Sea	Nabira- bu-balo- bu-balo- kane	Nabira- bu-balo- bu-balo- kan	Bi-hal
Ba	Doa	Nabale	Sire san- kum	Sea	Ko	Nyina	Nyema
Dem	Kye- kyem- bik	Diema	Diem	Sea	Nabiro- bu-baro- bukɔ- baro	Nabira- bu-balo- bukɔ- bira	Tɔlɔ-bala or Hel- bala
,,	Da-cɔp	,,	,,	Sea	Ko	Nyina	Nyema
Sanpɔy or Ma-tɔ pɔy-yɔ- dayɔ- pɔy	San-pɔk	Na-paga	Yan-pɔy	Sea	Nabira- bukɔ- bu-baro- kane	Nabira- bukɔ- bu-baro- kan	Bi-hal
Ba or Danyam	Doa	Nabale	Sire san- kum	Sea	Ko	Nyina	Nyema
Dem	Kye	Diema	Yan-sire	Sea	Nabira- bukɔ- bukɔ- biro	Nabira- bukɔ- bukɔ- bira	Tɔlɔ-bala or Hel- bal
,,	,,	,,	Pɔy-San- kum	Sea	Ko	Nyina	Nyema or Hel-bala
Yan	Da-nsa	Yan-tule	Yan-bie	Nana fofo or Sepo	Nao	Nao	Nihi-lere
Yab	Ko- Kwem- kpwake	Nabale	Sa-san kum	Nana or Da	Na or Nabalo	Nabalo	Nabalma

THIRD GENERATION OF DESCENDANTS (cont).

English.	Mole.	Mampelle.	Dagbane.	Kusal.	Nankane.	Dagare.
Son's son's daughter	Yageŋa-tuble-kyega	Yan-tob-kyea	Yan-teb-kyie	Yaŋ-yit	Yin-poka	Yan-tuloma
Father's father's father	Yab'-ka-sena	Yaba	Yaba	Yab-yit	Yaba	Sankuma
Daughter's daughter's son	Yageŋa-tuble-kyega	Yan-tob-kyea	Yan-teb-kyie	Yaŋ-yit	Yina	Yan-tuloma
Mother's mother's father, &c., all of this generation being similarly named	Yab'-ka-sena	Yaba	Yaba	Yab-yit	Yaba	Sankuma

GENEALOGY OF SPEAKER'S WIFE (Wife's generation)

English	Mole	Mampelle	Dagbane	Kusal	Nankane	Dagare
Wife's brother	Dakyea	Dakyia	Dakyia	Daki	Dakya	Dakyiɛ
Sister's husband	„	„	„	„	Dakya or Ta-sera	„
Wife's brother's wife	Dakye'-paya	Dakyia poa or Zoa-poa	Paya	Daki-poa	Dema or Dakya	Dakyiɛ-poyɔ
Husband's sister's husband	Sid'-da-kyea	Sira	Yidana	Sid-daki	Dema or Dakya or Pokya	Sere-da-kyiɛ or Dakyiɛ
Wife's sister	Paya or Dakyea	Poa or Dakyia	Paya or Dakyia	Daki, Poa	Dakya or Pɔy-kyema	Pɔyɔ or Dakyiɛ
Sister's husband	Sida	Sira or Dakyia	Yidana or Dakyia	„	Dakya or Ta-sera	Sere or Dakyiɛ

FIRST GENERATION OF ASCENDANTS

English	Mole	Mampelle	Dagbane	Kusal	Nankane	Dagare
Wife's father	Demba	Dema	Diem'-paya	Diema	Dema or Pɔya-sɔ	Diema
Daughter's husband	„	„	Diema	„	Dema or Pɔyoa-sera	„

Nabte.	Bulea.	Wale.	Loberu.	Gbanya.	Kasene.	Awuna (Fĕra).	Isal.
Yan	Da-lea	Yan-tule	Yan-bi-pɔy	Nana fofo or Bekye	Nao	Nao	Nihi-lere
Yab	Ko-kwem-kpwake	Nabale	Sa-san-kum	Nana or Kul	Na or Nabalo	Nabalo	Nabalma
Yan	Da-bik	Yan-tule	Yan-bi-deb	Nana fofo or sepo	Nao	Nao	Nihi-lere
Yab	Ko-kwem-kpwake	Nabale	Ma-san-kum	Nana or Da	Na or Nabalo	Nabalo	Nabalma
Daki	Kye	Dakyea	Dakyie	Coro	Kan-bɔna or Dɔɔ	Kan-nabɔ or Dɔɔ	Bagyeŋ
Daki or Tɔ-ser	,,	,,	,,	,,	Dɔɔ	Dɔɔ	,,
Dem or Daki-pɔy	Kye-pɔk	Dakyea-pɔyɔ	Dakyie-pɔy	Coro-bekye	Dɔɔ-kane or Tin-kane	Dɔɔ-kan	Bagyeŋ
Dem or Daki or Pɔy-kyi-ser.	Kye-kyem-bik	Dao or Sera-dakyea	Sire-dakyie, Pɔy	Kul sea	Dɔɔ	Dɔɔ	,,
Daki	Yoa or Kye	Pɔyɔ (yao or Kpɛma)	Dakyie or Sire	Coro	Kane	Kan	Hal
,,	Kye	Kpɛma (or Yao) o sera	,,	,,	Biro	Bira	Bala
Dem	Da-chɔp	Diema	Diem	Sea	Tinbaro	Kan'yina or Tin-balo	Hel-bal
,,	Kye-kyem-bik	,,	,,	,,	Bukɔ-biro	Bukɔ-bira	Bi (?)

FIRST GENERATION OF ASCENDANTS (*cont.*)

English.	Mole.	Mampelle.	Dagbane.	Kusal.	Nankane.	Dagare
Wife's mother	Dem'-poka	Dema	Diem'paɣa	Diema	Dema *or* Dem-poka	Diem-pɔyɔ
Daughter's husband	Demba	,,	Diema	,,	Dema	Diema

FIRST GENERATION OF DESCENDANTS

English.	Mole.	Mampelle.	Dagbane.	Kusal.	Nankane.	Dagare
Wife's brother's son	Dakye'-biga	Dakyi-bia	Dakyi-bia	Daki-bi	Bia *or* Dakya-dayoa *or* Dayoa	Dakyiɛ-bie
Father's sister's husband	Ba-dakyea *or* Pug'-duba-sida	Poroba-. sira	Pirib'-yi-dana	Puɣdub'-sid *or* Ba-daki	Puɣera-sera *or* Sɔ-ta-sera	Poro-sere *or* Sa-dakyiɛ
Wife's brother's daughter	Dakye-bi'pug'la	As above	Dakyi-bi'-puŋa	Daki-bi-puŋa	Dakya-pɔyoa *or* Pɔyoa	Dakyiɛ-pɔyɔ-ya
Father's sister's husband	Ba-da-kyea, &c.	,,	Pirib'-yidana	Puɣudub-sid, &c.	Puɣera-sera, &c.	Sa-dakyiɛ
Wife's sister's son	Paɣa biga *or* Dakye biga	Bia *or* Dakyi-bia *or* Poa-bia	Bia	Daki-bi	Dakya-dayoa *or* Dakya-bia *or* Dayoa	Bie
Mother's sister's husband	Samba	Ma (Kpem *or* Pira)-sira *or* Ba	Ba	Ba *or* Ma-daki	Ma-sera *or* Sɔ	Sa *or* Ma-sere
Wife's sister's son's wife	Dakye'-bi'-paɣa	Dakyi'-bi'-poa	Bi'paɣa	Daki-bi-poa	San-pɔɣa *or* Dakye *or* Dema *or* Dakya-dayoa-pɔɣa	Bie-pɔyɔ
Husband's mother's sister's husband	Samba	Danyana	Ba	Ba *or* Sid-ma-daki	Dakya *or* Dema	Sa *or* Sere-sa
Wife's sister's daughter	Paɣa bi'-pug'la *or* Dakye'-bi'-pug'la	Bia	Bia	Daki-bi-puna	Dakya-poyoa *or* Pɔyoa	Bie *or* Pɔya

Nabte.	Bulea.	Wale.	Loberu.	Gbanya.	Kasene.	Awuna (Fěra).	Isal.
Dem	Ɖa-nup	Diema-paya	Diem	Sea	Tinkane	Tinkan	Hel-hal
,,	Kye-kyem-bik	Diema or Dao	,,	,,	Tin-baro or Bukɔ-baro	Tinbalo	Bi (?)
Bi or Daki-dayɔ or Dayɔ	Kye	Dakyea-bie	Dakyie-bie	Coro-pibi	Dɔɔ-bu	Dɔɔ-bu	Bagyeŋ-bi
Ba	,,	Puro-sera	Pure-sere	Toto-coro	Nu-baro	Nu-bira	Nyema
Bi or Daki-pɔyɔ-yɔ or Pɔyɔ-yɔ	Kye-le	Dakyea-bie-paya	Dakyie-bi-pɔy	As above	Dɔɔ-bukɔ	Dɔɔ-bukɔ	Bagyeŋ-tɔlɔ
Ba	Kye or Ko	Puro-sera	Pure-sere	,,	Nu-baro	Nu-bira	Nyema
Daki-dayɔ or Bi	Pɔ-yoa (or Moa)-bik	Bie	Dakyie-bie	Coro-pibi	Kane-bu or Bu	Kan-bu	Bi
Ba	Ko	Ba	Ma-yeb-sire	Ni-coro	Ko or Nu-biro	Nu-bira	Nyema
San-pɔy or Daki or Daki-dayɔ-pɔy	Bi'-pɔk	Bie-pɔyɔ or Na-paya	Dakyie-bi-pɔy	Coro-pibi-bekye	Bu-kane or Bukɔ	Bu-kan	Bi-hal
Daki or Dem	Doa	Nabale	Sire-ma-dakyie	Kul-ni-coro	Ko	Nyina	Nabal-ma (?)
Daki-pɔy-yɔ or Pɔyyɔ	Pɔ-yoa (or Moa)-bik	Bie	Dakyie-bi-pɔy	Coro-pibi	Kane-bukɔ or Bukɔ or Dɔɔ-bukɔ	Kan-bukɔ	Tɔlɔ

FIRST GENERATION OF DESCENDANTS (*cont.*)

English.	Mole.	Mampelle.	Dagbane.	Kusal.	Nankane.	Dagare.
Mother's sister's husband	Samba	Ba	Ba	Ma-daki	So *or* Ma-yebega (*or* Kye-ma-sera)	Sa
Wife's sister's daughter's husband	Bi'sida *or* Demba	Dema	Diema	Diema	Dema *or* Pɔya-kyema, (Yebega) pɔyoa-sera	Diema
Wife's mother's sister's husband	Samba.*or* Demba	,,	,,	,,	Dema *or* Pɔya-ma-yebe-ga (Kye-ma (pɔyoa-sera	Diema

Nabte.	Bulea.	Wale.	Loberu.	Gbanya.	Kasene.	Awuna (Fĕra).	Isal.
Ba or Ma-pit (kpwɛm-ser)	Ko	Ba or Bile or Kpem-sera	Ma-yeb-sire	Ni-coro	Ko	Nyina or Tinbalo	Nyema
Dem or Pɔy-ma-pit (kpwɛm)-ser.	Le-coro	Diema	Dakyie-bie-pɔy-sire	Coro-pibi-kul	Bukɔ-biro	Tinbalo	Bi
Dem or Pɔy-ma-pit (kpwɛm)-ser.	Da-cɔp	,,	Pɔy-ma-dakyie	Bekye-ni-coro	Ko or Kan-ko or Tin-baro	Tinbalo or Nyina	Nyema

II

TERMS USED IN RELIGIOUS OBSERVANCES

IN pursuit of my endeavour to prove the affinities in language, custom, and religion between the diversely named tribes who inhabit the Northern Territories, I have, in the present chapter, grouped some of the terms used by them to signify particular aspects of their religious activities. I use the word 'religious' in the widest possible sense, to cover 'a belief in spiritual beings'. Such a classification will serve a double purpose. In the first place it affords a convenient method of comparison from a philological standpoint. Secondly, it brings prominently to our notice, thus early in this book, the close similarity between the terms which the tribes of these parts themselves use in their intercourse with the spiritual universe—that other world which influences their whole outlook upon life in a truly remarkable degree. My experience as a field anthropologist has taught me the importance of a clear understanding of such words. Unless we grasp what these imply to the African himself, we cannot help falling into the common error of grouping together or confusing many sides of primitive religion which the Native himself keeps more or less apart. The examples found here are not drawn from all the dialects or languages recorded in the previous chapter, but the selection given is sufficiently representative to show that the similarity already noted between the terms used to describe their relationships, extends also to other fields of thought and action. A critical examination of the terms found in these tables will occupy many chapters of these volumes. I therefore append here only a few notes which are mainly of etymological interest.

Sky-God: In both the Mole· and the Kasen'-Isal groups, the word used for the Sky-God is practically identical throughout. (In some of the dialects the word *Na* or *Nab'* (Chief) is prefixed.) The root of the word used by all these tribes for the Supreme Being is *we*. The word undoubtedly means simply 'the sun'. To distinguish the heavenly body from the Supreme Spirit, however, the former has generally some other word suffixed, e.g. *we-haya, wen-tan, wen* (or *wun*) *-teya*. Although it might thus appear that the Supreme God of all these people is the Sun, it would be quite misleading and erroneous to state that they are Sun-worshippers. The idea of the Sun *qua* Sun being a god simply does not occur to them. The name by which their chief deity is described seems rather to conjure up in their minds the whole firmament. *Wene* is the Sky-God not the Sun-God. 'The Sun falls in the evening time, but He is always there', said an informant, whom I was questioning on this subject.

It will be observed that in the Gbanya language a different root is found. *Ebɔre* is, I think, the Ashanti *Bɔrc-bɔre* (the Creator). The similarity of Gbanya to Ashanti has already been noted, and there are several other examples of this affinity even in the present short tables, and many more in the vocabularies which follow.

The Earth: In every dialect—in both the Mole group and the Kasen'-Isal group—the root in the word meaning 'land' is common to all, Gbanya, however, has *Esesar*. This is so like the Ashanti *Asase* as to be probably a corruption of that word or *vice versa*. The earth is a female, and is without exception regarded by all these tribes as the 'wife' of the Sky-God. Her cult, as practised by her chief priest, the *Tendana*, is one of the outstanding features of the tribal and political organization of these people.

Priest-King: The word I have translated thus is, in the original, composed of two words, *Teŋa* (or variant) 'land', and a suffix *sɔba*, *dan*, *dagena*, *tu*, or *tina* which in each case may roughly be translated by 'owner', the whole thus becoming 'owner of the land'. 'Owner' in this context means the person responsible to and for the land, its chief trustee, its high priest. This person is the spiritual head of the clan. I have decided to render his title by the compound word Priest-King. The Gbanya equivalent of *Tendana*, i.e. *Esesar-wura* (Ashanti *Asase wura*) has a similar meaning.

Shrine: *Bagare* (or one of its variants) is a shrine or habitation (potential or actual) of a spirit. This spirit may be human, or it may be that of an animal, or a nature spirit, or that of the Sky-God. In the Mole language group, Loberu appears to use a different expression, i.e. *tib-yin*, which possibly means the 'home of medicines'. I think it is very probable, however, that my informant in this case had not quite grasped my question. Gbanya has the word *kigwer*. *Ki* is a common prefix used with nouns in the Gbanya language; the exact derivation of *gwer*, I do not know. Kasene has the word *dwone* and Isal is *lelea*, the latter is just the plural of *lele*, which is the term also used for the spirit after death. The word comes thus by metonymy to be used for shrine. This word is *dwone* in Kasene.

Soul: The root in this word seems common all over West Africa.

Miss Kingsley found the word *sisi* farther west; the Ashanti *sasa* again is probably a variant, although that word has come to be used rather for a spirit after death. *Sia*, or one of its many equivalents, is the volatile soul which is capable of leaving the body even during life, and especially during sleep. It has a dangerous habit, as we see later on, of entering a newly made grave and remaining there after the hole has been closed, thus causing its owner to sicken and die. In Gbanya the word becomes *kelebe*, with the noun prefix *ki*. Kasene and Isal have *dworo* and *dema* respectively. The latter is also used for the little mud shrine on which the soul-owner will sacrifice to his *dema*. (Compare the Ashanti washing of the *kra*.)

Spirit of the Dead: *Kyima* or one of its variants is also used for spirit ancestors.

In Gbanya the word is *ebuni*, *e* being a noun prefix (compare Ashanti). In Isal, *lele* is the singular of *lelea* already noted. The Kasene *dworo* has the same root *dwo*, seen above in *dwone*.

Soothsayers: The soothsayer, oracle man, or diviner, as will be seen presently, takes a leading part in the everyday life of these people. He is consulted on almost every conceivable occasion. Hardly anything can be done until he has been asked. He is really a *medium*, a 'go-between' in the land of the living and the world of spirit ancestors. The root of the word used to describe this person is generally the same as that found in the word for shrine. The people consult him at some shrine, the spirit in which guides him and directs his answers. The soothsayer nearly always has a skin bag in which he carries his stock-in-trade. The soothsayer himself thus often comes to be spoken of as 'the soothsayer-bag' (*ba'kologo*).

Taboo: The root (*kyi*) in the vernaculars is very uniform throughout the whole of this region, extending right down into Ashanti.

Fairy: The root in the various dialects will be seen to be very similar throughout. Loberu has here borrowed from Isal.

Oath: The root throughout is again very constant. The Gbanya, *ntam* is pure Ashanti.

TERMS USED IN RELIGIOUS OBSERVANCES

English.	Mole.	Kusal.	Nankane.	Dagare.
Sky-God	Nwende	Nab'Wen or Wen	Wene or Yini or Na-Wene	Na Nwene
Earth (a goddess)	Teŋa	Teŋ	Teŋa	Teŋa
Priest-King	Teŋsoba	Tendan	Tendana	Tendagena
Shrine	Bagere	Bag'r	Bagere	Bogore
Soul (of the living)	Siga or Sega	Sig	Sia	Sia or Siɛ
Spirit (of the dead)	Kyima	Kpim	Kyima	Kpime
Soothsayer	Baga	Ba'a or Ba'-kolog'	Baga or Ba-kologo	Bogobura
Taboo	Kyisigo	Kisug	Kyisiri	Kyiruŋ or Kyiru
Fairy	Kinkiriga	Kinkirig	Kyinkyiriga	..
Oath	..	Pɔr	Pɔte	Pɔre

English.	Loberu.	Gbanya.	Kasene.	Isal.
Sky-God	Na Nwen	Ebore	We or Wea	Wea
Earth (a goddess)	Teŋ	Esesar	Tega	Tintai or Tinten
Priest-King	Teŋsob	Esesar-wura	Tegatu	Tintaintina
Shrine	Tib-yiri	Kigwer	Dwone	Lelea
Soul (of the living)	Sie	Kikelebe	Dworo	Dema
Spirit (of the dead)	Kpem	Ebuni	Kyiru	Lele
Soothsayer	Ba'bugere	Kpal, Ekpalpo	Voro	Vur'go
Taboo	Kyiru	Kishi	Kyuku	Kasan
Fairy	Kɔntɔn	Katinani	Kyikyirɛ	Kantɔn
Oath	Pɔre	Ntam	Dura	Dweaŋ

III

THE CARDINAL NUMBERS, VOCABULARIES, AND SOME NOTES ON GRAMMAR AND SYNTAX

IN the following tables the cardinal numbers are first given, followed by vocabularies which contain some three hundred words in each of the fourteen languages already examined. A dialect not hitherto noted is also now included, i.e. Talene (*anglice* Talanse). Talene is so closely related to the 'languages' in the Mole group (especially to Kusal) which have already been tabulated, as perhaps hardly to warrant a special vocabulary of its own. The tribe which speak this dialect have, however, so generally been regarded as belonging to a distinct group and as possessing a distinct language that it will be well to dispel this fallacy even at the expense of some repetition. The notes on syntax and grammar which are here included are also presented, in the first instance, in tabular form. Finally, the whole of this linguistic material has been subjected to a critical comparative examination by Dr. Westermann.

This will complete that portion of the present volume which deals almost exclusively with the languages spoken by certain tribes in the Northern Territories. I shall then be free to pass on to an anthropological survey of these same peoples, which, I trust and believe, will have an enhanced value as the result of these preliminary linguistic researches.

The following are some notes on the tables:

I. THE CARDINAL NUMBERS: The numbers up to 'twenty-one' are given consecutively; next the number for 'thirty', going up by tens to 'fifty', followed by the numbers for 'one hundred', 'two hundred', 'three hundred', and then the number for a 'thousand'. The reader, even without any previous knowledge of these languages, can easily construct the numerals which are omitted from the data thus placed at his disposal. In cases where any irregularities occur, these will be specially noted.

The Mole Language Group: In the ten dialects belonging to this group which are here recorded, not only are the cardinal numbers from 'one' to 'ten' derived from roots common to all, but the system of notation is, with one exception, identical. Bulea alone has not a decimal system. In this dialect we find separate numbers only up to 'five', after which we have 'six' expressed by 3+3; 'seven' by 3+4; 'eight' by 4+4; and 'nine' by 4+5. This appears to be the only language in any of the groups examined which have a quintanal system.

Talene and Kusal, it will be noted, have identical names for all numbers throughout. The letter *s* in one language sometimes becomes *h* in another, sometimes *r* (e.g. *nahe* and *nare* for *nase*).

There would appear to be generally an alternative for 'one'. This is, I think, the equivalent of our word 'single'. I omitted, however, to record it in every case.

The numbers from 'eleven' to 'nineteen' are formed thus: 10+1, 10+2, 10+3, &c. 'Twenty' is 10×2. Dagare, Wale, and Loberu borrow their number for 'twenty' from another language (*lezere* or a variant).

An interesting feature of these numerals is the variation caused by the addition of a 'class' or 'pronominal' prefix. I am convinced that all these dialects once possessed noun 'classes'. The tendency seems to be to discard them entirely or to retain only that one which was formerly used for persons, i.e. the *a* singular, *ba* plural 'class'. This in turn becomes used in a slovenly manner until the only trace of what were once half a dozen 'classes', each with a singular and plural, is often the singular number of class I, which is then employed indiscriminately for all 'classes' and for both singular and plural.

It may be noted, that in counting, when no particular object is specified, even in those dialects which still retain 'classes', the speaker tends to put the numeral adjective into 'class' I (*a–ba* class), and he is not particular whether he uses the singular or plural. In those languages which still use 'class' affixes, the old folk, at any rate, would use the proper 'class' were the numeral adjective qualifying a particular and specified noun.

I shall deal with these classes more fully later on under 'Syntax'.

The best example of what has been written above is afforded by Bulea. Here we may note the following. The numeral 'one' is *wanye*, 'two' is *banye*, 'three' *bata*, and so on. Here *(w)a* and *ba* are not really parts of the numerals but are respectively the singular and plural representative class prefixes of what I have later termed 'Class I', i.e. the class into which nouns denoting persons (among others) fall. In the remainder of the languages compared, the speaker has, either through carelessness, or because it has become the custom, put the singular 'class' prefix before the plural numeral adjective to form a

F

plural which has come to be used indiscriminately for all noun classes. In other dialects the fact that this prefix ever was a 'class' prefix is forgotten, and it becomes prefixed to singular and plural alike, and thus becomes merged with the numeral itself, e.g. *ayemle, ayibu*, &c.

The numeral given me for 'one' in Loberu is interesting, i.e. *Boyen*. *Bo* or *bu* is a 'class' prefix used in certain dialects when the numeral qualifies a noun which stands for an inanimate nameless object— a thing.

The Nankane numerals, in the above context, are also instructive. Nankane is one of the few languages which have retained 'class' affixes to a marked degree, although even here they are dying out before our eyes among the younger generation. Nevertheless the numerals given here are the stereotyped form used in other dialects which have abandoned pronominal prefixes.

The numbers for 'thirty', 'forty', 'fifty', &c., are, for the most part, formed by multiples of ten, but there are several exceptions. These occur in those dialects which have a distinct word for the number 'twenty'. In such cases 'thirty' becomes $20+10$, 'forty' 20×2, 'fifty' $20\times2+10$, 'sixty' 20×3, 'seventy' $20\times3+10$, 'eighty' 20×4, and 'ninety' $20\times4+10$. The roots in the words for 'one hundred' and 'one thousand' are identical throughout.

Gbanya: The resemblance of the cardinal numbers in this language to Ashanti are so striking as to be quite unmistakable and afford further proof of the affinities between them to which attention has already been directed. The numbers for 'four' and 'five' have also the same roots as those in the Mole and the Kasen'-Isal groups. The *a* and *ku* prefixes (the latter for the more usual form, *ki*) should be noted.

The Kasen'-Isal Group: The relationship between the roots in the numbers 'three' to 'seven' to those in the Mole group is clear. *Figa* and *piga* (ten), *do* and *yo* (the root in the *yobe, yobo*, &c.), are also possibly the same.

Awuna and Isal appear to have borrowed their word for 'twenty' from another language, i.e. *sapuga* and *mara* respectively. Like those languages already noted which have a separate and distinct word for 'twenty' in place of the multiple 'two tens', we have 'thirty' expressed by $20+10$; 'forty' by 20×2. Awuna then reverts to multiples of ten, and 'fifty' becomes 10×5 (*fenu*). Isal continues to use 'twenty' as the basis, and has $20\times2+10$ for 'fifty'. 'Sixty' in Awuna and Isal is *Sape' toa* and *Mahimmatore* respectively, i.e. 20×3. 'Seventy' in both languages is expressed by saying $60+10$ 'eighty' by 20×4; 'ninety' by

20×4+10. Isal has quite a distinct word for 'one hundred', i.e. zɔla and also for 'one thousand', *Boi*.

I once watched an old friend of mine called Gyapa (an Isala) counting. He held out his left hand, palm upwards, and with the first finger of the right hand he turned down each finger of the left hand in turn, until he reached 'five'; he then opened the hand and repeated the movements; on reaching 'ten', he placed the hands palms together; for 'eleven' he took the big toe of his left foot and gathered it up between the palms of both hands; for 'twelve' he gathered up the big toe and the next toe, and so on up to 'fifteen', repeating the operation up to 'twenty', when he placed both feet together and clasped his hands around them. He was sitting down during this demonstration.

II. Notes on the Vocabularies: The following notes are intended to draw attention to points of possible interest which might be missed in the bare recitation of such tables, by students wholly ignorant of any of these dialects. In most cases I have given the singular and plural of nouns and adjectives. Nouns and verbs, where these parts of speech are not clear from the context, are indicated by n. and v. respectively. In those dialects where *noun classes* still survive I have generally shown them, e.g., *fesega*, s. *ka*; *fese*, pl. *se*. *Ka* and *se* are respectively the singular and plural class prefix. These class-prefixes will be discussed later on in this chapter. In Bulea and Kasene 'classes' are already tending to disappear. In consequence, we need not expect to find them used with any degree of accuracy. In all cases, where I have not been reasonably certain of a word, I have omitted it. Each of these vocabularies was made in the only possible way by which even comparative accuracy may be hoped to be attained, namely, by travelling to the areas inhabited by the actual tribes whose languages were being recorded and settling down among them for a considerable period. The length of time and considerable expense these methods entail generally render such a *modus operandi* impracticable. Vocabularies have sometimes to be obtained by investigators, who are compelled for lack of time, funds, or opportunities to remain in one locality, and there to enlist the services of Africans who are often merely polyglot Natives. The average African has quite a remarkable gift for acquiring languages— up to a point. He may know half a dozen or more sufficiently fluently to make himself understood perfectly for all practical everyday purposes, but he may do this, while ignoring or being ignorant of the niceties of every language save his own. The very names by which the languages and tribes here tabulated have hitherto been recorded on our official maps and records have, for these reasons, seldom been the correct designations. It is, however (as any one with any experience in such work will testify), quite out of the question to expect complete unanimity—even among persons of the same tribe—as to how certain words should be pronounced. There is also often quite a marked difference in the way a language is pronounced and spoken by persons of the same tribe but of different generations, and even by persons of the same tribe and generations who inhabit different villages. I have myself noticed marked changes in a language during my twenty years in Africa.

Every unwritten language spoken in Africa is in this state of flux. There is always, therefore, to my mind, a possible danger for the African, when the European comes along, and with the best intentions in the world arrests this natural growth, and as it were, solidifies an African tongue by first recording it in writing. The stage at which a dialect or tongue is thus arrested, may not represent the more practical or perfect form towards which the language was progressing, and at which it would have eventually arrived had we left it alone. It behoves us therefore, I think, always to be tolerant, to take the wider rather than the academic point of view, and never to try to force upon the African (in our schools) a particular language or dialect just because it may happen to be the one which we have ourselves reduced to writing, or with which we may be familiar. It is here that the skilled philologist like Dr. Westermann can render such a great service to the African. With this word of warning I will pass on to the tables themselves, taking such words as I intend to examine in their alphabetical order.

Adam's Apple: The Mole word and those in most of the languages in this group are composed of the two words *koko* and *raugo* (*daugo*) or their variants and means literally 'male throat'. In Dagbane *kokole* is also used for 'voice'. In Nabte the word *kunkunyan*, lit. 'female throat', is used for 'gullet'. 'Female' and 'male' in this context, as is often the case, are used rather in the sense of 'weak' and 'strong', 'small' and 'large', than as denoting sex.

Adulterer: The word used in the majority of the dialects is a compound noun composed of the word for 'man' or 'woman' and the root of the word for 'to wander', 'roam about', the whole thus becoming 'a man, or woman, who wanders'. *Erega* in Nankane also means a 'wanderer'. In Nabte the word becomes, 'a wandering thing'.

Alarm: The Dagbane presents an amusing and interesting example of borrowing from another language. *Fan-fan-toa* is a corruption of the Ashanti talking-drum war signal *monka ntoa*.[1]

Arrow poison: The word *yabega* (or variant) does not strictly mean arrow poison. *Yabega* is the strophanthus plant. *Yibi* is the bean, and *yaam* the poison when prepared.[2] *Zelem* (or variant) is any poison.

Bastard: The derivation of the word *tampiri* (or variant), which is found in many of the dialects of the Mole group and also in Kasen', is interesting. *Tampiri* really means anything found on the land, which is without a master. It is from the roots *teŋa* (land) and *pise* (to find, to pick up). In many of these dialects, the meaning 'bastard' is of quite secondary significance, the word *tampiri* being more generally applied to a lost sheep or goat or cow, which becomes the property of the 'owner of the land', the Priest-King. Bastard in these dialects is generally more specially designated by a term meaning 'house child' (*yie-bie*, &c.) or 'sister's child' (*Tɔbi*, &c.), from the common practice of keeping a daughter at 'home' to mate with a lover who is in a prohibited degree of marriage relationship with her, in order to raise up seed for her own father's house. This interesting custom will be discussed fully later. Mampelle and Dagbane have a word which is borrowed from a root also found in Hausa. The word used in Isal means lit. 'child of a vagina', and that in Bulea and Dagbane 'lover's child'.

Beat: *Febe* and its variants mean to beat with a whip or lash; *nwe* is to beat with the fist or a stick. This distinction is common to all dialects which employ these words.

Boil: The words given me throughout mean 'to bubble', hence used of a pot boiling.

Butter: *Kam* and its variants besides meaning shea butter (which may be more particularly designated by *tana kam*) mean any fat or oil.

Cap: The word used means in most cases 'head covering'. In Loberu *kpa-wuo* means 'a bag for the back of the head'. Kasene has borrowed the word from the Mole group, *zu* becoming *yu*, *nyu* in Isal.

Carrying Pad: Note the modified *ü* in Bulea. This sound, it will be noted, occurs frequently in this dialect.

Castrate: The various words used to describe this operation refer to the different methods employed. *Lake* (Nankane) is to remove the

---

[1] See *Ashanti*, p. 256, footnote 2.
[2] For account of ceremony see Chap. IX, p. 175.

testicles entirely, compare *lehe* in Isal. *Gya* (and variants) and *za*, to beat between two stones. *Yish* (and variants) to remove entirely.

Chair: In Bulea and Kasene the word used shows that originally the chair or stool was a head-rest. These are still used in the Northern Territories and seem identical with those to be seen in East Africa. The Ashanti stool [1] was, I believe, evolved from the head-rest.

Chameleon: The following superstition with local variations is found among all these tribes. 'If you meet a chameleon coming towards you, it means some serious event (*yele*); if going away from you, good fortune (good head); if crossing your path from right to left, it is taking things from you; if from left to right it is putting something in your hand; if you meet two chameleons copulating, you will take them home to your compound and release them there; your house will then never break.' Certain female ancestral spirits appear to take up their abode in chameleons. This subject will be discussed later when dealing with the *segere* or guardian spirit of children.

Chin: *Lemde* (and its variants) refers really to underneath the chin, but is also loosely used for the chin itself, which is more correctly known as *teŋa-gore* (the sticking place of hair).

Come: In Mampelle the words for 'come' and 'go' appear to be identical. The word seems invariably to be accompanied by a gesture of the hand, beckoning or waving off the person addressed, according to the meaning to be conveyed.

Cow: *Na-nyaŋa* is a cow that has had a calf. A heifer is *na-saal* (or variants *saa*, *sar*). *Na-paha* is a heifer in Isal.

Cut: *Nwa*, *kuge*, *kye*, *kolege*, and their variants, mean respectively to cut with a knife, to slash at, to chop, and to cut the throat.

Day: A day is reckoned from sunset to sunset.

Deaf: *Wuŋa* and *muka* are used respectively for some one partially and completely deaf. *To-kpira* and *zɔlogo* have similar meanings. In Kusal *to-kpeda* means 'short ears'. *Zɔlogo* also means a deaf mute.

Debt: When all other means had failed, debts were recovered by doing what is described as 'descending into the valley' (*sig-boo*) to seize anything or anybody belonging to the debtor's town.

Doctor: The roots *tip* and *tim* (and their variants) which are used throughout are from the verb *tipi*, 'to treat' a person, and *tim*, medicine, respectively.

Egg: *Hál* (Isal) is an egg. *Hàl* with a falling tone is a woman.

Eye: 'To have an eye' in these dialects means to be a witch.

[1] See *Religion and Art in Ashanti*, Chapter XXVI.

Fall: Note the rising tone; *tò* means to die (Kasene).

Farm: *Pugo* (and its variants), *vaam* (Nankane), *talem* (Bulea), *kara* (Kasene), *baka* (Isal), mean farms in the 'bush' some distance from the compound. *Samane* (and its variants), *nanga* (Bulea), *langar* (Gbanya), *kaduge* (Kasene), *nwankaa* (Isal) are plots near the compound. *Za-nore-nakpar* (Mampelle), *kpikpia* (Kusal), *sensayle* (Nankane), are the names for the small plot cultivated by a son for himself in the evening when he has finished work on the family farm. *Talaya* (Kasene) is a tobacco farm.

Fast: 'To fast', in all languages and dialects, with the exception of Gbanya, is idiomatically expressed by 'to tie the mouth'.

Find: *Pisi*, and its variants, mean to find something that does not belong to the finder. All such things invariably (except where the prerogative has been usurped by Chiefs) belong to the land goddess, in the person of the *Tendana*.

Foot: Curious as it may seem, there is not any word to distinguish 'leg' from 'foot' in these languages, and the same applies to 'hand' and 'arm'.

Forget: *Suhu-vale* in Dagbane means literally 'to swallow the heart'.

Fry: *Hàl* (Isal) has a short vowel, *hàl*, also with a falling tone, but with a long vowel, means 'a woman'.

Glass: *Gisiga* (Bulea) and variants may just possibly be merely an attempt to pronounce the English word, but on the other hand the *kusal gotiŋ* is from the root *gos*, 'to look at'. *Be-na-ntere* (Isal) means literally 'look and see yourself'.

Gun: *Buglaudo* (and its variants) mean 'fire stick'.

Hailstone: The idiom in these vernaculars is 'storm (or rain) stones'.

Hair: The words *kobogo* (with variants), and *zobere* (and variants), which in some dialects appear to be used for hair in general, had, and still in some cases retain, distinct meanings. *Zobere*, as one of the roots show, means hair of the head, while *kobogo* is strictly the hair of animals, but is also used for pubic hairs.

Heart: This word in the vernacular is often also used for anger.

Hide (verb): *Fá* (Isal) with a rising tone means to run.

Hunger: In Dagbane *kùm* with a falling tone means death.

Hyena: The Kusal singular, *kora*, is like the Hausa, *kura*. Animals have so many *sobriquets* in Africa, that it is not surprising to find variations in these dialects for the name of the hyena which figures largely in their folk tales.

Kraal: *Bàgèrè* with falling tones is a shrine.

Lamp: In Bulea we find the same word as in Ashanti.

Light: In Isal and Gbanya the meaning is expressed by 'not heavy'.

Lip: This word in the majority of the dialects is made up of two words which mean literally 'mouth skin'. In Bulea and Kasene this becomes 'mouth leaf'.

Lizard: Note the falling tone in *banà* (Mampelle). *Baná* with a rising tone means a bangle. In Kusal, it will be noted, a lizard is described as a 'tree crocodile'.

Lock: Note the derivation of *day-kunkune* in Dagare. The word means literally 'wooden tortoise' and a similar expression is also used in Isal (*bor-golwal*).

Mad: In Mampelle and Dagbane *kpe* is the verb 'to enter'.

Market: Bulea has also a special word for a woman's market, *yaara*.

Marry: The common idiom is simply 'to eat a woman', i.e. to mate. Dagbane has, to take, to lift up, a woman.

Meat: The root in the vernacular in this word seems to be common right across the African continent.

Meet (v.): The words *pay* and *tur* (Loberu) and variants, mean 'to overtake' and 'to meet some one coming in the opposite direction' respectively. *Seye* and variations also mean to meet by overtaking.

Menstruation: The most common idiom is one which means literally 'to fall from the waist'. *Lwi seya* (or variants). Sometimes a circumlocution is employed as in Dagare where we find 'to put on leaves', or 'to change the waist'. Isal has also euphemistically 'leaves', and *men-cal* (*cal* is blood). Slang expressions are *m'ko la m' lodega* (or *ba' dɔ*) *zina* (I have killed my young bull (or my male dog) to-day).

Mid-day: The idiom is, 'sun-middle' or 'head-middle'.

Neck: Note that in Kasene and Isal, singular and plural are spelled alike. Isal, however, changes the tone from a low to a high for the plural. I could not detect any corresponding change in Kasene, but such possibly escaped my notice.

Needle: The idiom throughout is generally 'cloth (or coat) arrow'.

New: Note the tones in Dagare to distinguish singular and plural.

Nostril: Expressed by 'nose hole'.

Penis: In Dagbane *yólé* with a rising accent on both syllables means vain, worthless.

Pig: *Preko* in Dagare is the word used in Ashanti. The derivation is from the Portuguese *porco*. See also Gbanya.

Pipe: Idiomatically expressed by 'tobacco pot'.

Rainbow: The idioms are 'the chameleon of the storm', 'the knife of the storm', 'the chameleon's mark', 'the chameleon's bow', 'the strung bow' (Bulea).

Sand: Note the word in Gbanya means literally 'river earth'.

Sandal: Note the tones which are here used in Isal to signify the difference between singular and plural in words otherwise spelled alike.

Sieve (n.): The two words given in Isal are the names for a 'grain' and a 'beer' sieve respectively.

Small-pox: In Kusal it will be noted that the euphuism 'the Chief' is used for the dread disease.

Snake: *Wìrí* in Dagbane with a falling and a rising tone means a horse. I could not obtain any general name in Kasene for snake and the name given here is for the python. The word in Isal is possibly from the root *dem*, to bite.

Stink: *Pōge* and its variants mean literally 'to be rotten', hence, to stink.

Undress: The words given under this heading exhibit an interesting and, as far as I am aware, a hitherto unrecorded peculiarity in these languages. This is the existence of plural 'verbs'. Examples of these are: in Mampelle, *yee* and *pidige* to take off a single garment, *yese* and *pidisi* to take off several garments, so too in Nankane, *ye*, *yese*; in Dagare *yage*, s., *yagere*, pl.: Loberu, *ya*, s., *yar*, pl. Other examples of this interesting grammatical construction will be found in the notes under syntax. See also *lɔke*, s.; *lodege*, pl. (Mole); *lorege*, s.; *lorese*, pl. Nankane; *lore*, s.; *lori*, pl. (to untie).

Vaccination: The root in the majority of the words used is *da*, 'to buy'. A form of vaccination—by making an incision, generally on the wrist, and rubbing in some pus from a patient already suffering from small-pox—was practised by all these tribes from time immemorial. The pus had a market value and was bought and sold, hence the word. The Loberu expression *nwa . . . yan* means simply 'cut . . . put', as also does *kpare . . . he* (Isal).

Vagina: *Batoni* in Isal means literally 'the elephant's mouth'.

Wash: *Pɛke* (and variants) mean to wash pots, clothes, or the face, *su* to bathe the whole body. *Nar* and *sudi* (Bulea) are to wash pots and clothes respectively. In Gbanya *foro* is to wash the face, pots, or clothes, *birr* to wash the body. In Kasene *se* is to wash pots and clothes, *su* to wash the face, and *soe* to wash the body. In Isal *tisi* is to wash pots, *kyese* to wash clothes, *fo* to wash the person.

Wink: *Kahem* or *jahem* in Dagbane means to beckon, to make a sign; *gahem nu* to beckon with the hand, *kahem ni* to beckon with the eye.

III. Some Further Notes on the Grammar and Syntax. For fuller notes on Mole grammar and syntax I would refer the reader to my *Elementary Mole Grammar*; for Kasene to the treatise named on p. 11. There is also a grammar in Dagomba.[1] If further proofs were needed to show the close relationship between the languages of the Tribes whose vocabularies and classificatory nomenclature have now been examined, this is afforded by a comparison of the finer points in the grammatical construction and syntax of these same languages.

Classes: I propose first to examine these various languages to see how far 'classes'—or 'concords' as we used to term them in East Africa—are still employed. Classes appear still to be used in the following dialects, their prominence being in the order named: Nankane, Kasene, Bulea. In Mampelle and Dagbane there still remains a faint trace of their use, while in the remainder their former existence has to be assumed from indirect evidence alone. By 'classes' I do not here refer to the various classes into which nouns may be grouped for the formation of their plural, but to pronominal prefixes and pronouns, those concords which are also found in Bantu languages.

Concords or Classes in Nankane: The White Fathers at Navarongo have, I believe, been engaged for some years on the compilation of a Nankane grammar and dictionary. These have not yet been published, nor have I had access to their manuscripts. It is with some diffidence, therefore, that I append the following somewhat scanty notes on this difficult subject. So far as I have been able to discover, there appear to be seven concords or classes in Nankane, and these are tabulated as follows:

Class I. s. *A*, pl. *Ba*.

   e.g. *Nera a-yemna*, one person. *Nereba ba-yi*, two persons.

Class II. s. *ka*, pl. *se*.

   e.g. *Pɔka ka-yemna*, one woman. *Pɔkase se-yi*, two women.

Class III. s. *de*, pl. *a*.

   e.g. *Yire de-yemna*, one compound. *Yea a-yi*, two compounds.

Class IV. s. *bo*, pl. *i* (*yi*).

   e.g. *Wefo bo-yemna*, one horse. *Wiri i-yi*, two horses.

Class V. s. *ko*, pl. *to*.

   e.g. *Dɔɔ ko-yemna*, one log. *Dɔro to-yi*, two logs.

Class VI. s. *ka*, pl. *ba*.

   e.g. *Bia ka-yemna*, one child. *Koma ba-yi*, two children.

---

[1] *Dagomba Grammar*, by J. A. S. Okraku, Cambridge University Press, 1917.

Class VII. s. *ka*, pl. *to*.

    e.g. *Pugela ka-yemna*, one girl. *Puguto to-yi*, two girls.

These classes appear to be regularly prefixed to the numeral adjectives as here shown, but do not seem to be used with other adjectives, which form their plural apparently irrespective of the noun they qualify. (To this there appear to be some exceptions, e.g. in adjectives denoting colour, which will be noted presently.) I hazard the opinion that the omission of these concords before adjectives other than the numeral adjectives may be due to the striking change of form which the noun appears to undergo when it is qualified by, that is precedes, an adjective. Many years ago I noted exactly the same change in the noun in Mole, and what I then wrote, at a time when I was wholly unaware of the existence of class affixes in certain languages spoken in the Northern Territories, also equally applies to the change the noun undergoes when qualified by an adjective in Nankane. The reference is as follows:

'It has been seen that the same rules which govern the formation of the plural of nouns also in most cases apply to adjectives. This is the only inflexion the adjective undergoes, it having no gender inflexion. It is necessary, however, to note here the change the form of *the noun* undergoes when it is qualified by (i.e. in Mole, precedes) an adjective. This change is sometimes so marked as to alter the noun almost past recognition, indeed the present writer was so led astray at first by noticing these changes, as to imagine the altered form of the noun to be a concord or pronominal prefix.'

I have gradually come more and more to the conclusion that these concords in many Northern Territory languages are employed for euphonic reasons and are not in the nature of 'gender' categories into which certain nouns are placed because they are classed for some obscure reason in the Native mind as falling into a particular class or group. Even human beings, it will be noted, do not all necessarily fall in the *A, Ba* class, e.g. *Pɔka* has *ka*, s.; *se* pl. It would follow therefore, that when a noun suffers considerable euphonic change, in this case by elision of a whole syllable or of a final vowel, the reason for modifying the sound of the word which follows it, to conform with the sound of the original last syllable in the preceding word, no longer exists. This theory is only put forward as a tentative suggestion. Another possible explanation may be that what we call an 'adjective' may, to the Native be looked upon as a 'noun', and not therefore be subject to the adjective inflexion. This latter suggestion might appear to be borne out by the fact that when we have a noun coupled with a descriptive adjective and a numeral adjective, the latter still seems to retain the class prefix which the former lacks, although the noun has suffered the euphonic changes noted above, e.g. a white girl is *pɔ' pelega*, pl. *pɔ-pelse*, but one white girl, two white girls, become *pɔ pelega ka-yemna*, *pɔ-pelse se-yi*. There is, however, a further complication. As noted above, changes seem to take place in certain adjectives denoting colours (and possibly in others) and we have three distinct singulars and three distinct plurals which appear to vary *according to the class of the noun which they qualify.* Thus we have:

(*a*) *pelega*, s.	*pelse*, pl.	⎫		
(*b*) *pelego*, s.	*pelo*, pl.	⎬	white.	
(*c*) *pele*, s.	*pela*, pl.	⎭		
(*a*) *mɔlega*, s.	*mɔlse*, pl.	⎫		
(*b*) *mɔlego*, s.	*mɔlo*, pl.	⎬	red.	
(*c*) *mɔle*, s.	*mɔla*, pl.	⎭		
(*a*) *sablega*, s.	*sablese*, pl.	⎫		
(*b*) *soblego*, s.	*soblo*, pl.	⎬	black.	
(*c*) *sable*, s.	*sabla*, pl.	⎭		

Coupled with certain nouns we have:

> *Pɔ pelega*, a white girl. *Pɔ pelse*, white girls.
> *Ɣe pelego*, a white compound. *Ɣe pelo*, white compounds.
> *Ze*[1] *pele*, a white place. *Ze pela*, white places.

With *sablega* we have:

> *Nere sablega*, a black person. *Nere-sablese*, black persons.
> *Zo-sɔblego*, a black hair. *Zo-sɔblo*, black hairs.
> *Sagban sable*, a black cloud. *Sagban sabla*, black clouds.

I am inclined to think that in these cases the noun concord or class prefix, may possibly have become a class suffix. One more example, the only one I have been able to find, seems to bear out this supposition. A bad man is *nere beo*, but bad water is *Ko bebo*. *Ko*, water, is a *Bu*-class noun. A good man is *nere sona*, good water, *ko somo*. I leave further discussion of this very interesting problem to Dr. Westermann's expert examination, to pass on to a further investigation of those concords when coupled with other parts of speech.

---

[1] *Ze* is *de*, s., *a*, pl. class.

The classes next appear as nominative or objective pronouns, for *he, she, it, him, her,* and *they* and *them,* when they take the following form:

3rd person singular.	3rd person plural.
Class I. *e.*	*ba*
Class II. *ka*	*se, si*
Class III. *de*	*a*
Class IV. *bo*	*i*
Class V. *ko*	*to*
Class VI. *ka*	*ba*
Class VII. *ka*	*to*

e.g. *Iri wa de dela m'yiri,* this house it is my house, but *Ba wa ka dela m'ba,* this dog it is my dog.

We next find the classes coupled with the interrogative pronoun which? (*na?*), thus:

Class I.	s.	*e-na?*	pl.	*ba-na?*
Class II.	„	*ka-na?*	„	*se-na?*
Class III.	„	*de-na?*	„	*a-na?*
Class IV.	„	*bo-na?*	„	*i-na?*
Class V.	„	*ko-na?*	„	*to-na?*
Class VI.	„	*ka-na?*	„	*ba-na?*
Class VII.	„	*ka-na?*	„	*to-la?*

Wa is added to the above to form the demonstrative pronouns, *this, these.* The class prefix also appears in the relative pronouns, *who, which,* where it is suffixed to the particle *se.*

e.g. I saw the men who . . . , *M'nye nereba la seba . . .*
I saw the women who . . . , *M'nye pɔkase la sese . . .*
I saw the horse which . . . , *M'nye wefo (yefo) la sebo . . .*
I saw the house which . . . , *M'nye yiri la sere[1] . . .*
I saw the houses which . . . , *M'nye yiri la sei . . .*
I saw the sticks which . . . , *M'nye dɔɔ la seo or seko . . .*

An *n* sometimes appears to follow the relative, which is perhaps inserted for the sake of euphony.

The Concords in Kasene: In Dr. Cremer's posthumous work[2] on the 'Kassene' language five classes are recorded as follows:

---

[1] *Sere = sede.*

[2] This grammar was made from a manuscript found among Dr. Cremer's papers after his death and published under his name. The MS. was, I understand, not the work of Dr. Cremer himself but of Monseigneur Moran of the White Fathers'

Class I.	s.	*o.*	pl.	*ba.* ? ? *a.*
Class II.	„	*ka*	„	*se*
Class III.	„	*ko*	„	*te, ti*
Class IV.	„	*ko*	„	*de, di*
Class V.	„	*de, re.*	„	*ye, ya.*

My own investigations among this tribe were carried out at Paga, a few miles from the frontier of the French Haut Volta. Here I found four classes, Cremer's I, II, III, and V. His class IV is, I am inclined to think, the same as his class III, as I found *de* and *te* apparently interchangeable. This may of course have been due to carelessness on the part of my informants.

At Paga I noticed a very marked tendency to transfer the singular of all these classes to Cremer's class V, i.e. to make it *de*, while still generally retaining the correct plural class. When I queried this apparent inaccuracy, my informant would on second thoughts generally give the correct class prefix. Among the younger generation this irregularity was most marked and shows that the use of classes among them is tending to disappear.

The presence of almost identical classes in Nankane and Kasene is curious, as the general vocabularies of these languages do not appear to bear much resemblance to each other. The Kasena state that they acquired them by intermarrying with Nankane women, but I doubt very much if this explanation is correct.

Concords in Bulea: The following were noted:

Class I.	s.	*wa.*	pl.	*ba.*
Class II.	„	*ka*	„	*si, se*
Class III.	„	*de*	„	*y, ya*
Class IV.	„	*bu*	„	*n, na,* and also *ti.*
Class V.	„	*ko, ku.*	„	*ti.*

These classes are, however, used in a very lax manner and will, I think, soon disappear from the language. Singulars and plurals are already used almost indiscriminately; *y* or *ŋa* is much favoured for almost any plural, *ba* is often found used with a singular. These irregularities may be trying to the student who is attempting to frame systematic rules, but they are, on the other hand, particularly instructive as showing the intermediate stage between the systematic and correct use of classes

Mission at Navarongo, who had lent it to Dr. Cremer. These facts were not of course known to the editor, who naturally assumed that it was the work of the officer among whose papers it was found.

as in Nankane, their almost complete disappearance, as in Mampelle, Dagbane, &c., and their final extinction in Mole.

Concords in other languages: The only direct trace which I can find of classes in Mampelle and Dagbane is in the third person singular pronoun. The personal pronoun is *o*, but for animals and inanimate objects it becomes, in Mampelle *ka*, a relic of the *ka* (s.), *si* (pl.) class, and in Dagbane *de* or *le*, the Nankane *de* (s.), *a* (pl.) class. In Dagare again, we find, e.g. *Pɔgɔ-yene*, one woman, and *pɔgɔba-bayi*, two women, while for other nouns they still use a plural *a*, which the occasional use of *de* for the singular points to being the *de* (s.), *a* (pl.) class noted in Nankane. The singular of this class also survives in Dagbane (see above). This *de* (s.), *a* (pl.) class has also survived in Kusal, apparently to the exclusion of even the *ba* class plural, for we find *nid' deko* (one person); *poa deko* (one woman), *ba reko* (one dog), with plurals, *nit ayi, poa ayi, bas ayi*. In Mole the *a* prefixed to all numeral adjectives is, I believe, a remains of this class prefix, but it has here become part of the word and has lost all its former significance. In Isal, the only trace of class prefixes which I have noted are the *o* (s.), *ba* (pl.) class.

Gbanya presents some interesting features. The *ki* prefix in nouns is reminiscent of Swahili. There is also a distinct trace of former classes in the *ku* or *ko*, for the third singular pronoun as an alternative for *mo*, and the *a* as an alternative for *ba* for third person plural. So *mo*, means give him or her (a person), but *so ko*, means give it, when the object referred to is not a human being, with plurals respectively of *so bomo* and *so amo*. Loberu has lost all direct evidence of classes, but there is the usual indirect evidence that it once possessed them. Unfortunately, I omitted to make any notes about the presence or absence of classes in Nabte and Talene.

The Verb (the Future and Past Tenses): The future and past tenses in some of the languages and dialects here recorded exhibit some curious, and as far as I am aware, hitherto unrecorded grammatical features.

The Past Tense: An examination of the tables illustrating the grammar and syntax shows that in many of the dialects, the past tense is formed by a particle *da*. In certain of these dialects, however, e.g. in Mampelle, Dagbane, Nankane, Gbanya, there also appears a second or even a third particle *sa*, *de*, *ka*, or *zaan*. One might easily be tempted to pass over these alternative forms by assuming that they merely represented different ways of expressing the same idea, i.e. an action in the past, as indeed in a sense they do. They express more than this, however, for each particle, besides postulating an event which took place in time past, designates a particular time or date in that past. We have thus sometimes, e.g. in Dagbane, as many as three past tenses. These I have classified as follows:

(*a*) The particle *de*, used to describe events which took place on the day on which the facts are being related. This tense I shall call the Immediate Past.

(*b*) The particle *sa*, used to describe events which took place yester-day—the Less Immediate Past.

(*c*) The particle *da*, used to designate a more remote past than that of to-day or yesterday—the More Remote Indefinite Past.

Examples: *N'de nya bi ma*, I saw the child (some time to-day)
N'sa nya bima, I saw the child (some time yesterday)
N'da nya bima, I saw the child (some time in the past, but neither to-day nor yesterday).

Mampelle has retained two of the above, i.e. the particle of the immediate past, using *sa* for a past not later than yesterday and *da* for all other past events. In Nankane, also, two pasts are used, one expressed by *da* for the more remote past, and another *zaam* to express events of not later than yesterday's happening. Gbanya, too, has two pasts, a more remote expressed by *da*, and a less remote expressed by *ka*. In Mole no such distinctions are seen and we find only *da*. A more minute examination of the various particles which determine these finer shades of meaning is most instructive, and sheds some light on the lines on which a language is built up. Some, at least, of these forms *da*, *de*, *sa*, *zaan*, &c. which now appear as mere particles prefixed to the verb were, I believe, originally adverbs of time. *Da*, which denotes the past tense, was originally, I believe, the adverb *da*, formerly, once upon a time; *sa*, now only used in Mampelle and Dagbane for a past of yesterday, was originally, I think, *sɔhla*, *sɔ* (yesterday); *de*, was possibly *dare* (day). The Nankane *zaan* for past events of yesterday is probably the same word as *zaam* (yesterday).

The Future Tense: The suggestion made above, namely, that these particles which we now find joined to the verb to express the past tense were originally adverbs of time, seems further borne out by a careful examination of the future tense. Here again we find this tense divided into:

(*a*) A future of indefinite time, expressed by *na*, *ni*, *n*.

(*b*) A future time limited to to-morrow, *san*.

(*c*) A more remote indefinite future, expressed by *dan* (*kan* in Gbanya.) Thus we have a rather curious idiom, for we note that the same words are employed to express periods of time in the past and periods of time in the future, these times being as distant in the past from the present as they are distant in the future from the present.[1]

Here again we find that other dialects have dropped these refinements and employ a simple future. It may be noted, that for some reason which still remains obscure, the future tense appears often to have a separate negative particle of its own, distinct from the ordinary negative used with other tenses.

Plural Verbs: I have already mentioned plural verbs. The following are further examples of their use:

Yɛ fo fuo, take off your cloth. *Yɛse fo futo*, take off your cloths.

Korege noa wa, cut the throat of this fowl. *Korim nose wa*, cut the throats of these fowls.

Deke, pick up one thing. *Dekese*, pick up several things.

Pie, to find one thing. *Pise*, to find several things.

Nwelege, to twist once. *Nwelem*, to twist several times.

Nworege, to break one thing. *Nwore*, to break several things.

These above examples are taken from Nankane, but the majority of these languages either possess this idiom or show signs of once having done so. Once again (as in the case of classes), the tendency appears to be to drop such finer distinctions and to adopt one or other of what were once distinct forms using this as a transitive verb with an objective case, which may be singular or plural.

---

[1] This is exactly in conformity with another curious idiom where we find the same adverb of time used to signify the day before yesterday and the day after to-morrow. It would be interesting to discover if the two future forms in Hausa had a similar origin and meaning as the above.

I. THE CARDINAL NUMBERS

English.	Mole.	Mampelle.	Dagbane.	Kusal.	Nankane.	Dagare.	Nabte.
One	Ayemle	Yendam, ayene	Ayini	Ayen, Ko	Ayene, Yenta	Yenti or Ayeni	Ayeni
Two	Ayibu	Ayi	Ayi	Ayi	Ayii	Ayi	Ayi
Three	Atabo	Ata	Ata	Ata	Ataa	Ata	Ata
Four	Anase	Anase	Anahi	Anase	Anase	Anare	Anase
Five	Annu	Annu	Anu	Anu	Anuu	Anu	Anuu
Six	Ayobe	Ayobo	Ayobu	Ayob'	Ayobe	Ayobe	Ayobo
Seven	Ayopɔi	Ayapɔi	Ayopoŋ	Ayopɔi	Ayopɔi	Ayopɔi	Ayopɔi
Eight	Ani	Anii	Anii	Ani	Anii	Ani	Anii
Nine	Awai	Awai	Awai	Awai	Awai	Awai	Awai
Ten	Piga	Piya	Piya	Pig	Pia	Pie	Pu
Eleven	Pi'la'ye	Pi'ne ayene	Pi'ni 'yini	Pi'ne 'yeni	Pia la 'yene	Pie ne 'yeni	Pu ne 'yeni
Twelve	Pi'la'yi'	Pi'ne ayi	Pi'ni ayi	Pi'ne ayi	Pia la'yu	Pie ne ayi	Pu na 'yi
Thirteen	Pi'la'ta'	Pi'ne ata	Pi'ni ata	Pi'ne ata	Pia la'-taa	Pie ne ata	Pu n' ata
Fourteen	Pi'la'na'	Pi'ne anase	Pi'ni nahi	Pi'ne anase	Pia la-'nase	Pie ne anare	Pu n' anas'
Fifteen	Pi'la'nnu	Pi'ne annu	Pi'ni anu	Pi'ne anu	Pia la-'nuu	Pie ne anu	Pu n'a nuu
Sixteen	Pi'la'yo-be	Pi'ne ayo-bo	Pi'ni ayo-bu	Pi'ne ayob	Pia la-'yobe	Pie ne ayobe	Pu n'a yobo
Seven-teen	Pi'la'yo-pɔi	Pi'ne ayopɔi	Pi'ni ayo-poŋ	Pi'ne ayopɔi	Pia la-'yopɔi	Pie ne ayopɔi	Pu na 'yopɔi
Eighteen	Pi'la'ni	Pi'ne nii	Pi'ni anii	Pi'ne ani	Pia la'nii	Pie ne ani	Pu na 'nii
Nineteen	Pi'la'wai	Pi'ne awai	Pi ni awai	Pi'ne awai	Pia la'-'wai	Pie ne 'wai	Pu na 'wai
Twenty	Pishi	Pisi	Pisi	Pisyi	Pisyi or Pisi	Lezere	Pisyi
Twenty-one	Pish'la ye	Pis'ne 'yene	Pis ni ye	Pis'ne 'yen	Pis'la 'ye	Lezer ne 'yen	Pis'ne 'yeni
Thirty	Pishta	Pista	Pihita	Pista	Pisita	Lezer ne pie	Pista
Forty	Pishnase	Pisnase	Pihnahi	Pisnase	Pisinase	Lezer-ayi	Pisnase
Fifty	Pishnnu	Pisnu	Pihinu	Pisnu	Pisinuu	Lezer ayi-ne-pie	Pisnu
Hundred	Kwɔbaga	Kwɔbega	Kobga	Kobog	Kwɔbega	Kɔɔ	Kwoboɣ
Two hun-dred	Kwɔbsi	Kwɔbsyi	Kobsu	Kobsyi	Kwɔbsiyu	Kosayi	Kwobsiyi
Three hundred	Kwɔbsta	Kwɔbsta	Tobsta	Kobsta	Kwɔbsita	Kosayi	Kwobsiyi
One thousand	Tusuli	Tuhuli	Tuhuli	Tusur	Tushiri or Tusere	Turi	Tuhule

Bulea.	Wale.	Loberu.	Talene.	Gbanya.	Kasene.	Awuna.	Isal.
Wanye	Yente *or* Ayene	Boyen	Ayen	Kukonle, Eko	Kallo *or* Dodo	Kallo *or* Nodo	Kubala *or* Dian
Bayi	Ayi	Ayi	Ayi	Anyɔ	Lle	Lle	Lea
Bata	Ata	Ata	Ata	Asa	'Tɔ	'Tɔa	Tɔre
Banase	Anahe	Anan	Anas	Ana	'Na	'Nea	Nese
Banu	Anu	Anuu	Anu	Anu	'Nu	'Nu	Nɔŋ
Batanta (3 3)	Ayuobe	Ayoob	Ayob'	Ashe	'Do	'Do	Do
Batanase (3 4)	Ayopɔi	Ayopɔi	Ayopɔi	Asheno	'Pai	Pei	Pei
Nanin (4 4)	Ani	Ani	Ani	Aburuwa	'Nana	Nana	Cɔri
Na'u (4 5)	Awai	Awai	Awai	Akpeno	'Nogo	'Nogo	Nive
Pi	Pie	Pie	Pig'	Kudu	Fuga	Fuga	Fi
Pi la wanye	Pie ne 'yene	Pie ni boyen	Pi ne 'yeni	Kudu kako	Fuga dodo	Fuga nodo	Fi ri kobala
Pi la baye	Pie n'ayi	Pie ni ayi	Pi ne ayi	Kudua-nyɔ	Fuga balle	Fuga balle	Fibalea
Pi la bata	Pie n'ata	Pie ni ata	Pi ne ata	Kud'asa	Fuga bato	Fuga batɔa	Fibatɔre
Pi la ba-'nase	Pie n'-anahe	Pie ni anan	Pi ne anas	Kud'ana	Fuga bana	Fuga banea	Fibanese
Pi la banu	Pie n'anu	Pie ni anuu	Pi ne anu	Kudonu	Fuga banu	Fuga banu	Fibanɔŋ
Pi la ba-tanta	Pie n'-ayuobe	Pie ni ayoob	Pi ne ayob	Kudoashe	Fuga bardo	Fuga bardo	Fi baldo
Pi la ban-tanase	Pie n'-ayopɔi	Pie ni ayopɔi	Pi ne ayopɔi	Kudo-asheno	Fuga barpai	Fuga barpei	Fibalpei
Pi la nna-nin	Pie n'ani	Pie ni ani	Pi ne ani	Kudo-aburuwa	Fuga nana	Fuga nana	Firchɔri
Pi la nnau	Pie n'-awai	Pie ni awai	Pi ne awai	Kudo-akpeno	Fuga nogo	Fuga nogo	Firnive
Pisiyi	Lejare	Lizare	Pisyi	Adunyɔ	File	Sapuga	Mara
Pis la wanye	Lejare ane yene	Lizare ni boyen	Pis ne yeni	Adunyɔ ni eko	File do do	Sapuga nodo	Mara 'dian
Pista	Lejar ne pie	Lizare ni pie	Pista	Adusa	Filntɔ	Sapuga du fuga	Mara-r-fi
Pisnase	Leja 'ayi	Liza 'yi	Pisnase	Aduna	Filna	Sapelea *or* Sapile	Mahin-malea
Pisnu	Pisanu	Liza 'yi ni pie	Pisnu	Adunu	Filnu	Fenu	Mahin-malea-de-fi
Kwɔ	Kɔ	Kɔba	Kobog	Kalfa	Bi	Bi	Zola
Kwɔsiyi	Kɔsayi	Kɔbsayi	Kobsyi	Alfa nyɔ	Bielle	Bibalea	Zɔlbalea
Kwɔsta	Kɔsata	Kɔbsata	Kobsta	Alfasa	Bieltɔ	Bibatɔa	Zɔlbatɔre
Tusur	Tuse	Tur *or* Tus	Tusur	Kagbo	Moro	Moro	Boi

II. VOCABULARIES

English.	Mole.	Mampelle.	Dagbane.	Kusal.	Nankane.	Dagare.
Above	Dyiŋeli *or* Sa	Sa zugu	Zug saa	Sa zugu *or* Sa-go	Sa-zuo	Sa-zugu
Adam's apple	Kokorau-go, *s.*; Koko-rado, *pl.*	Kokodo, *s.*; Koko-dare, *pl.*	Kokɔle, *s.*	Kokɔrdaug, *s.*; Koko-doro, *pl.*	Kɔŋko-dɔŋo, *s.*; Kɔnko-dɔgo, *pl.*	Kɔkogalan, *s.*; Kɔkɔ-gone, *pl.*
Add	Pase	Pase	Pahi	Pes	Pase	Puɔ
Adhere	Tabene	Tabele	Tabli	Tabele	Tabele	Mare
Adulterer	Yoada, *s.*; Yoadaba, *pl.*	Poa-go-tere, *s.*; Poagota, *pl.*	Paɣa gɔrli, *s.*; Pa-gora, *pl.*	Goder, *s.*; Goda, *pl.*	Erega, *s.*, Ka; Erse, *pl.*, Se	Sensene, *s.*; Sense-neme, *pl.*
After	Pore *or* Nyaule	Nyana	Nyaŋa	Nyaaŋ	Poren	Pori
Agriculture	Kodo	Kobo	Kɔbo	Koob	Koa	Kwɔbo
Air	Pemsem	Pebsego	Pohum	Pebsug	Pemsem, Bo	Pensɔŋ
Alarm (war cry)	Kelanga	Kasego	Kuhi *or* Fan-fan-toa	Kasiɣ	Kasega	Kpɛle
Also	Me	Gba	Gba *or* Mi	Mi	Me	Meŋ
Alter	Lebege	Lebge	Lebege	Lebege	Lebege	Lie
Answer	Lokke *or* Lebse	Lebse	Labsi	Lebse	Lebese	Sage
Anus	Nyedega	Gbine, *s.*; Gbina, *pl.*	Nyiriɣ-vɔgo	Gbin, *s.*; Gbina, *pl.*	Fesega, *s.*, Ka; Fese, *pl.*, Se	Pare-biri, *s.*; Pare-bie, *pl.*
Approach	Kolege, *v.*	Pore	Miri	Pɔrr	Kolege *or* Pora	Sere-ta
Arm (upper)	Kanga, *s.*; Kamse, *pl.*	Kpun-Kpɔŋo, *s.*; Kpun-Kpana,*pl.*	Kbg'-Kpuŋ, *s.*; Kbg'-Kpana, *pl.*	Kpo-pɔŋ, *s.*; Kpim-kpama	Kana, *s.*, Ka; Kanse, *pl.*, Se	Kpan-kpane, *s.*; Kpan-kpama, *pl.*
Arm-pit	Bɔkpuga, *s.*; Baga-pushi, *pl.*	Bɔko-pune, *s.*; Bare-pune, *pl.*	Bɔɣ-loŋi, *s.*; Bɔɣ-lomani, *pl.*	Bɔk-puɣ; *s.* Baat-puɣ *pl.*;	Kyelin-poko, *s.*; Ko; Kyelin-pɔgero, *pl.*; To	Balugri
Arrange	Zemse *or* Mal	Sase *or* Male	Mali	Zemse *or* Male	Zemse *or* Male	Male
Arrow	Pim, *s.*; Pema, *pl.*	Pim, *s.*; Pima, *pl.*	Pem, *s.*; Pema, *pl.*	Pim, *s.*; Pɛma, *pl.*	Pim, *s.*; Bo. Pema, *pl.*, A.	Pĩ, *s.*; Pĩme, *pl.*

Nabte.	Bulea.	Loberu.	Talene.	Gbanya.	Kasene.	Isal.
Sa-zuɣ	Nwa-zuɣ	Sa-zu *or* Sa-iŋ	Zugen	Soso	Weyu	Wenyu
Kunkudɔ	Tutɔɣ	Kokɔlur	Konkoduŋ	Laŋtoro, *s.*; Alantoro, *pl.*	Kore-kyem	Yukɔro
Pas	Tem	Puɔ	Pahe	Dan so	Kra	Na—he (lit. take add)
Tabele	Maɣam	Mer	Tabl'	..	Kono	Mɛrɛ
Bun-goreg	..	Sen yaga	Goruŋ	Sakale, *s.*; Isakale, *pl.*	Kalaɣano, De, Ba	Bacɔrɔŋ, *s.*; Bacoromo, *pl.*
Pore *or* Nyaŋ	..	Pur	Dyaan	Kamaŋ	Kwaga	Hare
Kwɔb	Kpwar	Kwɔb	Koo	Kadɔ	Varim	Para
Pebhim	Veo, *s.*, Ku;Vata, *pl.*, Ti	Seseb *or* Piɛro	Pebsem	Afu	Fugo *or* Viu	Pel
Kaheg	Karea	Kyɛlɛ	Kahe	Kufol	Balara (of men), Ule (of women)	Kyiese (of men), Bunso, Kuli (of women)
Me	Mena	Me	Me	Le	..	..
Lebeɣ	Tagere	Leɛb	Lebeɣ	Kiligi *or* Car	Gyiga	Birime
Lebhe	Bisi	Saɣ	Lebs	Suli	Se	Sai; Saye
Gbin	Pe-tafik, *s.*, Ka; Pe-tafisa, *pl.*, Si	Per-voor	Gbin	Kifi, *s.*; Afi, *pl.*	Vula, *s.*; Vule, *pl.*	Boboa *or* Bolo-ni
Pore	Kpwaŋ	Ser-ta	Koleg *or* Pore	Tagato	Fufɔŋ yi	Kpwake
Punpɔŋ	Nisa, *s.*, Si; Nisima, *pl.*, Si	Kpaŋ-Kpaŋ, *s.*; Kpaŋ-kpame, *pl.*	Kpuŋ poŋ	Eno, *s.*; Enoana, *pl.*	Gyiŋa, *s.*, Ka; Gyea, *pl.*, Si	Nese, *s.*; Nesene *or* Nesea, *pl.*
Bɔgo-leŋ	Bulu-kupɔ; Bu, Ti	Balugur	Bɔ-leŋo	Kabar, *s.*; Mbar, *pl.*	Pelugu, *s.*, Ku; Peluru, *pl.*, Ti	Valuŋ, *s.*; Valushe, *pl.*
Zems	Neaɣ	Mal	Zems	Lɔŋe	Fage	Wase
Peem, *s.*; Pema, *pl.*	Peŋ, *s.*, De; Pema, *pl.*, N.	Pĩ, *s.*; Pĩme, *pl.*	Pim, *s.*; Peem, *pl.*	Kinyembi, *s.*; Anyembi, *pl.*	Kyene, *s.*, Di; Kyena, *pl.*, Ya	Hem, *s.*; Heme, *pl.*

II. VOCABULARIES (*cont*).

English.	Mole.	Mampelle.	Dagbane.	Kusal.	Nankane.	Dagare.
Arrow poison	Yabega *or* Zelem	Yabega	Pem-lɔyɔ	Yabek	Yabega, *s.*, Ka; Yabese, *pl.*, Se	Pĭ-zeloŋ
Ashes	Tempe-gelem	Tampea-lim	Tamplim	Tampele-gim	Tampeɣe-lim; Bo class	Tampeloŋ
Ask	Sukka	Bose	Bɔhi	Bose	Sɔke	Sogere
Ask for	Kwɔshe	Suse	..	Sus	Suse	Sore
Axe	Lare, *s.*; Laya, *pl.*	Leŋa, *s.*; Lensi, *pl.*	Lehɔ, *s.*; Lere, *pl.*	Lieŋ, *s.*; Liɛs, *pl.*	Lia, *s.*, Ka; Lise, *pl.*, Se	Lere, *s.*; Llɛ, *pl.*
Back	Pore	Nyaŋa	Nyaŋa	Dyaaŋ	Pore	Pori
Bad	Beaga, *s.*; Bese, *pl.*	Beo, *s.*; Beri, *pl.*	Beu, *s.*; Beri, *pl.*	Beog, *s.*; Beet, *pl.*	Beo, *s.*; Bero, *pl.*	Fa, *s.*; Fare, *pl.*
Bake	Sɛ̃	See	She	Sɛ̃	Sɛ̃	Sɛ̃
Bark	Wese, *v.*; Wesibo, *n.*	Wahabo, *n.*	Wahabu	Wese, *v.*; Wesib, *n.*	Wesiga *or* Yɛsiga, *n.*	Holo
Barter	Kosom, Tekere	Kɔse	Taɣe	Kosim *or* Teak	Kosom *or* Tere	Tegebo, *n.*
Basket	Peogo, *s.*; Peto, *pl.*	Peo, *s.*; Pere, *pl.*	Pièɣò, *s.*; Pièrè, *pl.*	Peug, *s.*; Peet, *pl.*	Peo, *s.*, Ko; Petto, *pl.*, To	Piɛ, *s.*; Pɛre, *pl.*
Bastard	Tampiri, *s.*; Tam-piba, *pl.*	Sege, *s.*; Sege-dema, *pl.*	Seɣe, *s.*; Seɣene-ma, p. *or*	Teŋa-boom; Yiwe-bi *or* Tɔ-bi	Tampiri; Yiye-bie	Sensen-bie
Bat	Zamzaŋ, *s.*; Zam-zanse, *pl.*	Zunzɔŋo, *s.*; Zun-zona, *pl.*	Bahɛrɛ nema; Zɔŋ, *s.*; Zɔna, *pl.*	Ziŋzɔŋ, *s.*; Zinzana, *pl.*	Zuŋzoŋo, *s.*, Ko; Zonzono, *pl.*, To	Zinzaŋa, *s.*; Zinzane, *pl.*
Bathe	Su, So	Su	Su-(Kom)	Su	So	So
Beat	Pabe, Nwe	Febe, Nwe	Dme, Febi	Nwe	Nwe, Febe	Nwe
Beard	Tweŋa, *s.*; Twemse, *pl.*	Teŋa, *s.*; Tensi, *pl.*	Teŋ-kɔbre	Tieŋ, *s.*; Ties, *pl.*	Teŋa, *s.*, Ka; Tense, *pl.*, Se	Tiɛne, *s.*; Tieme, *pl.*
	Singe	Pili	Pili	Pile	Pili	Pili
Belch	Zode	Boom	Djim	Eruŋ	Zoom	Geri

Nabte.	Bulea.	Loberu.	Talene.	Gbanya.	Kasene.	Isal.
Yabeɣ	Yam	Pī-zel	Yaam	Kubɔr	Vea	Susi
Tampeglim	Tuntuam, s., Bu; Tuntu-eta, pl., Ti	Tampolo	Tomperylo	Nsone	Sea	Twɔro
Bohe	Beɣ	Sorr	Bohe	Bishi	Bwe	Piɛse
Suhe	Jus	Zele	Suhe	Kule	Lore	Sɔllo
Leŋ, s.	Leaɣ, s., Ka; Lasa, pl., Si	Ler, s.; Lai, pl.	Lehu	Kanase, s.; Nnase, pl.	Doro, s., De; Dora, pl., Ba	Sa, s.; Sase, pl.
Dyaaŋ	Daŋ	Pur	Daaŋ	Kamaŋ	Kwaga	Hareŋ
Beog, s.;	Nalla (lit.	Fa, s.;	Beoɣ	Kilibi, s.;	Lɔŋo, s.;	Bɔŋ, s.;
Beet, pl.	not good)	Far, pl.		Alibi, pl.	Loano, pl.	Bɔma, pl.
Sɛ̃	Sɛ̃	Sɛ̃	Se	Tɔ	Wɔ	Wase
Wes, v.	Wusi, v.	Wore	Yehir	Abu	We, v.	Hosu, v.
Kohim	Diaɣ	Yɛrɛ	Kosem	Kachar, n.	Yollo	Yallo
Peoɣ, s.	Busuɣ, s. Ka; Busisa, pl., Si	Piɛ, s.; Pero, pl.	Pioɣ	Kalantaŋ, s.; Nlan-taŋ, pl.	Tutɔgɔ, s., Ku; Tutɔro, pl., Te	Sime, s.; Sinsi, pl.
Teŋapiri, s.; Yiye-bie,	Beata-gyana or Nɔŋ-bi, s.; Wa. Nɔŋ-bisa, pl., Ba	Sesen-bie	Timpiry	Kuyurebi Ayuribi	Tampiri, s., De; Tam-pire, pl., Ba	Menga-bi
Zenzɔŋ, s.	Gyanjaro, s., Ka Si	Zazaŋ, s.; Zazan, pl.	Ziŋzoŋ	Konkɔ, s.; Akonkɔ, pl.	Zuŋzuŋo, s., Ku; Zuŋzuno, pl., Ti	Gyeŋ, s.; Gyenne, pl.
So	So	So	So	Berr	Sõe	Fo
Nwe, Febe	Fɔ or Naɣe	Nwe, Pɔp	Nwe, Febe	Biri	Maɣe	Nwau
Teen, s.	Teeŋ, s., Ka; Teense, pl., Si	Tieŋ, s.; Tiene, pl.	Teŋ	Katur-kogye, s.; Ntur-kogye, pl.	Tone, s., Di; Tona, pl., Ya	Tɔŋ, s.; Tɔma, pl.
Pul	Pili	Tina, Tigil	Piil	Kar	Pulli	Boom
Bɔɔm	Berente	Ere	Boom	Gasi	Corom	Gese

II. VOCABULARIES (*cont.*)

English.	*Mole.*	*Mampelle.*	*Dagbane.*	*Kusal.*	*Nankane.*	*Dagare.*
Blind	Zoaŋa, s.; Zonshi, pl.	Zoma or Zomma	Zɔma, s.; Zomba, pl.	Zoŋ, s.; Zos, pl.	Foa, s., Ka; Fose, pl., Se	Zonɔ, s.; Zɔne, pl.
Bladder	Dudcugu, s.; Dudcudu, pl.	Dunsurugo, s.; Dunsursi, pl.	Dulumsurugu, s.; Dulumsura, pl.	Dunsuk	Dunduyuo, s., Ku; Dunduyura, pl., To	Durinwɔɔ, s.; Durinwore, pl.
Boil	Keda, Ke	Kpe	Kpee	Kot	Kɔre	Kpabo
Borrow	Peŋe	Peŋne	Paŋ	Peŋ	Peŋe	Pɛmo
Bow	Tapo, s.; Tabado, pl.	Toro, s.; Tarare, pl.	Tɔbo, s.; Tobri, pl.	Taraug, s.; Tarade, pl.	Tafo, s.; Bo; Tini, pl., I.	Tamo, s.; Tama, pl.
Brains	Zuputtu	Zuguputte	Zug'puri	Zuput	Zupurugu, s., Ku; Zuputtu, pl., To	Zupole, s.; Zupolo, pl.
Breast	Binshiri, s.; Bisa, pl.	Bishiri, s.; Bisa, pl.	Bihili, s.; Biha, pl.	Bisir, s.; Bisa, pl.	Bisiri, s., De; Bisa, pl., A.	Bere, s.; Berɛ, pl.
Build	Me	Me	Me	Mɛ	Me	Mɛ
Burn	Nyŏge	Nyŏ	Nyɔ	Nyo	Nyŏ	Nyŏge
Bush-pig	Deogo, s.; Deto or Dedo, pl.	Dea, s.; Desi, pl.	Dee, s.; Dehi, pl.	Deeg, s.; Dees, pl.	Dɛa, s.; Ka; Dɛse, pl., Se	Duo, s.; Dori, pl.
Butter (shea)	Kam	Kpam	Kpam	Kpam	Kam	Kã
Bury	Mwum	Pi	Pi	Pĭ	Pĭ, or Lae	Uŋu
Call	Bole	Bole	Bɔle	Bol	Yi	Bole
Cap	Pugula, s.; Puglesi, pl.; Zupugula	Zug-piliga, s.; Zugpilʃi, pl.	Zugpulugu, s.; Zug-pila, pl.	Zu-pebeg, s.; Zupebs, pl.	Zu-vokka, s., Ka; vogse, pl., Se	Zu-pili, s. Zu-pile, pl.
Carry	Tuke, Zi	Zi	Zi	Zi	Ze, Tukki	Gare
Carrying	Tusugo, s.; Tusudo, pl.	Tusuŋo, s.; Tusuŋa, pl.	Tizugu, s.; Tizuguri, pl.	Tesuuŋ, s.; Tesuun, pl.	Tusungo, s.; Ko; Tusunto, pl., To	Tanzuŋ, s.; Tanzune, pl.
pad						
Castrate	Nyaklande	Foa; Gya	Fog; Yihi, Za	Za or Yiʃ	Lake, Za; Gya	Iri (olene)
Catch	Nyake	Gba	Gbai	Gbae	Nyokke	Nɔge
Caterpillar	Zunzuri, s.; Zunzuya, pl.	Zunzure, s.; Zunzuya, pl.	Zinzuli, s.; Zinzuya, pl.	Zunzur, s.; Zunzua, pl.	Zunzuri, s.; De; Zunzua, pl., A.	Dunduli, s. Dundulo, pl.
Cease	Base	Base	Tʃela	Bahe	Base	Bare

Nabte.	Bulea.	Loberu.	Talene.	Gbanya.	Kasene.	Isal.
Zoom	Yie	Zoŋ, s.; Zon, pl.	Zoom	Tanipo, s.; Atanipo, pl.	Luleo, s.; De, Lulea, pl. Ba.	Nyɔlɔŋ, s.; Nyoloma, pl.,
Dunsug, s.	Sinsam-Liuɣ, s., Ko; Sinsam-luta, pl., Ti	Durukyee	Sugdundu	Kubɔfole-debe, s.; Abɔfole-debe, pl.	Fea-loŋo	Fila, s.; Felse, pl.
Kwɔt	Dig	Kare	Kwɔt	Daŋe	Cura	Wilimu
Peŋ	Peɛm	Peŋ	Peŋ	Kapaŋ	Gyene	Kyeŋ
Tap	Tɔm, s., Bu; Tuma, pl., N.	Tam, s.; Tame, pl.	Tab, s.	Kita, s.; Ata, pl.	Taŋa, s.; Tɛ, pl., Ku, Ti	To, s.; Toʃi, pl.
Zuput	Zupute, s., Ko; Zuputa, pl., Ti	Zupol	Pulinput	Mbɔ	Yu-kolpua	Nyu-konkɔl
Bihir, s.	Bisir, s., De; Bisa, pl., Ɖ.	Bir, s.; Birɛ, pl.	Bihir	Kagwene, s.; Ngwene, pl.	Yele, s.; De; Di; Yela, pl., Ya; Ye	Yel, s.; Yelea, pl.
Me	Se	Me	Me	Poro	Lɔ	Sa
Nyɔ	Nyoɣse	Nyek	Ɖwo	Choo	Zoe	Nyɛgɛ
Dee, s.	Deɔy, s., Ko; Dee, pl., Ti	Duo, s.; Dur, pl.	Dee	Libi, s.; Alibi, pl.	Togo, s., Di, De; Tɛrɛ, pl., Ya, Ye	Teu, s.; Teni, pl.
Kpwam	Kpwam	Ka	Kpaam	Nkũ	Sero nuga	No
Pi, La	Gu	Ũ	Pi	Puli	Ke	Wuge
Bol	Wi	Buɔl	Bol	Tɛrɛ	Bɔŋ, Bo	Yirɛ
Zu-pibig	Zutɔk, s.; Ka; Zutogsa, pl., Si	Kpa-wuo	Zu-pebeɣ	Kawuro, s.; Nwuro, pl.	Yu-puga, s., Ka; Yu-pwi, pl., Si	Nyunculo
Tu	Gi	Tuo	Zi	Sɔlo	Zila	Gyɔŋ
Tɛsuŋ	Tülik	Tɔsir	Tuhuŋ	Kikar, s.; Akar, pl.	Kazaga, s.; Ka; Kazɛ, pl., Si	Kankyeme, s.; Kankyema, pl.
Za, Foɣe	Na (kɔlog)	Ir lame	Fog; Ga	Lara	Loe or Ļ̃woe	Lehe (luro)
Nyok	Yik	Nyɔk	Gbae	Pɛ	Gya	Kaŋ
Zunzur	Nanzur, s., De; Nanzoe, pl., N.	Zanzul, s.; Zanzule, pl.	Zuzur	Kisisobi, s.; Asisobi, pl.	Kantini, s.; Di; Kantina, pl., Ya	Kuntuluŋo
Bahe	Base	Ber	Bahe	Yiga	Yaɣe	Lɛŋ

II. VOCABULARIES (*cont.*)

English.	Mole.	Mampelle.	Dagbane.	Kusal.	Nankane.	Dagare.
Chair	Gweile, *s.*; Gweila, *pl.*	Kuka, *s.*; Kugesi, *pl.*	Kuga, *s.*; Kugsi, *pl.*	Kok, *s.*; Kokes, *pl.*	Kukka, *s.,* Ka Kogse, *pl.,* Se	Kogo, *s.*; Kogri, *pl.*
Cheek	Yagale, *s.*; Yagase, *pl.*	Kpareŋo, *s.*; Kpa-rema, *pl.*	Kparin, *s.*; Kparima, *pl.*	Kpeder, *s.*; Kpeda, *pl.*	Yagere, *s.,* De ; Yaga, *pl.,* A.	Yàgèrè, *s.*; Yaga, *pl.*
Chest	Nyango	Nyõõ, *s.*; Nyare, *pl.*	Nyɔgo, *s.*; Nyori, *pl.*	Nyɔɔk, *s.*; Nyɔɔt, *pl.*	Nyõõ, *s.*; Ko ; Nyõõro, *pl.,* To	Nyaa, *s.*; Nyaare, *pl.*
Chameleon	Gomtiogo, *s.*; Gom-tido, *pl.*	Goma-cuwa, *s.*; Goma cusi, *pl.*	Guma-chugu, *s.*; Guma-churi, *pl.*	Dendeog, *s.*; Den-deet, *pl.*	Gomatia, *s.,* Ka ; Gomatise, *pl.,* Se	Gomatebo, *s.*; Goma-tere, *pl.*
Charcoal	Sala	Sala	Salla	San	Sane	Sala
Chew	Nwabe	Nwɔbe	Ɗobe	Ɔb	Obe	Ɔ
Chicken	Nobila, *s.*; Nobi, *pl.*	No-bila, *s.*; No-bisi, *pl.*	Nobla, *s.*; Nobihi, *pl.*	Nubil, *s.*; Nubilis, *pl.*	Nubila, *s.,* Ka Nubilse, *pl.,* Se	Nobila, *s.*; Nobile, *pl.*
Chin	Lemde, *s.*; Lema, *pl.*	Loŋo	Tieŋa, *s.*; Tiense, *pl.*	Leuŋ, Tengore	Lenne	Lene, *s.*; Leme, *pl.*
Choose	Tuʃe	Gamse ; yisi	Gaham	Gas ; Yis	Tusi, Gase, Loe	Turi
Circle	Giligi, *v.*	Gilige	Gilli	Gilig	Gyili	Gili
Clay	Yagado, *s.*; Yɔko, *pl.*	Yaare	Yaɣle	Yaat	Yɔgoro, *s.,* Ko ; Yɔkko, *pl.,* To	Yágéré
Climb	Du ; Zom	Du	Du	Do	Zon	Du, Zoŋ
Cold	Waodo	Ware	Wari	Ɔde	Ɔru	Ɔre
Collect	Laɣam, Tigiʃi	Laɣem Tigisi	Laɣam	Layse	Lagem, Tigisi	Lan—ta
Come (out from)	Yi	Yi	Yi	Yi	Yese	Yi
Come	Wa	Kyem	Kam	Kyem	Waam	Wa
Companion	Tudntaga, *s.*; Tudn-tase, *pl.*	Dolunpea	Kpie	Dolemtaa, *s.*; Dolem-tase, *pl.*	Tunta, *s.,* Ka ; Tun-tase, *pl.,* Se	Taba
Consent	Sake	Sake	Saɣe	Sake	Sake	Sage

Nabte.	Bulea.	Loberu.	Talene.	Gbanya.	Kasene.	Isal.
Kok	Zu-kpaka-lek, s., Ka; Zu-kpage-lesa, pl., Si	Kɔk	Kɔk	Kabe, s.; Mbe, pl.	Yu-tuŋu, s., Ku; Yu-tunu, pl., Ti	Kanjaŋa, s.; Kanjansa, pl.
Kperog	Nyo, s.; Ku; Nyoata, pl., Ti	Kokaŋ, s.; Kokame, pl.	Takperig or Takperek	Kataya, s.; Ntaya, pl.	Kellɛ, s., Di; Kella, pl., Ya	Can-kpaŋ, s.; kpana, pl.
Nyoog	Kusir	Nya, s.; Nyar, pl.	Nyŏŏɣ	Kagbene, s.; Ɖbene, pl.	Nyŏne, s., Di; Nyŏna, pl., Ya	Bɔye, s.; Bɔɛsɛ, pl.
Gumtiug, s.; Gane, pl.	Bunɔro, s.; Bu-nɔta, pl.	Gulatib, s.; Gula-tibe, pl.	Gomatioɣ	Dakareka, s.; Ada-kareka, pl.	Mala, s., Ka; Male, pl., Si	Koloŋ-gwene, s.; Koloŋ-gwense, pl.
Sana	Kara	Sala	San	Edundu	Cala	Hɔlɔ
Obeb	Nwab, Cam	Ɔb	Ob	Bagato	Tona	Caŋ
Nobil	Kpeaɣ, s., Ka; Kpɛsa, pl., Si	Lule, s.; Luli, pl.	Nu-bil	Koʃi-bi	Kyi-bie, s., De; Kyi-bia, pl., Ba	Gwiwie, s.; Gyiwisi, pl.
Leuŋ	Tan-kuru, s., Ku; Tean-kuru, pl., Ti	Tien, s.; Tiene, pl.	Leuŋo	Katoli-kogyi, s.; Ntoli-kogyi, pl.	Tutɔga, s.; Ka; Tutoe, pl., Si	Tanlaŋa, s.; Tanlaŋse, pl.
Lo	Lẅer	Tur	Tuɣ, Gahe, Lo	Tise, Lara	Kuri	Bɛrɛhɛ
Gilig	Gilim	Vile	Giliɣ	Kuliti	Gigilu	Golli
Yaɣede	Yak	Yagera	Yaɣd	Ebɔ	Dɔgɔ	Cɔro
Do	Dyur	Do, Zɔm	Do	Di	Dine	Gyel
Ɔde	Nwata	Ɔrr or Arr	Ɔɔt	Awo	Waro	Waro
Laɣam	Tigisi	Lan—ta	Ham	Kyala	Kɔgɔ	Hileme
Yim	Nyiŋ	Yi	Yim	Lar	Nɔŋ or Naŋ	Llei
Kyim	Dyan	Wa	Kyim	Ba	Ba	Kwɔ
Dolonta	Doa	Tuta, Poltable	Dolentaa	Tere, s.; Terana, pl.	Togɔdo, s. De; Togɔdona, pl., Ba	Torodɔŋ, s.; Torodɔse, pl.
Sak	Seaɣ	Sak	Sake	Suli	Sɛ	Sai

II. VOCABULARIES (*cont.*)

English.	Mole.	Mampelle.	Dagbane.	Kusal.	Nankane.	Dagare.
Cord (umbilical)	Nyuga, *s.*; Nyusi, *pl.*	Ḑyūwa, *s.*; Ḑyūsi, *pl.*	Nyugu, *s.*; Nyuguri, *pl.*	Nyuɣ, *s.*; Nyus, *pl.*	Nyua, *s.*, Ka; Nyuse, *pl.*, Se	Nyuo, *s.*; Nyuri, *pl.*
Corn (maize)	Kamana	Karwana	Kalwana	Kawener	Kamana	Kamani
Cough	Kɔsogo, *n.*	Kosuŋo, *n.*	Kohim	Kɔsog	Kɔsogo	Kɔrɔŋ
Cow	Naɣyanga, *s.*; Naɣnyanse, *pl.*	Nanyaŋa, *s.*; Nanyanse, *pl.*	Nahu, *s.*; Nigi, *pl.*	Na-ŋyaŋ	Naɣ-nyaŋa	Na-nyaŋa, *s.*; Na-Nyane, *pl.*
Cowrie	Lagato, *s.*; Ligidi, *pl.*	Laafo, *s.*; Ligidi, *pl.*	Laɣfu, *s.*; Ligidi, *pl.*	Lagf, *s.*; Ligidi, *pl.*	Lagefo, *s.*, Bo; Ligeri, *pl.*, I	Lebiri, *s.*; Lebie, *pl.*
Crested crane	Buluvaugo, *s.*; Buluvado, *pl.*	Kurunwaŋa, *s.*; Kurunwanse, *pl.*	Kulŋaŋ, *s.*; Kulŋama, *pl.*	Gbarenwau	Bugumnwabilega, *s.*, Ka; Bugumnwabilse, *pl.*, Se	Buruŋwao, *s.*; Buruŋwane, *pl.*
Cricket	Buguvare *or* Paŋa	Paŋa, *s.*; Panse, *pl.*	Paŋa, *s.*; Panse, *pl.*	Kpaŋ, *s.*; Kpams, *pl.*	Paŋa, *s.*, Ka; Panse, *pl.*, Se	Paŋa, *s.*; Pane, *pl.*
Crossroads	Sowedega *or* Sobadega	So-kyira *or* So-pulle	So-kyira	Sɔ-kyetig *or* So-puŋ	So-puŋa, *s.*, Ka; So-puse, *pl.*, Se	So-Kyɛrɛ
Crow	Gobogo	Kusunkoo, *s.*; Kusunkare, *pl.*	Kɔhoŋkwɔɣo, *s.*; Kɔhoŋkwɔre, *pl.*	Gago, *s.*	Gõ, *s.*, Ku; Gõro, *pl.*, To	Galangaa
Cup (calabash)	Liŋa, *s.*; Linse, *pl.*	Gare, *s.*; Gaa, *pl.*	..	Gar, *s.*; Gaa, *pl.*	Linka, *s.*, Ka; Linse, *pl.*, Se	Kɔlɔnkɔ, *s.*; Kɔlɔnkɔre, *pl.*
Curse	Tuse, *v.*	Tu	Yele noli	To	Tu	To
Cut	Kuge, Nwage, Kye, Kolege	Nwa, Kye, Korege	Nma, Kɔrige	Nwe, Kug, Kye, Kodeɣ	Kuge, Nwa, Kye, Korege	Nwaa

Nabte.	Bulea.	Loberu.	Talene.	Gbanya.	Kasene.	Isal.
..	Siug, s., Ku; Siuta, pl., Ti	Nyu, s.; Nyur, pl.	Nyuu	Kujopulo, s.; Ajopulo, pl.	Wuri, s., Di; Wurɛ, pl., Ya	Kawule, s.; Kawuliŋ, pl.
Karekyɛna	Twumben, s., De; Twumbena, pl., N	Kaman	Kareyena	Kuboye, s.; Aboye, pl.	Kamana	Koromea
Kŏhog	Kɔso	Kɔro	Koho	Ewose	Sisaro or Kukweru	Kɛhɛ
Na-nyaŋ	Na-sar or Na-nubi	Na-nyaŋ, s.; Ni-nyaŋ, pl.	Na-ŋyaŋ	Kina-kye, s.; Ana-kye, pl.	Na-kyebere, s., Ka; Na-kyebera, pl., Si	Na-hal, s.; Na-hala, pl.
Lagfo	Ligera, s., De; Ligri, pl., N	Libir, s.; Libie, pl.	Lagf, s.; Ligit, pl.	Kumasere-be-fuful, s.; Ama-serebe-fuful, pl.	Sabu, s., De; Sabia, pl., Ba	Morwi, s.; Morwie, pl.
..	Kunwao, s., Ku; Kunwata, pl., Ti	Buron-wan, s.; Buron-wame, pl.	Gbanwa-blego	Kumol, s.; Amol, pl.	Kunwao, s., Ku; Kunwaro, pl., Ti	Gama, s.; Gamse, pl.
Kpaaŋ	Paaŋ, s., Ka; Pansa, pl., Si	Paŋkyi, s.; Pan-Kyisi, pl.	Paŋ	Panse, s.; Apanse, pl.	Kyare, s.; Kyara, pl.	Lelea-poŋ, s.; Lelea-pomo, pl.
So-kedeŋ	Su-pɔkosa	Sorkyera, s.; Sor-kyese, pl.	So-puŋ	Ekpakye-rɛpe, s. or Kilarega, s.; Ala-rega, pl.	Co-grera or Co-kpwea	Wan-kparaŋ, s.; Wan-kpara, pl.
Gaog	Tagaro, s.; Ku; Tagata, pl., Ti	Gbagba, s.; Gbag-bar, pl.	Gao	Gaga, s.; Agaga, pl.	Cangao, s., Ku; Can-garo, pl., Ti	Gengaŋ, s.; Gengama, pl.
Liŋ	Leŋ, s., Ka; Lensa pl., Si	..	Gaaγe	Kawe, s.; Nwe, pl.	Kunkolo,s., Ku; Kun-kwalo, pl., Ti	Lloŋ, s.; Lloni, pl.
Tu	Le	Tob	Tud	Tege	Toe	Toso
Nwa	Gep	Nwa, Kɔr	Nwa, Kuu, Kye	Ku, Dɛ, Teŋ	Gweni or Goni, Zage	Kari, Ta

II. VOCABULARIES (cont.)

English.	Mole.	Mampelle.	Dagbane.	Kusal.	Nankane.	Dagare.
Dance, v.	Sao or Sau	Wa	Wa	Wa	Wa	Siɛre
Darkness	Lika	Lika or Zibsim	Liɣa or Zimsim	Lik	Lika	Lige
Day	Dare, s.; Dasema, pl.	Dare, s.; Dabsa, pl.	Dabsili, s.; Dabsa, pl.	Dar, s.; Dabsa, pl.	Da, dare, s., De; Dabsa, pl., A	Bie, s.; Bere, pl.
Deaf	Wuŋa or Muka	To-kpira or Zɔlogo	Tib-kpra, s.; Tib-kpralana, pl.	To-kpeda	Waŋa, s., Ka; Wase, pl., Se	Woŋo, s.; Woni, pl.
Death	Kum	Kum	Kum	Kum	Kum	Kum
Debt	Samde, s.; Sama, pl.	Samne, s.; Sama, pl.	Samli, s.; Sama, pl.	Sam, s.; Sama, pl.	Sane, s., De; Sama, pl., A	Sene, s.; Seme, pl.
Delay	Kɔsa	Yue	Yui; Yɔle	Yu	Yue	Kɔre
Descend	Sige	Sige	Seɣe	Sige	Sige	Sigi
Destroy	Sam	Saam	Saɣem	Saam	Saam	Sã
Dew	Melɛm	Mealem	Malgem	Mɛlegem	Mɛglem	Mɛloŋ
Diarrhoea	Saaga	Saa	Saa	Saa	Sã	Care
Die	Kyi	Kpi	Kpi	Kpi	Kyi	Kpi
Dip	Lose; Swi	Lose	Sugi	Los	Luse	Lɔre
Dirty, v.	Degem	Daɣre	Daɣri	Deɣat	Deɣe	Degere
Divide	Pwi	Purege	Prigi	Pudeg	Pu	Po
Doctor	Tipeda or Timsɔba	Timdana	Timlana	Tib or Tim, s.; Tib-dem, pl.	Tiba or Tim, s.; Tib-dema, pl., Ba	Tim-soba, s.; Tim-deme, pl.
Dog	Baga, s.; Base, pl.	Ba, s.; Base, pl.	Báá, s.; Bahe, pl.	Ba, s.; Bas, pl.	Baa, s., Ka; Base, pl., Se	Ba, s.; Bare, pl.
Donkey	Bwɔŋa, s.; Bwɔnse, pl.	Buŋa, s.; Bunse, pl.	Buŋa, s.; Buŋse, pl.	Boŋ, s.; Boms, pl.	Buŋa, s., Ka; Buse, pl., Se	Bɔŋo, s.; Bonni, pl.
Drag	Vugi	Vue; Vu	Dari	Vu	Vue	Vu
Dream	Zamse	Zasim	Zaham	Zasim	Zasem	Zane
Dress	Yelege	Yɛ	Ye	Yɛ	Ye	Yere
Drink	Nyu	Nyu	Nyu	Du	Nyu	Nyu
Drive away	Dige	Kare	Kare	Kare or Kade	Dige	Dige
Drop (of water)	Tokore	Tɔke	Tɔɣe	Tɔk	Tokore or Yule	Cono
Dumb	Muku, s.; Mugudu, pl.	Zɔlogo	Burugu, s.; Burugu-nema, pl.	Gaoŋ, s.; Gaam, pl.	Goŋo, s., Ku; Gono, pl., To	Mu, s.; Muri, pl.

Nabte.	*Bulea.*	*Loberu.*	*Talene.*	*Gbanya.*	*Kasene.*	*Isal.*
Wa	Gwɔk	Yaɣ or Se	Wa	Ca	Sa	Gwɔa
Lika	Leɣe	Lige	Lik	Tentembiri	Birim	Biriŋ
Dar	Dae, *s.,* De; Da, *pl.,* N	Bibir, *s.;* Bibie, *pl.*	Dar, *s.;* Dabsa, *pl.*	Kakye, *s.;* Nkye, *pl.*	Wepuli	Wehaya
Tu-kpira *or* Waŋa	Tu-kpara	Woŋ, *s.;* Won, *pl.*	Tu-kpira	Kpawu, *s.;* Akpawu, *pl.*	Zoa-kɔgɔ	Tɛŋɛ, *s.;* Tenea, *pl.*
Kum	..	Kun	Kuŋ	Luko; Ebune, *s.;* Bubune, *pl.*	Tone	Soo
..	..	San, *s.;* Same, *pl.*	Samt	Kukɔ, *s.;* Akɔ, *pl.*	Gyine, *s.,* Di; Gyina, *pl.,* Ya	Kyeŋ, *s.;* Kyema, *pl.*
Nyur	Ben	Kyele	Wue	Kyar	Dane	Dene
Sige	..	Sig	Sige	Bilekɛ	Too	Tu
Saam	Kase	Saŋ	Saam	Gyegye	Cɔge	Kyei
Mɛɣelɛm	Maglem	Beɛlo	Meaɣelog	Efurucı	Nyɔnɔ	Nyal
Saa, Nyẽã	Caro	Sa	Saa	Kifeɛ	Cɔrɔ	Churuŋ
Kpi	Kpi	Kpi	Kpi	Wu	To	Sõ
Luhe	Luse	Lɔr	Los	..	Dira	Tõ *or* Hɛ̃
Deɣhet	Daŋta	Deger	Daɣe	Eyurupi	Digeru	Disiŋ *or* Bisiŋ
Tõi	Necar	Po	Pu	Barka	Mmaŋ	Kpwa
Tiba	Tebedo, *s.,* Wa; Tebedeba, *pl.,* Ba	Ti-sob, *s.;* Ti-dem, *pl.*	Tiba *or* Timdan	Kuduru-wura, *s.;* Aduru-wura, *pl.*	Lerɛtu, *s.,* De; Lerɛtina, *pl.,* Ba	Dalinetina, *s.;* Dalihitina, *pl.*
Baa	Beaɣ, *s.,* Ka; Basa, *pl.,* Si	Ba, *s.;* Bar, *pl.*	Ba	Dwɔne, *s.;* Adwɔne, *pl.*	Kokure, *s.,* Ka; Kokuri, *pl.,* Si	Vaha, *s.;* Vase, *pl.*
Bɔŋ	Bɔneŋ, *s.,* Ka; Bɔnsa, *pl.,* Si	Bɔŋ, *s.;* Bon, *pl.*	Bɔŋ	Kuruma, *s.;* Akuruma, *pl.*	Benaga, *s.,* Ka; Benɛ, *pl.,* Si	Kakumo, *s.;* Kakuse, *pl.*
Vuu	Vur	Vu	Vu	Gbeɛ	Vaŋ; Turi	Lɛrɛ
Zahem	Gwadasa	Zan	Zahim	Edare	Dueem	Duoho; Doso
Yɛ	Yi; Dyo	Yɛre	Yɛ	Bu	Nzo	Lale
Nyu	Nyu	..	Ɖu	Nu	..	Nyoa
Kare	..	Dig, Kare	Karen	Dwɔ	Do; Zele	Kiri
Tɔk	Tokos	Yule	Tɔk	Dul	Lurɛ	Coru
Gaoŋ	Gaoŋ	Woŋ	Gaoŋ	Namu, *s.;* Anamu, *pl.*	Memao, *s.;* Memaro, *pl.*	Teŋe, *s.;* Teŋea, *pl.*

II. VOCABULARIES (*cont.*)

English.	Mole.	Mampelle.	Dagbane.	Kusal.	Nankane.	Dagare.
Ear	Tubele,*s.*; Tuba, *pl.*	Tuberi, *s.*; Tuba, *pl.*	Tebli, *s.*; Teba, *pl.*	Taber, *s.*; Taba, *pl.*	Tubere, *s.*, De; Tuba, *pl.*, A	Tori, *s.*; Tobo, *pl.*
Earth	Teŋa	Teŋa	Teŋa	Teŋ	Teŋa	Teŋe
Eat	Di	Di	Di	Di	Di	Di
Egg	Gelle, *s.*; Gella, *pl.*	Gyelle, *s.*; Gyela, *pl.*	Galle, *s.*; Galla, *pl.*	Gel, *s.*; Gella, *pl.*	Gyele, *s.*, De; Gyela, *pl.*, A	Gyeli, *s.*; Gyele, *pl.*
Elbow	Kantiga, *s.*; Kantise, *pl.*	Kantia, *s.*; Kantisi, *pl.*	Kpuŋkpangua, *s.*; Kpuŋkpanguhi, *pl.*	Kenkpantorik, *s.*; Kpenkpantoris, *pl.*	Kantoreŋa, *s.*, Ka; Kantorese, *pl.*, Se	Kpankpanbeli, *s.*; Kpankpanbele, *pl.*
Elephant	Wobogo, *s.*; Wobodo, *pl.*	Wobogo, *s.*; Wobere, *pl.*	Wobgo, *s.*; Wobre, *pl.*	Wobog, *s.*; Wobt, *pl.*	Wobogo, *s.*; Wobero, *pl.*	Wo, *s.*; Wore, *pl.*
Enter	Kye	Kpẽ	Kpe	Kpẽ	Kye	Kpɛ
European	Nasara, *s.*; Nasardamma, *pl.*	Nasara, *s.*; Nasaraba, *pl.*	Silmina, *s.*; Silminsi, *pl.*	Nasara, *s.*; Nasaranam, *pl.*	Nasara, *s.*, Nasaradema, *pl.*, Ba	Nasara, *s.*; Nasare, *pl.*
Everything	Bumfaa	Bunzaakam	Bunʃioŋkam	Buŋzaa	Buno-zaakama	Benzaa
Excrement	Bingu, *s.*; Bindu, *pl.*	Bine, *s.*; Bina, *pl.*	Bindi, *s.*; Bina, *pl.*	Bin, *s.*; Bina, *pl.*	Bino	Bine, *s.*; Binime, *pl.*
Extinguish	Cisi	Kpisi	Kpihi	Kpis	Chuse	Kpini
Eye	Nifu, *s.*; Nini, *pl.*	Nifo, *s.*; Nini, *pl.*	Nifu, *s.*; Nina, *pl.*	Nif, *s.*; Nini, *pl.*	Nifu, *s.*, Bo; Nini, *pl.*, I	Nimiri, *s.*; Nimie, *pl.*
Fall	Lwi, Lui	Lu	Lu	Li	Lu	Le
Fan, *v.*	Fibi	Vibi	Vebe	Kamfinug, *s.*; Kamfinit, *pl.*	Fili, *v.*	Figeri, *v.*
Farm	Pugo, *s.*; Puto, *pl.*	Pu, *s.*; Pure, *pl.*; Samane, *s.*; Samana, *pl.*; Zanorenakpar	Pu, *s.*; Pure, *pl.*; Sabane pu.	Pog, *s.*; Pot, *pl.*; Samaŋ, *s.*; Samana, *pl.*; Kpikpia	Vaam, *s.*, Ko; Votto, *pl.*, To; Samane, *s.*; Samana, *pl.*; Sensayle	Puo, *s.*; Puri, *pl.*

Nabte.	Bulea.	Loberu.	Talene.	Gbanya.	Kasene.	Isal.
Tobre	Tui, s., De; Tue, pl., N	Tober, s.; Tobe, pl.	Tobere	Kusɔ, s.; Asɔ, pl.	Zoɛ, s., Di or De; Zoa, pl., Ya or Ye	Degel, s.; Degela, pl.
Teŋ	Teŋ	Teŋ	Teŋ	Esesar or Kasawole	Tega	Tintei
Di	Di	Di	Di	Dyi	Di	Di
Gyel	Geŋ, s., De; Gena, pl., N	Gyel, s.; Gyele, pl.	Gel	Kofule, s.; Afule, pl.	Kyekyɛrɛ, s., De; Kyekyera, pl., Ye	Hál, s.; Hálla, pl.
Kpenkpaturg	Ninkuŋ s., Ka; Ninkunsa, pl., Si	Kpankpanyogbil, s. Kpankpanyogbile, pl.	Kpenkpaturɣ	Kabarekunko, s.; Abarekunko, pl.	Gyatogɔ, s., Ku; Gyatoro, pl., Ti	Na-toko, s.; Na-tokosi, pl.
Wɔbog	Yao, s., Ku; Yabta, pl., Ti	Wɔb, s.; Wober, pl.	Wɔboɣ	Kusɔl, s.; Asɔl, pl.	Tu, s., Ku; Turu, pl., Ti	Batuŋ, s.; Batuse, pl.
Kpẽ	Dyo	Kpɛ	Kpẽ	Luri	Zo	Djo
Selimi	Felek, s., Ka; Felsa, pl., Si	Nasal, s.; Nasalsi, pl.	Nasara	Broni, s.; Mbroni, pl.	Dasara, s., De; Dasare, pl., Ba	Nasara, s.; Nasaraba, pl.
Bunzãã	Gyamena	Bomeza	Bunzaa	Aseŋ-keke	Wenu	Kuŋ-kala
Biŋ	Biŋ, s., Ku; Binta, pl., Ti	Bin	Biŋ	Ebin	Benu	Baŋ
Kpes	Kpwems	Kpir	Kpes	Dum	Doe	Dirsɛ
Niho	Num, s., Bu; Nina, pl., Ɖ	Mimir, s.; Mimie, pl.	Nif	Kiniʃi, s.; Aniʃi, pl.	Yi, s., De; Yia, pl., Ye	Se, s.; Sea, pl.
Lu	Lo	Lo	Lu	Toro	Tó	Tel
Fib	Fu, v.	Figeri	Fib	Fo	Fulle	Vike
Pug	Talem, s., Bu; Tata, pl., Ti; Nanga, s., Ka Nangansa, pl., Si	Puo, s.; Pur, pl.	Puuɣ	Ndɔɔ, s.; Ndɔtɔ, pl.; Langar, s.; Alangar, pl.	Kara, s.; Kare, pl., Ka, Si; Kadugɛ, s., Ka; Kadui, pl., Si; Talaŋa, s., Ka; Talana, pl., Si	Baka, s.; Bakase, pl.; Nwankaa

II. VOCABULARIES (*cont.*)

English.	Mole.	Mampelle.	Dagbane.	Kusal.	Nankane.	Dagare.
Fast, *v.*	Loe nore	Loe nore	Lo noli	Lo nor	Lo nore	Le nore
Fear, *n.*	Dabeem	Dabeem	Dabiem	Dabeɛm	Dabeem	Dabie
Fight	Zabe	Zabe	Zabe	Zab	Zabe	Zɔre
Find	Pisi	Pii	..	Pii	Pie	Piri
Fire	Bugum	Bugum	Bugum	Bugum	Bugum (Bo class)	Vu
Fish	Jifu, *s.*; Jima, *pl.*	Ziŋa, *s.*; Zimi, *pl.*	Zina, *s.*; Zaham, *pl.*	Ziŋ, *s.*; Zime, *pl.*	Zifu, *s.*, Bo; Zim, *pl.*, I	Zɔmo, *s.*; Zuma, *pl.*
Fly, *n.*	Zoaga, *s.*; Zɔse, *pl.*	Zoa, *s.*; Zoʃi, *pl.*	Zoo, *s.*; Zɔhe, *pl.*	..	Zua, *s.*, Ka; Zuse, *pl.*, Se	Zoo, *s.*; Zoare, *pl.*
Flour	Zom	Zom	Zim	Zom	Zom	Zɔŋ
Fool	Yalma, *s.*; Yalmʃi, *pl.*	Gyerego *or* Yelema	Ƨerigo, *s.*; Ƨera, *pl.*	Gaoŋ, *s.*; Gam, *pl.*	Yalem, *s.*, Ka; Yalse, *pl.*, Se	Damboli, *s.*; Dambolo, *pl.*
Foot	Naure, *s.*; Nauwa, *pl.*	Nɔbere, *s.*; Nɔba, *pl.*	Nable, *s.*; Naba, *pl.*	Nɔber, *s.*; Nɔba, *pl.*	Naare, *s.*, De; Nama, *pl.*, A.	Gbɛre, *s.*; Gbɛ, *pl.*
Forehead	Dire, *s.*; Dia, *pl.*	Gbeo, *s.*; Gberi, *pl.*	Gberho, *s.*; Gberi, *pl.*	Gbeog, *s.*; Gbet, *pl.*	Dire, *s.*; Dia, *pl.*, De, *or* Gwere, *s.*, De; Gwera, *pl.*, A	Gbie, *s.*; Gbere, *pl.*
Forget	Nyim	Tam	Tam *or* Suhuvale	Tam	Tama	Yini
Friend	Zwa, *s.*; Zwaramba, *pl.*	Zoa, *s.*; Zoadema, *pl.*	Zɔ, *s.*; Zɔnema, *pl.*	Zɔa, *s.*; Zɔnam, *pl.*	Zɔ, *s.*, A; Zorema, *pl.*, Ba	Zɔ, *s.*; Zɔre, *pl.*
Frog	Pondere, *s.*; Pwona, *pl.*	Polɔre, *s.*; Polɔya, *pl.*; Pɔntere, *s.*; Pwona, *pl.*	Pololi, *s.*; Poloya, *pl.*	Poner, *s.*; Pona, *pl.*	Kampone, *s.*, De; Kampoma, *pl.*, A	Pɔntere, *s.*; Pontie, *pl.*
Fry	Kim	Kyim	Kyim	Kim	Kyim	Kyī
Funeral	Kure, *s.*; Kuya, *pl.*	Kuri	Kuli	Kur	Kure, *s.*, De; Kua, *pl.*, A	Kori, *s.*; Kue, *pl.*

Nabte.	Bulea.	Loberu.	Talene.	Gbanya.	Kasene.	Isal.
Lu nor Dabeem Zab Pii Bugum	Bɔb noa Yɔnsem Kpaleŋ Pisi Bolem	Lu nor Dembie Zebr Pil Vũ	Lu nor Dabeem Zab Pii Bugum	Kiʃi Kufu Kalo, *n.* Bente Ediɛ	Vɔgɔ ni .. Gyara Pu Mini	Vou ni Wolovo Hɛ yosuŋ Mɔla Nyiŋ
Ziŋ	..	Zim, *s.*; Zime, *pl.*	Ziŋa	Kabaŋe, *s.*; Mbaŋe, *pl.*	Yoni, *s.*, De; Yona, *pl.*, Ye	Camfile, *s.*; Camfilie, *pl.*
..	Nandyuŋ, *s.*, Ka; Na- ndyunsa, *pl.*, Si	Zoo, *s.*; Zor, *pl.*	Zoo	Kusu- msɔmbi, *s.*; Asu- msombi, *pl.*	Nandwoa, *s.*, Ka; Nandwɛ, *pl.*, Si; Zara, *s.*; Zare, *pl.*, Ka, Si	Naŋcoa, *s.*; Naŋcɔse, *pl.*
Zom	Zom (Bu class)	Zõ	Zom	Nyefu	Munu	Muŋ
Yalim *or* Gaoŋ, *adj.*	Kɔno, *adj.*	Dambol, *s.*; Da- mbole, *pl.*	Yaleɣ *or* Gaoŋ	Ewulpo, *s.*; Buwulpo, *pl.*	Gyoro, *adj.*	Yare, *adj.*
Nobere	Nantuog, *s.*, Ku; Nantata, *pl.*, Ti	Gber, *s.*; Gbe, *pl.*	Nabere, *s.*	Kea, *s.*; Aya, *pl.*	Naga, *s.*, Ka; Nĕ, *pl.*, Si	Na, *s.*; Nase, *pl.*
Gweog	Dir	Digir	Gbeog	Kaʃito, *s.*; Nʃito, *pl.*	Tiri, *s.*, Di; Tirɛ, *pl.*, Ya	Tile, *s.*; Tilli, *pl.*
Tam	Buti	Yir	Tame	Taso	Soe	Yo
Zɔ	Doa, *s.*, Wa; Doba, *pl.*, Ba	Ba, *s.*; Bare, *pl.*	Zɔ	Tere, *s.*; Terana, *pl.*	Bɛdo, *s.*, De; Bedoana, *pl.*, Ba	Nandɔŋ, *s.*; Nandɔse, *pl.*
Gwam	Bontɔr, *s.*, De; Bontoa, *pl.*, Ɖ.	Pɔntir, *s.*; Pontiɛ, *pl.*	Ponet	Pulo, *s.*; Apulo, *pl.*	Mantɔro, *s.*, Ku; Mantɔaro, *pl.*, Ti	Yeve, *s.*; Yevea, *pl.*; Sɔro, *s.*; Sɔrne, *pl.*
Kim Kur	Kyim Kup	Kyĩ Kur, *s.*; Koe, *pl.*	Kyem Kur	Ke Kali, *s.*; Nli, *pl.*	Kware Lua	Hàl Yoho

II. VOCABULARIES (cont.)

English.	Mole.	Mampelle.	Dagbane.	Kusal.	Nankane.	Dagare.
Garden egg	Kumere, s.; Komba, pl.	Kamne, s.; Kama, pl.	Kamli, s.; Kama, pl.	Komer, s.; Koma, pl.	Kune, s., De; Kuma, pl., A	Komiri, s.; Komie, pl.
Girl	Pɔgsada, s.; Pɔgsadaba, pl.	Poa-sa-rega, s.; Poa-sara, pl.	Bipuŋa, s.; Bi-puŋse, pl.	Poa-sader, s.; Poa-sada, pl.	Pɔg-saare, s., De; Pɔg-saara, pl., A	Pɔ-sera, s.; Pɔ-ser, pl.
Glass	Jetega	Masoasi	Digi, s.; Digse, pl.	Gotiŋ, s.; Gotis, pl.	Bisiga, s., Ka; Bise, pl., Se	Cana, s.; Cane, pl.
Go	Ceŋe	Kyem	Tce	Cem	Sene or Ceŋe	Ceŋ or Ga
Goat	Buga, s.; Buse, pl.	Bua, s.; Buʃi, pl.	Bua, s.; Buhi	Bug, s.; Buse, pl.	Bua, s.; Buse, pl.	Buɔ, s. Bore, pl.
Gold	Salema	Salema	Salma	Salem	Salema (Bo class)	Salema
Good	Sɔngo	Soŋo, s.; Soma, pl.	Suŋ, s.; Sima, pl.	Soŋ, s.; Som, pl.	Soŋa, s.; Suse, pl.	Vila, s.; Viele, pl.
Grain-store	Baure, s.; Bawa, pl.	Buri, s.; Boya, pl.	Kpacha-ɣalaga	Bur, s.; Buya, pl.	Bare, s., De; Baa, pl., A	Bugo, s.; Bugeri, pl.
Ground-nut	Suma or Namguli	Sunkpam, s.; Su-mpila, pl.	Simli, s.; Sima, pl.	Suma	Suma	Sankune, pl.
Guard	Gu	Gwose	Guli or Lihi	Gur	Gu or Bise	Gu
Guinea-fowl	Kɔngo, s.; Kini, pl.	Kpaŋo, s.; Kpimi, pl.	Kpaŋ, s.; Kpini, pl.	Kpɔŋ, s.; Kpini, pl.	Koŋo, s., Ko; Kyuŋi, pl., I	Kpaŋo, s.; Kpini, pl.
Gun	Buglaudo, s.; Bu-glado, pl.	Malfa, s.; Malfasi, pl.	Malfa, s.; Malfa-dema, pl.	Malfa, s.; Male, pl.	Bugumdo, s.; Bu-gumdoro, pl., To	Marfa, s.; Marfare, pl.
Hailstone	Sapilimde, s.; Sa-pilima, pl.	Sakugle, s.; Sa-kuga, pl.	Sakugli, s.; Sakuga, pl.	Sakuger, s.; Sakuga, pl.	Sakugeri	Sakugeri
Hair	Kobogo, s.; Ko-bodo, pl.	Zobere or Kwobere	Zɔbre or Kobere	Zobog or Kɔbog	Kobogo or Zobodo, Ku, To	Kɔgolɔŋ

Nabte.	Bulea.	Loberu.	Talene.	Gbanya.	Kasene.	Isal.
Kamre, s.; Kama, pl.	Komi, s., De; Koma, pl., Ŋ.	Kombiri, s.; Kombie, pl.	Kamre, s.; Kama, pl.	Katere, s.; Ntere, pl.	Kyelem, s., Di; Kyelɛ, pl., Ya	Kelen, s.; Keleme, pl.
Pɔ-sar, s.; Pɔ-sara, pl.	Nu-pɔy-leak, s., Ka; Ni-pɔg-lasa, pl., Si	Pɔg-sera, s.; Pɔg-sereba, pl.	Pɔ-saret, s.; Pɔ-sara, pl.	Sunguru, s.; Asunguru, pl.	Kakye, s.; Kakyoa, pl.	Ha-tɔlo, s.; Ha-tɔlie, pl.
Bisig	Gisiga	Cala	Dis	Diki, s.; Adiki, pl.	Zono, s., Ku; Zoono, pl., Ti	Be-na-nterɛ
Kim	Cen	Cen or Ceri	Cen	Yɔ	Vé	Mo
Buu	Bu, s., Ku; Boe, pl. Ŋ.	Buɔ, s.; Bor, pl.	Bu	Kaboi, s.; Mboi, pl.	Buno, s., Ku; Bonne, pl., Ti	Bon, s.; Bona, pl.
Salema	Salema	Saleme	Salema	Suga	Salem	Saleme
Son	Nala	Vila, s.; Vielo, pl.	Sona, s.; Soma, pl.	Wale	Lana	Zon, s.; Zoma, pl.
Bure	Bui, s., De; Bɔl, pl., Ŋ.	Bugr, s.; Buge, pl.	Bur	Kupuro, s.; Apuro, pl.	Tulɛ, s., Ka; Tuli, pl., Si	Virɛ, s.; Viriʃi, pl.
Sukpaam	Sunkpa, s., Bu; Sunkpata, pl., Ti	Sunkaa, s.; Sume, pl.	Sukpam	Kulonku, s.; Aku-lonku, pl.	Nawurɛ, s.; Ka; Nawuri, pl., Si	Gyosi, s.; Gyone, pl.; Si, s.; Sie, pl.
Gur Kpɔno, s.; Kpini, pl.	Gis Kpɔn, s., Ku; Kpina, pl., Ŋ	Gu, Pige Kan, s.; Kyin, pl.	Wule or Gur Kpon, s.; Kpim, pl.	Pete Kikya, s.; Akya, pl.	Ni Sugu, s., Ku; Suni, pl., Ti	Pɔ Su, s.; Suuni, pl.
Bugundɔɔ	Kabo-nduɔ, s., Ku; Ka-bondata, pl., Ti	Bonda or Malfa	Marfa	Marfa, s.; Amarfa, pl.	Kpeyɔ, s., Ku; Kpɛrɔ, pl., Ti	Marfa, s.; Marfase, pl.
Sakuger	Nwarotan	Sabikur	Sakuger	Bore-gyombo	Dubane, s., Di; Du-bana, pl., Ya	Duontave, s.; Duon-tavea, pl.
Kobog	Zukzüsa	Zukɔblo	Kɔboɣ	Emen, s.; Emenana, pl.	Wuwa, s., Ka; We, pl., Si	Pon, s.; Pona, pl.

II. VOCABULARIES (cont.)

English.	Mole.	Mampelle.	Dagbane.	Kusal.	Nankane.	Dagare.
Hand	Nugu, s.; Nusi, pl.	Nuu, s.; Nuʃi, pl.	Nuu, s.; Nuhi, pl.	Nuug, s.; Nus, pl.	Nuo, s., Ka; Nusi, pl., Se	Nu, s.; Nuri, pl.
Hang up Head	Yagele Zugu, s.; Zuttu, pl.	Yaale Zugu, s.; Zugere, pl.	Yili Zugu, s.; Zugri, pl.	Yaal Zug, s.; Zut, pl.	Yagele Zuo, s., Ko; Zuto, pl., To	Yagele Zu, s.; Zuri, pl.
Hear Heart	Wum Suri, s.; Suya, pl.	Wum Sufo, s.; Suhuri, pl.	Wum Suhu, s.; Suhuri, pl.	Wum Sur, s.; Suya, pl.	Wum Suri, s., De; Soa, pl., A	Woŋ Suri, s.; Sie, pl.
Heat	Winge, v.; Tulugo, n.	Tulege, v.; Wologo, n.	Tulum, n.; Wolgo, n.	Tulik, s.; Tulug, n.	Tulege, v.; Tulugo, n.	Tole, v.
Hide, n.	Goŋgo, s.; Gando, pl.	Gbaŋo, s.; Gbana, pl.	Gbaŋ, s.; Gbana, pl.	Gboŋ, s.; Gbana, pl.	Goŋo, s., Ko; Gana, pl., To	Gane, s.; Geme, pl.
Hide, v.	Lili or Solige	Lili or Soa	Lili or Soɣe	Lus or Soa	Lile; Soɣe	Lini, s.; Sogole, pl.
Hill (rock)	Taŋa, s.; Taŋse, pl.	Zore, s.; Zoaya, pl.; Kugere, Tetare	Zoli, s.; Zoya, pl.	Zoa, s.; Zoya, pl.; Taŋpi, s.; Tampis, pl.	Taŋa, s.; Tase, pl.; Ka; Zore, s.; Zoa, pl., De, A	Taŋa, s.; Tane, pl.
Hippo-potamus	Yemde, s.; Yema, pl.	Nyemne, s.; Nye-ma, pl.	Damli, s.; Dama, pl.	Pĩ, s.; Pĩs, pl.	Ene, s.; Ema, pl., De, A	Eŋ, s.; Ene, pl.
Hunger Hyena	Kom Katere or Soasa	Kum Kunduŋo, s.; Kunduna, pl.	Kúm Kuŋduŋ, s.; Kunduna, pl.	Kom Kora, s.; Koranam, pl.	Kom Saseŋa, s., Ka; Sase, pl., Se; Gbingbere, s., Be; Gbingbia, pl., A	Koŋ Gboŋbori, s.; Gboŋ-bor, pl.
Ill (to be) Immerse	Be Lose or Kome	Be Lose	Be Lim	Bɛt Los	Be Luse	Be Lore
Impudent	Titam	Kara-mbani (Hausa)	Karambani (Hausa)	Titalem	Muŋa or Tentalim	Nimi-kuna, s.; Nimi-kumo, pl.

Nabte.	Bulea.	Loberu.	Talene.	Gbanya.	Kasene.	Isal.
Nuug, s.	Nisa, s., Si; Nisima, pl., Si	Nu, s.; Nuru, pl.	Nuuɣ, s.	Eno, s.; Enoana, pl.	Gyeŋa, s., Ka; Gye, pl., Si	Nɛhẽ, s.; Nesea, pl.
Yagle	Payik	Yagle	Yagle	Saga	Pale	Sakɛ
Zug	Zuk, s., Ku; Zuma, pl., D.	Zu, s.; Zuru, pl.	Zuɣ	Komu, s.; Amu, pl.	Yu, s., Ku; Yuni, pl., Ti	Nyuŋ, s.; Nyusi, pl.
Wum	Wum	Wob	Wum	Nu	Ni	Ne
Suri	Sui, s., De; Suɛ, pl., D.	Sur, s.; Suge, pl.	Suri	Agbo, s.; Nbo, pl.	Bakyarkili, s., De; Baykarkila, pl., Ye	Wiese, s.; Wiesi, pl.
Tulig, v.	Tolen, v.	Tolo, v.	Tuleg, v.; Tulug, n.	Tuſe, v.; Kuwulo, n.	Lone, v.	Laŋ, v.
Gboŋ	Gbaŋ, s., De; Gbana, pl., D.	Gan, s.; Game, pl.	Gboŋ	..	Tɔnɔ, s.; Toano, pl.	Tɛŋ, s.; Tenni, pl.
Lil or Sɔγe	Suk	Sɔgle	Lil; Sɔɣ	..	Sɛgɛ	Fà
Taŋ or Taŋpii	Peŋ, s., Ku; Pena, pl., D.	Taŋ, s.; Tan, pl.	Taŋ	Kibie, s.; Abie, pl.	Peo, s., Ku; Pero, pl., Ti	Kandolo, s.; Kandoli, pl.; Pel, s.; Pelle, pl.
Emere	Nyinyen, s., De; Nyinyema, pl., D.	Yɛn, s.; Yene, pl.	Emere	Curu, s.; Acuru, pl.	Coŋo, s., Ku; Choano, pl., Ti	Lle-naŋ, s.; Lle-nese, pl.
Kwom	Kwɔm	Kɔ	Kwom	Akoŋ	Kana	Losu
Gbingᵂere	Piuk, s., Ku; Piŋa, pl., D.	Gbonbor, s.; Gbonbo, pl.	Gbingwere	Kuŋtuŋ, s.; Akuntuŋ, pl.	Wiru, s., Wira, pl., Ba	Gungurɔ, s.; Gungruſi, pl.
Bẽ	Yuɔk	Bier	Be	Llɔ	Wela	Welo
Lohe	Lus	Lor	Loke	Polɔ	Dira	..
Muŋ	Kanjanta	Cegero	Muŋ	Karambani (Hausa)	Kajane	Toakɛro

II. VOCABULARIES (*cont.*)

English.	Mole.	Mampelle.	Dagbane.	Kusal.	Nankane.	Dagare.
Immense	Berle, *s.*; Beda, *pl.*	Karege, *v.*	Tatali	Bedog	Kate, *s.*; Kara, *pl.*	Berɔŋ, *s.*; Bɛre, *pl.*
Intestines	Nyaugo, *s.*; Nya-do, *pl.*	Nyõõ, *s.*; Nyõre, *pl.*	Nyogo, *s.*; Nyore, *pl.*	Nyog, *s.*; Nyot, *pl.*	Nyoo, *s.*, Ko; Ny-oro, *pl.*, To	Nyɔbɔ
Iron-worker	Saya, *s.*; Saba, *pl.*	Sainya, *s.*; Saba, *pl.*	Mana, *s.*; Mana-nema, *pl.*	Sai, *s.*; Sab, *pl.*	Sa, *s.*, A; Saba, *pl.*, Ba	Kurkuro, *s.*; Kur-kurubo, *pl.*
Join	Tɔnge	Tuge, Toŋe	Tugi	Nal	Toŋe *or* Nal	Tone
Jungle	Mõge, Weogo	Mõne	Mɔyoni	Mõõg	Mõõ, *s.*; Mõõro, *pl.*	Moa *or* Wie
Kick	Tɔ	Tabe	Tab	Teb	Tɛbe	Tiɛ
Kneel	Nyigimde	Gbane	Gbane	Igen	Yigele *or* Kure	Gbi
Knife	Suga, *s.*; Suse, *pl.*	Suwa, *s.*; Susi, *pl.*	Sua, *s.*; Suhi, *pl.*	Suuk, *s.*; Suus, *pl.*	Sua, *s.*; Suse, *pl.*	Suɔ, *s.*; Sɔre, *pl.*
Kraal	Bagéré, *s.*; Baɣa, *pl.*	Na-baare, *s.*	Na-kpahe	Zanpak, *s.*; Zanpas, *pl.*	Naɣa-dene, *s.*, De; Naɣa-deme, *pl.*, A	Zagere *or* Na-daŋ
Knock, *v.*	Ka, Nwe, To	Kpasa	Kpahi	Koŋ	Koŋe, Kue *or* Nwe	Kori
Lame	Wɔbega, *n.*	Wɔbega, *s.*; Wɔbse, *pl.*	Wobga, *s.*; Wobse, *pl.*	Wɔbeg	Wabega, *s.*, Ko; Wabse, *pl.*, To	Wɔ, *s.*; Wɔre, *pl.*
Lamp	Fitila, *s.*; Fitilse, *pl.*	Filla, *s.*; Filla-dema, *pl.*	Frila, *s.*; Fril-rema, *pl.*	Filla, *s.*; Fita, *pl.*	Fila, *s.*, Ka Filse, *pl.*, Se	Fentila, *s.*; Fentena, *pl.*
Laugh, *v.*	La	La	La	La	La	La
Laughter,	Lado	Lare	Lari	Laat	Laro *or* Loro	Lare
Lay (eggs)	Lobe	Nye (gyella)	Nye (galla)	Lob	Lobe *or* Nye	Nye (gyeli)

Nabte.	Bulea.	Loberu.	Talene.	Gbanya.	Kasene.	Isal.
Karog	Kpweem	Bero, s.; Berɛ, pl.	Berog or Karog	Kubɔŋbo, s.; Abɔŋbo, pl.	Daga	Bal, s.; Bala, pl.
Nyog	Nẅeta	Nyager, s.; Nyage, pl.	Nwoɣ	Kupunibi	Loro	Lobie
Sayɛ	Kyeok, s., Ku; Kyeɔta, pl., Ti	Sakpere	Saye	Bayipo, s.; Abayipo, pl.	Luru, s., De; Lurɛ, pl., Ba	Liviru, s.; Liverɛ, pl.
Toŋ	Tɔm	Cok	Toŋ	Kye...so	Tɔŋe	Pe
Mõg	Sakai	Muɔ or Ẅiɛ	Mõg or Yeoɣ	Kopuŋ	Gao	Gire
Tɛbeg	Toŋ	Teb or Very	Tɛbeg	Sala	Tɔ	Ye
Kun	Kwi dunduna	Gure	..	Gbirr	Kuni	Tokuii
Suu	Gebeg, s., Ka; Gebsa, pl., Si	Suɔ, s.; Suor, pl.	Sugu, s.; Suu, pl.	Kasaŋe, s.; Nsaŋe, pl.	Seo, s., Ku; Ku; Seno, pl., Ti	Sea, s.; Sesɛ, pl.
Zanpak	Na-kpwem, s., Ka; Na-kpensa, pl., Si	Na-zak, s.; Na-zager, pl.	Zanpak	Kulu, s.; Alu, pl.	Na-boo, s.; Ku; Na-boro, pl., Ti	Na-dea, s.; Na-disɛ, pl.
Kɔ	Nuk	Nwẽ or Kpale	Koŋere	Biri	Maggɛ	Mwau
Wɔbog	Gbwaneŋ, s., Ka; Gbwansa, pl., Si	Woba	Wɔbeg	Kileŋ, s.; Aleŋ, pl.	Gwana	Jussi
Fila	Kanea, s., Ka; Kanasa, pl., Si	Fitila, s.; Fitilse, pl.	Fila	Fitina, s.; Afitina, pl.	Mezoŋo, s., De, Ku; Mezoano, pl., Te, Ti	Caŋ, s.; Cana or Canse, pl.
La	La	Lara	La	Muse	Mɔne	Mɔŋ
Laat	Lata	Lar	Lare	Emuse	Mɔano	Momɔŋ
Lob	Lob	Lɔb	Lobe	To	De	Llo

II. VOCABULARIES (cont.)

English.	Mole.	Mampelle.	Dagbane.	Kusal.	Nankane.	Dagare.
Lazy	Kwima, s.; Kwimba, pl.	Zimyaare-dana, s.; Zimyaa-dema, pl.	Zinyaɣle or Vin-yaɣle or Gbinyaɣle	Zennyaɣer, n.	Zannya-gere, n.	Entuo
Lead, n.	Namdo	Darema	Dalma	Nam	Nɔŋo	Kpwana
Lead, v.	Wiligi	Bigse or Wulse	Biele	Paal	Paale	..
Leaf	Vaugo, s.; Vado, pl.	Vɔ, s.; Vare, pl.	Vɔgo, s.; Vare, pl.	Vao, s.; Vad, pl.	Võõ, s., Ku; Voto, pl., To	Va, s.; Vare, pl.
Left	Gwɔboga	Gwɔboga	Gobga	Gɔbog	Gɔbega	Gɔ
Lick	Lelem	Lele	Leli	Leɛl	Lele	Lene
Lie	Ziri	Ziri	Ziri	Maɣ	Parem, v.; Ziri, n.	Ziri
Lie down	Gane; Gande	Doone	Dooni	Dɔɔn	Gare	Gan
Lift	Zeke; Dike	Kpeke	Kpoɣe	Zaŋ	Zeke or Deke	Zege or De
Light, adj.	Faugo, s.; Fado, pl.	Faalega	Faka-faka	Fasug	Fooŋo, s.; Foono, pl.	Fõ, s.; Fõne, pl.
Lip	No-gongo, s.; No-gando, pl.	Na-ŋgban-pebere	Naŋgbon-peble	No-gban, s., No-gbana, pl.	Nogane, s., De; No-gbana, pl., A	Na-gbene, s.; Na-gbeme, pl.
Listen	Kelege	Wum	Wum	Wum	Kyelese	Kyele
Little	Bilifu; Fifu	Bela	Biela	Fii; Beɛla	Fii; Bila	Bile
Lizard	Selemde, s.; Sele-ma, pl.	Baɲà, s.; Banse, pl.	Baɲle, s.; Baɲa, pl.	Ti-ba-ndaug, s.; Ti-ba-ndat, pl.	Bandɔɔ, s., Ko; Ba-ndɔro, pl., To	Bɔŋa, s.; Bɔne, pl.
Load	Zibo, Tedo	Zire, s.; Zia, pl.	Zili, s.; Zia, pl.	Zib, s.; Zit, pl.	Zeo, s.; Ze-ro, pl.	Tobo
Lock	Kuloŋnifu	Baŋ-bia, s.; Ban-bisi, pl.	Kpare	..	Kwaresega, Ka, Se	Daɣ-ku-nkune
Love, v.	Noŋa, Datta	Bɔ	Yu	Som, Nɔŋ	Son, Non	Nomo, n.
Lover	Dolle, s.; Dolleba, pl.	Maam, s.; Mamade-ma, pl.	Mam, s.; Mam-ne-ma, pl.	Saboa, s.; Saboos, pl.	Zaba, s., A; Zabdema, pl., Ba	Sene, s.; Se-neme, pl.

Nabte.	Bulea.	Loberu.	Talene.	Gbanya.	Kasene.	Isal.
Zinŋaɣere	Nyinworo or Kpi-kpeak	Yaŋtuo-sob	Zenŋaɣere	Etɔlpo, s; Botolpo, pl.	Kokwao, s.; Kokwaro, pl.	Pimperebu, s.; Pi-mperebe, pl.
Nam	Kpwamak	..	Nɔŋ	Epal	Mau	Sankpe-renbí or Marfa-tavea
..	..	..	Paal	Gberege	Kɛ...yiga	La...sepa
Vog	Veok, s., Ku; Vata, pl., Ti	Va, s.; Var, pl.	Vug	Afanta	Vɔ, s.; Vɔro, pl.	Pepaa, s.; Pepaaro, pl.
Gɔbog	..	Goba	Gɔbog	Bana	Gya	Goa
Lele	Lele	Lere	Lel	Dente	Dellim	Lenni
Maɣe	Velem or Kyesa	Ziri	Maɣe, v.	Kontɔmpo	Fɔva	Wai, Nyɛa
Dɔone	Duɔk	Ga	Doone	Dese	Pane	Paŋ
Zek	Kwɔt	Kpag; Zek, De	Zake or De	Ta	..	..
Fag	Valeŋ	Kalfal	Faɣ	Ku-mu-wogwɛ	Bɛ duna	Be-yun or Ve-yun
Nagban	Noeveok, s., Ku; Noevata, pl., Ti	Nobiri	Nogwane	Kalo-piribi	Nivɔ, s., Ku; Nivɔ-ro, pl., Ti	Ni-piŋ, s.; Ni-pine, pl.
Wum	Wum	Kyɛle	Wums	Nu	Niɛ	Nei or Ne
Fii, Bela	Maka	Bile	Beɛla	Gberɛ, Fibi	Balaŋa	Wie, s.; Wisi, pl.
Bandog	Baŋ, s.; Bansa, pl., Ka, Si; Yug, s.; Yuta, pl., Ku, Ti	Banda	Bandog	Kiti, s.; Ati, pl.	Belaga, s., Ka or De; Belle, pl., Si	Haval, s.; Havala, pl.
Ziri	Gib, s., Bu; Gib-ta, pl., Ti	Tur, s.; Toe, pl.	Ziri	Esolo, s.; Esolana, pl.	Zile, s.; Zila, pl.	Cokà, s.; Cokose, pl.
Kwareseg	Lika, s., Ka; Lig-sa, pl., Si	..	Kpareseɣ	Kradua, s.; Akradua, pl.	Bor-kyegga	Bor-gol-nwal, s.; Bor-gol-nwala, pl.
Som	Yaga	Nɔne	Som	Sa	Sɔe	Coŋ
Zaba	Nɔŋ, s.; Ku; Nɔ-nta, pl., Ti	Sen, s.; Senbɛ, pl.	Gab	Gyipo, s.; Gyipoana, pl.	Bɔlɔ, s., De; Bɔla, pl., Ba	Hela, s.; Helava, pl.

II. VOCABULARIES (*cont.*)

English.	Mole.	Mampelle.	Dagbane.	Kusal.	Nankane.	Dagare.
Lung	Fulfugu, *s.*; Ful-futtu, *pl.*	Sofua, *s.*; Sofushi, *pl.*	Sapugu, *s.*; Sapuri, *pl.*	Sofut	Fulunfo, *s.*, Ko; Fu-lumfuro, *pl.*, To	Falanfugeri, *s.*; Falan-fugu, *pl.*
Mad	Genga, *s.*; Gemse, *pl.*	Kpe ... ye-yaare, *v.*	Kpe ... yi-nyare, *v.*	Zoluk, *s.*; Zoŋ, *pl.*	Zologo, *s.*, Ko; Zollo, *pl.*, To	Yenyaa, *s.*; Yenyaare, *pl.*
Make	Mane *or* Male	Maale	Maale	Mal	Eŋe, Male	Male
Male	Dauwa, *s.*; Dappa, *pl.*	Dowa, *s.*; Dapa, *pl.*	Doo, *s.*; Doba, *pl.*	Daog *or* Daug	Doo, *s.*; Doro, *pl.*, Ko, To	Do, *s.*; Do-bo, *pl.*
Mane	Gede, *s.*; Geto, *pl.*	Gbere, *s.*; Gbea, *pl.*	Gbem	Gbere, *s.*; Gbɛa, *pl.*	Gyebego, *s.*, Ko; Gye-bero, *pl.*	Gberɛ, *s.*; Gbɛ, *pl.*
Market	Daga, *s.*; Dashe, *pl.*	Daa, *s.*; Daase, *pl.*	Daa, *s.*; Dahi, *pl.*	Daa, *s.*; Das, *pl.*	Daa, *s.*, Ka; Dase, *pl.*, Se	Da, *s.*; Dare, *pl.*
Marry	Loe-furi	Amre (Hausa) Di poa	Kpoɣe-paɣa	Di poa	Pama (*or* di) poɣa	Kyɛre
Mat	Pili, *s.*; Pia *or* Piya, *pl.*	Zane, *s.* (Hausa); Zana, *pl.*	Soŋ, *s.*; Sondi, *pl.*	Soŋ, *s.*; Soŋ, *pl.*	Soŋo, *s.*, Ko; Soŋo, *pl.*, To	Pili, *s.*; Pile, *pl.*
Meat	Nemdo	Nomne	Nimdi	Nim	Neŋo, *s.*, Ko; Neno, *pl.*, To	Nene, *s.*; Nema, *pl.*
Meet	Seɣe	Tuse, Pa	Tuhe	Tus	Tuse *or* Seke	Tore
Mend	Za, Sɛn, Sukuli	Tuge	Male	Lasig	Ligi	Liri *or* Sugi
Menstruation	Lwi seɣa	So, *v.*	So, *v.*	Li sea	Lu sɛa	Sie vare *or* Tie sie
Micturate	Dude	Dune	Dun-dulum	Duun	Durɛ	Dore
Mid-day	Winto-sukka	Wuntaŋa-zugo-saa	Wuntaŋ-zug-saa	Winbulin	Wunteŋa-teŋa-soka	Nwina-are-zusonsugo
Middle	Sukka	Susuka	Sunsuuni	Suu	Suka	Sonsugo
Milk, *v.*	Pɛ̃	Pe	Pe	Pɛ̃	Pɛ̃	Pɛ̃
Mix	Damme *or* Jedege	Gyɛre	Gare	Jedeg *or* Gudug	Jerege *or* Dame	Doŋ
Moon	Ciugu, *s.*; Cisi, *pl.*	Nwarega, *s.*; Nwarse, *pl.*	Goli, *s.*; Goya, *pl.*, *or* Ciri, *s.*; Cira, *pl.*	Nwadeg *s.*; Nwa-des, *pl.*	Nwarega, *s.*, Ka; Nwarse, *pl.*, Si	Cu, *s.*; Curi, *pl.*

Nabte.	Bulea.	Loberu.	Talene.	Gbanya.	Kasene.	Isal.
Safug	Zuzuk, s., Ku; Zuzuta, pl., Ti	Fulafur	Soput	Farfara	Fulaŋfuŋo, s.; Fulanfuno, pl.	Cofosɛ, s.; Cofosa, pl.
Zalog	Yisin	Yanyaar, s.; Yanyadem, pl.	Galog	Ebom, s.; Bubumpo, pl.	Cuco, s.; Cucoru, pl.	Nyinyɛtina, s.; Nyinyɛtema, pl.
Ene	Nye or Neaɣ	Mal	Eng	Worɔ	Ke	Da
Dɔg	Dɔba	Deb, s.; Deber, pl.	Dɔɔg	Nyeŋ, s.; Banyeŋ, pl.	Baro, s., De; Bara, pl., Ba	Belle, s.; Belli, pl.
..	..	..	Gbebeg	Egbelema	Vao or Bao, s.; Vado or Bado, pl.	Gbɛso,s.; Gbɛsene, pl.
Daa	Yaba, s.; Yababa, pl.	Da, s.; Dar, pl.	Daa	Kibe, s.; Abɛ, pl.	Yaga, s., Ka; Ye, pl., Si	Yauwa, s.; Yause, pl., or Yɔva, s.; Yɔse, pl.
Di pɔɣo	Far	De-pɔg	Di-pɔɣɔ	Furu	So kane	Gya
Suŋ	Teak, s., Ka; Tasa, pl., Si	Pil, s.; Pile, pl.	Soŋ	Kalaŋ, s.; Akalaŋ, pl.	Sara, s., Ka; Sare, pl., Si	Bɔhɔ, s.; Bɔhɔne, pl.
Niuŋ	Lam	Nen, s.; Nene, pl.	Numd	Ebalan	Nane, s., De; Nana, pl., Ye	Namea, s.; Namese, pl.
Tus	Tua	Paɣ or Tur	Saɣe	Sar, Tu	Gyera or Yi	Kyen, To
Lig	Lik	Page	Lig	Ti	Nyane	Yɛrɛ, Wase
Lu sɛ	Nisa	Lu sie	Lu see	Di kir	Ka lugu	Meŋ-cal or Peparo
Lur	Sam	Dure	Dur	Bɔfol	Fea	Fe
Wunteŋteŋsok	Kantuem sunsum	Zusɔg	Nintensuk	Epeni-bukumu-so	W̌ea-tetare	Wehaisiese, Weatutuavan
Sok	Sunsum	Sɔgolesɔg	Suk	Bargato	Tetare	Pɛkɛ, Tutuavan
Pẽ	..	Pɛ̃	Pe	Nyaŋ	..	Cake
Jerim	..	Dam	Jerim	W̌eto	Gware, Yũ, Solle	Goli, Kosi
Nambɔɔ	Kik, s., Ka; Kisa, pl., Si	Cu, s.; Curi, pl.	Namboo	Kofɔl, s.; Afol, pl.	Kyena, s., Ka; Kyene, pl., Si	Kyɛnɛ, s.; Kyense, pl.

II. VOCABULARIES (*cont.*)

English.	Mole.	Mampelle.	Dagbane.	Kusal.	Nankane.	Dagare.
Mosquito	Duŋa, s.; Dumsi, pl.	Duŋa, s.; Dunse, pl.	Duŋa, s.; Dunsi, pl.	Dum, s.; Dums, pl.	Doŋa, s., Ka; Dose, pl., Se	Duŋo, s.; Dune, pl.
Name	Yule, s.; Yuya, pl.	Yure, s.; Yuya, pl.	Yuli, s.; Yuya, pl.	Yuur, s.; Yuda, pl.	Yure, s., De; Yura, pl., A	Yune, s.; Yie, pl.
Neck	Nyubula, s.; Nyubelsi, pl.	Nangori or Nyingori	Ɗyingɔli, s.; Ɗyiŋgɔya, pl.	Niŋgɔr, s.; Ningɔya, pl.	Nyugela, s., Ka; Nyugelɛse, pl., Se	Nyu, s.; Nyuri, pl.
Needle	Fupim, s.; Fupema, pl.	Kpar-pim, s.; Kparpima, pl.	Ɛeriga, s.; Ɛersi, pl.	Kpar-pim, s.; Kparpema, pl.	Fupim, s., Bu; Fupema, pl., A	Kparo-pi, s.; Kparopime, pl.
Nest	Tukko, s.; Tɔgodo, pl.	Teo, s.; Tere, pl.	Teɔ	Teuk, s.; Teet, pl.	Tuko, s., Ko; Togero, pl., To	Cogo, s.; Cogoli, pl.
New	Paalaga, s.; Palse, pl.	Palega, s.; Pale, pl.	Palle, s.; Pala, pl.	Pal, s.; Pala, pl.	Palega, s., Ka; Palse, pl., Se	Pàla, s.; Pála, pl.
Nose	Nyore, s.; Nyoya, pl.	Nyõre, s.; Nyõya, pl.	Nyie	Nyõr, s.; Nyõya, pl.	Nyore, s., De; Nyoa, pl., A	Nyore, s.; Nyɛ, pl.
Nostril	Nyo-bɔko or Nyovore	Nyo-vore, s.; Nyovɔya, pl.	Nyie-vɔli, s.; Nyievɔya, pl.	Nyõ-vor	Nyo-vore	Nyo-bɔge, s.; Nyobɔgeri, pl.
Okro	Mande, s.; Maana, pl.	Mane, s.; Mana, pl.	Maani, s.; Mana, pl.	Maan, s.; Maana, pl.	Maane, s., De; Mana, pl., A	Maani, s.; Maana, pl.
Old	Kudugu, v.	Kuruge, v.	Kurugi, v.	Kudue, v.	Kuruge, v.	Kore, s.; Kora, adj.
Orphan	Ciba or Kiba, s.; Cibise or Kibise, pl.	Kpibiga, s. Kpibsi, pl.	Kpibga, s.; Kpibsi, pl.	Kpebig, s.; Kpebis, pl.	Cibiga, s., Ka; Cibse, pl., Se	Bikpibɛ
Open, v.	Pake	Yoe	Yoi, Kparɣe	Yoog	Pake or Yuɛ	Yuo
Pant	Sesaga, Vuse	Vuse	Vuhi	Vus	Vose	Vure

Nabte.	Bulea.	Loberu.	Talene.	Gbanya.	Kasene.	Isal.
Dums	Duuŋ, *s.*, Ka; Dunsa, *pl.*, Si	Duŋ, *s.*; Dun, *pl.*	Dums	Epini	Bɔna, *s.*, Ka; Bɔne, *pl.*, Si	Bomo, *s.*; Bosi, *pl.*
Yure	W̌e	Yur, *s.*; Yoi, *pl.*	Wure	Keterɛ, *s.*; Atere, *pl.*	Yere, *s.*; Yera, *pl.*, De, Ye	Yerɛn, *s.*; Yera, *pl.*
Nangore	Dir, *s.*, Ku; De, *pl.* Ti	Nyu, *s.*; Nyur, *pl.*	Ningore	Kubɔ, *s.*; Abɔ, *pl.*	Ba, *s.*; Ba, *pl.*, De, Ye	Banà, *s.*; Baná, *pl.*
Kpare-pim	Garo-pen, *s.*, De; Garo-pema, *pl.*, N	Mesiŋ, *s.*; Mesine, *pl.*	Serig	Kanaledi, *s.*; Daledi, *pl.*	Goroleo, *s.*, De; Gorloa, *pl.*, Ba	Garhɛŋ, *s.*; Garhene, *pl.*
Teuk	Tuk, *s.*, Ku; Tuta, *pl.*, Ti	Cogo, *s.*; Cor, *pl.*	Tuk	Kisa, *s.*; Asa, *pl.*	Zun-pogo, *s.*, Ku; Zun-poro, *pl.*, Ti	Dɛlɛ, *s.*; Dɛllɛ, *pl.*
Palega	Palk	Pala, *s.*; Pale, *pl.*	Paleg	Popɔro	Duŋo, *s.*; Duno, *pl.*	Fɛle, *s.*; Fɛlea, *pl.*
Nyŏre	Nyor, *s.*, De; Nyoe, *pl.*, N	Nyuɔr, *s.*; Nyɔe, *pl.*	Dore	Kamuna, *s.*; Mmuna, *pl.*	Mumwɛ, *s.*, De; Mumwa, *pl.*, Ye	Mesɛ, *s.*; Mesa, *pl.*
Nyo-vore	Nyo-ve	Nyɔ-vage, *s.*; Nyɔ-vagse, *pl.*	No-vore	Kamuna-man	Mumwɛ-bone, *s.*, De; Mumwɛ-bona, *pl.*, Ye	Me-boi, *s.*; Me-bɔye, *pl.*
Maan	Dwae, *s.*, De; Dwaana, *pl.*, N	Salo	Maan	Kagwene, *s.*; Ngwene, *pl.*	Porri, *s.*; Porra, *pl.*, De, Ye	Nweŋ, *s.*; Nwene, *pl.*
Kurig, *v.*	Soma	Kura, *s.*; Kure, *pl.*	Kurig	Dara, *v.*	Kwea, *s.*; Kwe, *pl.*	Heaŋ, *s.*; Heɛse, *pl.*
Kpibig	Kwiŋ, *s.*, Ka; Kwiŋsa, *pl.*, Si	Kpweb, *s.*; Kpwebe, *pl.*	Cibig	Kumunibi, *s.*; Amunibi, *pl.*	Bu-taro, *s.*; Butara, *pl.*, De, Ba	Bi-sime, *s.*; Bi-sinsi, *pl.*
Yoom	Lak	Yuo	Woe	Buge	Pore	Suri
Vos	Vusim	Voro, Hele	Vos	Fote	Siu	Wesu, Wese

II. VOCABULARIES (cont.)

English.	Mole.	Mampelle.	Dagbane.	Kusal.	Nankane.	Dagare.
Partridge	Kwadaŋa, s.; Kwadanʃi, pl.	Kwɔreŋa, s.; Kworensi, pl.	Kɔriŋa, s.; Kɔrinse, pl.	Kodiŋ, s.; Kodis, pl.	Kwareŋa, s., Ka; Kwarense, pl.	Kɔroŋa, s.; Kore, pl.
Pass	Loge	Gare	Gare	Gade	Tole	Gare
Pay	Yau	Yɔ	Yɔ	Yoa	Yɔ	Yɔ
Penis	Yole, s.; Yoya, pl.	Yɔre, s.; Yɔya, pl.	Yɔli, s.; Yoya, pl.	Yuor, s.; Yɔda, pl.	Yoore, s., De; Yɔra, pl., A	Yoore, s.; Yoɛ, pl.
Pepper	Cipare-nga, s.; Ciparense, pl.	Nanzua, s.; Nanzuʃi, pl.	Nanzuli, s.; Nanzua, pl.	Nanzug, s., Nanzus, pl.	Nanzuŋa, s.; Ka, Nanzuse, pl., Se	Siemani
Permission	Basbo	Sore	Soli	Baseg	Basega	Sori
Perspire	Yita tulogo	Puse wɔlogo	Wolgo	Ɔsur pus	Muregere	Wale
Pig	Kurkuri, s.; Kurkuya, pl.	Kurcu, s.; Kurcudema, pl.	Kurucu, s.; Kuri, pl.	Kur, s.; Kurkur, pl.	Kurikuri, s., A; Kurikuridema, pl., Ba	Preko
Pinch	Tɔbege	Fiŋe	Fiehe, Nyeŋ-yeɣo	Fiŋ	Tɔbege, Kyi	Iɛ
Pipe	Tabruko, s.; Tabrugudo, pl.	Tabduko, s.; Tabdugere, pl.	Tabadoɣo, s., Tabaduɣre, pl.	Tabruk, s.; Tabduk, pl.	Tabadoko, s., Ko; Tabadogoro, pl., To	Tɔla, s.; Tɔlare, pl.
Place	Ziga, s.; Zise, pl.	Zia, s.; Zisi, pl.	Saani or Zaʃie	Zii, s., Ziis, pl.	Zia	Zina, s.; Zizina, pl.
Porcupine	Semde, s.; Sema, pl.	Semne, s.; Sema, pl.	Σelŋle, s.; Σelma, pl.	Seɛm, s.; Seema, pl.	Saanè, s., De; Saana, pl., A	Sieni, s.; Sieme, pl.
Possess	So	So	Su	Su	Sɔe	Soo
Pot	Duko, s.; Dɔgodo, pl.	Duko, s.; Dugere, pl.	Dugu, s.; Dugri, pl.	Duk, s.; Dugut, pl.	Doko, s., Ko; Dogoro, pl., To	Doge, s.; Doere, pl.
Poverty	Nɔngo	Noŋo, Fara	Namo, Fara	Nɔŋ	Nɔŋo	Nɔŋ
Precede	Deŋe	Daŋe	Daŋ	Deŋ	Deŋe	Daŋ
Prepare	Segele	Seaase	Σiri (Hausa), Neŋ, Niŋ	Maal	Sege, Gomse	Segeli
Press	Di	Disi	Dihi	Diis	Di	Dii
Prick	Kwɔʃe	Kuse	Kuhi	Kus	Voŋe	Coge
Pull (along ground)	Vuge	Vu	Vo	Vu	Vue	Vu
Pull (up)	Vike	Vuke	Vɔ	Voe, Vik	Vike, Tu	Voɔ

Nabte.	Bulea.	Loberu.	Talene.	Gbanya.	Kasene.	Isal.
Kwodeŋ	Yeŋ, s., Ka; Yeŋ-sa, pl., Si	Kɔre, s.; Kɔresi, pl.	Kworiŋ	Doboi, s.; Adoboi, pl.	Luga, s., Ka; Lui, pl., Si	Yohó, s.; Yosi, pl.
Gaare	Ta	Tɔl	Gari	Co	Kɛ̃	Bal; Keli
Yom	Tuŋ	Ya	Yɔ or Wɔ	Ka	Tini	Tiŋ, Tim
Yɔɔre	Yoar, s., De; Yoa, pl., N	Yɔr, s.; Yɔe, pl.	Wore	Kotutu, s.; Atutu, pl.	Pɛne, s., De; Pena, s., Ye	Peŋ, s.; Pɛne, pl.
Nanzun	Nwareba-zum	Selman	Nanzuu	Gyantere	Namena-gyua, s., Ka; Na-menadẅe, pl., Si	Nangyohɔ
Bas-nor, v.	..	..	Bas nori, v.	Ekpa	Coŋa	Waneŋ
Mudigere	Wulim	Hana	Wɔlɔg	Kibile, n.	Luluŋo	Soluŋ
..	..	..	..	Preko, s.; Apreko, pl.	..	Dea-teau, s.; Dea-teni, pl.
Kyii	Dwan	Yeb	Fiŋ	Fin	Cɔ	Lɔye
Tarog or Tadog	Tacen, s., Ka; Ta-censa, pl., Si	Tebla, s.; Teblare, pl.	Tarog	Katabale, s.; Nta-bale, pl.	Tadoa, s., Ka; Ta-doe, pl., Si	Tɛnɛ, s.; Tɛnsɛ, pl.
Zii	Jigini	Zie, s.; Zir, pl.	Zii	Do, Kakpa	Gyeŋa, s.; Gye, pl.	Dehɔno
Seemere	Saan, s., De; Sa-ma, pl., N	Sien, s.; Seme, pl.	Sameri	Etu, s.; Etuana, pl.	Sene, s., De; Sina, pl., Ye	Sam, s.; Sama, pl.
Su	Sɔa	So	Su	Wɔ	Gye	Te
Duk	..	Dook, s.; Door, pl.	Duk	Kapuli, s.; Npuli, pl.	Kanbia, s., Ka; Ka-nba, pl., Si	Pupoi, s.; Pupɔye, pl.
Nɔŋ	Nenam	Naŋ	Nɔŋ	Kitir	Zore, v.	Sŭm, Sŭ
..	Liŋ	Daŋ	Deŋ	Daŋ	Kɛ̃, Yiga	La...sepaŋ
Sɛye	Goms	Cɔbere	Mahet	Lone	..	..
Dihi	Duŋ	Dí, Nɛ	Dihi	Yiſi	Zi	Nyakɛ
..	..	..	..	..	..	..
..	Tẅup	Cɔr	Wore	Cote	Zɔ	Tou
Vug	Vur	Vu	Vug	Gbɛ	Ture	Lɛrɛ
Vŏ	Tu	Vuɔ	Voe	Tia	Gwɔ	Curi

II. VOCABULARIES (*cont.*)

English.	Mole.	Mampelle.	Dagbane.	Kusal.	Nankane.	Dagare.
Pumpkin	Yɔgore, s.; Yɔga, pl.	Yoare, s.; Yoa, pl.	Yɔyle, s.; Yɔya, pl.	Yɔar, s.; Yoaa, pl.	Yogere, s., De; Yɔga, pl., A	Yɔgere, s.; Yɔgɔ, pl.
Push	Tuse	Daae	Daai	Daae	Zaɛ	Daa
Quickly	Marsa	W̌emw̌em	Yomyom	Wɛɛnwɛɛn	Toto Kale-kalem	W̌eŋw̌eŋ
Quiver	Loko, s.; Logodo, pl.	Lɔkko, s.; Loare, pl.	Lɔyo, s.; Lɔyri, pl.	Lok, s.; Loat, pl.	Loko, s., Ko; Logo-ro, pl., To	Logi, s.; Logeri, pl.
Rain	Saga	Saa	Saa	Sa	Saa	Sa-
Rainbow	Sag-go-mtirgo	Saa-suwa	Saa-sua *or* Saa-gani	Dendeo-gboe	Gumatiata-fo, s., Bo; Gumatia-tini, pl., S	gon-gono
Rat	Dayuga, s.; Da-yusi, pl.	Dayuwa, s.; Da-yuse, pl.	Dayugu, s.; Dayure, pl.	Dayuk, s.; Dayut, pl.	Dayuo, s., Ko; Dayu-ro, pl., To	Dayu, s.; Dayuri, pl.
Raw	Kado	Kahere, s.; Kasa, pl.	Kahali, s.; Kaha, pl.	Kasere, s.; Kasa, pl.	Kasere, s.; Kasa, pl.	Kare
Razor	Balaga, s.; Balse, pl.	Barega	Puloŋ, s.; Pulma, pl.	Barig, s.; Bars, pl.	Barega, s., Ka; Bar-sese, pl., Se	Bera, s.; Bɛre, pl.
Reach	Ta	Pa	Pai	Pa	Pae	Ta
Reap	Wuri, Cɛa	Kye	Ce	Cɛa	Sɛ, Cɛ	Cɛ
Red	Miyugu, s.; Midu, pl.	Zia, s.; Zese, pl.	Zie, s.; Ziehe, pl.	Zia, s.; Zes, pl.	Mologo, s., Ko; Molo, pl., To	Zie, s.; Zire, pl.
Refuse	Todoge, Zagese	Zayse	Zagse	Zayas	Todage *or* Zagse	Zagere
Rice	Mwi	Mui	Sinkafa (Hausa)	Mui	Mui	Mi
Rise up	Yikki	Isigi, Do	Yegse	Duom	Isige	Iri
Road	Sore, s.; Sɔya, pl.	Sore, s.; Soya, pl.	Soli, s.; Sɔya, pl.	Sore, s.; Soya, pl.	Sore, s.; Soa, pl.	Sori, s.; Soe, pl.
Roll	Bilim	Bilim	Bilim	Bilim	Bilim	Billi
Ruin	Dabogo, s.; Dabo-do, pl.	Daboo, s.; Dabaare, pl.	Dabɔyo, s.; Dabare, pl.	Daboog, s.; Daboot, pl.	Dabɔɔ, s.; Dabɔro, pl.	Dabori, s.; Dabe, pl.
Salt	Yamsim	Yaarem	Yalim	Yarim	Yarim	Yarɔŋ
Salute	Puse	Puse	Puhe	Pus	Puse	Pori

Nabte.	Bulea.	Loberu.	Talene.	Gbanya.	Kasene.	Isal.
Yɔyere	Per,. s., De ; Pe, pl., Ꭰ	Yɔgfo, s.; Yɔge, pl.	Wɔyet	Kiŋama, s.; Aŋama, pl.	Gaane, s.; De ; Gaana, pl., Ye	Kaaŋ, s.; Kaama, pl.
Daa	Tus	Daa	Daae	Nyiŋ	Yigi	Yigi
Tɔtɔ	Nwuli-nwuli	Kpeŋ	Yemyem	Malam	Lala	Lemma, Lailai
Loko	Llɔk, s., Ku ; Lɔgtaa, pl., Ti	Lok, s.; Logr, pl.	Loko	Kafɛ, s.; Mfɛ, pl.	Coŋa, s., De ; Tẅe, pl., Ye	Huoŋ, s.; Huoni, pl.
Saa	Nwaro	Sa	Saa	Bore	Dua	Duoŋ
Ndeugzu-bok	Nagottɔn, s., Bu ; Nagortuma, pl., Ꭰ	Sa-gogo	Gumatiug	Ebore-ka-saŋe	Dua-siu, s.; Ka ; Du'-seo, pl., Si	Duoŋ-sea, s.; Duoŋ-sesɛ, pl.
Dayug	Dayu, s., Ku ; Dayuta, pl., Ti	Denyu, s.; Denyur, pl.	Dawoo	Sobɔi, s.; Asobɔi, pl.	Bayue, s.; Bayua, pl.	Sanyun, s.; Sanyuma, pl.
Kahere	Gyaben	Kɛr, s.; Kere, pl.	Kahere	Kubumbu	Bege, Gwa	Huo, s.; Horu, pl.
Barig	Ponen, s., Ka ; Ponsa, pl., Si	Bera, s.; Bereʃi, pl.	Barig	Kaʃɛ, s.; Nʃe, pl.	Fana, s., Ka ; Fane, pl., Si	Nyu-fona, s.; Nyu-fonse, pl.
Pa	Pae	Ta	Paa	Fɔ	Yi	Yi
Cɛ	Cɛ	Cɛb	Cɛ	Ku	Zage	Ta
Zeg	Monen	Zie, Zir	Zeug	Kepeper	Seŋa, s.; Se, pl.	Feaŋ, s.; Feesɛ, pl.
Zags	Zere	Zager	Zags	Kini	Ve	Ve
Mui	Moe	Mui	Mui	Ɛinkafa (Hausa)	Mumune	Miriŋ
Dɔɔ	Yir	Ir	Du (sazug)	Koso	Zaŋ	Ɛi
Sore	Siu, s., Ku ; Siuna, pl., Ꭰ	Sɔr, s.; Sɔye, pl.	Sore	Ekpa, s.; Ekpana, pl.	Coŋa, s., Ka ; Coe, pl., Si	Waŋ, s.; Wase, pl.
Bilim	Bilim	Bili	Bilim	Bilti	Bebile	Bilim
Dabog	Gu, s., Ku ; Guta, pl., Ti	Dekpol, s.; De-kpole, pl.	. .	Kilambore, s.; Ala-mbore, pl.	De-dɔŋo, s., De ; De-doeno, pl., Te	Di-wolo, s.; Di-woli, pl.
Yarim	Yesa	Nyaro	Yarim	Mfɔl	Yɛ	Yesɛ
Puhe	Puse	Pur	Puhe	Corɔ	Zaŋ, Ke peɣe	Po (dea)

II. VOCABULARIES (*cont.*)

English.	Mole.	Mampelle.	Dagbane.	Kusal.	Nankane.	Dagare.
Sand	Binʃiri	Bisego	Bihigu	Tanbisi	Tombisigo *or* Bisere	Bire
Sandal	Naudre, *s.*; Nau-da, *pl.*	Namtere, *s.*; Na-mna, *pl.*	Namdili, *s.*; Namda, *pl.*	Taadere, *s.*; Taada, *pl.*	Tagete, *s.*, De; Tage-ra, *pl.*, A	Na-tire, *s.*; Na-tie, *pl.*
Shade	Masom	Masim	Maham	Masim	Maasem	Maru
Sheep	Pesego, *s.*; Pisi, *pl.*	Peo, *s.*; Pesi, *pl.*	Pɛgo, *s.*; Pɛre, *pl.*	Peuk, *s.*; Peɛs, *pl.*	Pesego, *s.*, Ko; Pisi, *pl.*, Se	Pire, *s.*; Piire, *pl.*
Shut	Page	Yo	Yɔ, Kpare	Yoa	Yu, Kpare, Ga	Pɔge
Sieve, *v.*	Yoge, *v.*	Te	Te	Teɛm	Tɛ	..
Sieve, *n.*	Lepere, *s.*; Lepa, *pl.*	Tea, *s.*; Tesi, *pl.*	Tie, *s.*; Te-he, *pl.*	Tea, *s.*; Teɛs, *pl.*	Tea, *s.*, Ka; Tɛse, *pl.*, Se	..
Slap	Pyeka	Pɛka	Tepaga	Peak	Pɛka	Nwe lempe-gere
Slippery	Salaga	Salega	Salgida	Sal	Salega	Saloŋ
Slowly	Balem	Balem-be-la	Balim	Baan	Baalam	Baluŋ
Small-pox	Gyaneba *or* Pa-msɔba	Zuŋzona	Tcakpandi	Nab	Zonzoŋo	Gyalema
Snake	Wafo, *s.*; Wisi, *pl.*	Wafo, *s.*; Wigi, *pl.*	Waho, *s.*; Wiri, *pl.*	Waf, *s.*; Wigi, *pl.*	Wafo, *s.*, Bo; Wiri, *pl.*, I	Wabo, *s.*; Wire, *pl.*
Snail	Garweo-ngo, *s.*; Garwe-ndo, *pl.*	Gengare, *s.*; Genga-ya, *pl.*	Gingalyɔgo, *s.*; Ginga-lyɔri, *pl.*	Wiluk, *s.*; Wilit, *pl.*	Kateyigele, *s.*, De; Kateyige-la, *pl.* A	Gerewene, *s.*; Gere-weme, *pl.*
Sour	Miki, *v.*	Mi	Miha	Mi	Mie	Miruŋ
Spear	Kande, *s.*; Kana, *pl.*	Kpane, *s.*; Kpana, *pl.*	Kpane, *s.*; Kpana, *pl.*	Kpan, *s.*; Kpana, *pl.*	Kanne, *s.*, De; Kana, *pl.*, A	Kpane, *s.*; Kpama, *pl.*
Spit	Tubʃi	Tuse	Tuhi	Tubs	Tubsi, Cebsi	Tore
Stammer	Bidi, *v.*	Bire	..	Biit	Bire	Bire
Stink	Pŏge	Nyŏ	Nyɔ̆	Poɛ, Nyusit	Pŏe, Fĕĕ	Pɔ̃ɔ̃, Nyuro
Stone	Kuguri, *s.*; Kuga, *pl.*	Kugeri, *s.*; Kuga, *pl.*	Kugli, *s.*; Kuga, *pl.*	Kugr. *s.*; Kuga, *pl.*	Kugere, *s.*, De; Kuga, *pl.*, A	Kuri, *s.*; Kugo, *pl.*
Suck	Moge	Moa	Mɔye	Mogm	Mõge	Mŏge
Surpass	Yida	Gare	Gare	Gar	Gana	Gaŋ

Nabte.	Bulea.	Loberu.	Talene.	Gbanya.	Kasene.	Isal.
Biheg	Tambusiŋ	Bire	Bihigo	Ebonto-esasar	Kasulo-bona	Hɛgelɛ bumbu-gulo
Tayert	Nüsir, s., De; Nü-sa, pl., Ḍ	Nafage, s.; Nafagse, pl.	Tayert	Kisabeta, s.; Asabe-ta, pl.	Naterɛ, s., De; Nate-ra, pl., Ye	Nantèbè, Nantébé, pl.
Mahem	Yɔgsim	Kparo	Masim	Kayul	Woro	Fealuŋ
Peog	Pɔso, s., Ku; Pisa, pl., N	Pero, s.; Piir, pl.	Pehuk	Kobolepo, s.; Abole-po, pl.	Piɛ, s., Ka or De; Pe, pl., Si	Piesu, s.; Piesɛ, pl.
Yθ	Lik	Pag	Ga	Boso	Pe	Tɔ
Tɛ	..	..	Tɛ	Gbaŋgbaŋ, v.	..	..
..	Kyagasik, s., Ka; Kyagasi-sa, pl., Si	Kpocura, s.; Kpo-curse, pl.	Tɛre	Gbaŋgbaŋ-de, n.	Yɔlɔ, s., De Yɔalo, pl., Te	Mun-kyehɛ, San-coro
Pɛk	Fɔp	Kpa, Kpa, Gba	Pek	Kpa ... taŋ	Lo pepɔŋo	Mwau
Saleg	Satega	Sansalo	Salog	Ferege	Sesɛrɛ	Sesɛrɛ
Bug	Maɣa	Balo	Bug	Gbɛrɛ gbɛrɛ	Fefe	Moamoa
Ziŋzɔŋ	Tambola	Gyenbe	Zeŋzɔŋ	Abibigbom	Tambɔlla	Saŋkpɛn-bisi
Waf	Wap, s., Bu; Wi-ga, pl., Ḍ	Wab, s.; Wir, pl.	Waf	Kowa, s.; Awa, pl.	Deo, s., De; Dena, pl., Ba	Dem, s.; Dema, pl.
Gareyighle	Kunkolog, s., Ku; Kunkota, pl., Ti	Wir, s.; Wei, pl.	Gariyeoŋ	Konte, s.; Akonte, pl.	Kunkɔre, s., De; Kunkɔra, pl., Ye	Kunkɔluŋ-mawe, s.; Kunkɔ-lunmawe, pl.
Mii	Mika	Miru	Mii	Nyaŋ	Nyɔna	Nyala
Kpan	Gbalog, s., Ku; Gba-ta, pl., Ti	Kpaŋ, s., Kpame, pl.	Kpaŋ	Kokpa, s., Akpa, pl.	Tw̌utw̌e, s., De; Tw̌u-tw̌a, pl., Ye	Tiŋ, s., Timme, pl.
Tubes	Kyese	Cir	Tubes	Tu	Toe lelero	Tő
Bire	Bege	Bulle	Bire	Kubaba, n.	Bebego, n.	Bambosɔŋ, n.
Pőe	Nyum	Puo, Nyur	Pőg	Dufe	Loe	Sworo, Poa
Kuger	Bontae, s., De; Bo-ntana, pl., N	Kuʃer, s.; Kuʃɛge, pl.	Kuger	Kujombu, s.; Ajo-mbu, pl.	Kandoɛ, s., De; Ka-ndoa, pl., Ye	Tave, s.; Tavea, pl.
Moɣe	Nwos	Mɔgre, Ere	Moɣe	Pipe, Nyepo	Nwɔge, Mu	Wase, Mosɛ
Gare	Gan	Gaŋ	Garog	Cɔ	Doe	Ka

II. VOCABULARIES (*cont.*)

English.	Mole.	Mampelle.	Dagbane.	Kusal.	Nankane.	Dagare.
Tail	Zuri, *s.*; Zuya, *pl.*	Zure, *s.*; Zuya, *pl.*	Zuli, *s.*; Zuya, *pl.*	Zur, *s.*; Zuya, *pl.*	Zuri, *s.*, De; Zoa, *pl.*, A	Zore, *s.*; Ziɛ, *pl.*
Tale	Solomde, *s.*; Soloma, *pl.*	Solemne, *s.*; Solema, *pl.*	Saŋle, *s.*; Sɔlma, *pl.*	Solem, *s.*; Solema, *pl.*	Solene, *s.*, De ; Solema, *pl.*, A	Sekpɔgere, *s.*; Sekpogɔ, *pl.*
Tear, *n.*	Nintam	Nintam, *s.*; Nintama, *pl.*	Nintam, *s.*; Nintama, *pl.*	Nintam, *s.*; Nita-mnam, *pl.*	Nintam	Nintoŋ
Testicles	Lande, *s.*; Lana, *pl.*	Lane, *s.*; Lana, *pl.*	Lane, *s.*; Lana, *pl.*	Lan, *s.*; Lana, *pl.*	Lane, *s.*, De ; Lama, *pl.*, A	Lene, *s.*; Leme, *pl.*
Thigh	Gele, *s.*; Geya, *pl.*	Gbar-pune, *s.*; Gbar-puna, *pl.*	Gbale-pini, *s.*; Gbale-pina, *pl.*	Gwer, *s.*; Gwea, *pl.*	Gye-pune, *s.*, De ; Gye-puna, *pl.*, A	Gbere-kpɔŋ, *s.*; Gbere-kpomo, *pl.*
Thin	Fage, Wa-gere, Ba-laga	Balega, *s.*; Balse, *pl.*	Balle	Baleg, *s.*; Bals, *pl.*	Baelga, *s.*, A ; Balse, *pl.*, Se	Balss, *s.*; Bale, *pl.*
Thing	Bumbu, *s.*; Bundu, *pl.*	Buŋ, *s.*; Buŋa, *pl.*	Buni, *s.*; Bunyarse, *pl.*	Bun, *s.*; Bunam, *pl.*	Zogo, *s.*, A; Buno, *pl.*, Ba	Bene, *s.*; Buma, *pl.*
Think	Tẽge	Tẽse	Tehi	Tẽẽs	Tẽẽse	Tiɛrɛ
Thirst	Kom-yudu	Koŋ-yure	Kon-yuri	Konyuut	Konyuro	Konyuri
Thorn	Gwaga, *s.*; Gwose, *pl.*	Goa, *s.*; Goʃi, *pl.*	Goo, *s.*; Gɔhe, *pl.*	Gŏa, *s.*; Gŏŏs, *pl.*	Gŏa, *s.*, Ka; Gŏse, *pl.*, Se	Guɔ, *s.*; Gore, *pl.*
Tickle	Ligem	Logero	Nyaɣele	Ligem	Leghem	Legere
Tongue	Zilimde, *s.*; Zilima, *pl.*	Zulune, *s.*; Zuluma, *pl.*	Zinli, *s.*; Zilma, *pl.*	Zelim, *s.*; Zelima, *pl.*	Zelinne, *s.*, De ; Zele-ma, *pl.*, A	Zille, *s.*; Zilla, *pl.*
Tooth	Nyende, *s.*; Nye-na, *pl.*	Nyine, *s.*; Nyina, *pl.*	Nyini, *s.*; Nyina, *pl.*	Nyiŋ, *s.*; Nyina, *pl.*	Nyene, *s.*, De ; Nyen-na, *pl.*, A	Nyene, *s.*; Nyime, *pl.*
Tree	Tiga, *s.*; Tise, *pl.*	Tia, *s.*; Ti-ʃi, *pl.*	Tia, *s.*; Ti-hi, *pl.*	Tiig, *s.*; Tiis, *pl.*	Tia, *s.*, Ka; Tise, *pl.*, Se	Tiɛ, *s.*; Tire, *pl.*
Twist	Nwenege	Nwelege	Dmɛle	Nweleg	Nwelege	Nwele
Undress	Pidigi	Yɛɛ, Yɛse, Pidige *or* Pidisi	Yee, Pirigi	Pidig	Ye, Yese, Piligi	Yage, Ya-gere
Untie	Lokke, Lo-dege	Lorege	Lorge	Yidig	Lorege, Lo-rese, Yi-dege	Lorè, Lorí
Urine	Dudom	Dunom	Durum	Dundunom	Dundurum	Durom

Nabte.	Bulea.	Loberu.	Talene.	Gbanya.	Kasene.	Isal.
Zur	Dwuk, s., Ku, Dwu-ta, pl., Ti	Zogr., s.; Zoge, pl.	Zurt	Kabul, s.; Mbul, pl.	Nabile, s., De; Nabi-la, pl., Ye	Dohõ, s.; Doʃi, pl.
Solmere	Susuer, s., De; Su-suela, pl., N	Sole, s.; Soleʃi, pl.	Maɣa	Kisere-kpaŋ, s.; Asere-kpaŋ, pl.	Sonsoala, s., Ka, De; Sonsoale, pl., Si	Sensa-mporo, s.; Sensa-mporesi, pl.
Nintam	Ni-nyeam	Kyiru	Nintam	Kpeɛ	Kucula	Selero, s.; Seleraŋ, pl.
Lan	Kolobir, s., Ku; Kɔla, pl., N	Laŋ, s.; Lame, pl.	Lan	Kuwɔlebe, s.; Awɔle-be, pl.	Mankyale, s., De; Mankyala, pl., Ye	Luru, s.; Lurɔ, pl.
Gbere	Kosuk, s., Ku; Ko-sa, pl., N	Gber-kpe, s.; Gbɛ-kpere, pl.	Gbere	Ebɛŋ, s.; Abɛŋ, pl.	Twe, s., De; Twa, pl., Ye	Napwi, s.; Napuo, pl.
Baleg	Deak	Bale, s.; Bali, pl.	Baleg	Bɛ	Kwara, s.; Kware, pl.	Gyɛkɛ, v.
Bon	Gyap, s., Wa; Ɖa-nta, pl., Ti	Bom, s.; Bome, pl.	Bum	Kusɔ, s.; Asɔ, pl.	Ɖo, s.; We-nu, pl.	Kɔŋ, s.; Kea, pl.
Tẽs	Ter	Tiera	Tẽs, Tihi	Tama	Buŋe	Bene
Konyurt	Nyanyura	Konyur	Koŋyurt	Acukom	Nanyɔ̃	Llenyoose
Gõõ	Mun, s., Ka; Mu-nsa,pl.,Si	Guɔ, s.; Guor, pl.	Gõõ	Ewi, s.; Awi, pl.	Sabɔra, s., De; Sabɔ-re, pl., Si	Sɔu, s.; Sɔse, pl.
Leɣem	Luksi	Kilkile	Legem	Nyenyeŋ	Lologe	Lugsi
Zelmere	Gengelloŋ, s., Ko; Gengele-nta,pl.,Ti	Zel, s.; Ze-le, pl.	Zelemert	Kudɔndulo, s.; Adɔ-ndulo, pl.	Dindelim, s., De; Dindelɛ pl., Ye	Nandelin, s.; Nande-lime, pl.
Nyiŋ	Nyi, s., De; Nyi-na, pl., N	Nyem, s.; Nyime, pl.	Nyin	Kinyi, s.; Anyi, pl.	Yele, s.,De; Yela, pl., Ye	Nyel, s.; Nyelea, pl.
Ti	Tib, s., Bu; Tisa, pl., Si	Tuɔ, s.; Tor, pl.	Tii	Kadibi, s.; Ndibi, pl.	Teo, s.; Te-ro, pl., De, Ti	Tea, s.; Tɛ-sɛ, pl.
Nweleg	Nwelim	Nwele	Nweleg	Kito	Gyugyugi	Mileme
Yɛ	Yɛr	Ya, Yar	Yɛɛ	Gbaŋ	Le	Wuri
Lorg	Fɔl	Loro	Lorig	Saŋe	Bɔ.i	Puri
Durum	Sensam	Duro	Dundurin	Ebɔfɔl	Fea	Fero

II. VOCABULARIES (*cont.*)

English.	Mole.	Mampelle.	Dagbane.	Kusal.	Nankane.	Dagare.
Vaccination	Dabo *or* Kyisibo	Dabo *or* Kyihiri	Dabo	Da (nab)	Daa, Kye-siga	Nwabo
Vagina	Cinde, *s.*; Cina, *pl.* Pare, *s.*; Paya, *pl.*	Pyene, *s.*; Pyena, *pl.*	Pani, *s.*; Pana, *pl.*	Pen, *s.*; Pena, *pl.*	Pene, *s.*, De; Pena, *pl.*, A	Pare, *s.*, Pe, *pl.*
Vomit	Wobe	Ti	Ti	Tï	Ti, Okke	Ti
Waist	Sɛaya	Σea, *s.*; Σesi, *pl.*	Σie	Sea, *s.*; Sesɛ, *pl.*	Sɛa, *s.*, Ka; Sɛse, *pl.*,Se	Siɛ, *s.*; Siire, *pl.*
Wait	Gu	Gure	Guli	Gu	Gu	Gu
Wake	Neke	Neɛ	Nee	Niɛ	Neɛ	Seɲi
Wash	Pekke, So	Peɛ, Su	Paɣi, Su	Pie, So	Pee, So	Pɛge, So
Water	Kom	Kom	Kom	Kom	Kom (Bo class)	Kɔɔ
Well, *n.*	Buluga, *s.*; Bulse, *pl.*	Bulega, *s.*; Bulsi, *pl.*	Kobilga, *s.*; Kobilsi, *pl.*	Bulik, *s.*; Bulis, *pl.*	Bulega, *s.*, Ka; Bulse, *pl.*, Se	Bullo, *s.*; Bulli, *pl.*
Whisper	Walem	Wahe	Sɔyyele	Nyaam	Wasem	Walo
Whistle, *v.*	Fili, Pebe	File	Vuli	Peɛb	Fule, Pebe	Piɛle
Widow	Pokore, *s.*; Pokopa, *pl.*	Poa-kore, *s.*; Poa-koya, *pl.*	Pa-koli, *s.*; Pa-koya, *pl.*	Pu-kor, *s.*; Pu-koya, *pl.*	Pu-kore, *s.*; De; Pu-kope, *pl.*, A	Pɔgo-kore, *s.*; Pɔgo-kɔbɔ, *pl.*
Widower	Dakore, *s.*; Dakopa, *pl.*	Da-kore, *s.*; Da-koya, *pl.*	Da-koli, *s.*; Da-koya, *pl.*	Da-kor, *s.*; Da-koya, *pl.*	Da-kore, *s.*, De; Da-kopa, *pl.*, A	Da-kore, *s.*; Da-kɔbɔ, *pl.*
Wind, *n.*	Sebego	Bebsego	Zagu, Po-hom	Sebeog	Sebego	Sasiɛ
Wink, *v.*	Kabse	Kamse	Kahem-ni	Ams	Kabse	Kogeri
Wipe	Nyĕse	Nyehe	Nyehe	Es	Duse	Yɛre
Wood	Daugo, *s.*; Dado, *pl.*	Do, *s.*; Dare, *pl.*	Dɔɣo, *s.*; Dari, *pl.*	Doog, *s.*; Dat, *pl.*	Dɔɔ, *s.*, Ko; Dɔro, *pl.*, To	Da, *s.*; Dare, *pl.*
Work, *v.*	Tum	Tum	Tum	Tum	Tum	Tum
Yam	Nyuri, *s.*; Nyuya, *pl.*	Nyure, *s.*; DꞶea, *pl.*	Nyuli, *s.*; Nyuya, *pl.*	Nyur, *s.*; Nyuya, *pl.*	Nyure, *s.*, De; Nyua *pl.*, A	Nyur

Nabte.	Bulea.	Loberu.	Talene.	Gbanya.	Kasene.	Isal.
Da	Mɔboka	Nwa... yaŋ	Da	Kacule	Zagge ta-mbola	Kpare... hɛ
Pen	Badeag, s., Ka; Ba-dasa, pl., Si	Par, s.; Pai, pl.	Pen	Katopo, s.; Atopo, pl.	Mɛne, s.; Mɛna, pl., De, Ye	Meŋ, s.; Menɛ, pl., Batoni
Tï	Tulisi	Tir	Ti	Kwɛ	Tɔne	Twose
Sɛ	Kyeak, s., Ka; Kye-asa, pl., Si	Sie, s.; Sir, pl.	See	Kasar, s.; Nsar, pl.	Teŋa, s.; Te, pl., Ka, Si	Teŋa, s.; Tense, pl.
Gurum	Limse	Gu	Guri	Dwo	Kyɛge	Gbɛrɛ
Neem	Yiti	Siŋ	Nee	Tiɲi	Zaŋ	Kyesɛ
Pe	Nar, Sudi, So	Peg, So	Peem, So	Foro, Birr	Se, Soe, Su	Tisi, Kyɛsɛ, Fo
Kɔom	Nyɛem	Koɔ	Kom	Ncu	Nna	Lle
Bulig	Bulik, s., Ka; Bul-sa, pl., Si	Bule, s.; Bulʃi, pl.	Bulig	Kuturubi, s.; Aturu-bi, pl.	Vule, s.; Vula, pl., De, Ye	Vilboa, s.; Vilbose, pl.
Was	Wase	Wale	Wahum	Kuli	Susea	Nyimsi
Peb	Pie	Fole	Peb	Kafole	Fore, Fole	Mõ
Pakor	Pu-kɔye, s., De; Pu-kɔga, pl., N	Po-kɔr, s.; Po-kobe, pl.	Pa-kori	Ekulpo-kye	Ka-dene, s.; Kadena, pl., De, Ba	Yo-hal, s.; Yo-hala, pl.
Dakor	Da-kɔ, s., Wa; Da-kɔsa, pl., Si	Da-kɔr, s., Da-kobe, pl.	Da-kori	Ekulpo-nyeŋ	Ba-dene, s.; Ba-de-na, pl., De, Ba	Yo-bal, s.; Yo-bala,
Sabeog	Veɔk	Seseb	Sanpephog	Afu	..	Pel
Ams	Kamse	Kabr	Kabs	Dwoke	Bugese yie	..
Dus	Düsi	Yier	Dus	Pata	Pe	Pisa
Dog	Duɔk	Da, s.; Daar, pl.	Dug	Kadibi	Da, s.; De, pl., De, Si	Da, s.; Dase, pl.
Tum	Tɔm	Toŋ	Tum	Sun	Tuŋe	Ten
Nyur	Nyur, s., De; Nyul, pl., Ɗ	Nyur, s.; Nyie, pl.	Ɗyure	Kujɔ, s.; Ajɔ, pl.	Pe, s.; Pea, pl.	Pi, s.; Pea pl.

III. GRAMMAR AND SYNTAX

English.	Mole.	Mampelle.	Dagbane.	Kusal.	Nankane.
ADVERBS					
Here	Ka	Kpa	Kpe	Na	Kela, Kyela
There	Be	Bene, Sa	Sa, Ni	Sa	Bila
Near	*Expressed by verbs,* peya *and* kolege, Yamyam	Pɔre (*v.*)	Miri	Erege (*v.*)	Pɔre, Kolege (*v.*)
Far	Zara (*v.*)	Waalogo	Katena	Lal	Zae
Where?	Yai?	Yene?	Ya?	Ya?	Bɛ?
Wherever	Jifwa	Logere kam	Ʃel kam	..	Zia woo
On the right	Ditigo	Dirego	Dirigu (nu)	..	Zuo, Ditigo
On the left	Gwoboga	Gwɔbogo	Gwobga, Za	..	Gɔbega
Before	Taure	Tone	Toni	Tuon	Nena
Behind	Pore	Dyaana	Nyana	Nyaan	Pore
On top	Nyinili	Sa zugu	Zug sa	Gol	Zuo
Under	Tenele	Tenne	Tenle, Gbini	Gyegbe	Tena, Tenele
Inside	Puye	Pune	Púní	Puge	Puam
Upwards	Sa, Runde	Sa zugu	Sa zugu	..	Zue, Zuo
Outside	Yina	Yina	Yina, San-bani	..	Yina
Over there	Kaʃene	Sa	Niha	..	Sa
To-day	Dunna	Zunna	Zuno	Zina	Zina
To-morrow	Beogo	Beo	Beoyni	Beog	Bere
Yesterday	Zame	Sohla	Sɔh'la	Suas	Zaam
Day after to-morrow	Dayita	Dare	Dare	Dar	Dare
When?	Dabule?	Bondare?	Bondali?	Bondar?	Dandena?
Always	Darfwa	Dabzaa	Dabazaa, Sahakam	Dabsawoo	Dabsa
Formerly	Pinna, Da	Daa	Daa	Kudeme	Korome, Da-seresa
Not yet	Nan-ka-ye	Na . . . bo	Na . . . be	Na...po...e	Nan . . . ka
First	Ddene (*v.*)	Dan (*v.*)	Dan	..	Dene, Yia
After	Nyaule (*v.*)	Nyaana	Nyana	..	Pore
In vain	Zalem	Nyɔre	Yoli, Yɔli	Zaalem	Zana
Again	Lebe (*v.*)	Lan (*v.*)	..	Leb (*v.*)	Le (*v.*)
Much	Wusugo	Pam	Pam	Babeg	Zoe
Little	Bilifu, Fifa	Bela	Bela	Fĩfũ	Fi
Well	Nele	Vela	Vela	Som	Sona
Badly	Wenga, Nwe-na	Be vela	Be vela	..	Ka sona
How much?	Nwanna?	Ala?	Ala?	Ala?	Nwana?
Straight	Tiriga	Tontoaa	Tuhe	Totoaa	Tentɔ, Tɔ
Thus	Woto, Boto	Lala	Lala, Dɔ	Wela	Bala
Like	Dwenna	Dwan	Dwane	Nwan	Nwona
Different	Tɔre	Kokɔba	Kɔn-kɔba	Kõkõ	Tɔka

Dagare.	Bulea.	Loberu.	Gbanya.	Kasene.	Isal.
Kye	Dewa	Ka	Mfe	Yo	Raha
Be	De	Be	Ndɔ	Yiga	Daha
Yenyeŋ	Kpwaŋ	Yɛyɛ	Takito (v.)	Bole	Pwaka
Tɔre	Niŋ	Zaa	Kufɔ	Yiga-yiga	Bolie
Yen?	Bɛ? Bea?	Nwene?	Nɛ?	Yɛm?	Ne?
..	..	..	..	..	..
..	Dwuwa	..	Gyisa	..	Na-di
..	Gala	..	Bana	..	Na-goa
Tɔre, Wie	Niŋ	Niŋ	Aniʃito	Yiga	Sopa
Pore	Taŋaŋ	Pur	Kamaŋ	Kwaga	Hareŋ
Zu	Sum	Zu	Esoso	Baŋa	Nyuŋ
Puli	Pasu	Puli	Kaseto	Kuri	Beboa
Puɔ	Nyoro	Puɔ	Tŏ	Pugɛ	Toa
..	..	..	..	..	..
..	Yerepo	..	Kawoshina	..	De-jale
Kyeseŋ, Beseŋ	Degaŋ	Kaseni	Ndo	..	..
Zine	Gilla, Ginla	Diɛ	Kabere	Zem	Jenaŋ
Bie	Twum	Bio	Ekyefo	Gyoane	Kyie
Zaa	Deem	Zaa	Nderɛ	Diim	Dia
Dayere	Vɔnum	Deyere	Ekalade	Gyɔayiga	Kyie-dɔn
Dabo?	Dinpoa?	Dabor?	Samo?	Do?	Ky'ave? Wu?
Biezaa	Damena	Yerelekpo	..	Demama	Tapulakala
Saŋa	Pilinka, Pilindi	Daŋdaŋ	Saŋgena, Da	Deem	Cala
Nam . . . ba	..	..	Mo-da	..	..
..	Liŋ	..	Daŋ	..	..
Pore	Vaka (v.)	..	Kamaŋ	..	..
Zala	Killa	Zagla	Jaga	Kafai	..
Le (v.)	Ɖwana	Le (v.)	Na	..	..
Yaga	Yega	Yaga	Gaŋ	Daga	Yuga
Bilaŋ	Maga	Bila	Gberɛ	Fɛ̆	Moa
Vele	Nalla	Vela	Ku-wale	Lana	Zɔma
..	N'alla	..	Ku-mu-wale	..	..
Awula?	Dina?	Anwen?	Afene?	Bagera?	Nwai?
Tori (v.)	Yɔr	Tori	Kiniŋi	Yɔri	..
Le	Dila	Lɛ	Le	Tɔnto	Nla
Yila (v.)	Nes (v.)	Iŋa	Duli	Nyera	..
Tɛtɛ	Tɔka	Tora	Koro	Ba nyera	Dɔndɔn

III. GRAMMAR AND SYNTAX (cont.)

English.	Mole.	Mampelle.	Dagbane.	Kusal.	Nankane.
PREPOSITIONS AND CONJUNCTIONS					
With	Ne	Ne	Ni	Ne	La
Except	Kal, Dil	Se	Fase	..	Se
Because	Nyiŋa	Bonzugu	Dama	..	Bezuo, Beŋa
Until	Hal	Hale	Hali	..	Hal, Bela, Ta . . . pa
That	Ti	Te	..	Ka	Te
And	Ne	Ne	Ni	Ne	La
Or	Bi	Be	Be	Be	Bi
If, when	Sa	Yi	Yi	Ya	San

PRONOUNS

(1) *The Personal Pronouns when standing alone*

English.	Mole.	Mampelle.	Dagbane.	Kusal.	Nankane.
I (me)	Mam	Mani, ma	Mani, ma	Mane, Man	Mam, Ma
Thou	Fom, Fo	Nyini, Yi, 'I	Nyini, Yi, A	Fo	Fom, Fo
He (him), &c.	Nye, A	Nwana, O, Ka	Duna, O, *or* De, le	Ɔn, Ɔ	Ɛna ɛ, &c., &c.
We (us)	Tondo	Tirema, Ti	Tinima, Ti	Tinam	Toman, To
You	Nyama	Yedema, Ya	Yinima, Iya	Yinam	Yaman, Ya
They (them)	Bama, Ba	Bana, Ba	Bena, Ba	Banam	Bama, Ba, &c.

(2) *Personal Pronouns when coupled with the Verb*

English.	Mole.	Mampelle.	Dagbane.	Kusal.	Nankane.
I	M'	M', N'	M', N'	Mam, M'	M'
Thou	F'	Yi	A	Fo	F'
He (she, it)	A	O, Ka	O *or* De, Le	O, De, Re	A, &c., &c.
We	Tond',' Ton', Td'	Ti	Ti	Te	To
You	Nyam, Yi	Ya	Yi	Yi	Ya
They	Ba', Eb', B'	Ba	Ba	Ba, A	Ba, &c., &c.

(3) *Emphatic and Reflexive Pronouns*

English.	Mole.	Mampelle.	Dagbane.	Kusal.	Nankane.
I, myself	Mam meŋa	Mam maŋa	Man meŋa	Mam meŋ	Mam meŋa
Thou, thyself	Fo' meŋa	'I maŋa	A meŋa	Fo meŋ	Fo meŋa
He, himself, &c., &c.	Nye (*or* A) meŋa	O maŋa	O meŋa	O meŋ	A meŋa

(4) *The Possessive Pronouns*

English.	Mole.	Mampelle.	Dagbane.	Kusal.	Nankane.
Mine	Mam-dilla *or* Mam-so	..	..	..	..
Thine	Fo-rilla, &c.	..	..	..	..
His, hers, its	Nye'-rilla, &c.	..	..	..	..
Our	Ton'-dilla, &c.	..	..	..	..

Dagare.	Bulea.	Loberu.	Gbanya.	Kasene.	Isal.
Ne	Le	Ne	Ne	De	Arr
..	Karo (v.)	..	Bɔ se ne	..	..
..	Dila nyiŋ	..	So	..	Bewea
..	..	..	Hale	..	..
Ka	Ti	Ka	..	Se	..
Ne	Le	Ne	Ne	De	Arr
Bi	Ya	Bi	No	A	..
Ka	Gya	Ke	Ni	Na (?)	De
Ma	Mi, Me	Ma, Me	Ma	Amɔ̀	Mena
Fo	Fi, Fe	Fo	Fo	Mmo	Nna
Ɔna, Ɔ	Wa, &c.	Ɖa, O	Mo, Komo	Omo, Umo, &c.	Ona
Te	Tama, Ta, Te	Tom, Ti	Anye, Nye	Deban, De	Lana
Ye	Nama, Na, Ne	Nyom	Benye	Aba	Mana
Bana, Ba	Ba	Beŋa	Bumo, Amo	Bamo	Bana
M', N'	M'	M', N'	M', N'	À	Me
Fo	Fe	Fo	Fo, Fu	M	N'
Ɔ, De	Wa, O, &c.	O	E, Ku	Ɔ, &c.	O
Te	Ta	Te	An	De	La
Ye	Na	Nyom	Bi	Á	Ma
Ba, A	Ba, &c.	Bel	Bu, A	Ba, &c.	Ba
Ma meŋa	Mi dek	Man meŋa	..	Amo tete	Mena tetea
Fo meŋa	Fi dek	Fo meŋa	..	Umo tete	Nna tetea
Ɔna meŋa	Wa dek	Ol meŋa	..	Omo tete	Ona tetea
..	..	Ma-so	Me-ye	..	..
..	..	Fo-so	Fe-ye	..	..
..	..	Ol-so	Mo-ye	..	..
..	..	Tom-so	Anye-ye	..	..

III. GRAMMAR AND SYNTAX (*cont.*)

English.	Mole.	Mampelle.	Dagbane.	Kusal.	Nankane.
Your	Nyam' dilla, &c.	..	..	..	..
Their	Bam' dilla,&c.	..	..	..	..

(5) *The Interrogative Pronouns*

Who?	Aai? Ana?, Aairama? *pl.*	Nwane?	Ɖuni? *s.*; Banema? *pl.*	Anon?	Ane? *s.*; Bana? *pl.*
What?	Boi?	Boa?	Bo?, Bɔ?	Bo?	Bim?
Which?	Bugo?	Deŋ?, Keŋ?	Deŋ?, Dini?	..	Ena?, &c., &c.

(6) *The Indefinite Pronouns*

Any one	Ned fwa	So-kam-zaa	So-kam-zaa	Nid-faa	Mina
No one	Ned-fwa-ka-ye *or* Ka-ye	So-ka-ne	So-ka-ne *or* Pa-so	So-pe-be	Mina-saan-kai *or* Kai
All	Fwa (Fa)	Zaa	Zaa	Zaa	Zaa
Another	Ato	Soa	So *or* Ɛeli	..	Ato, Ato-dana
Each	Ned-kamfwa	..	..	..	Woo, Nera woo *or* Nera-kama
One...another	Aye...Aye	..	..	Abon... abon	Abono... abono
Everything	Bumfwa	Bone-zaa	Ɛel-kam; Ben-zaa	Bon-zaal	Bono-zaa *or* Bono-kama
Nothing	Bum-ka-ye	Sel-ka-ne	Pa-ʃeli; Ɛel-ka-ne	Siɛl-ka	Sela-ka *or* Zaŋa
So-and-so	Zagala	Zaala	Zaɣla *or* Ɖo-ne-ŋo	..	Azagala, Abono

(7) *The Demonstrative Pronouns and Adjectives*

This, This one	Nyaŋwa, Ada; Kyaŋa, *pl.*	Nwoŋwa, *s.*; Banwa, *pl.*	Ɖo	Ɔŋa	Eŋawa, *s.*; Banawa, *pl.*, &c., &c.
That, that one	Rilla, Nyenna	Nwoŋwa *or* Kanwa	Dina Kano	Ɔna	Eŋlawa, *s.*; Bamlawa, *pl.*, &c., &c.

(8) *The Relative Pronouns*

Who, whom	Sẽ	So, *s.*; Ɛeba, *pl.*	So, *s.*; Ɛeba, *pl.*	Se	Se, *s.*; Seba, *pl.*, &c.

THE VERB

Perfect *or* Aorist Tense	Formed by suffixing *nya* or *ya* to the simple form of the verb	*Nya* or *Ya* before the simple form of the verb	*Nya* or *Ya* before the simple form of the verb	Formed by suffixing *ya* to the simple form of the verb	Formed by suffixing *ya* to the simple form of the verb

Dagare.	Bulea.	Loberu.	Gbanya.	Kasene.	Isal.
..	..	Nyom-so	Bin-ye-ye	..	..
..	..	Bel-so	Bumo-ye	..	..
An ?, *s.*; Amine ?, *pl.*	..	An ?	Ane-na ?, *s.*; Bomo-na ?, *pl.*	Wɔmu ?, &c.	Kove ?, *s.*; Koveva ?, *pl.*
Bɔŋ ?	..	Bo ?	Me-ne ?	Bɛmu ?	Beko ?
Bo ?	..	..	..	..	Kove ?
Nebɔ-zaa	..	Be-zaa, Ne-be-zaa	Eka-ma	Nɔŋ-ama-ma ?	Nɔ-kala
Ne'-za'-ce-be	..	Ne-zaa-ka-be	Eka-ma-wo-tɔ	Nɔŋ-tera	No'-to
Zaa ; Ozaa, Oto	..	Zaa	Keke	Mama	Ba-kala
Otɔ	..	Atɔ	Eko	..	..
..	..	..	..	..	..
Yene ... yene	..	Ne-bon ... ne-bon	..	Odo ... odo	De ar de
Boma-zaa	..	Bom-zaa	Aseŋ-kekɛ	Wenu-wuu	Kon-kun-kala
Bene-zaa-ce-be	..	Bom-zaa-ka-be	..	Ku-tera	Kun-to
Zagala	..	Zagele	Kutiʃina	Agyanwe	Nyanwe
Ɖa	Wa	..	Kedɛ	'Nto	Deŋ
Ɖa	Wa	..	Kedɛ ndo	Nto	Nereŋ
Na	..	Na	Wo	..	Se
..	..	..	Expressed by suffixing *ya* to the simple form of the verb	Expressed by suffixing *ya* to the simple form of the verb	Expressed by suffixing *ya* to the simple form of the verb

III. GRAMMAR AND SYNTAX (*cont.*)

English.	Mole.	Mampelle.	Dagbane.	Kusal.	Nankane.
Past Tense	Formed by *da*, before the simple form of the verb	Formed by *da*, or *sa* before the simple form of the verb	Formed by *de*, *sa*, *da*, before the simple form of the verb	Formed by *di* before the simple form of the verb	Formed by *da* or *Zaan* before the simple form of the verb
Future Tense	Formed by *na* before the simple form of the verb	Formed by *san* or *dan* or *ni* before the simple form of the verb	Formed by *san*, *nan*, *ni*, *ya*, before the simple form of the verb	Formed by *na* before the simple form of the verb	Formed by *wan* before the simple form of the verb
The Locative verb *to be*	Be	Be	Be	Be	Bo
The Copulative verb *to be*	Ya, Yi	Yela	Yela	Ale (neg, ka)	De, dela, dena
The verb *to have*	Tara, Tala	Mara	Mali	Mɔro	Tara

THE NEGATIVE

English.	Mole.	Mampelle.	Dagbane.	Kusal.	Nankane.
Negative Imperative	Expressed by *da* before the simple form of the verb	Expressed by *de* before the simple form of the verb	Expressed by *de* before the simple form of the verb	Da	Da
Negative of Locative verb *to be*	Ka	Ka	Ka	Ka	Kai
Negatives with other verbs	Ka (*or* Pa)—Ye *Kon* with future	Be, Ko, with future	Be, Ku, Pa, Ku *or* Ko is neg. used with the future	Ko, Po	Ka

Dagare.	Bulea.	Loberu.	Gbanya.	Kasene.	Isal.
Formed by *da* before the simple form of the verb	Formed by *pom* before the simple form of the verb	Formed by *da* before the simple form of the verb	Formed by *ka, da,* before the simple form of the verb	Formed by *na* before the simple form of the verb	..
Formed by *na* before the simple form of the verb	Formed by *le* before the simple form of the verb	Formed by *na* before the simple form of the verb	Formed by *n, kan,* before the simple form of the verb	Formed by *wo* before the simple form of th verb	Formed by *gya* before the simple form of the verb
..	..	Be	Wɔ	O, ora	..
Ela, E	Kaa (neg. is *da*)	Ine, I.	Nele, le	Ye (neg. *da*)	Ne
Ta	Ta (neg. is Ka)	Tɛre	Wɔ, kɔ	..	..
Ta	Ka, kan	Expressed by *Ta* before the simple form of the verb Ka	Expressed by *Sa, san* before the simple form of the verb Mo wɔ	Expressed by *yi* before the simple form of the verb Te, tera	Expressed by *se* before the simple form of the verb
..	..				..
Ba	M, n ; kan	Be	Ma, m (ma is used with the future)	Be	Bo

APPENDIX

In this appendix will be found some short vocabularies and a few notes on the grammar and syntax of five languages which have not yet been recorded in these pages. These are as follows:

1. *Vagale*: the language of the Vagala.
2. *Tampolem'*: the language of the Tampolense.
3. *Anufɔ* or *Chakosi*: the language of the Chakosi (*Anglice* Chokosi).
4. *Moare*: the language of the Moab' (*Anglice* Bimoba).
5. *Kpokpale*: the language of the Kpokpama (*Anglice* Konkomba).

Three of these dialects are of particular interest. Vagale and Tampolem', as will be observed by an examination of the tables, are very closely related both to each other and, as has already been noted, to a third language, Isal. Although now found widely separated, there is no doubt that the Isala, Vagala, and Tampolense were originally one stock. The traditions of all three tribes, not less than their linguistic affinities, all go to prove that such is the case. The existence of these two tribes (Vagala and Tampolense) seems hardly to have been known to us. Their names do not appear either in official 'language' or 'tribal' maps or in the last (1921) census reports, yet in the western and more central area marked 'Gonja' on the map, the tribe whose name is thus given to the whole area, only comprises the upper ruling classes. The mass of the people are Vagala[1] and still talk that language and retain their own customs. The latter will be examined in detail in a later portion of this volume.

The Tampolem' vocabulary which appears here was compiled at Langwinse (*Anglice* Kambonaba), not far from Gambaga. Here, among the so-called Mamprusi, were discovered a small colony of the Tampolense, occupying seven villages, speaking their own language, endogamous, in that they would not marry out of their own tribe and, surrounded as they were by strangers, yet retaining their very distinctive customs. Other members of this tribe bearing the same name are to be found near Daboya. Their customs and history will also be dealt with in a later chapter.

The remaining three languages, of which very brief vocabularies are given, do not, strictly speaking, belong to the Northern Territories, but are to be found spoken chiefly across the frontier in what is now the Mandated Area of Togoland. Chakosi, it will be seen, is a language closely related to Akan. It would not be easy to find a better example

---

[1] Including Tampolense.

of the pitfalls which beset the path of those who would attempt to unravel the secrets of West Coast migrations and origins. Here, in the remote north-eastern corner of the Gold Coast, are to be found a compact and self-contained little tribe numbering over 12,000 who talk an Akan dialect. They also possess all the physical and other characteristics of that race. Without a record of how the Chakosi came to occupy their present habitat, it would almost certainly follow that we would draw wrong conclusions from their presence in this area. We could certainly be excused for assuming that they probably represented a remnant of the parent Akan stock who had been left behind in a migration of this people southwards towards the Coast. Nothing, however, would be further from the truth. These Chakosi are, it is true, of Akan stock, but their present position does not indicate the line of any march coastward by the Akan. They arrived at their present home from the Coast, not on their way thither. Their ancestors had been brought from the south as mercenaries by the Dagomba or Mamprusi in the reign of Na Atabea some centuries ago. Instead of returning, they settled down where they found themselves when the campaign was at an end.

The following is the story in their own words. It was given me by the son of the Chief of Chereponi. 'Our ancestors came from Mango Ture where the white kola-nuts come from. We were formerly the Anufɔ. We had been hired to fight for them by the Ngbanjam (Gonja) and later by the Mamprusi who were quarrelling about the Chieftainship in the time of Atabea. We went from Gonja to Naleregu (northern Mamprusi). After the war was over, Atabea said that he had nothing to pay us with, so that we could fight the neighbouring tribes for what we could get. We fought the Bimoba and the Kpunkpamba (Konkomba) and settled in a place which we called Sansane-Mango [Sansane means a camp]. We used to send back slaves to our former home.' The new name given to them, which they now bear, was explained as follows: *chan*, to go, to wander, *kohe*, to sell, i.e. the people who go about selling slaves. Another version of the same tradition, which I obtained at Gambaga, gave a similar reason, and date, for the arrival of these people where they are now settled, but it stated that they came from a place called *Anɔ* near Botuku (Bontuku, French Ivory Coast). Mango, which was mentioned in the first tradition and gave its name to the new settlement, is sometimes stated to have been in Wassaw.

With regard to Moare (Bimoba) and Kpokpale (Konkomba), Dr. Westermann, even with the very scanty data given here, will possibly be able to link them up with one or another of the languages already tabulated.

Even now these vocabularies do not exhaust all the dialects spoken in the Northern Territories. There remain, among others, Nchumuru and Kratchi[1], which are, I think, dialects of Gbanya. Mo is spoken in the extreme south-west and also across the border into Ashanti. I made a short vocabulary of this language some years ago, but have, at the time of writing, unfortunately mislaid those notes.

The following brief notes amplify the material contained in the tables.

The Numerals: Vagale and Tampolem' both possess many 'loan words' among their cardinal numbers; e.g. *kalfa* (100), and *kagbom* (1,000) appear as *kalfa* and *kagbo* in Gbanya. The word *toko*, used for 'twenty' in Vagale, is of interest. In a previous volume, *Ashanti Law and Constitution*, written some years ago, appears the following in a footnote on page 110. 'They (the Ashanti) then commence again with *aduduotwe*, lit. 80 days; going back again, they count as before for "40 days", when they call the period *noha toku*, which is the first half of the year. This last word does not appear to be Ashanti.' It is now clear that *toku* in the above phrase means 'twenty', the expression *noka toko* thus reading 'one hundred and twenty'. The Chakosi also use the word *toko* or *toku* for a string of twenty cowries.

Words used for numerals appear among the least constant and the most subject to borrowings, more especially among the higher numbers.

In the classificatory terminology, although here again all these dialects exhibit signs of borrowing from neighbouring languages, the connexion between Vagale, Tampolem', and Isal is clearly indicated, and also between Chakosi and Akan.

Moare (Bimoba) and Kpokpale (Konkomba) both appear to fall into the Mole language group. The vocabularies do not call for any special comment, except to note that the majority of the words in Vagale and Tampolem' are from Isal roots and those in Chakosi from Akan. The personal pronouns (when standing alone) in these four dialects are as follows:

Vagale:

I,	*Man.*	We,	*Yama.*
Thou,	*Hen.*	You,	*Mma, Ima.*
He, &c.,	*One.*	They, &c.,	*Bama.*

[1] Also spelled Chumuru and Krachi.

Tampolem':

I,	*Mam.*	We,	*Ya.*
Thou,	*Hen.*	You,	*Ma.*
He, &c.,	*One.*	They, &c.,	*Ba.*

Chakosi:

I,	*Mene.*	We,	*Ye.*
Thou,	*Woro.*	You,	..
He, &c.,	*Ahe.*	They, &c.,	..

Moare:

I,	*Me.*	We,	*Tim.*
Thou,	*Fe.*	You,	*Yim.*
He, &c.,	*Ona.*	They, &c.,	*Be.*

Kpokpale:

I,	*Me.*	We,	*Tim.*
Thou,	*Fe.*	You,	*Tim.*
He, &c.,	*Ona.*	They, &c.,	*Ba.*

Concords or Classes: Vagale still retains the two plural classes *Ba* and *A*. It uses the former for persons and the latter for all other nouns, e.g.

Han kpan, one woman.   *Hana ba-niɛ*, two women.

Hal kpan, one egg.   *Hala a-niɛ*, two eggs.

I have not any information about classes in Tampolem', as I unfortunately omitted to investigate this part of the grammar.

There appear to be traces of the survival of several noun classes in both Moare and Kpokpale, as the following examples indicate.

Det ti-le, two rooms (Moare.)

Diug ko-ba, one room.   *Dir ti-le*, two rooms.   (Kpokpale.)

Po yen, one woman.   *Po banle*, two women.   (Moare.)

Pi oba, one woman.   *Pi-be-le*, two women.   (Kpokpale.)

The Chakosi, like their kinsmen, the Akan, have a week of seven days, with a special name for each day, e.g.

Chakosi.	Akan (roots).
Mone	*Memene*
Kyise	*Kwese*
Gyore	*Dwo*
Mana	*Bena*
Ohoe	*Wuku*
Ya	*Ya*
Foe	*Fi*

A somewhat curious point, however, is that the Chakosi appear to be one day behind in their reckoning, or putting it in another way, they have transposed the names of the days. It is not a case of mistaking the date, thinking, for example, that Sunday is Saturday. They know it is Sunday, so to speak. Sunday in Akan is *Kwese-(da)*, which becomes *Kyise* in Chakosi, but this word in Chakosi is used to designate Monday not Sunday, Sunday being called by the word which in Akan would mean Saturday. That the above does not arise owing to a mistake in the day of the week, which any of us might make, is proved by the fact that the Mohammedan Friday, which is well known, and is *Fi-(da)* in Akan, becomes *Ya* in Chakosi.

VOCABULARY

English.	Vagale.	Tampolem'.	Anufɔ (Chakosi).	Moare (Bimoba).	Kpokpale (Konkomba).
NUMERALS					
One	Kpan, Kpe	Beɣam, Dige	Ko	Koa Yen	Oba
Two	Anie	Alle	Nyɔ	Banle	Bile
Three	Ahoro	Atora	Nza	Banta	Beta
Four	Anazo	Anase	Nna	Bana	Bema
Five	Anoe	Anyu	Nnu	Banmu	Bumu
Six	Anumbel	Anora	Nze (nzie)	Balob	Belob
Seven	Anidanie	Anope	Nzo	Balole	Belele
Eight	Anidahoro	Nwenasa	Motwe	Banni	Ini
Nine	Kabel or Ani-danazo	Sandoso	Ngona	Banye	Bawe
Ten	Fi	Fi	Buru	Pik	Pirr
Eleven	Fi de kpan	Fi de kobe-ɣam	Buru ne ko	Pik ayen	Pig le ba
Twelve	Fi da nie	Fi de alle	Buru ne nyɔ	Pikbanle	Pig i le
Twenty	Toko	Fomlle	Abura nyɔ	Pinle	Pile
Thirty	Toko ne kporogo	Fomtora	Aburasa	Pinta	Pita
Forty	Toko anie	Fomnase	Aburana	Pina	Pina
Fifty	Adunu	..	Aburam	Pimu	Pimu
Sixty	Toko ahoro	..	Aburase	Pilob	Pilo
Seventy	Toko-ahoro ne-kporogo	..	Aburaso	Pinlole	Pilele
Eighty	Toko anazo	..	Aburamo-twe	Pini	Pini
Ninety	Toko anazo ne kporogo	..	Aburangona	Pinye	Pir i we
Hundred	Kalfa	Kwoɣwa	Aburonu	Kwobeg	Kwobeg
Two hundred	Kalfa bonie	..	..	Kwobile	Kwobyile
Thousand	Kagbom	Tusuga	Ya	Kutir	Tudir
CLASSIFICATORY SYSTEM					
Husband	Gyare	..	Hu	Soro	Kyer
Wife	Han	Han	Yi	Po	Po
Elder brother	Kpɛma	..	Goro	Yoro	Kpwer
Younger bro.	Niwie	..	Nema	Waro	War
Father	Mie	Nyena	Si	Ba	Ba
Son (child)	Bie	Bie	Wa	Biɣ	Biɣ
Mother	Ma	Nina	Ni	Na	Na
Son	Bie	Bie	Wa	Biɣ	Biɣ
Father's sister	Nyana	Naha	Nika	Poro	Por
Brother's son	Bie	..	Goro wa	Por bir	Por bir
Mother's bro.	Nara	Nera	Nwe	Ye	Weja
Sister's son	Nara or Bie	Nere	Nwe	Ye biɣ	Weja
Mother's sister	Ma bie (or zen)	..	Ni	Na (waro or yoro)	Na (kpwer or war)
Sister's son	Bie	Nere	Nwe	Biɣ	Biɣ

English.	Vagale.	Tampolem'.	Anufɔ (Chakosi).	Moare (Bimboa).	Kpokpale (Konkomba).
Father's father	Nabal	Nawal	Na	Yagya	Yagya
Son's son	Na	Niha	Anoma	Yabon	Yabil
Daughter's husband	Hela	..	Sibie	Diam	Tchoar
Wife's father	,,	..	,,	,,	,,
Wife's brother	Dakea	..	Sibie	Gyeseni	Kyingya
Sister's husband	,,	..	,,	Gyesib	,,
Wife's mother	Hela-han	..	Sibie	Diam (po)	Tcoar pi
Daughter's husband	Hel'-bal	..	,,	,,	,,

TERMS USED IN RELIGIOUS OBSERVANCES

Sky-God	Koro-aweze	Koro-wosa	Nyeme	Yonu, Yen-du	Nwe
Earth (a goddess	Here	Tiene	Aseno	Tin	Tin
Priest-King	He'ohen	Toha-tina	..	Tindano	Tinda
Shrine	Vog *or* Vok, Doma	Vera	Tie amoi	Pater	Bawol
Soul (of living)	Weze	Σiʃima	Awewe	Naren?, Yeyun?	Gyingyun
Spirit (of dead)	Lale; *pl.* Lala	Lelea, Lele	Nome	Kpemo	Okpwir
Soothsayer	Vogere	Vota	..	Gyaba	Obuo
Taboo	Ki	Kyiu, *v.*	Kyire	Lekoa	Koo
Fairy	..	Konton	Gyina	..	..
Oath	Hiezo	Hiese, *v.*	Ndie, Tam, *v.*	Po	Po

English.	Vagale.	Tampolem'.	Anufɔ (Chakosi).
VOCABULARY			
Arrow	Hem, *s.*; Hema, *pl.*	..	..
Back	Har	..	..
Bad	Coga	..	..
Bear	Lol	..	Wo
Beard	Tan-lona	..	..
Beer	Sen	..	..
Belly	Lore	..	..
Bite	Dom	..	..
Blood	..	..	Bongya
Bow	Ho, *s.*; Hoze, *pl.*	..	..
Bring	..	..	Fa ... bra
Bury	Huko	..	..

VOCABULARY (*cont.*)

English.	Vagale.	Tampolem'.	Anufɔ (Chakosi).
Buttocks	Zepum	..	..
Cat	..	..	Gyaramo
Chest	Bempiri	..	..
Chief	..	..	Feme, *s.*; Fenem, *pl.*
Climb	Zenne	..	..
Cloth	Wagye, *s.*; Wagyese, *pl.*	Garo	..
Come	Ba	..	Bera
Cook	Hon	..	..
Cow	Nau, *s.*; Naune, *pl.*	Noha, *s.*; Nohe, *pl.*	..
Cowries	..	Marebi	..
Crested crane	Kumol, *s.*; Kumola, *pl.*	..	..
Crocodile	..	..	Alene
Death	Seo	..	..
Die	..	..	Wu
Dog	Noahen, *s.*; Nosehena, *pl.*	Vaha, *s.*; Vasa, *pl.*	Ca, *s.*; Cam, *pl.*
Donkey	Kawe, *s.*; Kaweze, *pl.*	Kakuma, *s.*; Kakusa, *pl.*	..
Eat	Di	..	Di
Egg	Hal, *s.*; Halla, *pl.*	Hal, *s.*; Halla, *pl.*	..
Elephant	Bala, *s.*; Balaze, *pl.*	Bwola, *s.*; Bwolsa, *pl.*	Sui, *s.*; Suim, *pl.*
Enter	Zo	..	..
Eye	Siwi, *s.*; Siwe, *pl.*	..	..
Fan	..	Kafene, *s.*; Kafena, *pl.*	..
Farm	Ko, *s.*; Koni, *pl.*	Nwaha, *s.*; Nwana, *pl.*	..
Fat	..	..	..
Fire	Nin	..	Si
Food	Diwe	..	Dire
Go	Dala	..	Ko
Gun	Marfa	..	..
Head	Nyo, *s.*; Nyone, *pl.*	..	Oti
Horse	Zako, *s.*; Zagoro, *pl.*	Zaga, *s.*; Zana, *pl.*	..
House	..	..	Awuru, *s.*; Awurum, *pl.*
Kill	..	..	Kue
Leopard	Lol, *s.*; Lola, *pl.*	..	Awoba, *s.*; Awobam, *pl.*

VOCABULARY (cont.)

English.	Vagale.	Tampolem'.	Anufɔ (Chakosi).
Male	Bal, s.; Bala, pl.	..	..
Market	Yawa	..	..
Mat	Kalan, s.; Kalanze, pl.	..	..
Meat	Oll	..	..
Moon	..	..	Sara
Name	Soan	..	..
Navel	Ule, s.; Ulize, pl.	..	..
New	Kon-fale	..	..
Nose	Meze, s.; Mezeze, pl.	..	..
Person	Newe, s.; Newea, pl.	..	..
Quiver	Hon, s.; Honi or Haze, pl.	..	..
Red	Kon-amo	Ka-sheam	..
Refuse	Ve	..	..
River	Mo, s.; Mone, pl.	..	..
Road	..	..	Ati, s.; Atim, pl.
Room	Dea, s.; Dene, pl.	..	..
Sandal	Gao, s.; Gawa, pl.	Natau, s.; Natausa, pl.	..
Sheep	Piezi, s.; Pieza, pl.	Pisa, s.; Pisi, pl.	..
Skin	Hwon, s.; Hwona, pl.	Toan, s.; Tona, pl.	..
Sit	So	..	Tana
Slave	..	..	Akoo
Sleep	Tco	..	..
Smoke	Nyoze	..	..
Snake	Dom, s.; Doma, pl.	Dom. s.; Doma, pl.	..
Spear	Kanda, s.; Kandaze, pl.	Tim, s.; Tima, pl.	..
Stick	Da-kpala	..	..
Sun	Weze	Woha	We
Thief	Nwen, s.; Nwena, pl.	..	..
To-day	..	..	Nyoma
To-morrow	Kere	..	Ahema
Tongue	No-zone, s.; No-zona, pl.	..	..
Tooth	Nyen, s.; Nyena, pl.	..	..

VOCABULARY (*cont.*)

English.	Vagale.	Tampolem'.	Anufɔ (Chakosi).
Town	Bol, *s.*; Bola, *pl.*	Toha, *s.*; To-sa, *pl.*	..
Tree	Da, *s.*; Daze, *pl.*	..	Baka, *s.*; Bakam, *pl.*
Waist	Chara	..	..
Want	Nyini	..	..
Water	Nee	Ni	Nzoe
White	Kon-hono	..	..
Woman	Han, *s.*; Ha-na, *pl.*	Han, *s.*; Ha-na, *pl.*	..
Worthless	Pie	..	..

IV

SOME NOTES ON THE FOREGOING LINGUISTIC MATERIAL

BY D. WESTERMANN

IN the following short notes, I employ for the names of languages and language groups, the terms under which they are generally known in the linguistic literature; these are in a few cases different from those used by Dr. Rattray, who always gives the (more correct) names by which the Natives themselves call their language.

The languages represented in Dr. Rattray's collections (except Gbanya and Chakosi) belong to the so-called Gur (Goor) group of Western Sudanic languages. The name Gur has been given to the group because this syllable occurs in names of several of the languages belonging to the group.

The territory of the group extends approximately between 5° western and 5° eastern long., and between 8° and 24° northern lat., that is to say, in the Northern Territories of the Gold Coast, North and Middle Togo and Dahomé and the adjoining French territory farther north.

The Gur group is divided into the following sub-groups: (*a*) Mosi-Dagomba (Mole-Dagbane) sub-group, (*b*) Grusi sub-group, (*c*) Gurma sub-group, (*d*) Tem sub-group. Other branches are Kiliŋa and Bargu in Dahomé, Bargu reaching into the north-western corner of Nigeria; and the Senufo or Siéna group on the Ivory Coast. Of these sub-divisions, the first three are represented in Dr. Rattray's material.

The languages belonging to the Gur group form a definite linguistic unit, they reveal strong affinities in vocabulary as well as in grammatical structure. It is true that every sub-group and every individual language has its own characteristics, in grammatical peculiarities, word forms and in the words used, but Dr. Rattray is perfectly right in saying that it is possible 'to regard the Northern Territories of the Gold Coast as a more or less homogeneous cultural and—to a lesser extent—linguistic area, rather than as a mosaic comprising a welter of tongues and divergent customs'. This fact explains the easiness with which Natives acquire a second language of their group and the natural way in which the more important of the languages are spreading. In the case of the Northern Territories of the Gold Coast and the adjoining Mandated Togoland, the spreading language is, of course, Dagomba (Dagbane).

In point of grammar the characteristic feature of these languages is that nouns are divided into classes, mostly by means of suffixes, in a similar way as in the Bantu languages noun classes are formed by prefixes. In the Gurma sub-group, and partly also in Tem, both nominal prefixes and suffixes are used, while in the Central Togo group (Avatime, Akpafu, Santrokofi, &c.), which is the nearest relative to the Gur group, classes are formed almost exclusively by prefixes. The class division and class concord in both these groups is, however, not so well developed as in most Bantu languages (see also Rattray, p. 56.) In certain cases the prefix or suffix of a noun may be dropped, compare, e.g. the combination of a noun and its adjective on p. 58. Also the fact that some languages use pre-eminently suffixes, others (as Guang and the Central Togo group) prefixes, and again others (as the Gurma sub-group) prefixes and suffixes, shows that the affix system is more movable, less rigid than in Bantu languages.

It may be noted here that rudiments of class division by prefixes exist also in the languages farther south, such as Akan, Gã, Ewe, Yoruba, and, most of all, in Guang.

A few examples will show how the principle of class division works.

Dagomba (Dagbane)[1] *uses suffixes*

num-ga,   pl. *num-si,* bird.
kwe-ga,   ,, *kwe-se,* head-dress.
dir-gu,   ,, *dir-te,* spoon.
kpal-ugu, ,, *kpal-a,* Hausa gown.
teb-le,   ,, *teb-a,* ear.
kɔb-ele,   ,, *kɔb-a,* bone.
kum-bu, crying, from *kum,* to cry.
kwo-m, water. *kpa-m,* fat. *bihi-m,* milk.
nir-a,   pl. *nir-ba,* man.
kpar-a,   ,, *kpar-ba,* farmer.

While in the Mosi-Dagomba sub-group nominal classes are formed by suffixes, the numerals take prefixes, e.g. Dagomba, *a-yi,* two, *a-ta,* three, *nira ba-yi,* two men, *nira ba-ta,* three men.

Likewise the interrogative pronoun 'which?' has prefixes; comp. the examples given by Dr. Rattray in Chap. III, p. 59.

[1] The orthography used is that recommended by the International Institute of African Languages and Cultures. Comp. Memorandum I, *Practical Orthography of African Languages.* Revised edition, London, 1930.

Gurma uses pre- and suffixes

li-nyin-li,	pl. *a-nyin-a,*	tooth.
li-tub-li,	,, *a-tub-a,*	ear.
li-tan-le,	,, *a-tan-a,*	stone.
o-nu-lo,	,, *bi-ni-ba,*	man.
o-pua,	,, *bu-puo-ba,*	woman.
o-dyawa-l	,, *bi-dyawa-ba,*	boy.
o-tafa-go,	,, *ti-tafa-de,*	foot.
o-fa-gɔ,	,, *ti-fa-de,*	leaf.
bu-kpale-bɔ,	,, *ti-kapale-si,*	cloth.
n-nyi-ma,	water.	
n-sɔ-ma,	blood.	
n-nya-ma,	salt.	

Guang, like the Central Togo sub-group, uses class prefixes
In the Nkunya dialect of this language they are as follows:

o-nyi,	pl. *a-nyi,*	mother.
o-bisi,	,, *e-bisi,*	rat.
o-bu,	,, *a-bu,*	house.
ɔ-ba,	,, *a-ba,*	companion.
ɔ-kaŋ,	,, *ɛ-kaŋ,*	fish.
ɔ-fɛ,	,, *e-fɛ,*	thread.
a-bobi,	,, *m-bobi,*	bird.
a-bo,	,, *m-bo,*	arrow.
e-bo,	,, *a-bo,*	stone.
e-bia,	,, *m-bia,*	chair.
ɛ-fɛ,	,, *m-fɛ,*	axe.
ɛ-datobi,	,, *n-datobi,*	nail.
i-bu,	,, *a-bu,*	hut.
i-fuli,	,, *a-fuli,*	corpse.
m-fɔle, salt.	*m-fɔ,*	oil.
n-tsu, water.	*n-ta,*	palm wine.
n-sibi, eye.	*n-dobi,*	small farm.
ka-nyirɛ,	pl. *bɛ-nyirɛ,*	warrior.
ke-bi,	,, *nye-bi,*	child.
ke-bande,	,, *a-bande,*	wall.
ke-babi,	,, *a-babi,*	finger.
ke-puta,	,, *a-puta,*	bag.
ha-dzibi, food.	*hɛ-dɛ,*	fire.
hɛ-nɔ, arm.	*hɛ-fɔr,*	rope.

Class concord (i.e. the repetition of the nominal class affix before or after the predicate and the attribute) is not altogether lacking, but it is in most languages defective and some do not seem to have it at all. Dagbane e.g. has no concord, the only distinction it has in the pronoun is that between persons and things: *ɔ nya*, he, she sees, *de nya*, it sees; *o du*, his house; *de du*, its house.

But the following examples from Akasele (a Gurma dialect) show a real class concord:

o-nyi o-mama,	red person,	pl.	*be-nyi be-mama-be.*
o-ta o-mama,	red horse,	,,	*i-ta i-mama.*
di-ɲufɛ-re de-maman-de,	red nose,	,,	*a-ɲufɛ a-mama.*
bu-tyi bo-mamam-bo,	red tree,	,,	*i-tyi i-mama.*
ki-nyimi ke-mama,	red bird,	,,	*i-nyim i-mama-m.*
ko-koko ko-mama,	red feather,	,,	*te-koko te-maman-te.*
n-yɛ m-mama,	red fruit,	,,	*i-yɛ i-mama.*

The demonstrative pronoun *nɛ* exhibits the following forms:

o-tya nɛ-o,	this stranger,	pl.	*be-tya-mbe nɛ-mbɛ.*
de-kpokpo-re nɛ-ndɛ,	this leaf,	,,	*a-kpokpo nɛ-ɲe.*
bu-tyi nɛ-mbo,	this tree,	,,	*i-tyi nɛ-i.*
ki-budya nɛ-ɲkɛ,	this buck,	,,	*m-budya-m nɛ-m.*
ku-di nɛ-ɲko,	this house,	,,	*ti-di-ti nɛ-ntɛ.*
m-bo nɛ-ɲ,	this wound,	,,	*i-bo n-ɛi.*

Similarly in the relative pronoun:

o-tya wa,	the stranger who,	pl.	*be-tya-mbe ba.*
di-nyimi-li da,	the eye which,	,,	*a-nyi-m ya.*
bu-tyi bwa,	the tree which,	,,	*i-tyi ya.*
ki-nyimi ka,	the bird which,	,,	*i-nyim wa.*
ko-koko kwa,	the feather which,	,,	*te-koko ta.*
n-yɛ wa,	the fruit which,	,,	*i-yɛ ya.*

I agree with Dr. Rattray in attributing the ten languages mentioned by him on page 2 to the Mole (Mosi-Dagomba) sub-group. Only in the case of 'Bulea' one might doubt whether it should be placed here or in the Grusi sub-group; it shows obvious affinities with both.

Kasene, Awuna (also called Atyulo), and Isal (Isala, Sisala) belong to the Grusi sub-group. Again I believe Dr. Rattray is right in including 'Tampolem' and Vagale in this sub-group, although the material at hand is somewhat scanty for a definite statement.

Moare (Moba, Moab, Bimoba) and Kpokpale (Konkomba), of which Dr. Rattray gives short vocabularies, are languages of the Gurma sub-group, other representatives of which are Gurma, Akasele, Tobote, all spoken in the Mandated Territory.

Languages of a different type are Chakosi and Gbanya, both belonging to the Akan stock. The origin of the Chakosi colony has been explained by Rattray on page 113. The people themselves call their language Anufɔ.

Gbanya or Gonja (also Gbanja, Ngbanya, Ngbanye) is spoken north of Ashanti and south of the habitat of Dagomba. It seems to stretch through the whole breadth of the Gold Coast, although probably interspersed with languages belonging to the Gur group; the linguistic situation of this region is not yet sufficiently known. But Gbanya is no doubt an important language; properly speaking, it is only a section or a dialect of a language which is spread over a considerable part of the Gold Coast and of Togoland, and is known by the name of Guang. Other dialects of this language are spoken in Chumuru and Kratchi (see Rattray, p. vii, preface), in Kyerepong and Late, and in parts of Togoland (Nawuri, Atyoti, Anyaŋa).

Chap. I, p. 5.

bia, little, and bia, child, both contain the root *bi*, which means 'child' as well as 'small'; the same root occurs again on page 6 in Bulea *na-bik* (where *-k* is a suffix, shortened and altered from *-ga*; the same suffix is *-a* in *bia*, the original form being *bi-ga*, this becomes *bi-ya*, and finally *y* is dropped, while in *na-bik* the vowel *a* has been dropped and thus *-ga* changed to *-k*. The root *bi* for 'child' is common to all the languages of the group and to many other West African languages.

Chap. I, p. 9.

The relations between the Ashanti and the Ngbanya (Gonja) represent a difficult problem, because we know little or nothing about the history of the tribes. The Akan tribes (Ashanti-Fante-Twi) immigrated into their present abodes not later than in the fifteenth century (Delafosse in his *Langue Agni*, p. 185, dates the beginning of the immigration back to the twelfth century). According to their own traditions they came from Nta, N.W. of Salaga, i.e. from Gonja country; it may be assumed that their march towards the coast was due to pressure from the north. It is very likely that long before they arrived, the main population of the present Gold Coast and Ashanti were the Guang tribes, of which the Ngbanya (Gonja) are one section. We know nothing about the original language of the immigrating Akan tribes, very likely it was akin to Gbanya, since they came from that country. As Dr. Rattray has repeatedly pointed out, Guang and Akan are closely related; in a number of cases, however, Guang has older word-forms than Akan, and the latter shows certain peculiarities which are alien to the other languages of the sub-group (Gã, Ewe, Guang), so that one might be justified in saying that Akan is a side-branch of the original Guang, altered by a foreign element (represented by the immigrating Akan tribes). If then the Gonja state that when they first settled in the Gonja country, they found the Ashanti and married their women, this would mean that a group of men (mostly without women) came into Gonja country as foreign invaders, and their descendants naturally adopted the language of the country, viz. Guang.

CHAP. I, p. 11.

The root *bal-* for 'male person, husband' occurs in a number of languages of the group, -*o*, -*a* are suffixes. Comp. also Akan *ɔ-bari-ma* male person.

CHAP. II, p. 44.

The original meaning of *kyima* in Dagbane and *ebuni* in Gbanya is dead person; the forms *ebuni* and *ebuno* also occur in eastern Guang dialects, e.g. in Anyaŋa.

Same page. The root *ki*, *kyi*, to avoid, to keep as taboo, is found in the following languages: Akan *kyi*, *kyiri*, Ewe *kli*, *tsri*, Agni (Ivory Coast) *kyi*, Gã *tſi*, Guang *kisi*, Dagbane *kyi*, *kyihe*, Tem *kisi*, Senufo (Ivory Coast) *ki*.

CHAP. III, p. 48.

In Awuna *sa-pu-ga*, -*pu-ga* is evidently the numeral ten.

p. 52. *tim*, medicine is the root *ti*, tree, with the class-suffix -*m* denoting liquids, *ti-m* is tree-water; *tip* is possibly a variant of *tim*. The root *ti*, tree, is spread over a large part of West Africa and of the Bantu area.

On page 53. Words for 'foot' and 'hand'. The languages have one word which designates the fore-arm, i.e. from the elbow to the tip of the fingers, and another for the upper arm from elbow to shoulder;

likewise with the lower extremities, where the knee corresponds to the elbow.

p. 56 ff. *Classes.* There is no doubt that the adjectives given by Dr. Rattray on page 58 have real class suffixes: *pele-ga*, pl. *pele-se*; *pele-go*, pl. *pel-o*; *pele* (*pel-e*), pl. *pel-a*; *-ga*, *-go*, *-e* are singular suffixes, and *-se*, *-o*, *-a* are plural suffixes. Also the pronominal forms as given on page 59 show class concord.

But the interesting fact is that, as is clearly to be seen from the examples given on page 58, the combination of a noun and an adjective is considered as a close unit, and, corresponding to this, the class-suffix of the noun is not expressed after the noun, but after the adjective; e.g. *pɔ-ga* is girl or woman, *pele* is white, and *pɔ pele-ga* white girl; likewise in plural: *pɔ-se* girls, but *pɔ pel-se* white girls. *Nere son-a* is a good man, *ko somo* good water; the root for good is *son*, to this is added *bo*, the class suffix for liquids: *son-bo*, this changes by assimilation to *sombo* and finally becomes *somo*.

p. 60. *Examples of Noun Classes in Kasene*:

Class 1. *non-o*, pl. *non-a*, man.
  „   2. *sar-a*,   „ *sar-e*, mat.
  „   3. *kul-u*,   „ *kul-lu*, hump.
  „   4. *ti-o*,   „ *ti-ni*, village.
  „   5. *per-e*,   „ *per-a*, present.
With an adjective: *la* 'good' *non la-o* 'good man'.

p. 61. *Conjugation of Verb.* The particles *sa* and *da* are adverbs, *sa* meaning 'yesterday' *and* 'to-morrow', and *da* meaning 'the day before yesterday' *and* 'the day after to-morrow'; this double meaning of each of the two particles explains the surprising fact that they both may express past as well as future tenses. The real meaning of *sa* is 'the nearest day', no matter whether passed or to come, and *da* is 'the nearest day but one'. In many African languages the expressions for 'yesterday' and 'to-morrow' are identical, and in fact the word from which the English 'yesterday' is derived, had formerly both meanings, (Gothic *gistradagis* is 'to-morrow', Old Nordic *igaer* means 'yesterday' and 'to-morrow').

Thus *n sa nya bi ma* is literally: I to-day saw the child, *n da nya bi ma* I the day before yesterday saw the child. (*ma* is a demonstrative pronoun, used as a definite article.)

The future is expressed by *ni*: *n ni nya* I shall see; *n sa ni nya* I to-morrow shall see.

Chap. III.

Numerals.

Kalfa in Gbanya is the Arabic *'alf*, thousand with the *ki-* prefix.

Appendix

The numerals in Anufɔ (Chakosi) show the softening of a consonant following a nasal (*nza* from *nsa*, *nze* from *nse*) which is characteristic of the western Akan dialects (Baoule, Nzema, Agni) to which Anufɔ is most closely related.

For fuller information the reader is referred to the following studies:

R. Bluzet: *Vocabulaire de la langue du Mossi, précédé de notes grammaticales*, Paris.

F. Dubois: *Vocabulaire Gourma.* Paris, 1898.

I. Cremer: *Grammaire de la langue Kassena ou Kassené.* Paris, 1924.

R. Fisch: *Grammatik der Dagomba-Sprache.* Berlin, 1912.

F. Frogen, *Étude sur la langue des Massi.* Paris, 1910.

E. Funke: 'Vokabular der Kussassi-Sprache im Westsudan'. *Mittlgn. d. Sem. f. Oriental. Sprachen*, xxiii–xxv.

——: 'Die Isala-Sprache im Westsudan'. *Mittlgn. d. Sem. f. Oriental. Sprachen*, xxiii–xxv.

B. Groh: 'Sprachproben aus zwölf Sprachen des Togo-Hinterlandes'. *Mittlgn. d. Sem. f. Oriental. Sprachen*, 1911 (short vocabularies of Chakosi, Dagbane, Mamprusi, Moba, Gurma, Konkomba, Basari, Loso, Kabere, Sokode).

P. Müller: 'Beitrag zur Kenntnis der Tem-Sprache.' *Mittlgn. d. Sem. f. Oriental. Sprachen*, viii.

Okraku:

R. S. Rattray: *An Elementary Môle Grammar, with a Vocabulary.* Oxford, 1918.

D. Westermann: 'Die Mossi-Sprachengruppe im westlichen Sudan.' *Anthropos*, viii, 1913.

——: 'Die Grussisprachen im westlichen Sudan.' *Zeitschrift für Kolonialsprachen*, iv, 1913–14.

——: *Die Sprache der Guang in Togo und auf der Goldküste, und fünf andere Togosprachen.* Berlin, 1922. (Containing outlines of three Gurma dialects and of Bargu.)

——: *Die westlichen Sudansprachen.* Berlin, 1927. (Pp. 121–43: Die Gur-Sprachen. With bibliography.)

V

INTRODUCTORY NOTE

IN this, and in the chapters which immediately follow, an African (Victor Aboya by name; see Fig. 1) has recorded for us in his own words[1] and from an African's point of view, a series of pen pictures of Native life in a Nankanse village. The characters, sometimes designated by name, sometimes merely described as 'a man' or 'a woman', or 'a child', are in every case real persons. The sights and scenes he has described were actual happenings in the everyday life of the narrator's village. The writer is a Nankani who at an early age, in a time of famine, had been exchanged by his uncle for a few baskets of grain which were to help in keeping the remainder of his family from actual starvation. In other words, he had been sold as a slave. After various adventures he had found himself free and adopted by kindly missionaries of Basel, by whom he was educated and taught to read and write. Many years later, following that 'homing' instinct, which is so strongly developed in the African, he returned to his native village. Here it was I first met him. He was persuaded to record various events in the village life. He has done so, faithfully and without any attempt to impress us by airing or dragging in his later acquired European knowledge.

The various sketches, dealing, among other subjects, with birth, puberty, marriage, and death, not only throw many side-lights on tribal customs and mentality, but they also afford (in the original specimens selected) a good example of one of the most interesting perhaps of the various dialects which have now been recorded. So far as I am aware these are the first published specimens of the Nankane language. The whole will, I trust, serve to link up the early chapters of this volume, dealing exclusively with linguistics, with the later portion of these books, where the religion, customs, and constitution of the peoples who speak these languages are recorded, in this case, as seen through the eyes of a stranger.

Victor Aboya's prologue to these later series of descriptions is as follows:

---

[1] The originals, of which the following chapters are translations, were written in Nankane.

Fig. 1. Victor Aboya

The Birth of a Child

If a Goreŋa[1] man mates with a woman, and she continues to walk about for a long time (without having conceived), that is a thing that spoils his heart exceedingly. He wanders about consulting (sooth-sayers) ceaselessly, (to find out) if his father (i.e. the spirit of his father) is a thing which is lifeless. He (the husband) is always standing beside the shrine of his father's spirit continually soliciting him, telling him that he (the spirit) has a sour belly; telling him that he is not kind; telling him that he is pulling down the compound, for are not children the building up of a house? Many times he puts mouths (i.e. makes vows). He is also always to be found before his own and his wife's *sega* (guardian spirits) asking their aid also. He does all this until he will arrive at the true position (*zia*) and his body become cool. 'The true position' is that the woman 'falls from the waist' (has her menses), recovers and remains thus. This truly is conception[2] (lit. a belly). There are some women also who have a miscarriage (*se liya*). That means that about four or five moons later when she is still walking about and every one thinks that she has conceived, then suddenly there falls much blood. Then she causes her husband to become weak. Such a case often brings a rising of the heart (*sunsua nyim*) between the woman and her husband. If it so happens that the woman has already had a child somewhere, before she knew her present husband, it will not be so bad for them. If the man also has two wives, and if one of them has a child already, it will be still better. If neither of these things are, then they stand in the dark (as to whose fault it is); they are quarrelling every day and if the woman does not look out she will be running away to marry some place[3] and leave that one (that man) and he will again seek for a new wife. Others, when it happens so, cool themselves properly (are patient) and the male seeks soothsayers without ceasing, killing (i.e. sacrificing) fowls, goats, sheep, and makes, I don't know how many, mouths (vows) until he will see that his wife has given birth. When he sees her with a belly, he will

[1] See p. 398.

[2] When a woman becomes pregnant for the first time, an old woman is sent for, and she comes secretly and stands inside the girl's compound. She calls the pregnant girl by name, and as soon as she comes out to see who it is who wants her, the old woman blows ashes over her off the palm of her hand, saying 'I have whitened you'.

[3] In such a case the man will be entitled to the return of the hoes and the cock (but not among the Nankanse), and all presents given by the husband to his wife. An impotent husband will often allow his wife freedom to have intercourse with other men in order to raise up seed for him. This custom is called *galsego* or *tua*.

stand by the shrine of that spirit which had told him that his wife
would conceive, consulting it and sacrificing to it often, in order that
its belly should be washed (i.e. that it should be happy) and that it
might do him good; in order that when the woman comes to deliver
she should not feel pain; in order that she may not struggle for people
to hear her. When a woman is pregnant, she may not sleep in a cold
place, she may not eat cold food. Why? Because such things cause
much blood on the day of delivery. She may not sleep on her
stomach, she may not sleep on her back, lest when her belly is ripe she
injure the baby inside. She may not run, but this she will know herself,
because she will be weak. She may not dance, lest she cause injury
to the child. A pregnant woman may not eat honey,[1] or eat the flesh
of the *eo* (antelope). The husband of such a woman may not touch
a corpse; he is not allowed to kill any wild animal; he may not build
a new hut. The woman observes her husband's taboos but he need
not respect hers.[2] If, when she comes to give birth, she keeps
struggling, they will upbraid her, telling her it is because she failed
to observe these rules. This is why they try like this. It is, in order
that when something bad happens, the neighbours may not say,
'There is no good house-spirit there', when all the time it was disobedience caused it (the difficulty in bringing forth). When the
woman is in the midst of labour, the owner of the house runs with
'water' (really flour and water) to give his spirits, those spirits which
have already said that they would 'have' (look after) her, saying, 'The
woman, whom you spoke about saying that you would "have" her, is
in labour, hold her now and let her "lay" on an earthen dish because
a calabash is a noisy thing.'[3] When she has delivered, the owner of the
house again runs with water for his ancestors' spirits and tells them
that the woman has delivered, and he gives them *fura fura* (thanks)
and tells them that they (the spirits) should 'have' (look after) the
stranger (*sana*) until the small tree becomes a big tree. Should the
child be a girl, the mother comes outside in four days, if a boy, in
three days, after delivery.[4] The afterbirth (*yala*) is placed in a small
pot, in which a hole has been knocked, and in this the navel cord

---

[1] Compare the Ashanti, see *Religion and Art in Ashanti*, p. 54.

[2] He will not wantonly violate them.

[3] Laying in a calabash is synonymous with having difficulty in delivery; an easy
delivery is called 'laying in an earthen plate' (*lobe laŋ*).

[4] Here we have the first example of the association of these numbers with the two
sexes, which will be noted repeatedly throughout these volumes and is common to
all the tribes.

(which has been cut a middle finger's length from the navel) is also placed, and the pot is buried at the foot of the kitchen midden. Another hole is also dug there, and over it the mother is bathed, and after her, the child. The woman is not allowed to sit where there are many people until the days already mentioned have passed. On the 'coming forth day' (*yesega dare*) the mother and an old woman (who had been in constant attendance upon her) will rise up 'morning night night' (very early in the morning) and gather up the ashes from the fire of the room where mother and child have been and put them in a potsherd and place the broom, with which the room had been swept out, on top, and they go and empty all away at the cross-roads on the path leading to the woman's town. The woman will now be allowed to walk about outside and make food and go to fetch water. The young mother is not allowed to drink cold, only hot, water. She also only eats hot grain food and does so for many days until they know that 'bloody days' are past, then she will commence drinking cold water.

There are some people alive, who taboo food cooked by a woman who has lately given birth. This is on account of their possessing some 'medicine' (*tim*) whose taboo it is. Such will neither eat nor drink anything that comes from such a room (*deo*) until many days have passed. There are others who, if they eat 'young mother's food', will vomit. Such people have bad gullets and they will seek for some medicine, which those who bury corpses possess (*baya tim*, sexton's medicine) after which they will not be sick any more.[1]

If a woman is just a young girl and she has delivered a female child, the husband takes a female fowl and goes off to report to her 'house-people'. If it were a male child, he will go with a male fowl and a stick. When they (the wife's relations) see him, they know that their daughter has delivered a female or a male child. They will not ask about it; they themselves know (the sex) according as to whether it is a female or a male fowl.[2]

There are some other houses where, when a woman goes out for the first time, the child does not go out. It is left in the room until it can crawl and go out itself.[3] After this happens the mother may take it out. The bringing up of such children is difficult, for in the very hot weather it is hard not getting outside. The sun descends

---

[1] As we shall see later, entering graves is frequently considered a treatment for persons afflicted with delicate stomachs.

[2] As will be noted later, silence on the part of all concerned is generally enjoined on such occasions.   [3] Variations of this custom will be seen to exist.

hotly and every one wants to sit where the wind casts itself, but behold it is taboo for the child to go out, and mother and child are forced to remain in the heat, and they do not know what to do.

When a child has been born and they have finished cutting its navel cord, they are wont to seek for some one whose hands are bitter.[1] He will go and fetch a leaf called *puo*. *Puo* is a kind of leaf which has latex (*sira*). This *puo* leaf is taken by the one whose hands are bitter, and he touches all round the navel cord with it and smears on the latex. They also keep oiling the cord with shea butter until it drops off. On the 'day of its falling' they will seek for the shell of a shea butter nut, put the navel string inside, scrape a hole above the doorway of the inner room, and place the shell in it, plastering it over, the outside of the shell remaining visible. Every child's navel string is 'stuck' there, and when you enter into this room, if you know this custom, you know that the number of children delivered is the number of shea nuts.

Now the child becomes black and learns how to sit up, crawl round the walls, but as yet still does not know outside.[2] On account of this, the mother will resort to a plan. She will arrange secretly with a *poyablega* (a woman from her own village) to come on purpose to take the child outside. The mother no sooner sees that this woman has one leg across the threshold, but when too late to stop her, than she cries out 'Don't go out, Don't go out', but the child is already outside. The reason for all this is that a spirit (*kyima*) cannot quarrel with a mistake made by a *poyablega* and not any fault of the mother. It is as if the spirits had done it themselves. Should this (subterfuge) not be done, the child continues thus (crawling about the hut and yard). The mother will sit by it in the *naγ' dene* (cattle-kraal),[3] and one day the child will crawl outside itself. That is a sign that the spirits have agreed, and have themselves taken the child out. Did the woman do so herself *tulugo* (fever) would catch the child, and when they went to consult the soothsayer his wand would make it clear what she had done. (In such a case) they will return and ask the woman and she will speak the truth, then they will appease the spirits, saying, 'We had strayed off the path', and the sickness will leave the child.

There are some 'new' children who are not at first allowed to

[1] Some persons have supernatural power in their hands and can cause sickness by a slap.

[2] The child is allowed in the yard but not outside the main entrance of the compound. [3] See plan of compound, p. 248.

sleep upon a mat or even to have the *mia* grass (from which mats are made) 'peeping' in, much less a real mat, until some custom has been performed. Some man will come to lay the child on a mat (for the first time), after which it is no longer taboo for it to lie upon one. The man who first lays such a child upon a mat, and afterwards the infant dies, is finished with that. His hands are not good. The one who 'lays' a child, and that child does not die, he possesses good hands. The 'laying' of a child is thus: The one who 'lays'[1] rises up between morning and night night (i.e. very early) and before the rays (of the sun) have climbed, to find roots. The name of the roots is *am-nyagere* (*am*-roots). When he reaches the house where the infant is, he takes the *am*-root and cuts it into four pieces; they take down a new mat from where it is hanging up and spread it in the middle of the *zi-nzaka* (yard). This man, who is about to perform the ceremony, takes a piece of the root, and places it at the head of the mat, another of the pieces on the right, another on the left, and one below, where the feet of the child are placed. He also cuts *sensase* grass and places it at the 'head' of the mat. He now takes the child and places it between the roots. He watches the sun rise, and when it climbs very red, he catches up the child and climbs the wooden steps (leading to the flat roof) holding the child in both hands, he lifts it up, holding it forth to the rays. Then he brings it down and rests it again upon the mat.[2] Again he takes it up and mounts the ladder and holds it forth and again descends and places it in the middle of the roots. If it is a male child, he will hold it up three times, if a female child, four times. The taboo has now been 'lifted up' (*dikke*). The child and its mother are now able to sleep on a mat. This is the custom among children of *Ten'dama* (Priest-Kings).

The heads of some children must not be shaved until they become full-grown men or women. This is because of some taboo imposed by their *sega* (guardian spirits). Before the hair of such persons is cut they must not have sexual intercourse. When the head of such a child has been shaved this removes the taboo, but some other girl or boy must be given to their *segere* in their place. At the shaving of the head beer will be cooked and fowls and guinea-fowls be caught and may be even a beast (goat or sheep) and a sacrifice made to the guardian spirit (*segere*).

---

[1] *Yae*, the word used, also means to take a drowning person out of the water.

[2] The following detail has been omitted. Between each holding forth, the man mounts again on the ladder and smokes a few puffs from a long pipe. Complete silence is observed.

There are some other customs in connexion with this ceremony which I do not know properly.

Predestination: There are some children who (before birth) have spoken 'badly' with God,[1] saying that they did not want a father or a mother, or that they did not wish to benefit by their food, or perhaps that they did not want ever to marry.[2] If the soothsayer's bag reveals all this in time they will know what to do, and they will take things and make the necessary sacrifices, and good will result. If they do not do so, the boy or girl will die or become sickly or spoiled. There was a male child from God (*Yini*), who said he did not want to marry. His parents inquired into the matter from the soothsayer's bag in order to know about it and find out if it were possible to remove the evil or not, or if it were one which could be counteracted. They particularly asked about the kind of fowl, what kind of 'feathers' it must have (i.e. its colour) and the kind of beast, and the kind of corn (to offer to *Yini*). Unless this ceremony was performed, he might not marry. When (his parents) even talked about marriage 'it' would go and strike him; it was the smell of death, and they desisted, then fresh air blew. There was the case of —— who became ill every time he married, and at last died. He had (before birth) declared that he would never marry. Such a one has already lain with a woman above, when with *Yini* (the Sky-God). Another lives in our land called A. N.; he married a wife but he has never known her. When the sun entered (set) he hid himself from her. To-day his younger brother has the woman, and he, the husband, has the children begotten by his younger brother.

There are, again, other kinds of children who have declared before *Yini*, that they do not want *nyere*[3] (younger brothers or sisters). If this is revealed in time, when the child is still in babyhood, and if they do what is necessary, it will be better. Why? Because then they will perform the necessary customs. If they did not hear of the matter, when the mother came to deliver other children, they would continue to die. After, perhaps, the death of the third child, the soothsayer's bag will be called in to make the case known among many men. The necessary rites will be performed and the woman will be delivered and 'have' (i.e. the child will remain alive).

Training of Children: They perform all these small customs until

---

[1] Compare the *Ashanti*. Vide *Ashanti Proverbs*, note under *Nkrabea*, p. 25.

[2] In such a case the husband or wife will die. The spell will, however, be broken after the death of the third spouse.   [3] See p 8.

an infant is grown, until it is able to fetch a thing and has learned to
work for itself. A male child will learn how to herd live stock, to
follow sheep, and after learning how to do that, cattle.[1] A girl must
learn to work in the house, learn how to grind flour, sweep up refuse,
wash pots and calabashes. Next she learns how to break firewood and
get grass for mats and do other women's work. When a boy has followed the sheep and next the cattle and learned to do work other than
the following of animals, he will now turn to farming with his father.
He will have his own *sensayere* (small plot for grain crops); his own
sukalaneya (plot for ground-nuts); his own *sunlaliya* (plot for hard
ground-nuts), his own *lala-pese-vugse* (plot for Nankane potatoes).[2]
He will also learn hunting with his neighbours.

Preference for Male Children: When a Gorena man is of age to have
a child, but has not got one, this causes him to feel inferior to others.
Even when he has a daughter, but not a son, he feels inferior. Even
if he has a son, and he is only yet a boy, he is better than ten big
daughters. When you are old enough to have a son, but have not
got one, your neighbours do not respect you; they will call you a
bon-basela (a worthless thing), even relatives on your mother's side
(*sōō*) will address you saying, 'You, what are you?' Another will say,
'I shall in future receive water (when a spirit) and you (when you are

---

[1] In the old days, there was much friendly rivalry among the young lads who acted
as cattle herds. They competed in wrestling, shooting with toy bows and arrows and
slings. Youths who attempted early sexual intercourse or masturbation, lost their
prowess and skill, and were derided. The girls looked forward with pride to being
found chaste at the incision ceremonies. 'Now,' stated my informant, 'a Chief's son
may get hurt in these rough and tumbles and he runs and complains to his father and
the Chief will contrive to punish the parents of the boy who hurt his son, so that we
are now afraid to play these games.'

[2] The following are the names for various kinds of farms (sometimes involving also
various forms of tenure) among the Nankane:

(*a*) *Samane*: This is the farm land around a *yiri* (family compound). Among the
Nankanse it is generally divided up among the brothers, each plot is then called a *loya*
(pl. *lonse*). Each married female in the compound has a small garden patch (out of the
samane) called *nanginkuku* where she plants *nangina* vegetables. The eldest brother's
loya is generally in front of the compound entrance.

(*b*) *Vaam*: It is a plot in the bush owned by the *Ti-dana*, head of the compound,
and worked by him assisted by his sons. After the *Ti-dana*'s death, it may be divided
into *lonse*. The *Ten'dana* (Priest-King) will be approached before a new *vaam* is made.

(*c*) *Sensayere*: The plot belonging to a man's son during his father's lifetime which
the son works in his spare time and when not working for his father. It is not carved
out of the *samane*, but has been cleared and cultivated by the son from the beginning.
All food grown on it belongs to the son.

dead and have become a spirit) will come and attach yourself to me for a drink, for as for you, you would not get one otherwise.'

If you have not got a son, when you become old and are only able to drag your buttocks along the ground, and have still to work for yourself, what will you do? You will eat only pity; you will fall down (i.e. die) like some light thing and they will not even know that some one is dead. Only sons-in-law will come with things and assemble for the 'burning'[1] and the funeral will not have any 'head'. They will make it carelessly and off they will scatter. If such an one had brothers, it would not be so bad.

When a Goreŋa man marries, he wishes, if God consents, to beget plenty male children, rather than female children. Why? Because the girls will scatter to people's houses (as wives). Some one may marry many wives and beget many male children in his house. In the place where men meet to talk, they have him for a topic of conversation, saying that So-and-so has 'built a house'. Such an one will always be standing up 'cutting' (i.e. sacrificing), not missing a day. When he hears that a soothsayer is in a town, off he goes there (to consult him about what he must do so as not to lose his children). He becomes *wogologole* (skinny) and never becomes fat. Thoughts about his children fill his house; he will eat wonderful medicine called *noadogoro* (mouth pots), also *luse* (tying medicine),[2] in order to protect his house. A man so situated forbids his children to talk impudently (to their superiors).

Another man may always be boasting about his children and too proud to see any one else, saying that whatever happens, he will be able to face it. Such a man is a fool, and does not respect any one, or consider a person to be 'a thing'.

When a man has many sons, corn cannot fail in his house. Why? Because they are many. When going to the bush farm,[3] soon they have finished, passing on to the next; when this farm fails, that one does not. On account of this, they do not ever fail to have corn. Such people are better off than their neighbours. Starving people's best goats, sheep, the biggest of the heifers, find their way to their place in exchange for corn; their belly is washed (i.e. they are happy because not in want) and you have to agree to what they give you (in exchange for your live stock).

---

[1] See p. 185.   [2] See *Ashanti*, pp. 310–11.   [3] See footnote, p. 137.

VI

COURTSHIP, MARRIAGE, AND DIVORCE

COURTSHIP: When a man has sons, he tries to teach them farming; he does not wish them to idle about; he wishes them to look after cultivation, the rearing of winged creatures, and live stock, instead of wandering about foolishly. He wishes them to regard work in which there is profit. Some people do not mind about all this and they begin early to follow after women. Some men, too, allow their children to walk about and have lovers so that they squander the things that they have, because if a youth goes and visits his lover, he will take tobacco and salute the senior woman (*deo-dana*) in that compound, and present her with it, and do the same with the master of the house, and if there are many people in the house, he will salute them all and give them all tobacco. They will call the girl whom he loves, to come for him to greet her. He will salute her and say, 'I want to speak with you and I know what I am going to say will be a belly washing word for you (i.e. make you happy).' He says, 'Do you want me, or do you not want me?' He says, 'The ancients have measured (*make*) (i.e. pondered over certain matters) and declared that it is necessary to tickle a dumb person in order to know the words which are in his inside. If I remain silent and say to myself that you would never agree to love me, would that not be foolish? It is on account of this, that I sit with you thus, that we may know each other's bellies (i.e. thoughts), that I may know if you consent, or do not consent.' Perhaps the girl will answer and say, 'Does one person refuse to converse with another? I never expected that you would agree to open your mouth and say that you love me. Did you expect that I would open mine and say that I don't love you? Such things cannot be. Come, let us talk, and if our converse becomes good, and the spirits unite and agree to give us, we will be united.' If, however, a girl does not love you, but is shy to tell you so, she will speak and say, 'Follow my father and my mother, it is their consent that matters, I am powerless to jump over something before they do. Their consent is my consent. If I say "I consent", then it is as if I owned myself. Let us listen to them.'

Another girl, when she does not want a man, and herself is lacking in sense (*yeam*) will speak more plainly and say, '*Ee*, I don't know what to say, I am not quite old enough for such a thing. I—a little thing like this, how can I be expected to know about such matters? If you want a girl, are women lacking?'

One who has no sense speaks thus, and if she continues to do so (to all her suitors), some day one of them will not understand her and consider that she has no respect for people and that she is conceited. If he has power, he will make medicine and spoil that girl and cause sickness to enter. He does not realize, that she has not yet acquired enough sense and that that is the cause of her manner of speaking. By her refusal of men in this manner she causes others to laugh at her (disappointed) suitors. They talk about them and say, 'This thing (person) and that thing went to seek the daughter of So-and-so and she has refused them.' For shame's sake, a Gorenja man does not like to seek for a girl and fail.

The boy, on the second day on which he returns to court the girl, will have a guinea-fowl in his hand. He calls the *deo-dana* (lit. owner of the room, i.e. senior woman in the house) and she comes and he salutes her. He will give her some tobacco and present her with the guinea-fowl. The master of the house (*Yi-dana*) will be called and given some tobacco. He (the suitor) will salute them all and also greet the girl herself. If she happens to 'drink' a pipe (i.e. smoke), he will also give her some tobacco.

If the girl loves him, she will reveal the fact to her *tadana* (her favourite girl friend) and next time her lover comes to visit her this girl will 'come round' and talk with the youth. If she smokes she will take her pipe with her (see Fig. 52). He is expected to fill it for her, and if he fails to do so, they will ask him for some (tobacco), without fear of shame. If, however, they are too shy to ask (outright), they will take their empty pipes, and give them to him saying, 'May we give you these?' They are only making fun of him talking thus, and assuredly there is no charm against ridicule, and he must fill the pipes with tobacco. If he has no tobacco, he will put a cowrie in the pipes, instead of tobacco. If he does not give all the things I have mentioned, they will be a debt for a future day which he will return and pay. Matters go on like this. Next time he returns, he will bring three or four guinea-fowls.

It is on account of all this that some people do not agree to their children beginning early to seek for women, or wander to a place where there are girls, because they are only wasting things. A man may tell his son all this, but still the child's ears may not hear, and if the father does not want all this to go on, he will seek for some one's pretty daughter and arrange for a formal marriage between her and his child. He does so in order to compel his son 'to enter a room' (i.e. remain at home).

Oaths: If the son's ears are still closed and he does not agree to leave off (his wanderings) he, the father, will swear an oath upon him, saying: 'Behold, you are not yet old enough for marriage, yet I have found you a wife to prevent you going out. You say you will not listen to me, saying, "Who am I?" and you go out and leave some one's daughter (i.e. your girl wife) to seek a wife more attractive than the one whom I have given you. Now if you go out again and sleep out again with some person's daughter (here follows the conditional curse) (by) my father (who was slain) with an arrow, if you again take one step to go and sleep in some one's house to seek a wife, my father take a wooden club—. May they carry you home in a mat, or failing that, may you step on a snake on the ground (and may this befall you) because you consider that I am so insignificant and not fit to have begot you.'[1]

When a son hears this, he knows that his father is not playing. He will stop, and will not again step outside (the family compound).

Another may swear, 'My mother with small-pox'. This means that his mother had died of small-pox. Others swear by their *bura* (clan) and say, 'My ancestor and a fowl'; or 'My ancestor and a goat', or 'crocodile', or 'water lizard', or say, 'My grandfather with a white gown and three cowrie shells'.[2]

There are others, again, who do not object to their children doing all this, but let them wander about to other people's houses and do what they wish.

Seeking for a Wife: When a man sees a woman for the first time and thinks that he would like to have her as a wife, when he meets her outside somewhere, he will converse with her and ask her many things —whose daughter she is, the name of her house (i.e. ancestor), her father's name, the place her mother came from. All this is on account of taboos, in order to know if there is any cause of avoidance. If there is nothing to prevent it (marriage), he will one day go out well dressed. If he is shy, he will have a companion, if not, he will go alone.

---

[1] Instead of actually mentioning an arrow, the tragedy is sometimes euphemistically expressed by saying, 'My father who was wounded with a thorn'. The one who swears such an oath must go away and eat some charcoal and make an offering of flour-water on his ancestor's shrine.　　　　　　[2] See p. 392.

When he reaches her town, he will ask where So-and-so's house is, and some one will say, 'Here it is'. He will go there, 'reach' there, and enter. If there are a number of *deto* (separate women's quarters), he will ask which is that of the girl's mother, and he will climb down to the place where they sit. When he sees a comfortable place to sit down, he will not sit there, but sits down at the foot of the ladder (*dorogo*) which he has descended. When the people near by see him, and if they like his looks they will say, '*A-a-a*, don't sit there, that is not a sitting place.' He will remain silent, sitting there, in his fine attire. If the girl likes him, she will quickly spread a mat and tell him to pass inside. He will rise up, remove himself, and go to where they have allowed him a mat. If they all like him, they will do everything for his welfare. Very quickly water and a calabash drinking-cup will reach him that he may drink, as he will be thirsty after having walked there. He, too, even if he is not in need of water, must drink. Why? Because, if he were to refuse it, then after he had departed, they would say that he had not any respect for other people and only considered himself, and many words would be laid against him. That is the reason he must drink, whether he wants to or not. When he had first descended (into the yard), they had greeted him saying, '*Zare*'.[1] All the folk in the compound, when they hear that a stranger is there, descend and give him '*zare*'. After he has been sitting down for a little he will say, 'Owner of the room, let us greet each other', and the 'room owner' will come and salute him. After these salutations it (i.e. the cause of his visit) will come from his mouth. 'When thirst takes hold of you, and you hear that water is to be found here and there you will set off without delay, because you are suffering. I am now suffering for want of water and I kept asking for it and I heard your name. That is the reason my foot came here. I wish to talk to you about my need. Perhaps you may be one of those persons who takes pity on people.' The *deo-dana* (owner of the room) answers, 'You talk thus, and say that thirst has seized hold of you; you have asked for and heard the name of the owner of this compound. You have said it is my name which you have heard, but does a woman kill a snake and cut off its head (that is a man's job). What you mean is that you wish to tell the owner of this compound (*yiri-dana*) about your need, perhaps he will be better off than you are.'

The stranger says '*E*' (yes, that is so). The *deo-dana* (owner of the

---

[1] A greeting to some one whom you have not seen for a long time; derivation, *zara*, far.

room) continues, 'Oh, that is not too much to ask. You have already come, and you will see how matters stand (lit. how things are). The master of the compound (the male head of the household) now greets him, and he (the stranger) tells him the same thing. Now a *Yi-dana* is a *Yi-dana*, and he cannot give an immediate answer. He will reply, however, saying, 'What you ask is not enough, but let us wait a little while.' Then he gets up and goes out. The owner of the room will then call the girl herself and they will talk together. The man says, 'Thirst had taken hold of me and I inquired and was told that there was good water here. Before an arrow has entered, it is not difficult to pluck it out. If you do not agree, I will return home, where I will still be the same ugly fellow you think me, in the eyes of him who owns me.'

The girl replies, 'Oh! oh! oh! I never thought that you would accept something from my hands, or that I should consider myself important enough to scoop water for you, come and let us talk and follow what my household will tell you, that is the best thing to do.'

The man will then go home. If he truly loves the girl, in three days he will be back with something in his hand (tobacco for her parents). He will arrive, and salute them, talk with them, take leave (*suse*) of them and again go home. Three days later, he will return again with a guinea-fowl and tobacco, greeting the *deo-dana* first,[1] next the *yi-dana*, next his brother, but not his sons, and last of all the girl herself. Then he returns home. One day the youth will ask his male friend to accompany him to the girl's home saying, 'The red ants say that number makes for strength.'[2] Once they have arrived, this companion owns all things that day (i.e. does all the talking).

In a case where the father wishes to give his daughter to some one to marry, but the girl and her mother do not like the man, the women will remain silent and await the day when the 'wife-seeker' comes to the compound. When he arrives, they will immediately rise up and begin to break shea butter nuts. When the wife-seeker sees them breaking shea butter nuts, he will not return, he has 'hit a bad foot', and it is as if he had been poisoned.[3] This puts a stop to his going to see that girl, for if he were to continue doing so and were to marry

---

[1] It is a severe breach of etiquette to greet a man before having first saluted his wife when inside the compound. Inside a compound is considered the woman's domain. Immediately without the compound, the reverse is the case, the male must be saluted first.   [2] *Sansia yete alayam gubi nde kweyo.*

[3] The making of shea butter and cooking of beer is part of a funeral custom.

her, he would not derive any profit from it; he would not beget any children. This is a taboo among the Gorense, to marry a girl at whose house you arrive, while they are making shea butter.

(To continue.) Two or three days later, the two men will again return with two or three guinea-fowls [1] and some tobacco. When the number of these guinea-fowls has reached six to eight, the seeker after a wife will cease going to the girl's compound, and thereafter, either his elder brother, or a 'younger father' (i.e. his father's younger brother) will take charge (of the subsequent proceedings). He will take four hoes and three guinea-fowls [2] and go and greet the girl's household, and he will continue these visits until they tell him 'a good word'. Then they will tell him to bring the *bagere bono* (lit. the things for the ancestral shrine).

[Here the writer again digresses to tell us what happens in the event of there being several suitors for the girl's hand. He states:] When 'the seekers' are many and all had been encouraged by the girl's parents and they do not know what to do, they will tell these suitors (individually) to bring along the full bride-price, before they allow their daughter 'to go out'. This will cause those who have not the means to stand aside and there will remain the 'owners of hands' (*nuse dema*) (i.e. those who are prepared to come forward at once with the number of cows asked for by the parents in exchange for the girl. These cows are not generally asked for at the time of the marriage, indeed they are sometimes not claimed for twenty or more years.[3])

The remaining suitors will vie with each other, and the one who brings the full number of cows asked for, that one possesses the girl, and is told to bring the *bagere bono* (the things for the shrine of the spirits). Where the girl is an eldest daughter, these *bagere bono* consist of a ram with a fine body, and corn for making beer, which is put in a good-sized basket. These things are taken along with a cock, hen, and a guinea-fowl, to the girl's compound, and a day is settled upon for making the sacrifice. If the bride's father does not 'own himself', but there is some one who is 'heavier' than he, the corn goes to him and the sacrifice too is made at his place.

[1] Among the Nankanse, as also is the case among the majority of these tribes, grown-up women do not eat fowls.

[2] These guinea-fowls when taken are already killed, plucked, cleaned, and have been smoked and dried over a fire. Should the 'engagement' become broken off for any reason, the girl's family will offer to return them to the rejected suitor.

[3] The bride-price claimed before the girl 'goes out' is called *leɣe*; when paid subsequently to the marriage, it is called *sulle*.

The Sacrifice at the Ancestral Shrine: Wherever the shrine may be, in a room,[1] outside, or it may be a *tingani*,[2] or a *tobega*,[3] wherever it is, there the *bagere bono* are taken. Now this shrine is never anything else but that of the *segere* (guardian spirit) of the bride. Before they sacrifice to this spirit, however, they will report to the spirit which owns the compound and first brought child-bearing into that house. They will draw some beer from one of the pots and 'reach' this spirit.

He who is going to make the sacrifice sits in front of the shrine, and those who should be present are also sitting there. He removes the potsherds from the shrine,[4] some flour is added to the beer, and the owner of the shrine (*bagere-dana*) speaks to the people and says: 'I am going to sacrifice to the shrine.' They reply, 'Yes, sacrifice.' The owner of the shrine says: 'So-and-so (addressing the spirit), there is a custom common to every living thing. A man begets a child and gives her to some one (in marriage). Our ancestors did so, and we have continued doing so up to now, and the compounds stand many, for that is how houses are founded (lit. built). You own this entrance and it stands firm and prospers; if it is destroyed, its destruction lies with you. You made its foundations, then you melted like shea butter and descended into the ground and we remained and took charge. The house is still not yet worn away. There remained a small child (the speaker) and he has not failed to have a female child. People came and "whitened me",[5] and when one comes up against a wall, what can one do? We had told lies (to the various suitors for the girl's hand) and did not know what to do next, so we told them all to bring cows. Some failed and stepped back, but one refused (to be put off any longer) and said he would "whiten" me; his cows are now in the place where the cattle are, and he did not fail to bring a hoe; his sheep for the shrine is standing here; a basket of corn has been ground (for beer); his basket of flour, his two fowls and a guinea-fowl are here, and we are all assembled. A man cannot marry his own daughter. We told this man (the successful suitor) to bring the *bagere bono*, saying that, as she is your eldest child, she cannot be "taken out" without these things, if she were, perhaps you would fight with us, and it would

[1] Among the majority of the Nankanse the shrines of male ancestral spirits are outside the entrance of the compound, those of the female, inside, just as, during life, are their respective spheres of influence. [2] Sacred grove. See p. 307.

[3] See p. 310.

[4] Placed to keep fowls, &c., from walking over it.

[5] 'To whiten' any one is the Nankanse idiom for to force a person to reveal what his intentions are, or what he has in his mind.

become a headache and belly-ache matter.[1] Here I sit, and here all the rest are standing that we may give you your daughter's beer as an offering, so do not let us hear of headache or belly-ache in this, my house, do not let any one shake a foot (be bitten by a snake). My father, receive your beer and these scratching things (*pereba*), reach to her guardian spirit, that her going may be a good going. When she gets there (to her husband's home), may she stumble with a good foot (i.e. conceive) and turn into a house bug (*bubsere*), which is always to be found at home. Let her off-spring be numerous so that the man (her husband) may not say that he has thrown away his cows in the long grass. May I never hear that she or her husband has headache or belly-ache. May their mouths not disagree together. May they not make a loud noise and people hear them quarrelling in their houses. If you are indeed a thing, you will surely "have" (i.e. look after) them; you are a builder up of compounds.'

Now, he lays both his hands upon the shrine, saying, 'Well, my father, receive beer, you yourself know (what we wish); it is not I, who tell you to do this and that.' When the beer has been given, he will give the cock, saying, 'Well, my father, if you have received the beer, now accept your cock, he (the bridegroom) has caught a fowl without grudging it; he wishes you to do him good; here is a guinea-fowl in addition; all these things are for you.'

He then 'cuts' the fowl and blood falls on the shrine, and when the fowl begins to flutter, he casts it down, and the fowl beats on the ground *pa-pa-pa* and turns over and lies on its back. Every one claps their hands, because the spirit has accepted. Every one's belly is washed, but those of the in-laws more than all the rest.

If the fowl 'refuses' (i.e. does not fall on its back) it means that the spirit has refused (the offerings). They will rise up and go to the soothsayer to consult in order that the spirit may tell them what is wrong. Then they will return and remove that wrong before they do anything else, and again kill a fowl, and when it is received, they know that the spirit has now agreed to what they asked.

They next sacrifice the guinea-fowl, saying: 'Receive also your guinea-fowl; a poor man's guinea-fowl is a goat; accept it, I cannot repeat all again; in the manner in which your belly has been washed, let theirs also be washed. A man does not do good to you, in order that you may spoil him.'

---

[1] All the ills that the flesh is heir to are summed up in this phrase.

Children take the fowl and guinea-fowl and pluck the feathers, and the Elders now move on to the spot where the one who owns the shrine of the girl's guardian spirit lives. They take with them another pot of beer, the sheep, and the (remaining) fowl and arrive at the place where the owner of the shrine is sitting before it and they sit down beside him. They give him the calabash used in making offerings, and one man takes some flour and puts it in and pours some beer on top from the pot.

The owner of the shrine removes the pieces of broken pottery from the top of the shrine, lays both hands on it and calls out the name of such and such a spirit, and calls out the name of the spirit to whom he has already sacrificed, saying: 'You have received yours, to-day the sacrificial things stand here in plenty, do you now set out and reach her guardian spirit (*segere*). It has been able to look after her well and she has survived until to-day, the owner of a nose (i.e. of life) and we are arranging her marriage to-day, so come hither both of you and receive your daughter's beast.' When he has finished saying this, he again lays hold of the shrine with his two hands, saying:

'On the day when the child was delivered, you received something and became her guardian spirit. Before her mother had fallen from the waist (i.e. had her menses) for the last time, you had begun to declare that you were the owner of the seed which was in her womb. Of a truth she was delivered and you refused to change your mind and continued to say that you owned it. I too, I did not strike the mouth strings (i.e. argue) but took her and gave her to you and you have guarded her until to-day. She has become a maiden and is ready to go to a person's house, and it is on account of this that the seekers after a wife kept coming here. I kept driving them away, saying that she was not old enough, but without avail . They were numerous and every 'head' of them (every one) hit himself on the chest (boasting about his possessions) and I did not know what path to follow, since it is not our custom to consult the soothsayers before giving our daughters in marriage. That is why I told them to bring the bride price (*leye*) in advance. This they said they would do, and some failed, but there was one who refused to be shamed (*nyane*) and did all I asked, and reached whiteness (a clear mutual understanding). Thus I came up against a wall and was compelled to tell him, "Drive your cows hither". Because she is an eldest child, he has brought your offerings, and a cow now stands in the cattle kraal. He has poured out corn into a basket for making beer; corn for making grain cakes he has poured out into a basket. The corn has been ground. He retained in his hands two fowls and a guinea-fowl. Your sheep was among them. All these matters I have reported to those who should be told and they agreed and ground the corn and put it into water the day before yesterday that I might be able to give you (beer) to-day. That is why I have called you, that you too may summon those who ought to be called and that you may assemble in one place and receive your things. Well, receive a calabash of beer and drink, and receive your ram which stands there and go and reach this one and that one (other spirits).'

When he has finished speaking thus, he stirs with his middle finger the beer, mixes it, and pours it on top of the shrine, saying, 'Receive, receive, and hold her firmly', and those who are sitting around clap their hands. When this is finished, they give her *segere* the fowl, cutting its throat and letting the blood drip on the shrine, *twu-ru-ru-ru*; it flutters and he casts it down and it flaps about *pa-pa-pa-pa* and lies on its back, visible to all, and they all clap their hands because the guardian spirit has accepted it.

Next comes the ram; one holds 'here', another holds the head, another has the earthen plate to catch the blood. Here is one with a knife; it is set on the ram's throat and the blood flows into the earthen plate. When it has almost finished flowing, they pass the ram to the owner of the shrine, who receives it with both hands and holds it over the shrine so that the blood falls upon it, and again he says, 'Receive your ram.' He lays it down, and those whose duty it is to skin it, skin it, and cut up the meat in portions, and take away the parts that are to be roasted. These are, the liver, a piece of meat off the hind leg, a piece off the back. All the rest of the meat is put inside the skin and this is placed against the shrine that it may receive its meat. The meat that was for roasting is roasted by children, and when this has been done, the owner of the *shrine* offers it to the spirit, and if his belly has been washed about the marriage (i.e. if he is pleased about it) he gives it the liver, in addition to the meat off the hind leg. The remainder of the meat is shared out, omitting nobody, however small the portion has to be (to make it go round). The two fowls and the guinea-fowl are put on a fire (and cooked whole, *vule*); the entrails are then removed, but the liver is put back in each. The flesh of the sheep and of the guinea-fowl is cooked inside the compound by the women; male children cook the fowls outside, because women when full grown, are not allowed to touch a fowl. They make soup (*sele*) of the blood; they make grain food (*sayabo*). The portion for the shrine, which will later become the share of the head of the compound, consists of grain food, on top of which is placed a hind leg of the ram and its liver, the livers of the fowls and of the guinea-fowl, and a small piece of the flesh off the leg of each. When he is given these he will again 'sit down upon his toes' and make his offering as before. First he will give (the spirit) some cold water, next he takes some of the grain food, some of the liver, and meat off the hind legs, and squeezes all in his hand and dips it in the blood soup and offers it. Next he takes some dry food (*gaare*) and says 'Accept this too, and any one who gives you *gaare*, you too give him *gaare*.' Again, he pours cold water on top of the shrine, saying, 'Receive cold water and wet your mouth.'

Before the shrine has had its offering, no one must take any of the food and put it in his mouth.

All this takes place before dark, because after the ceremony at the shrines and the eating of the food, the girl will 'go out' and follow the 'strangers' (i.e. the bridegroom's representative and his relatives) home. The portions are shared according to custom; an elder, a hind leg, next in seniority (*tarima*), a foreleg; the owner of the shrine, a hind leg, that one from which a small piece of meat has been cut for the spirits. The fowl's flesh will be shared among the young children (of both sexes). If the women are many, the senior wife of the master of the compound takes a leg of the guinea-fowl. The eldest son takes a leg of the fowl. When there is not enough for others, the neck and heads and feet are given to them.

When they are sharing out the grain food, one portion is set aside for the stranger[1] and the girl, and they put the two together in a room, or in the kitchen, to eat. The *yi-dana* now tells the *deo-dana* to allow the strangers to return home because it is getting dark.

The girl's mother gathers together her child's belongings, her leaves, waist-strings, beads, and all are put in a small calabash (*wula*).[2] When all is ready, the *deo-dana* will tell the *yi-dana*, saying, 'I have finished.' The strangers will rise up and take their leave, saying, 'We shall return now', and they answer, 'Oh, if it must be so, you must return some other day and we shall talk together again.'

---

[1] During the whole ceremony, the bridegroom is not present, but is represented by either his brother, or his father's younger brother.

[2] On divorce, this has to be returned by her husband's family to the girl's family, see p. 151.

When they have finished saying good-bye, they leave the compound, and the *yi-dana* rises up and embraces his 'father' (i.e. his shrine) with both hands and says, 'Eh! my father, the girl will go out, follow her, that she may stumble well (i.e. soon conceive); do not let me hear about her having headache or belly-ache or she will not be able to work. When she reaches where she is going and "her waist falls", let it do so only once; well, father, accept my congratulations.'

They now set out for the husband's home. The mother and the sister of the girl may accompany her a little of the way. When she reaches the village (of the bridegroom) they make her enter the house of 'an elder sister' of hers, a *poyablega*.[1] There she remains three days before she goes to her husband's house. During these three days her husband may send his best friend (a man) to stay with her. This man may sleep on the same mat as the girl. He will not touch her, that is a black taboo. The husband may accompany his friend, and all three lie on the same mat. After three days she enters her husband's home. Her husband's neighbours play and dance many kinds of dances for many days. When the girl enters her new home for the first time they give her the hospitality due to a stranger, but when she is getting this (special) treatment, if she loves her husband, she will start working and not take any notice of her privileges as 'a stranger', but try to work herself. She will help the others to grind grain; she will descend to the river to fetch water, she will sweep up refuse, doing all these things as it were before daybreak (i.e. before it is really expected of her). Any misgivings they might have had about her are removed and they know that they have got a real woman. In a few days she will descend into the kitchen with her 'mother' (her husband's mother).

When she comes among (her new relations) she will not call her husband's father by his real name; she will call him 'my father'. Her husband's brother she will call 'lover' (*zaba*). They too will not address her by her real name, but will take her town's name and call her by it.[2]

The First Visit of the Bride's 'Brothers' to their Newly Married Sister: A few days later her 'brothers' will follow her,[3] and her husband's family will kill the things known as *beseno bono* (the going-after-some-one's-things). When they arrive, they cannot enter the compound

---

[1] Any woman from the bride's village of her generation is so called.

[2] See p. 3.

[3] If the bride were the last of the daughters of a family, only her mother, accompanied by a small girl, will visit her on this occasion.

before the family have brought out a fowl and flour and water.[1]
If they have the necessary things to kill for the visitors, they must
show these to them first, and if they are not satisfied with them,
because perhaps they are not fat enough, they (the 'brothers') may
tell them to add a well-fattened dog, or a fat male goat. Should the
visitors see any fat animal which they have not produced, they will
keep on refusing any other, until they bring that one. The strangers
do what they like in the compound. If the compound folk make some
mistake, the bride's 'brothers' may refuse to accept anything, and will
tell them that they only killed the things in order to eat them themselves, in which case their brother-in-law will have to appease them
by giving them a fowl.[2]

When they have finished eating—not sharing anything with their
hosts and only giving the women who have cooked for them the
stomach of one of the animals tied round with its intestines—they
set off to return home, led by their *isiga*,[3] who accompanies them
some of the way, receiving a foreleg from them, before he turns
back—the share of an *isiga* is always a foreleg, he may not have
a hind leg. When the bride's 'brothers' are nearing home again, they
sit down by the side of the path and take all the meat which they
have not eaten from their bags and share it out according to custom.

Divorce, and the part taken by the Wula *Calabash in the Marriage
Ceremony*: The *wula* calabash which was given to the girl on the day
of her 'going out' is an important thing. When the girl reaches her
husband's home, and they fail to keep her because her 'doings' are
not good—if, for example, she shows laziness; has ears that do not hear;
tells tales; is slovenly; is barren; and, in addition has a long hand
(*nu woko*), i.e. steals—this calabash, which was given to her by her
mother, and she took to her husband's home, will be taken by the
Yi-dana (of the husband) and sent back with the wife to her parents.
If they are very angry with her, they will send her back with it. If
afraid to do so, they will wait until a day when she is paying a visit
to her people, when they will return it by the *posigera*.[4] This means
that the husband has divorced her.

Sandono in the Marriage Ceremony: A few days after the bride's
'brothers' have returned home after visiting their 'sister', the bride-

---

[1] These gifts are called *loko yere bono*, i.e. the things to remove the quiver from the
shoulder.

[2] There is clearly a privileged familiarity about the whole occasion, see p. 336.

[3] See p. 282.   [4] See p. 149.

groom will seek for a guinea-fowl, kill it, pluck it, and clean it, add some tobacco and a live cock, and send the *posigera* with them to go and perform the *sandono* ceremony (*lu loka la sandono*).[1] This ceremony is to show that they (i.e. the husband's family) have now married the girl and own her hands and feet. The *posigera* will set out to the bride's home, and when he reaches there, will go to the house of the bride's father's half-brother (*sɔ-bia*). He will salute him, and give him the cock, saying that he has come to 'let fall' So-and-so's *sandono*.

The Elder receives the fowl. There still remains the guinea-fowl and the tobacco. Setting off again, the *posigera* goes to the compound of those who owned the bride. When he reaches there he climbs down (into the yard) and greets her mother, takes the dead guinea-fowl and the tobacco and says, 'Here is my "mother's"[2] (the bride's) *sandono*.' He also greets the head of the house and says the same thing. The *deo-dana* will cook him some grain food and allow him to return home in the evening.

After this ceremony has been performed the woman is no longer considered as a *yi yea* (a member of that household, i.e. her parent's household). She has now become 'some person's' wife.[3] That man is now responsible for the woman (her debts and actions). Unless the *sandono* has been made, the woman is not a wife, she is just 'a house person'.

In the event of divorce, the *wula* calabash is handed by the *posigera* to the one to whom he had given the *sandono* cock, and he is informed that her husband's people say that they do not want the woman and that if her relations do not come quickly and take her away, and should anything happen to her, that they (her husband's family) will not be responsible. He will send a boy at once, to tell the girl's father that they (her husband's people) do not want his daughter any longer. The father will send at once to her husband's village to inquire the reason, asking, 'Does she steal or fly?' (i.e. is she a witch). They reply, 'No, she does not steal, nor does she fly, only we don't want her.' Then they rise up and return home, and when the *wula* calabash is sent back the husband's people know that they no longer own her, but that her own house people possess her once more.[4]

---

[1] This, it will be noted, is the essential part of the legal ceremony of marriage.

[2] The *posigera's* own mother must always be a woman from the same town as the bride.   [3] *Pɔya* = wife; *pɔka* = woman.

[4] If a wife is an old woman, her husband may not divorce her, or if she is sick. If she had children, and the man had demanded back his cows, the wife's relations would in turn demand the children.

The Mating of Lovers:[1] Girls, who are kept as lovers only, but not married, are those whom we address as 'sisters' (*tapa*), but they are not children of our own father or mother but women of the same town (*teŋa*) who have the same taboos as ourselves and belong to a section founded by a *sɔ-bia* (half-brother) of the first ancestor. These are they whom we call *tapa*. The method of seeking a wife and seeking a lover are the same, the only difference is that you cannot marry a *zaba* (lover), and you do not give hoes (or cows), and that children born of such unions belong to the girl's parents. [Here follows a description of the courting of such a woman at her own compound. It is done quite openly with the full consent of her parents and the story follows the lines of an ordinary courtship already described. The narrator thus describes a dialogue between the man and the girl:] The throat of the male is heard saying: 'See, you are my *tapa* (sister in the classificatory sense). I may not marry you any day at all, but a man learns how to make love to women from his "sister". If one does not seek one's sister, how will he understand the finding of wives and avoid being laughed at by them. On account of this, I looked and saw you alone near this our dwelling-place, a good girl, whom my sense and soul (*sia*) prefers; Well, I will finish speaking. If you do not want to hold conversation with me, I know where I came up' (referring to the wooden ladder he had climbed to get over the wall leading into her yard).

[The man continues visiting the girl's compound, always taking tobacco and guinea-fowls and trying hard to ingratiate himself with her parents, and especially with the *deo-dana* (senior woman in the house); Aboya describes a scene between the suitor and this dame caused by the former having failed to salute the latter before noticing any one else.]

When you salute some one else first, you have spoiled your case. If she can control her anger, it will be the better for you, and she may do so if you happen to be an old acquaintance of hers and you know

---

[1] We have not any exact equivalent of the custom about to be described. It is not concubinage nor is it promiscuity. It really arises from the fact that the girl and the youth who fall in love with each other happen (according to tribal law) to be in a prohibited degree of marriage relationship with each other. They are from the same 'town' and of the same age class and are thus in the classificatory sense 'brother' and 'sister' and may not contract a legal marriage. Whether what is here described results from a breaking down of tribal authority, or whether the custom actually had the parent's authorization in ancient times, it is not easy to state. I am inclined towards the latter opinion.

each other's bellies (i.e understand each other). If, however, you are only a new comer and are guilty of such an impertinence (as to salute some one else first) she will 'wash your eyes for you' and you will begin to know that all people are not equal. She will say, 'Because no one respects you, do you come to look upon me as also as small (of no account), and do the people of your household have these manners? Who am I to possess a *deo* (room)? Who am I to waste your salutations upon? I did not call you to come here.' When she addresses you thus, you do not know where to rise up and go. You sit there hanging your head and feeling light and like a thief who has stolen a goat.

[In course of time the man is given a room at the girl's compound.] He will sleep there and they will give them a separate mat and a separate room in order that they may be able to talk freely and shyness not have them. He can now go there any time he wants. If the girl has not yet been 'cut',[1] she will not agree to the man having sexual intercourse with her. If she loves him very much perhaps she may agree. In the latter case, when the time approaches for the ceremony, she will tell her lover and let him know the day, and her mother, who knows that her daughter has loved much, will not hide the day from him.

On the day when the *pukubega* (the man who performs the operation) arrives, the man will go to him quickly when no one sees and pay him about one thousand cowries (value about 1*s*.) or a hoe, telling him that the girl is his lover and that he had 'known her' (*mi ka*). He will say to him, 'When you come to cut her and find that she has lost her virginity (*suuliŋo*),[2] be silent, don't tell any one but say she is a white *yablega*.' If he had not been given this payment of one thousand cowries and a hoe he would reveal her great shame before many people and they would laugh at her very much. She would hide herself among her neighbours and they will spread the news everywhere that she is not a virgin but had known a man before 'cutting'.

The one who led her into shame and did not attempt to help her, he will fail ever to get her again and will no more go to her home. On that day the father and mother of the girl will blame her and call her a rascal, but it is too late to abuse her.

When a girl has been cut and is still confined to her room, it is

---

[1] The Nankanse, like many other of these tribes, practise incision; in this case, the operation is performed about the age of puberty. See p. 165.

[2] *Ka suulia*, she is spoiled.

taboo for her to speak to her lover until she has 'washed her hands'. Hand washing is this: The man will seek four hundred cowries, catch two to four guinea-fowls and send these things to the *deo-dana* and she will give the one who is attending to the *yabega* (girl who has been 'cut'). The guinea-fowls and some grain food are cooked, and the man and girl are put in a room. Four of the cowries are taken and put into the water in which they are going to wash their hands. They wash their hands and eat the food. The four cowries are then taken out and put on a string and tied round her waist. If this were not done she would always have a grievance against him. Four days after being 'cut', she may sit in public. On that day her lover will catch about six guinea-fowls and ask about eight of his friends to go and fetch firewood. He will buy waist-strings; if he is able he will buy 'leather leaves'[1] and salt and *dawa dawa*,[2] and his mother will make shea butter. All these things he will take to his lover.

Thus the man and his 'sister' hold converse until the day when she will be married, or until she steals a belly ('to steal a belly' is said of an unmarried girl who becomes *enceinte*) with her lover.

As soon as she knows that their work has come to light, she is very anxious to get married. If those who own her do not know and do not hasten (to find her a husband) she will run off to some place to marry. Such things cause some girls to marry in haste. Some girls, however, will never allow their lovers to have intercourse with them before they are 'cut'. Such a one will say, 'do not be in such haste, let me get "cut" first, for I don't wish to get "cut" and be disclosed to be *suuliyo* (not a virgin) and have people laughing at me.' The male may say, 'Cannot I pay (bribe) the *pukubega* ?' 'No,' she says, 'for if you do not happen to be there on that day (when the incision ceremony is performed) who is going to bear the brunt of all this; oh! you are in such a hurry, are you going away anywhere; have you never heard that to do a thing in a hurry may make up for the want of the relish but it does not appease the real hunger ?'[3] The man replies, 'How can a fowl sleep with a grain of corn without eating it ?' But the girl will refuse, until the day of her 'cutting' and come forth from the ceremony a white *yabega*. On that day her parents will praise her lover, and say he is a live man, for they do not know that he had fought and been defeated.

When the girl has finished all her 'cutting matters', what excuse

---

[1] See p. 332.   [2] *Parkia filicoidea.*
[3] *Atɔtɔ mare la valega gye ka maara kom.*

will she make now for not giving herself to her lover? If she continues to make excuses the man will go away and leave her.

When the day comes for the girl to marry, that day is sour for them both. The man does not want his lover to marry, the girl does not want to leave her lover. Seekers after her in marriage, when they perceive that her lover has influence over her, offer him presents to advance their suit. The lover may try and persuade her to marry some one from whom he has received payment, instead of the man arranged by her parents, in order to spite them all. Or, again, if he has no real power over her, he may deceive her, saying, 'Let us go here'; he will have told the wife-seeker where they are going, and he will go there and seize the girl and carry her off. When the man returns home, he will say, 'As we were returning from the market, we were stopped and your daughter was carried off. I was alone, what could I do against many?'

If the girl does not like the man who has carried her off she will run away from him; if she does, she will return home and tell her mother, saying, 'It was a good compound, but I came back on account of you'. The man will follow her and visit them and they will give her to him as a wife.

Custody of Children in the event of Divorce, and certain other Matters arising out of Divorce: When a woman marries some place and bears a male child there, and later 'goes out' (i.e. is divorced) and marries again somewhere else, and there bears only daughters by her second husband, this second marriage is a cause of sadness to her son. Why? Because he will never own the things (i.e cows) which will be received for them should they live. These will belong to his half-sisters' father's family and not to his own father. His mother too, who bore this male child, does not own him if his father (her first husband) is still alive.[1]

He has nothing to do with the house-people of that place (i.e. of his mother's new home). Even were he to go and stay with them and work for them, he cannot get any profit there, only his food. They are not concerned to find a wife for him; even if he finds one for himself, they (his mother's second husband's people) will not perform the *malego* or *beseyo* ceremony and kill a small fowl to take off the quivers (*ye loko*).[2] All this will cause him (the son by the first husband) to be annoyed at his mother getting a divorce and thus causing him to

---

[1] After the death of his father, he will visit his mother, but not during the lifetime of his own father, for 'he and the second husband are enemies'.

[2] See p. 150–51.

'eat poverty'. It will not be so bad for this child if his own father dies and leaves plenty things. In that case he will not return to his mother.

As for the mother, if she does not bear a child by her second husband, she will want to return to her first husband's family; if her second husband does not treat her properly, she will certainly go back to her son, leaving her daughters whom she had by the second husband. She will do so because she knows her son is the one to give her 'water' when she dies.

Should the woman bear both male and female children by her second husband, she will remain where she is, but failing that, she is going (eventually) to return to her first husband's compound where her son is. When she does so, it may be that her first husband's people do not care to have her back and they may open their mouths, and what she had done in the past may come forth. They may say, 'You, who go wandering about, and return to trouble us, why don't you get out and go back whence you came.'

Another man, when his wife, whom he loves much, leaves him, is up at every daybreak wandering to consult the soothsayers until the sun enters again. If he has it in his power, he will make (lit. do) medicine to kill his enemy (the man she has run off to). If he has not power in his own kindred group, he may go somewhere else and 'put his mouth' (make a vow) to some one's shrine saying, 'If you kill my enemy I will give you a dog and a goat.' If the shrine consents and sends medicine 'to cut the throat' of that person, when he hears that his enemy is dead, he will run with what he had promised, in order to redeem 'his mouth' (i.e. his vow).

When a man marries a woman who was (until he took her) another man's wife, he may go with her to a shrine called *pɔyɔ-kwem-dokko* (strong wife pot) and make medicine and both will eat it. When they have done so, and the first husband wants to send medicine to kill them, it will not do them any harm.

VII

THE MAN WHO MADE A VOW TO A RIVER

THERE was once a man who went and put a river in his mouth (i.e. made a vow to a river), saying that if he begat plenty male children so that the quiver-hanger in his house broke,[1] he would give it (the river) a human being. Of a truth he begat and 'built a house' and the quivers hung on the peg *zororo*. His sons also married and begat grandsons, and great-grandsons. Now, one day as he was sitting there, the *zalega* peg broke and his children ran and told him saying, 'Father, the quiver peg has broken'. He sat with his hand resting upon his chin and said, 'What is that you say?' They again said, 'The *zalega* (quiver) peg has broken.' He remained silent and slept without eating food and it was as if he were crying. When others were talking in the house he did not know that they were talking at all; he was as if a bone had stuck in his throat. Now his eldest son, the one who sat with him and did not move from him, looked at what he was doing and did not understand, and he asked, saying, 'Father what has possessed you?' He is silent. He again asked, 'Father what is your heart saying, it is time now you told me?' The man opened his mouth to speak and tears flowed, then the son began to know that the matter was serious. He continued asking him, refusing to sleep until his father said, 'Do not you see that this compound has been built up so large, now it only remains for it to fall down. I once went and made a vow to the river saying that if I built up a house and it became filled with male children and came to possess so many quivers hanging up, that the *zalega* peg broke with their weight, I would give it a human being. Behold it has broken. This has spoiled my heart.'

Now the name of the river was *Akwakule*. The son answered, 'If that is so, let it be, do not let your heart spoil too much.' He called his neighbours (i.e. his brothers) together in front of the father and told them what had happened, and he said, 'Find a good sheep and give me', and the father gave the son a good ram, and he said they should kill it. They killed and skinned it and cut the meat in pieces. He told them to take the stomach, and they took it and emptied it

---

[1] The quivers of a father and his sons are all hung up on a single peg called *zalega*. To say that this breaks, implies that a man has such a large number of male children that the peg cannot support the weight.

of grass. He said they must cook the sheep and take the blood and make *selle*. So the women took the blood and made *selle* and also prepared grain food. The son washed out the sheep's stomach with water, and they brought the grain food and cut it in small pieces and put it in the stomach, and he took the fat of the sheep and put it in the sheep's stomach, and he also put its flesh inside. The soup made out of blood was also put there. Then he tied up the stomach and he said, 'Get the horses ready', and they did so quickly. The father rode one, and the son too rode one. They set out, taking the stomach of the sheep which had been filled with meat, *selle*, grain food, and they reached the river, and he (the son) told his father to call the river. And the father called out:

Akwakule O!

Akwakule O!

The river answered, and he said: 'Once I said with my mouth, that if I built a house and male children came to hang their quivers so that the *zalega* peg broke, I would give you a human being. Behold, here is your person here.' They took the sheep's stomach and let it fall into the water, *twiriti*!

They then went back to the compound. Akwakule mounted the river bank, shouting 'Hey! Hey!', but they went on without looking behind.

Akwakule also called his companions to assemble and told them all that had happened. They told him to bring the stomach for them to see. Akwakule brought the stomach containing the meat, *selle*, and grain food, and placed it before them. 'Mm, Mm,' they said, 'Akwakule, you know the truth but want to trouble us, now who eats grain food except a person, and *selle* meat, and fat; you have received your man, killed him, and chewed all, and now you are only troubling people, you said you never received a person, then where did you get a person's stomach from? You did get a man; they have paid you; you have no longer any debt.'

If a man does not remember to return and fulfil his vows, his house, people, children, girls and boys, wives, cows, sheep, donkeys, and winged creatures, will soon be lost and his walls easily pulled down.

No one will know the cause. A soothsayer will eventually reveal it, but by that time the people will be finished. You must remember your vows, and give quickly what you promised, and thus save your house. If you do not do so, it were better that you had not made any promises.

In a house where a spirit has killed, because of broken promises, all the private property (*logoro*) is gathered together and becomes the property of that spirit; it becomes its *bagere bono* (shrine things). If even a small thing remains, it is as if the debt had not been paid. After all has been paid, there is peace.

The Man who would not give a Cow to his Father

A Goreŋa man is fonder of having children than anything else. The one reason for this is, that when he is dead he has many sons remaining to sacrifice to him, and people will continue saying, 'That is the house of So-and-so'. If you die, and have no sons remaining, you will not get 'water' to drink.

There was once a man who died and he left nothing, but his son, by hard trying, got a cow. His father (i.e. his spirit) asked for it, but the son gave him only fowls. The father asked many times, but without success. At last he said he would kill his son. Now, there was a man living there who could see the spirits of the dead. One day a number of spirits assembled and sat down, and all those whose children had given them cows had taken the skins and were wearing them. The father of the man who was always giving his father fowls also came and sat down with his head a wild mass of fowls' feathers. They discussed what they had come to talk about and were rising up to go away, when a big wind blew, and hit the father on his head and blew all the feathers about. All the spirits laughed heartily. The child's father gathered himself up and fetched a *kurugu* (wooden mallet) and in spite of opposition from the rest of the spirits was going to strike and kill his son. They repeatedly held him back, and at last succeeded in dissuading him. The man who had been watching them went and told the son and advised him to give his father a cow, but he was wholly of another mind, saying that it could not be 'worked' (*tone*). The man said to the son, 'Follow me', and he went, and there were the spirits sitting in a line. The wind blew again, and the fowls' feathers blew all about the father's head, and again the spirits laughed heartily. The father again rose up and fetched a wooden mallet to go and kill his child, but the remainder of the spirits again succeeded in stopping him.

The man said to the child, 'That is your father struggling with the wooden mallet to hit and kill you, because you do not give him a cow. Cannot you see his neighbours wearing cow skins, and the wind carrying about the feathers of the fowls you are always giving your father? If you do not kill this cow, you know that you are a dead thing.'

So the child returned home and caught a cow and killed it for his father. Now, when he had finished killing the cow and taking the skin and cutting up the meat and setting it down (at the shrine), the man again took him to stand in the former place. There they were, coming with the meat, walking in a long line, with his father in front with a tail in his hand walking proudly, while they (the remainder of the spirits) followed.

When the child saw all this he wished to rush off to take back some of the meat, but the man said, 'The meat has not gone from where you left it at home.' So they returned home, and of a truth, there was the meat lying just as it was before, none of it had been taken. After that the child's father did him good; he farmed and bought many cows, and filled the cattle-yard full.

This is the reason why Gorense always want children beyond all else.

Female Children

Now, there is something to say about female children. These grow up, marry, and their family receive cows and in turn get wives with these cows. If you have only male children, it is difficult to secure wives for them.

When one sees some one's child and loves her, her parents will speak against him, saying that his house has no daughters, and even if she runs off to him, they will bring her back quickly and not permit her to conceive, for in that case they could not bring her back.[1] For such a family, there is nothing for them to do but hard work on the farms to get enough for eating and have enough left over to allow beasts to be bought. First they will rear fowls and guinea-fowls to exchange for goats and sheep; goats and sheep breed and are in turn exchanged for cattle and all things necessary for marriage.

The Children of a House-person (*Ỹi-yeen bia*): When a Goreŋa man has only got girls, it is as if the house was to become a ruin, because they will all scatter and go away to people's houses leaving their father and mother sitting there on their toes.

Sometimes a man who has no male children allows one of his daughters to sit in the compound and mate like the animals and bear a male child. [The father of the child will be some man in the girl's own section, or in a prohibited degree of relationship to her, which will prevent him marrying her legally and thus claiming the child.]

[1] Once a wife has conceived, she may neither be sent back to her parents by her husband, nor taken back by her own people. Should a man try to send his wife home when in this condition, the parents will say, 'First take out your own arrow' (*foe fo pim*).

An eldest daughter is never allowed to sit in the compound and bear children [1] so long as her father and mother are alive, that is taboo; the children 'behind' her may do so. Those who seek her go there, and she chooses him whom she loves, and sits at home and bears children. [2] [These 'house-person's children', as they are called, will be the same clan as their grandfather. The mother will not take a lover out of the same kindred 'section' [3] as she herself belongs, but from another 'section' of the same kindred group, e.g. one founded by a half-brother of the original common ancestor.]

This is not a marriage. It is only a sowing of seed. Such a child may never become the head of a 'section'. A daughter who sits at home and has given birth to two or three male children will then try and get a husband. She will not wish always to remain in her parents' compound because the household have not any real respect for her. 'Sister's children' [as a house-person's children are also called] have no position and cannot ever gather power (kyeɲo). The children 'behind' them will gather power which they have not tasted (vege). When a sacrifice is made, a Goreɲa's eldest child receives a hind leg, but as for 'sister's children', however old or large they are, they can never receive more than a foreleg until they die. It is on account of all this that our daughters do not care 'to sit in the house' and bear children. As long as such children's grandfathers and grandmothers are alive, things are not so bad for them (lit. it is a little better), but they go away with 'their part of life' and it is a sorrowful thing for the survivors. They then become helpless people. However many they become, they never have any real status. They cannot sacrifice to their grandfather, only to their grandmother. She then takes the offering and 'reaches' her husband and they eat. Sometimes, however, the grandfather may become Ɣini [4] to his grandson, in which case he may sacrifice to him directly. Otherwise the grandfather's spirit cannot go directly to his grandson, as he could if he were his own son.

A 'sister's child' when it grows up will always reproach its mother because she has brought him low status (torogo).

---

[1] She may not, even if legally married, ever have intercourse with her husband in her parents' compound.

[2] The zaba (lover) will work for the girl's grandfather and also bring presents for the girl's parents. He will not cohabit with her openly, but will come by stealth at night. He has not any claim over the woman or children.

[3] See footnote, p. 202. [4] See pp. 307–8.

VIII

SOME FURTHER CUSTOMS CONCERNING SPIRITS. THE EDUCATION OF GIRLS. INCISION. THE GIVING OF *SANDONO* IN MARRIAGE. *PAALA* (DESTINY OR PRE-DESTINATION). A *KUMPIO*, THE CALABASH IN WHICH REPOSES A WOMAN'S SOUL DURING HER LIFETIME

AS I have already told you, when a woman has given birth to a female child, she may, on the fourth day, go out into the yard of the compound and walk about among people. The reason why she comes out on the fourth day is because the number four is the woman's number, while three is the number for the male.

On that day the ashes from her room are taken, together with an old broom, to the cross-roads leading to the woman's country, and here the ashes are poured out and the old broom placed on top and a potsherd placed on top of all. After this she returns and shaves her head all round the base of it.

Now, during all the time the woman had been pregnant, the *Yi-dana* (head of the house)[1] had been going about consulting sooth-sayers, and on the day the girl had been delivered he had run with 'water' to give to the shrine whose spirit he had been told by the soothsayers would become the newborn child's guardian spirit (*segere*). He tells it that the girl has been delivered, and asks it to take proper care of the mother and the child and allow the infant to grow up in order that she may herself live to thank her guardian spirit for having protected her and her mother during birth. He also asks the *segere* to see that the mother has good milk that the child may never fail to get food. When the baby comes to grow a little, she is presented to the shrine (*bagere*) which possessed her when she lay in the womb and had life, which has now become her *segere*.

At the shrine of a guardian spirit is a pot containing roots soaked in water. Some of this water is given to the infant to drink. There are some infants, however, whose *sega* (plural of *segere*) do not permit them to be forced to drink; if such a child is forced, it will die. There are many children whose heads are shaved on the day on which they are given to their *sega*. 'Water' is continually given to the

[1] Not necessarily the woman's husband.

segere until the child is about three years old. After that the mother will stop suckling it, begin again to have her menses, 'see' her husband, and unite with him once more.

About eight years of age, when a girl can work and use reason, her mother is always showing her how to sweep out the rooms and yard, and how to wash plates and calabashes. The girl herself will also learn little things from her companions—how to twist *kenkase* grass bangles, how to wear her leaves properly; she will at first only wear leaves behind, *vokapela*, *kenkarega kenkalega*, *nyea*, and *lua* leaves.[1] When she nears puberty and 'strikes' having breasts, she learns how to weave and wear *visi* in place of always wearing leaves. If her mother is a potteress or a basket-maker, the girl will sit and watch her mother at work and the mother will also instruct her a little. She will follow her mother in the rainy season time, when the shea butter trees bear fruit and learn how to collect the nuts and make shea butter oil. She learns how to grind corn and fetch water; the making of grain foods and how to make soup stews, in order to know how to do all these things in the future. Her mother shows her how girls should sleep on a mat with a man who is not her husband.[2] The mother teaches her daughter thus, and if she follows her advice, people will say that So-and-so has a good daughter. She advises her not to run after boys, telling her that if a girl always runs after boys she will be called a *bon-bareŋa* (a worthless thing). She says, 'Do not be of a flighty character, such conduct causes the good in a person to be wasted. When you and your companions are together somewhere, don't let your mouth rise higher than theirs, that is how a person gets a bad character given her, and how bad characters are formed. You do not want people to say that you are not a good girl. That will "pour you out" and cause the loss of your things and of ours. If you are talking with a person, let sense live in what you say, that will keep your head high, and you will be able to live with a husband and enjoy your things. Do not laugh at old men or old women, or if you see a person with part of his body crooked. When you laugh at such people they will "do" you and not say that you are some one's good daughter.' When she learns dancing with her companions the mother says, 'Beware of wildness in dancing, and of dancing new steps on your own, that will only bring you the reputation of being a lighthead; conduct such as that pours everything away.'

When she follows her companions to attend an incision ceremony,

---

[1] See also pp. 331–2   [2] See pp. 169 and 280.

her mother instructs her how to behave in a strange town, so that a bad report of her may not be brought back among the compounds. Her mother says, 'Be gentle that my heart may not be sick.' If a girl has sense she will follow this advice. Her mother will buy her wrist bangles, elephant teeth bangles, beads, waist-strings (*valese* and *sebese*) and everything a woman needs.

Now the girl will think about nothing else but dressing up, and when she hears that there is dancing somewhere, she will not fail to be there. She will now have many suitors, and tobacco and guinea-fowls and many other things will be brought to the mother. These are the fruits and profits of her child-bearing.

Incision[1]: The girl is now ripe and full grown and is old enough to 'cut'. She herself will go and break firewood and make it into a good bundle and place it in her mother's room, ready for the time she will be cut. When they reap the early millet and find there is enough to make the custom, they inform the *pokubega* and he comes to cut the girls. When he cuts a 'white' *yabega* (a virgin) every one praises her and says she is 'a living girl', but when a girl is found not to be a virgin, people laugh at her and her mother is considered a light-headed person for not having trained her daughter properly. In such a case, the *pokubega* (operator) charges a higher fee than for one who is a virgin. When a girl comes out from the *yabega* room (where she has been confined after the operation) her suitor will be told to fetch the *bagere bono* (the offerings for the shrine of her *segere*)[2] and she is now given in marriage[3] (as has already been described).

Adultery: After *sandono*[4] has been made, a girl is no longer a *yiri-yea* (some one belonging to a compound) she is a *yi'-pɔka* (a woman of a compound). If some one now seeks her, and the owner of this woman discovers him, there will be a quarrel.[5]

Bride-price: When the *sandono* ceremony is completed, the master of the bride's household (i.e. her parent's household) may ask about the 'beasts' or *sulle* (the bride-price), four head of cattle and four hoes.

---

[1] See also page. 168–70. [2] See p. 293.

[3] The full bride-price among the Nankanse is reckoned at one bull and three cows, but often one bull, two cows and seven or eight sheep are accepted.

[4] See pp. 152 and 282.

[5] It will depend upon who the adulterer is what action will be taken. If he is a townsman of the husband's, that is a clansman, the case will probably be settled before the Elders. If a stranger, he is likely to be killed if actually caught, or if he escapes, the husband will 'descend into the valley' (*siɣe bɔɔ*) and seize anything (person or cows) belonging to the adulterer's town.

From the day on which a bride is 'whitened',[1] she begins to wear leaves in front as well as behind. At this time (i.e. when she has become pregnant) her husband, or his father if he still sits with a nose (i.e. if alive), will go to the house of his in-laws and he and the girl's father will go together to the soothsayers to consult and find out what the woman had talked about in front of Yini,[2] the Sky-God, before her birth. They do so, lest perhaps she had said that during her pregnancy she did not wish to see her father, or mother, or sisters, or brothers. They will also find out whether she had declared that she did not want any children. They inquire what her *segere* has to say about it. Her husband then returns home and takes a guinea-fowl and a cock and hen (symbolizing a male and female) and puts them in his skin bag, and goes with them to his parents'-in-law's house. One of the fowls is given to the shrine of the girl's grandfather and the cock and the guinea-fowl are given to her *segere*. If it is taboo for her parents to visit her during pregnancy, then in all subsequent pregnancies until she becomes old, the taboo continues to be observed. The manner such taboos are removed is thus. The soothsayer will tell them to bring a white goat, a white fowl, and a brown guinea-fowl and water mixed with indian corn, or early millet. These are offered, and the unfortunate utterances which the girl had made to the Sky-God return to him.

When a woman has had a child by her husband and known that 'he is a person' and will be able to look after her, she will go back to her mother's place 'to take things'. These things consist of a *zaleya* (a string net), a calabash known as *kumpio*, a head-rest (*zaleya tusunko*) and a red *kaleya* pot.

Kumpio: A *kumpio* is where a woman keeps her valuables, beads, &c., and is also the shrine of her soul (*sia*) during her lifetime. The soul of a male, during life, resides in his grain store or in his leather bag. The *kumpio* also contains things which will only be used on the owner's death in connexion with her funeral custom—dried fish, dried okro, dried meat of a hare, a large bead called *pera nifo* (ram's eye). It is kept inside the *zaleya* net between two large calabashes upon which others are placed (see Fig. 2). A woman does not permit any one else to touch her *kumpio* or look inside;[3] should any one do so and the owner, or even her child, sicken and die, the one who did so is accused of being

---

[1] See footnote, page 145.

[2] There is another kind of destiny known as *Paala* which is inevitable and cannot be altered or avoided.

[3] An eldest son or daughter are forbidden ever to put a hand inside the grain store

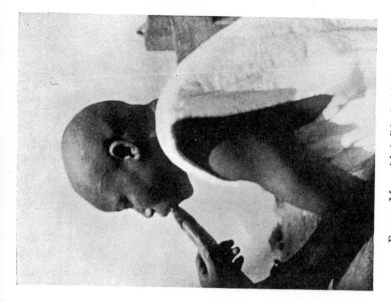

Fig. 2. Showing *zaleya* net containing the *kumpio*

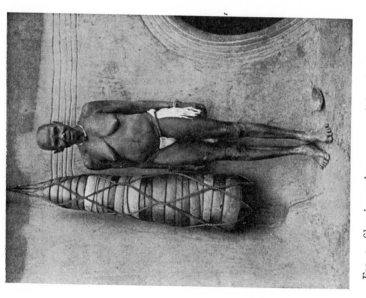

Fig. 3. Man with 'talking' whistle

a witch. She will be caught and have to undergo the ordeal of arrows (*pema lua*).

When a woman dies, her daughter inherits her things, but if she had goats or cowries, her son will take these and not her father's brothers, but, if she brought any property with her on her marriage, her brothers will claim it if they are bad people, otherwise her son will take it. On her death, however, her 'brothers' and 'sisters' will come and take her *kumpio* and carry it home and perform the *poyablega* or *kutotere* funeral custom with it at the girl's own home. Her eldest daughter will carry it and try to prevent it shaking (lest she disturbs the soul within) and she will not speak with any one while carrying it.

The husband's people will kill a beast before the *kumpio* is taken away, and when it reaches the girl's home, her relatives will hold a second funeral custom.

The reason why they take away a woman's *kumpio* after her death is because her soul is living inside during her life, and when she dies is still living there until they have finished the funeral custom, after which it departs to 'its going place'. The funeral custom of a married woman is thus made twice, that of a male once.[1]

The Custom of Incision: [Clitoridectomy, and also, I believe, the cutting away of the *labia* are still practised by the majority of the tribes in the Northern Territories of the Gold Coast.

The Nankanse and Kasena perform the operation about the age of puberty, and with them it is the prelude to marriage.

Other tribes do so much earlier, at ages varying from a week old to six years. The Namnam, Talense, Dagbwandaba, and Mamprusi do not, as far as I know, 'cut' their women at all. This is a custom, which (in spite of its being to some extent an incentive to early chastity among those tribes which observe the rite at puberty), should, in my opinion, be firmly but tactfully suppressed by the Administration. When the operation is performed during infancy, it is possibly less dangerous,

during their father's lifetime, nor may a son ever put a hand in his father's bag or wear any of his articles of apparel.

[1] Really in two places at the same time; at her husband's home where she is buried, and at her own parents' home. A mother's spirit is supposed to follow her eldest son. Aboya suggested, that as a woman leaves her parents' home virtually as a 'bought' person, on her death she is first freed, and will then return as 'a person who owns herself'. He adduces as evidence of this suggestion, the fact that only one funeral custom is held for a female slave unless the owner had given the slave to another man in marriage, in which case, the real master will send for his female slave's *kumpio* on her death, as if the woman had been his daughter.

cruel, and painful, but in such cases there is not even the excuse that it serves as a deterrent to early sexual intercourse. When performed at puberty, the fear of ridicule at being found to have lost virginity undoubtedly has served and still serves to encourage prenuptial chastity. In this case, however, the operation becomes so cruel and even dangerous—fatal results are known to occur—as quite to outweigh any scruples we might have concerning its abolition on the grounds of any indirect good purpose which this custom may serve. To abolish it would meet with at least the silent approval of all those directly concerned, and would not, I believe, meet with any opposition in other quarters. One factor alone should make our veto more easily accepted. In a few years, these tribes whose life is here depicted will almost without exception have abandoned their nudity; no one will be so poor as not to be able to afford a cloth. Nakedness and this practice are I believe very closely associated, if not actually a case of cause and effect. No one could read the account which now follows without feeling that the sooner this ruthless custom is definitely forbidden, the better it will be for all concerned. It should not be beyond the ingenuity of schools and missionary bodies to make use of and adapt the good precepts which this otherwise barbarous rite enjoins upon its initiates.]

Before a woman marries, she must undergo the cutting ceremony. The time for cutting women is when they are fully developed, and their breasts fully grown, i.e. when they are ready to marry. If a woman 'cuts' too soon, she will suffer from a sickness called *pukuno*. These days, women do not wait until they are matured enough, and one sees girls who are not full grown seeking 'the cutting place'.

Not all girls are 'cut'; for some it is a taboo of their guardian spirit; some, who know they are not virgins, avoid the operation because they fear ridicule; others again are merely frightened. Any girl, however, who is not cut is laughed at all the time by other women. 'If you step across my *yoka* pumpkins you will spoil them', they will say to such an one.

This ceremony takes place after the cutting of the *nara* (early millet). The *pukubega* (the man who performs the operation) is given a present for each *yábègà*[1] (the initiate at this ceremony is so called) whom he cuts. This consists of a fowl and grain in the case of virgins, and a thousand cowries (about 1*s.*) or a hoe in the case of a girl who has had intercourse with any man, even her own husband, before the ceremony.

---

[1] Plural is *yabse*. *Yabégá* is the strophanthus plant.

Should a woman have already married and conceived before the operation, the *pukubega* will have to be given a goat. A stranger may not understand what is meant by 'cutting'. There is something that women are shy about, when they do not wear any clothes. When they are just young girls, it does not matter so much, but when they have 'known' men, they do not like to go about as formerly, what can be seen is 'a load on their head' and this causes them to wish to be 'cut'. Any girl who is not 'cut' is much talked about among the women. When a girl, during the operation, is found not to be a virgin, she will be shamed amongst her neighbours. Young men will call her 'a worthless thing'. On account of this, it is very difficult to get a young girl to consent (to intercourse) before she has been cut. As young girls and boys are often sleeping together on the same mat, it follows that sometimes a girl will weaken. In such a case, when the time for cutting comes, her *zaba* (lover) [1] pays (bribes) the operator to save the disgrace following the exposure of her condition. [That his action is not wholly disinterested is seen by what follows.] A girl who is found not to be a virgin is called *sulim*; one who is, is called a *yab' pelego* (a white *yábègà*). (In the former case), her lover too, it is shameful for him among his companions; they will tell him that he has destroyed the girl. [The following is a description of this custom as performed at Winkoŋo on 26th August 1928.]

A man sat down outside the compound beneath the shade of a tree and the girl to be operated on sat between his outstretched legs with her back to him. The man forced open her legs by twisting his own around hers. The *pukubega* [2] squatted down between the girl's legs facing her. He took his left hand and covered the girl's front with it to prevent those looking on from seeing it, only removing his hand to rub his fingers over with earth to prevent them slipping. He then quickly took hold of the part to be cut [3] and severed it as if he were cutting an enemy (*datene*). He then dug a small hole with the razor which he was using and buried in it the part he had cut off. Again he applied the knife to the other side. . . . The women who were standing by raised the shrill *kyenkyelese* cry to make the girl's heart strong, that she might not cry out on account of the pain. The girl struggles, but is

[1] The relationship is that described in Chapter VI. It appears to be a recognized custom for young unmarried girls to lie on the same mat with a young man. I was invariably informed that it is the exception for impropriety to take place. See also Chapter XXIV.

[2] The derivation of this word is said to be *pɔya* a woman and *kubega* to hurt.

[3] Called *zan-kabere*.

held firmly by the man who grips her from behind until the *pukubega* has finished. A woman comes forward with a *birego* [1] leaf and binds her up with *biro* fibre passed between her legs. They then let her go and the girl stands up dazed (*gam*).

The wounds were not dressed for three days, when an old woman came and washed the sores with a decoction made of *dawa dawa* husks. It was now found that the operation had not been successful, and another *pukubega* was called to perform another cutting. The girl wept, but many people seized her and the knife was again set against the place which remained to be cut.

The treatment with *dawa dawa* is continued for two days, when it is changed for *petere* leaves and *pintuba* and *yilim* roots which are boiled, and this water used for dressing the wounds until they are healed. When she has recovered, the old woman takes ashes on her open palms and blows them over the *yábègà*,[2] [this custom is known as *pebelego*], after which the girl may walk about once more. She will now wear the leaves of the *wantuyo* [3] until the time comes for the cere-mony of 'throwing away the roots'. The girl's suitors now vie with each other in bringing presents which the old woman who is attending to her helps in putting in her bag (in pocketing). [If she had a *zaba*, the hand-washing ceremony,[4] already described, is carried out.]

The ceremony of throwing away the roots (*nyegere basega dare*) is as follows. On that day beer will be boiled. All the presents which her suitors have brought are divided into two, half for the girl's mother, half for the old woman. Good food is cooked which the old woman will carry home with her. The girl's father will also give her a hoe.[5]

All these roots which the old woman used for medicine must be collected and not thrown away until the *dawa dawa* trees are in bloom. Should any of the *yabse* (initiates) die, the old woman is not paid any-thing. All the dressings used are kept and carefully burned, this cere-mony being called *suguru nyoa*. When the time comes for doing this, a basket of *kyea* [i.e. grain at the fourth stage in the brewing of beer], a basket of grain, and guinea-fowls are taken 'to burn the dressings' and a sacrifice is made to the girl's *segere*.

In 'the cutting of women' girls risk their lives.

---

[1] An edible plant; the stalks supply fibre.   [2] The initiated one is so called.
[3] Lit., the calabash pumpkin.   [4] Called *nuse peere*.
[5] A hoe is still almost regarded as currency; its value, until recently, being that of a goat; a cow was formerly worth ten hoes.

IX

SOME HUNTING CUSTOMS. *PENTIA*, THE SHRINE OF LIFE. THE MAKING OF ARROW POISON

THE thing that gives most pleasure to a Goreŋa's child is hunting. When a boy is full grown, he will never forget his bow, never forget his farming, never forget the cattle and the driving of herds home in the evening. A father's ambitions (*potere*) are centred in his child, and he is never unmindful of him. A good parent teaches his son to handle a quiver, and the boy is never missing when his neighbours go hunting. For the kind of hunting called *perega* (a game drive), men go forth with dogs, bows and arrows, and throwing sticks. They seek out the bush things, and the men and dogs catch some and at others they throw sticks, or, when they are too far away, shoot arrows. The throwing-sticks are hurled at hares, partridges, wild guinea-fowls, and those they kill, they put in their leather bags. Such game are of no importance, and need not be handed over to the ones in authority (*yi'-zu kyema*) (lit. heads of compounds),[1] but the 'head' of a real beast belongs to him, and not to the 'fathers' of those who kill it, unless the latter also happen to be the heads of compounds. Otherwise a father will only hear that his son has killed such and such a beast, but will get no share in it. When they kill what is known as a *dun sabela* (lit. a black beast),[2] then a medicine pot must be 'set' on the fire for it.

The animals for which a pot must be 'set' are *koo* (hartebeest); *nafo* (buffalo); *yoka* (?), *sebega* (roan); *molifo* (bush buck?); *isiga* (duyker); *gambua* (a species of small antelope).

The time for hunting is after the harvest has been gathered in and people have descended to work on the tobacco farms in the hollows. When this season arrives, they begin to smear their arrows (with poison) and the *wore* or *wo-dana*[3] (the one in charge of the hunt) makes ready, asking advice of his shrine and doing all it demands. Those others, too, who have *katin woŋa* (hunting shrine calabashes), will follow their advice carefully and kill many things (i.e. make many

---

[1] See Chapter XXI.

[2] Compare the Ashanti *sasa boa*, see *Religion and Art in Ashanti*, p. 183.

[3] The 'medicine' of the *wo-dana* is a magic horn which he blows and leads the hunters. This horn is called *wure*, so that *wo-dana* probably means the owner of, the master of the horn; elsewhere he is known as the *go-dana*; see also p. 378.

sacrifices to them) before all is ready for the hunt. The starting out of the *wo-dana* is the signal for all to set off; he goes in front sounding his horn and following a path leading to the bush. The only people who remain behind are infirm people and women and children.

They will sleep in the bush three or four days before returning home. If they kill a big beast, such as a hartebeest, it is skinned, cut up, and every one carries a portion (*nandase*). The one who carries the head goes in front, strutting with the horns like the very beast itself, glancing from side to side as he walks. Whistles, *wise* and *liteŋa* (see Fig. 3) sound the praises of the hunters, mentioning such and such an one. They walk one behind another with the meat, and when they are coming among the compounds, some one has already run on in front to the house of the one who had killed the animal, in order that the *santegero* (the outlets for rain water to run off from a yard or on a flat roof) may be closed up. Now, the women sound the *kyinkyelense*, *le-le-le-le*! Those who carry the meat, visit the houses of the section heads. They dance the war-dance (*dea*) and their bellies are washed, and you cannot compare it with anything else; on such a day a Chief is of no more importance than the hunters. When they have finished going round the compounds of the *zu-kyema*, they will come with the meat to the head of the compound to which the man who killed the beast belonged. Here it is put down. A man now climbs on the wall of the compound and stands straddling the entrance. He calls loudly to the spirit, of which a hunting calabash (*katin-woŋa*) is the shrine:

'Bono O!

'Bono O!

'I call thus, that if you are at Adogwire,[1] if you are here, if you are there, you may come hither.' When he calls thus, and there is any animal which the hunters had wounded but which had escaped and died somewhere, and some one had found it and taken it to eat, that person will see something. He will become blind, or some sickness catch hold of him.

When he has finished proclaiming thus, he next calls the *yiri la kyim'-dema* (house spirits) saying:

'Anude, if you have heard, reach Avila and both of you go to Akongoe (another ancestor) and thence to Anaba who is the eldest of you all, and join together and come hither to the *zenore*[2] of So-and-so,

---

[1] A place in the uninhabited bush between *Naga* and *Winkoŋo*.

[2] The open space immediately outside a compound where the men-folk foregather to smoke and talk.

because a stranger (the dead hartebeest) has entered into his compound. On account of this, I call you to hear. If it is a bad thing, which will ruin this house, and pull it down, and result in people not being born, as you own this compound, drive it away that it may return to Manmilima or Adogwire or to Sabakalesaka, because it is there its neighbours live. If it is a good thing which will found (lit. build) a new house, and cause children to be born, cause good corn harvests, new marriages, rearing of live stock, if it will do these things, do you, who own this house, receive it and let it enter.'

He then comes down from the wall; every one scatters, and there remain only those 'who own themselves' (i.e. the Elders).

The meat is then portioned out, and the one entitled to a portion takes it.[1] Those who are not entitled to a whole *nenda* receive lesser portions cut off. The wife of the hunter who killed the beast is given a portion cut off the neck 'to sit upon' and mix with grain food, and some of the meat is put aside for making *kale* (meat boiled and mixed with flour).

The man who is going to 'set the pot', who is called 'the master of the roots', has also a foreleg sent to his compound. He will bring medicine (*tiim*) to treat the one who killed the beast. If this were not done, the beast would make him sick, or kill his wife and children, or destroy him, or make him thin and weak. That is why they treat him. This man—the one who killed the animal—when he finds that he has the necessary fowls and corn for making beer, will assemble the people for the 'pot-setting'. The 'pot-setting day', ah! that is a great festival; no one will be absent unless he is sick. On that day, the owner of the roots will come, the whistle-blowers will come, those whose throats are sweet and who are not shy will come to sing and get cowries. When a sufficient number of people have assembled, they will take a pot and dig a hole at the foot of the kitchen midden. There the pot is 'set' and filled with beer. Then the whistlers (see Fig. 3) and the singers begin singing and mentioning the name of the hunter.[2] On this day, only those who have themselves killed an animal and understand the rite take part in it. They first go outside the compound one by one and take a drink out of the *sere* pot, lapping from it like an animal. As they come out of the *nay dene* (cattle-kraal) they go on hands and

---

[1] A carcass is considered as consisting of six *nenda*, pl. *nendase*; or main portions—two hind legs, two forelegs and the remainder divided into two. Each is a *nenda*.

[2] There is a whistling language among many of these tribes. Compare the Ashanti Drum language, see *Ashanti*, Chapter XXII.

knees (like an animal) glancing all round as a beast does when walking. They put their mouths down to drink, stop drinking, hold up their heads, look about them to find out if some one is hiding somewhere to shoot them. Then the sound of a bow is heard twanging *pae*! and they run back into the compound. A pot containing *kal' sabele* (black *kale*) was also set beside the beer pot, and those old hunters who have killed a beast will eat some, but it is forbidden for anyone who has not done so. When all those who already 'know' have finished, last of all comes forth the man on account of whom the ceremony is being performed. Around his forehead are bound four *kara*. These are small pieces of the skin of the animal killed, cut in the shape of a bow and sewn into little leather bags in which has been placed powdered medicine. These appear 'white, white', on his head; his eyebrows are painted, and down the centre of his nose is a white line to resemble the markings of the animal he has killed. On that day this man is more than anything which lives; all eyes look only at him; all ears are listening to 'the words' of the whistle-blowers and the praise is beyond compare.

This is the reason that those who enter the bush (as hunters) are many. Men will stand on trees night and day for the sake of getting such praise.

When a beast has been killed, the one who killed it does not receive any of it except the *kale*. He incurs many expenses in addition to the hardships of hunting which he has already undergone. Fowls have to be caught to give the one who 'sets the pot'; cowries have to be paid to the whistle-blowers; the women who sing about him will be paid; it is because of his name that they do these things.

The *kara* are later put on the hunter's quiver, and when people see it, they say 'This one is a man'.

When men go hunting in parties, they know the rules of precedence; they know him who is higher than another; they understand when one says 'I speak, you remain silent'. Before men go hunting, they consult the soothsayers, because there are dangerous things in the bush, and a small quarrel may bring many arrows. Mouths (vows) will be made before they set out. In hunting, when an argument arises and one does not know how to speak properly, there will be shooting of arrows. One may try to stop another from drinking water; or again, one may throw at a beast 'white, white,' for all to see (i.e. clear for all to see) and knock it down, and yet another may try to claim it from him. If he does not look up and see some one who can make him feel that he has 'a load on his head', he will try to take it by force.

Pentia [1]: Before the arrival of Europeans (and there was fighting between the tribes) there was a very bitter custom for some girls. They were made 'to enter *Pentia*'. Why should this be bitter for a girl? Because *Pentia* is the shrine of life, with it men guard themselves when they fight with arrows. This shrine has taboos which the girl (who waits upon it) must follow very carefully as must all those others (men), who have 'entered *pentia*'. The one who violates any of its taboos will quickly receive an arrow when he goes into the valley of arrows. When the girl who has 'entered *pentia*' goes with the men to the shooting of arrows, she hangs the *pentia* shrine round her neck and follows the warriors into the valley. If she has observed all its taboos—never known a man and not even sat on a mat with a male—then, even when one of them receives an arrow, he will get life. If this girl has sense, she will remain thus (chaste) not knowing a male at all until she feels strong. When they consider that such a girl should be given in marriage, they will sacrifice to the *pentia* and 'sweep' her away.

The Making of Arrow Poison: If you wish to 'smear arrows', you will first of all seek for or purchase *yiba* seeds (strophanthus seeds). Then a day is appointed, and all who have arrows to smear tell each other. On that day they will seek for sticks of the *dawa dawa* tree to make a fire. They will rise up very early (lit. morning night night) and set the poison pot upon it, and into this pot are put the seeds which have been ground. Now the thing which must be avoided, beyond everything, in the making of *yabégá* (arrow poison) is uncleanness, which includes stealing. If two men have had intercourse with one woman, and they meet together to smear the arrows, that quiver of arrows is a dead quiver; a beast shot with an arrow from it does not die. Therefore, when they are smearing arrows, they will inquire into all such matters and call to mind if So-and-so and So-and-so had ever followed after the same woman. [2] All such will be sought out and driven away. They will continue boiling the poison until the sun is turning towards the west and until it is properly boiled and has a proper *loko*. [3] The arrows

[1] The root of this word is probably *pema*, an arrow.

[2] Among many of these tribes, it is thought that if one of two men, who have both had intercourse with the same woman, falls sick, the other man must on no account look on him, or the sick man will surely die.

[3] *Loko* generally means a quiver, but the word is used in other senses. It often stands for bow, arrows, and quiver; it also means the pain felt when the poison takes effect, and as here, the poison property of the decoction.

are smeared by dipping a stick in the pot, and smearing the arrows with it; then they set them to dry, after which they are put in the quivers. Three days later they will take the ashes from the fire which they had kindled and enter the bush to wander and see if the *loko* is good. If they shoot a beast and it dies, it is good.

X

MARRIAGES, PROHIBITED AND ALLOWED. SOME CUSTOMS RELATING TO *KYISA* (SPIRITS). THE MAKING OF A *YINI* SHRINE

WE do not marry into our own clan (*tumso; bura*). We do not marry whence we originated. Our father's *sōō*[1] relations (i.e. on his mother's side) we do not marry.

If our *ma bi'a* (mother's sister) marries somewhere and bears children, we may not marry them. Our father's mother's house (where we call the people *aseba* although not really so, *aseba* being your mother's brothers) we do not marry into that group, or even into any of its sections (*yi'zuo*). If you want any woman on your father's mother's brother's side, you may not even have her as a lover; if you want to, they will not agree, and all you can do is to 'cool your throat' and converse together. Even this the Elders are always trying to prevent, and if you do not obey them, you must do that in secret, but as for marriage, you will not dare to do so. There are some others who possess cunning, and want you to suffer in vain. They will be silent while you squander your things (on presents), by going there, while they eat up your gifts, then, when they have received enough from you, they will tell you that the marriage (you were contemplating) is prohibited and explain the relationship which prevents you marrying. If knowledge does not come to you in time, and the marriage has already been entered upon and children are born, it causes confusion, the children will die. In such a case, the Elders will summon the wife's *po'sigera* (witness to the marriage) and he will take a calabash and climb on top of the flat roof. The man and his wife are standing in the room below, and each takes hold of a corner of the calabash which he holds through a hole in the roof and pulls it asunder, each retaining half. This breaking of the calabash in two parts divides the relationship which existed at the time of the marriage and caused the resulting evil consequences (*yelege*). The *sōō* relationship is separated. The couple are now 'strangers';[2] there is no longer any difficulty; it is now a correct marriage. You may not marry your mother's brother's daughter (*aseba pɔyoa*) or any of that *tumsum* (line?). You

---

[1] See p. 240.   [2] See footnote, p. 183.

may not marry into the section of your mother's mother's uncle's daughter's house, but may do so into another section of that town. If a man marries two wives, and the descendants follow on for many generations and become 'a big people' far away, the descendants of these two women may marry, but only if the two ancestresses were not originally of the same family, and if it was a long way back. If a man marries only one wife, and she bears children—in such a case, the descendants of these may not marry. If they do so by mistake— because the relationship goes back to long ago—and not because of 'the shortness of their ears' (i.e. disobedience) or the strength of their arms, they will only return the girl to her parents, but if the couple are determined by the strength of their arms to have their own way, then they will 'break the calabash'. The reason why they do so is because their *kyisiri* (taboo) is the same. This *kyisiri* may be a fowl, or crocodile, or dove, which all descendants of the original ancestor swear by, do not eat, do not kill, or even direct any one towards it. If you direct any one to it, and that person kills it, it is as if you yourself had killed it, and you will have to make amends, or death will kill you, and what you have done will only be revealed after you are dead by the soothsayer; or you may only become sick, or impotent, or your farming may not prosper, or your live stock, or you may not be able to get women in marriage. Your having done so (i.e. harmed your *kyisiri*) will drive all success away. You will have to give offering after offering until you have lost all your hair (i.e. possessions). Those whose *kyisiri* is a crocodile, it will not harm them. On the day when it does so, it is because they have done something wrong, it would not have harmed them otherwise. People whose *kyisiri* is a crocodile do not harm it, or kill it. If such a person dies, he turns into a crocodile, that is why if you kill a crocodile you kill a person. At that place where they have the crocodile for a *kyisiri*, you will see old old crocodiles; they become so old that their colour changes. When a crocodile dies, they will make a funeral custom and bury it as if it were a man. When any one wants to trouble a crocodile, they will not agree, only a European may do so; the people do not know what to do, so remain silent. In the case of all these *kyisiri*, when a man does something bad against them, not long after, 'the owner' will suffer. If a stranger does so, it does not matter so much. Sometimes we think that a certain person is always in trouble, but there will be a reason for this. All those who swear by a crocodile, do not marry each other, their *tumsum* is one, e.g. the Black and Red *Ten'dama* of Danweo. The *kyisiri* of the Winkoŋo people is a fowl, and they do not intermarry except into the Alabisi [1] section.

The proper place to marry is where you are not related [2] and neither your *kyisiri* nor ancestral shrines are in common, that is the straight place for marriage; there is nothing unclean (*deko*) there. The place where the *tun* or *solom* is, or the *kyisiri*, that is not the place for marriage.

The Kyisiri *of the People of Winkoŋo*: Winkoŋo people taboo a fowl. Our first ancestor begat a child and it was laid in a hut with a grass roof (*deo tini*). Every one had gone out, when fire caught the house. A female fowl was sitting on her eggs inside the hut, and when the room was on fire, it left its eggs and covered the baby with its wings. When people rushed into the room to save the infant, they found the fowl protecting the child. They brought out the child and the fowl. On account of this our ancestor said, 'I cannot take an oath that I shall never eat a fowl, but my eldest children, male and female, shall never eat a fowl'. That is why our eldest sons and eldest daughters never eat a fowl and why they swear by a fowl. When such persons eat a fowl by mistake, they will become thin and their cheek-bones stick out unless they are given a decoction of roots known as *yaba tiim* (ancestor's medicine), when they will become proper persons. This is the reason Winkoŋo people (eldest sons and eldest daughters) have a fowl for their *kyisiri* and why they swear by a fowl to this day. Those who taboo a fowl thus, live at Bonobaluŋo and Boŋo. Some of the Moshi also taboo a fowl. Other Nankanse taboo goat (the Zare people), others *danwane* (dove), *ebega* crocodile, *woo* (a water lizard ?) Io (?),

---

[1] Alabisi means children (here in sense of descendants) of Ala. Ala was a 'father's sister's child', or *ma yenta bia*. Ala's mother married a man from the town of Wachia, but for some reason did not remain there, and returned to Winkoŋo (her parent's town) and there bore many children as a *yi yeen bia* (see p. 161). The descendants of these became a group, by themselves, and those who were descendants of the original common ancestor's other wife are not forbidden to intermarry with this group. The following genealogical table will make this clearer:

A. Original ancestor.

B and C. Co-wives; each calls the other *Yenta*.

D. A daughter of A and C and mother of Ala.

E. The Wachia man whom D first married.

F. Ala, a son born to D who returned to Winkoŋo.

G and H, the descendants of these two lines.

[2] The word used in the original is *kyin*, which means 'pinched off' of something pinched or taken of the flesh.

pesego (sheep; *mone* (a kind of harmless snake); *Kole-tuka-zifu* (fish from a certain pond).

How the Black Ten'dama came to have the Dawane (*Dove*) *for their* Kyisiri: When a Black Ten'dana has a child male or female, its *kyisiri* is *dawane* (the dove). The reason for this is (as follows). Their ancestor once went to the bush and saw the hole of a *tenanboŋa* (badger ?) (lit. land donkey) and he went into the hole. Now, this animal had dug a second hole (tunnel) branching off from the first, and while the man was down one tunnel, the beast was in the other, and it came and cut off the retreat of the man and he could not get out. But he was a lucky man; a bird had seen him—a dove. The bird flew *ta, ta, ta,* to the man's compound, and when it reached there, it stopped on top of the wall and cried so much that it became a thing of wonder, and people had their senses (*yam*) opened and became aware that it was not crying like that for nothing, besides they had been searching for the man for three whole days and all their thoughts (*potere*) had been set on what had happened, so when the bird behaved like this, it dragged their sense (minds) in that direction. So they went out with their quivers hung on their shoulders. When they got outside, the dove sat on a tree, and when the people got near to that tree, it flew off again and continued doing so until it reached the place where the hole was; here it descended and scratched and made a small hole, and the man saw the light, and they also who had gone there said, 'Let us dig here, because the actions of this bird are very wonderful' (*kyerese*). So they dug and saved their *yaba's* (ancestor's) life. That is why all Black *Ten'dama* have the dove for their *kyisiri*.[1]

The Making of a Yini Shrine: There are certain women, who, when they marry a man, bear only female children. As soon as they bear a male child, he is dead.

There was a certain woman who had given birth to two boys and had had to bury them both in the ground. On account of this, her husband went after soothsayers who told him that his wife had once, during the time she was 'in God' (*Yinin*), had speech with Him (*tara Yini* or *tara koa*), saying that she did not wish ever to have a male child, and it was this 'utterance' of hers that was killing her male children and causing her seed on the male side to be unsatisfactory (*butta*). The soothsayers said that if she wished to see male seed, they

---

[1] This and the previous account are typical examples of a score or more which might be given, to account for one aspect at least of totemism in these parts. This subject will be dealt with fully elsewhere.

must find—a black goat, a brown guinea-fowl (lit. a brown 'room' guinea-fowl, but not really a guinea-fowl at all, but a small house-bat called *denon-kaan-dokko*,[1] a red cock, a house maggot, some earth from the hole of a house mouse,[2] and a root called *soa*, in order to take back the 'utterance' which she had made and thus obtain male seed. The soothsayers also said that they must brew beer. Now, the Gorense really believe that every person who is born and becomes full grown and gets possessions, had spoken during the time he was 'in God', saying that he desired these possessions. Should a man lack possessions, they believe that when such a person was 'descending' he had declared that he did not want them.

'I want this, but I do not want that,' is what we call *Yini*. One who 'makes it a pair'[3] (*ta*), that is what we call *paala*. Nothing can be done to change that, but *Yini* may be made all right (by the performance of certain ceremonies).

As soon as the woman's husband heard this and knew that it was an 'utterance' (*koa*), he sought for these things. They 'boiled' beer[4] and filled a large pot and a small pot. This small pot of beer is called *da-beobo* (lit. bad beer), no one at all must touch that except one who 'has *Yini*'. This beer is taken 'to meet God'. The husband of the woman also boils beer, but that is only for 'the strangers' (i.e. his in-laws) to drink. He also seeks for a beast in order to prepare 'water' (i.e. food) for them. When the sun is about to 'fall', the strangers are arriving with all the things which the soothsayers have named—the black goat, the brown 'room' guinea-fowl (i.e. the small house bat), the red cock, the house maggot, earth from the hole of a house mouse, a pot of beer in addition to 'the bad beer', and the *soa* roots—and they enter the compound and salute (the occupants) and descend into the kitchen of the woman who 'has *Yini*'. They take her food pot, soup pot, food calabashes, food plate, porridge stick, calabash spoon, firewood, the stalks of grain (used for lighting the fire) and a pot of water, and bring them all out into the yard. He who is to perform the *Yini* custom now rises up, holding a rattle; the woman's mother stands

---

[1] Ordinarily called *kyinkyilina*.

[2] All these things, it will be observed, are things about the house.

[3] I am not quite sure as to the exact meaning of this idiom; it may mean that every one has one choice, i.e. one wish, but no more, and if this number is exceeded, then the second or third wish becomes irrevocable and is destiny and 'kismet'. My informants could not throw any further light on the subject.

[4] This beer, together with all the other things have to be found by the woman's 'brothers'.

behind him; behind her stands the husband's mother; next behind her, the husband; behind him, the woman herself, followed by her two daughters, all in a line. They all march out to the cross-roads. Here the master of the ceremonies (*malema-dana*) draws a cross upon the ground with the handle of his rattle and picks up some earth with his left hand; the mother of her who has *Yini* spits on this; next the mother of the husband spits on it; every one spits on it in turn, four times, except the woman's husband who does so only three times. The *malema-dana* then puts this earth in a potsherd. They now all rise up (they have been squatting or sitting down) and return to the compound in the same order in which they had set out, enter the compound and pass on into a room. They now take all the things which had been brought from the kitchen and put them in this room, over the doorway of which a cow skin is hung. The master of the ceremonies now goes outside into the yard, beating a rattle, and calls out three times:

Yini, O woe! (Sky-God, O, woe!)

The husband [1] asks, 'Who is calling?' The man answers, 'I, the son of the chief consulter, am calling'. The husband again asks 'Why are you calling?' The soothsayer answers:

'Once, you have said that you did not want to build a house; did not want to bear children; did not want to rear animals; did not want to tend fowls; did not want to marry; did not want to farm; and therefore I, the son of the chief soothsayer, have come to withdraw this "mouth" (vow) and let a house be built; and let children be born; and let cattle be reared; and let fowls be fed; and let marriages be made; and let corn be cultivated.' Each time something is named, the husband says '*Muu*', until the speech is finished. The doorway is now uncovered and the kitchen utensils brought out again into the yard. The earth which had been spat upon is now emptied on to the floor of the yard and moistened and built up. The 'brown room guinea-fowl' [2] is lifted up and shown to the Sky-God, the soothsayer saying: 'Sky-God, Sky-God, Sky-God! descend and receive your brown room guinea-fowl which you have asked for.' He kills the bat with a knife on the clay mound—it bites him just before he does so. Next, the red cock is taken. He calls out as before; the fowl is killed and is 'received' (i.e. lies on its back). Then the goat is killed. Before this was done, some of the 'bad beer' to which flour was added had been offered on

[1] A woman may not 'consult' (among the Nankanse), hence the husband is here speaking for her.　　　　　　　　　　　　[2] Really a bat.

the shrine. The remainder of this 'bad beer', which also contained the roots, was given to the *yına dana*[1] to drink; no one else touched this beer. The large pot of beer was given to the 'house-people', and they in turn gave it to the strangers[2] (i.e. the brothers and mother and sisters of the woman who had '*Yini*'), and they drink out of each other's calabashes.

During this time, others are cooking the things which were killed. The people of the house kill six guinea-fowls to make food for the 'strangers'. A basket of flour which the 'strangers' have brought is taken to make grain food, and offer to the (new) shrine. Other grain food is made in the kitchen for the 'strangers', and after they had finished eating, they are given a pot of beer. They are also given a hind leg, the liver, 'the small stomach', all being put inside the skin of the goat. They now ask permission to return home and they allow them to do so.

The 'strangers' tell the house-folk that they must not allow a single thing which they have sacrificed in the name of God to remain and stand over until day-break, for that is taboo. The house-people now take the beer which was left over and of which they have had enough, and the food which is left over, together with all the feathers and sweepings off the floor, and call on God and empty it all on the clay mound, and throw all away outside the same night so that nothing remains in that house.[3] The beer which the strangers have taken away with them, they cannot finish, so they send for others to come and drink it, for it is taboo to take any home. The 'bad beer' is finished by those who have *Yini*, and they also rub their heads with the powdered roots which it contains.

---

[1] *Yina* is a plural of *Yini* and *yina dana* means those persons who already own such shrines as that now being consecrated, and in this case also, the husband and two daughters of the woman.

[2] *Sana*, stranger, really means any one not belonging to the speaker's own town, e.g. a sister goes out and marries elsewhere, she and her husband become *sana* to the speaker.   [3] It must either be eaten or thrown away.

XI

FUNERAL CUSTOMS

A Chief's Funeral. The Funeral of an Old Woman

WHEN a person falls ill, the first thing to do is to seek a medicine-man to treat the sick person. When he comes, he will say, 'Get a fowl with feathers of a certain colour (for example, a red cock, a black hen, a red hen, a grey guinea-fowl, or perhaps a black goat, and other things, including cowries. If the patient is a male, the cowries must number three hundred and thirty-three, if a female four hundred and forty-four;[1] a hoe must also be brought 'to place on top of the (medicine) pot'. When these things have been brought, the doctor will cut the middle 'toe' of the fowl and allow the blood to drop on his roots. Now, he follows the usual treatment. He burns some of the roots, allows others to stand in water. Some of this the patient is given to drink; the powdered medicine he rubs where the sickness lies. Sometimes the sick person recovers, sometimes the sickness destroys him. If it destroys him, as soon as he falls down and it is ended, those who possess him will fetch water. His daughters assemble from where they live (i.e. married daughters) and they support him and bathe him, and place the body on a new mat in his wife's room. They will report the funeral and seek for *gulugu* and *luse* drums, and singers, and catch a sheep to pay the workers who dig the grave. They consult the sooth-sayers and kill a cow for the dead man. They dance the war-dance called *dea*. When they go to bury the body, they will walk round the grave, and the eldest son of the deceased will peep inside. Not just any one may dig a grave; there are special people, called *bayase*[2] (s. *baya*) who do so. They have been taught many many things, and learned them, and have thus become *bayase*. There is a difference between a good *baya* and 'a thing' which 'merely lives'. When they have finished digging a grave, a good *baya* will look inside and take out the souls (of living people) which are descending into it. Some-times he will be unable to get a soul out. In that case, he will take that person's 'soul thing' (i.e. the favourite possession of the owner of the soul) perhaps his favourite arrow, or in case of a woman, a bangle, and he will then be able to entice the soul with it to come out.[3] Other

---

[1] See footnote, p. 131.   [2] Sextons.   [3] See also p. 186.

bayase are bitter-bellied; they see a soul in a grave, and grind it, as one whom they hate.

If the deceased were 'an old thing', on the day of his burial they will beat a fowl to death on the flat roof, and guinea-fowls and a sheep. The funeral custom will now be postponed for a year. When the year comes round, they will make the second funeral custom called *woore*. They will seek for the corn required. Sons-in-law, grandchildren, his own sons, 'the house-people', all assemble and gather plenty of things, and now the real funeral custom is made. *Kyenkyera* and *kamsa* cakes are made. *Tuntu*[1] seeds and beans are cooked and many other kinds of food. The bow and quiver of the deceased is burned and other things are done before they 'break' the funeral custom. If this funeral custom is being held in the wet season, they will not dance the *dea* dance, because they would trample down the crops; they dance the *yoyo* dance. Young boys dance the *kologo* and women the *seyaya*.

When they have finished 'burning the funeral', there remains the washing of the entrance to the compound. The widows put on the widows' leaves, and eat widows' medicine. The orphans make the *dono*.[2] The 'making of the *dono*' is with guinea-fowls and goats, or if they cannot get these, then a hoe. These things are for the old woman who fastens the strings and, later, takes them off again.

Sons-in-law of the deceased will pour out cowries, and those who were his friends and want a name, will boil beer, in order to make the untying of the *dono* a big festival, but this will only be when the deceased was a very old man. When they have finished the custom, the one who is next to the dead (i.e. in seniority) will gather in the (ancestral) shrines, but a son will take that of his own parents and also the medicine, he, the father, used to eat. These will all come to the eldest son.[3]

A Chief's Funeral Custom: When a chief dies it is bitter for a man to hear, only the *bayase* (sextons) and the people in the Chief's house know of it. They dig the grave in the house, kill a cow, skin it as if it were a goat (i.e. it is skinned like a bag), and cover the body with it. He is buried, and many days will elapse, then little by little they will

[1] Seeds of the baobab tree.

[2] String made of a couple of strands of *bero* fibre. On males, it is fastened round the middle finger of the left hand and then round the wrist. On females, it is fastened round the neck, then passes down the middle of the back and round the waist. 'Black' *dono* string is put on the first-born and last-born children of both sexes.

[3] This account only touches several interesting customs which are more fully explained in the writer's succeeding narrative.

whisper, and people will hear that the Chief has 'descended behind the house'. The body is taken, covered with the cow skin, to the grave, and when it has been laid inside, they take a cloth as a mat and roll it for resting his head upon. They take a stone which is large enough to cover the entrance to the grave and collect the soil which had been taken from the grave and cover the stone with the earth until it cannot be seen, to keep in the smell. The skinning of the cow, as a goat would be skinned, and the resting the head on the cloth is different from an ordinary burial, but 'the burning' of the funeral custom is the same. Three days after, as is the case after every burial. the grave is opened again in order that the *bayase* may take out any souls which, on the day of burial, had run and gone inside the grave. If they fail to get one out, they will take the *sia loko* (soul-quiver) of that person and 'fix' it there in the grave and leave it there. That will prevent the person dying.[1]

The Death of an Old Woman: When an old woman becomes sick, or an old man (for that matter), boys and girls and women, and all those who just like dressing up in fine things, have their 'belly washed' (i.e. are happy) because they hope to see dancing and playing. If she recovers, it is a thing which will not 'wash their belly' (i.e. they will not be glad). When to-morrow becomes clear (i.e. at dawn) their conversation is about this only, and when the event happens, they are really pleased. Then one who has a fine loin-cloth (*lebere*) will seek it out from its resting place, or a good head cover, or a good cloth, and the women who have not any nice leaf front covers seek them, and *vallese* (waist-strings), and fine beads and head-bands (*bobega*), and bangles and ivory bangles, and brass anklets. All these are sought out on account of the (impending) dancing.

The funeral custom for an old woman and of an old man is very much alike, but we do not speak of 'burning' in the case of women, but 'breaking' (*woregere*),[2] her calabashes and pots. If the old woman is the senior old woman of the section, then 'her grave is dug with a sheep' (i.e. the sextons, *bayase*, are given a sheep). A cow is slaughtered and placed at the entrance to the compound (*zenore*), and they will kill a beast (*duŋa*), and a fowl for the ceremony called 'cutting *nanwoo*'.[3] The flesh of these animals is eaten by the sextons, only a leg

---

[1] This would appear rather an illogical proceeding, but such is the custom. As long as the article buried remains in good condition, the living owner is supposed to keep fit and well. Such a custom might throw a new interpretation on the reason for such articles being found in graves.

[2] But the latter expression is also used in connexion with the breaking of a man's pots.

[3] *Nanwoo* is the word used in connexion with the method employed of placing

cut off the fowl is buried in the grave. If the deceased were 'the owner of hands' (i.e. well off), they will fetch *gulugu* and *luse* drums and stand on the flat roof and beat drums until to-morrow's dawn. The corpse will remain in the house three days. At 'the mouth of evening', when the sun is slanting, the sextons (*bayase*) will have assembled in numbers and they will dance *dea*, or if it is the wet season, *yoyo*. Then the corpse is covered with a mat and tied round with string and covered with a cloth.[1] Her eldest son climbs on the flat roof[2] (*gosogo*) and calls out his mother's name:

'A! he! Mother So-and-so, if formerly when you were alive, you were catching people and were a bitter-bellied witch, killing people, taking food, and handing little bits to your neighbour's child (instead of inviting it to eat out of the same dish) because you did not want your neighbour to have anything, if it is on account of such things that *Yini* (the Sky-God) killed you, come hither quickly.'

While he is speaking thus, the *bayase* have taken the corpse on their left shoulders and they are standing there.

He again calls out:

'Oh! if your days have 'reached', and your father and your mother have received you and your husband's father and your husband's mother (*deyandema*) and *Yini* (God) received you, then come hither quickly.'[3]

The corpse comes boldly forward and 'walks' towards the entrance. They all cry out together and they and the corpse circle the compound four times—three times if a male— after which the *bayase* carry the corpse to the grave and bury it. The corpse is buried naked; the mat in which it was wrapped is burned with fire.

The *bayase* then go and bathe their bodies, and those who were in the house with the corpse wash their hands with cow dung (*bili*). Those whom the deceased called her '*dayose*' ('sons' in the classificatory sense) mount on the *gosogo* (flat roof), with many beasts, guinea-fowls, and fowls; other people are in the yard (*zinzaka*) below. A 'son' who was already an orphan[4] before the death of the deceased, kills his things first. The sheep and goats are killed by suffocation or strangulation, and the fowls and guinea-fowls by beating their heads on the owner's identification marks on guinea-fowls. This is done by cutting their claws in a certain way. Innumerable combinations are thus made possible.

[1] This cloth is called *ganka*; every family, however poor, possesses one, which is used again and again, not being buried with the corpse.

[2] In case of a male, he climbs on the wall at the entrance to the *zoyo* hut.

[3] Compare 'carrying of the corpse'; see *Religion and Art in Ashanti*, Chapter XV.

[4] Known as *kyib-kyɛma*, senior orphan.

wall. After he has done so, every one 'beats' his things; sons, grandsons, sisters' sons; these are they who 'beat'. They who were her 'husbands' have no concern in all this. When they have finished the 'beating', they continue playing for three days. Meanwhile they consult the soothsayers to find out what the dead will say has to be done.

When they have finished consulting, now come the important things. On that day, they tie the *dono* strings on the eldest son, eldest daughter, and also on the wives of the sons (*sanpoy'ba*). The grandchildren shave their heads in the manner called 'grandsons' half'. They will continue to wear them (the *dono* strings) until the 'breaking'—in the case of a funeral of a male, the 'burning'—of the funeral custom, when they will be untied. Once the 'fresh corpse day'[1] has passed, the funeral custom 'sleeps' for a year. Even then, if they cannot find the grain, they may delay 'burning' it for two or three years. When the time comes and it is decided to celebrate it, they will, in good time, (*tele*) put sufficient corn in water and tell the daughter of the deceased and the husbands of her daughters also to immerse *kyea*. All her *tunsim*[2], wherever they live, will come with things in their hands in readiness for the day, and when everything is ready the senior people and all those who ought to be informed are asked to choose a day. When this comes, every one assembles when the sun 'enters', and the drums will again 'climb' on the flat roof and beat, and people will say 'They are beginning to make So-and-so's funeral custom.' Next morning they pour out the corn for the *poyablese*[3] and for the *yi'poyaba*[4] to grind. The *poyablese* grind their corn for beer outside the deceased's compound, and the *yi'poyaba* inside the compound.[5]

Next morning the beer will be strained and boiled a second time and pots filled. The following day they bring a soothsayer (*bakologo*) to hear what the deceased has to say from her mouth. On that day they will unfasten the *dono* fibre. The eldest son and eldest daughter of the deceased must pay a goat, or if they cannot afford this (lit. have not strength) then a hoe.

The youngest son and youngest daughter also give a goat or a hoe,

---

[1] *Ku'masere dare* as opposed to *ku'chaka-dare*.

[2] *Tunsim* or *tumsum* here are the *sōō* relations, descendants of grandmother, mother, mother's sisters, sisters' sons; all through the female line.

[3] *Poyablega* (pl. *poyablese*) are all women born in one town.

[4] *yi'-poya* (pl. *yipoyaba*) are the women of a town who have become resident in it by marriage.

[5] For this special occasion, the locally-born women assume the honorary position of males, *vis-à-vis* the 'foreign' women. See footnote, p. 143.

and the remainder of the sons and daughters, a guinea-fowl, each. No one whose father or mother is not dead may touch (i.e. eat) these things. Food is then cooked and placed in calabashes which are called 'the calabashes of the orphans'. Shea butter will be made, ground nuts, beans, and *kyinkyira* cakes in plenty. All these things are for the funeral custom.

While the funeral custom is being made, the women of the town from which the deceased came before her marriage, who are known as *kupugereba*, come and remain three days. On the third day they are told to choose a lover, and each one does so, and the man whom a girl chooses takes her off to his compound. Only unmarried girls actually go off with these lovers, the married women choose their men and receive the presents they bring, but do not sleep with them.[1] The presents are called *akka*. These women know that they must set out for home before the 'breaking' of the funeral custom. It is their taboo (*kyisiri*) to be 'overtaken' by the custom in the deceased's town. Next day in the night they perform 'the breaking'.

When a (married) woman dies, because she was a *poyablega*[2] in a certain town (before she came to live in her husband's town) her husband's people are compelled to report her death to her household before they bury her. The deceased may have been given to a *tobega*[3] who was her guardian spirit (*segere*), in which case they will have to sweep (*pie*) her,[4] to separate the *segere* from her body before burial, or there may be a shrine at her house to which a sacrifice has to be made.

When the funeral custom is quite finished, the 'house-people' of the deceased will come (to her husband's town)'to receive the funeral' (*toe kure*[5]). When they arrive at the deceased's town, a goat and sheep are killed for them, and flour and ground-nuts given them, and the women will again choose 'lovers' and again receive gifts, and then return home.

All those who married the deceased[6] will lead her (the dead woman, as represented by her *kumpio*) home, and her own house-people will again make her funeral custom.

'A town woman's' funeral is thus made twice, that of a male only once.

---

[1] See also footnote, p. 392, where a similar custom is practised by the Kusase.
[2] See footnote, p. 188. [3] See p. 203. [4] See pp. 391, 394, 421.
[5] That is, to take away the deceased's *kumpio*. See p. 166. The word *kumpio* is not permitted to be spoken during a funeral custom.
[6] These include her own husband and all his 'brothers'. That marriage is considered, at least in theory, as a corporate affair, is well illustrated in the above.

XII

FUNERAL CUSTOMS (*continued*)

Care of the Sick. Funeral Custom of an Old Man

WHEN sickness catches some one, first they will get to know what the sickness is. When they know, they will search for the one who possesses its roots and treats such a disease. If they do not know any one, they will inquire until they find out. They will send some one to summon him to come, saying, 'A sickness holds our person and we have heard that you treat such diseases, and because of that we have come to you.'

They take a fowl with them when they go to the doctor (*tiba*) and give it to him in order that he may notify his spirits before he comes. Why do they do this? Because, even if his roots are good roots, if the doctor offends his house-spirits, then, when he comes to treat his patient, what he prescribes will do him no good. That would only cause a waste of things. The doctor will accept the fowl, saying, 'People really hate doctors, but they do not dislike sextons, but I cannot refuse to come; you may return home while I dig for this and for that root; I shall first consult a soothsayer, and after I have wandered about and "seen", I shall arrive at such-and-such a time.'

The doctor will then go to the home of the soothsayer and ask if he ought to go. The soothsayer will tell him what he ought to do, and when he returns home after consulting, he will give his spirits flour and water and also report the matter to his *segere*,[1] giving it flour and water. His *Ƴini* shrine he will also give water before he sets out. When he reaches the patient he will tell what he requires, perhaps a red cock, a female fowl, a guinea-fowl. Perhaps he will ask for a goat and also three hundred and thirty three cowries (if his patient is a male) or four hundred and forty-four (if a female). Some lying doctors make this fee into three thousand and thirty-three and four thousand and forty-four[2] in order to get much money, but when they act thus, the roots 'will not follow' the sick person.

The doctor now cuts up his roots into pieces. He will take the red cock and tell the *yi-dana* (head of the house of which the sick man is an inmate) to report to his ancestral spirit. The *yi-dana* answers him, saying, 'Oh! it seems that I have no spirit when such

[1] See p. 135.   [2] About 4*s*.

things can happen', but he takes a calabash of water and addresses the spirit saying: 'My father, you have failed to keep this house well, that has necessitated this heap of roots, receive this water and add to, and enter, these roots, so that even if they are not good (efficacious) roots, it may not be necessary for me again to call in the doctor.'

After this, the doctor asks for permission from the *yi-dana* to begin, saying, 'May I commence that we may see (the result)?' The doctor then says: 'My father,[1] these roots are those which I take to treat my patients everywhere; you also are behind me and cause my roots to be real roots, living roots. When a man is ill he seeks everywhere for one to cure him, so they have mentioned my name, and come to me with a fowl—a *tim-dae-noa*, a smearing-medicine-fowl. I have reported to you already in my own home and told you to go on in front. I have now arrived and they have given me the things for treatment. Nothing remains; here is their red fowl; a guinea-fowl is among the things, also a female fowl; there stands a goat and a pile of cowries. Well, enter into the roots and make this patient sleep soundly this very morning, then shall I know indeed, that you follow me until the end.' He holds the calabash containing the flour-water, and lets a little drop upon the ground. He then takes a knife and cuts off a piece of the middle claw of the fowl. The blood flows and he lets it fall on the roots. Some doctors kill the fowl outright, but this may cause the patient's death soon after, for when a man is sitting with tears, and some one comes and kills a fowl before him, that may cause him to have cold shivers (*mumulego*) and puts a weight on his head.

Now, if the doctor is a (proper sort of) person, this red cock—the blood of which he has sprinkled on the roots—he will leave behind (with the family of the sick person) in order that he may look a little while and see how the patient goes on. Why? Because sometimes the medicine will not act, and the patient may seek for a new doctor; only when the medicine does good should he take away the fowl.

When he has finished with the fowl's blood on the roots he will soak (*po*)[2] the roots in water for two days, some he will burn (*kābe*)[3] and some he will pound into a powder. The roots which are put

---

[1] On any ordinary occasion, if a man wishes to sacrifice to his father when away from his own home, he must go out to the path leading to his own 'town'. He must never, except in this case or in the making of a new soothsayer's shrine, do so in the compound of another.

[2] *Po*, to ferment, also used in the making of beer.   [3] *Kābe* is to sacrifice.

in a pot to soak, remain there until the third day. If the doctor orders the patient to bathe with the medicine, they (the roots) are first put into a pot filled with water, and this is covered with a plate and placed near the *santeko* (the hole for rain water to run off from the flat roof or yard). There they remain for two days. On the third day they are uncovered, and are then used to bathe the patient. The roots, which were burned, will perhaps be given him to eat, and the powdered roots be used for rubbing. After three days the doctor will come back again to see the sick person, and will bring some other medicine.

On the first day on which the doctor had commenced to treat the patient he had said, 'If the patient becomes cured, you will make beer "to throw away the roots".' Truly the days have barely reached two (i.e. soon) when the patient is able to rise and again 'has eyes' and a clear face. This happens if the medicine has agreed with him.

When the patient recovers, the doctor has a white belly (is glad), and the house-people do everything and their hearts do not grudge the expense because again they have seen the eyes of their patient. They will seek for the doctor that same male fowl from which he had dropped the blood on the roots, the guinea-fowl and the goat, and the three hundred and thirty-three cowries[1] and will add more presents on account of his 'white belly' (kindness). Now, they will select a day, seek out corn for making beer, and call the doctor to come that he may cast away his roots. On that day he will be given 'the male's number of fowls' (i.e. three) and perhaps also a hoe, and they will catch a guinea-fowl and make soup for him and the pots of beer will perhaps be three. They will cook *tuntu* seeds. All these things they will set before the doctor (*tiba*),[2] saying, 'Here stand your treatment things'.

If the roots are to be burned on the midden heap, he (the doctor) will take a pot of beer and one plate of food, with meat on top. These he takes and goes to the kitchen midden and empties the roots at the foot of it and pours out some beer and puts a little of the meat and food into the hole he has made. He prays (*ka*) and takes a hoe and earth[3] and covers over the roots. Other doctors bury the roots where the black ants live, taking them there to do so.

---

[1] All these had been given the doctor on the first day as his fee, but it is not etiquette for him to take them away with him until his patient has recovered.

[2] *Tiba* really means to treat a complaint.

[3] *Tontono* is soil, as opposed to *teŋa*, land.

The Funeral Custom of a Very Old Person: When a person has become very old and his head white, *pagee !*, and he is older than any one else, so that no one can say, 'This one may be older than he', then, when such a person is lying ill, boys and girls and women and all those who are of an age to be dressing up (*none bute*) have their bellies washed (i.e. are happy) because he is lying thus and will die and they will get dancing. Their talk is only about the sick man. They have him for a topic of conversation with their neighbours. Even when some one goes to some other town, he will say, 'I think that there will be dancing in our country one of these days, because the old man in our town "who owns himself" is lying ill, and can you expect an old man who has an illness to rise up again?' The other person will ask, 'Who? Who?' or if he already knows the one mentioned, will cry out saying,

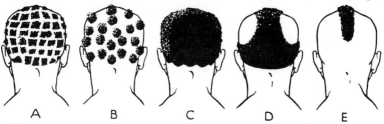

A   B   C   D   E

'Oho! indeed there is going to be dancing at your town; we shall come.' When day breaks, they keep their ears open to hear news of this; nothing else interests them. They follow each other and meet at the house of the old man to hear how things are going. When matters are long delayed, every one is now saying, 'When he does die, people will only regard it as something of no value which has got lost; now a proper death is one which strikes down and takes away, but to lie and give trouble before you die is an unseemly thing (*vesa*) for an Elder to do. Why should an old thing lie for a long time like this, has he eaten the medicine of life (*vom tiim*)?'

When at last they hear that the old man is dead, that is belly-washing news. They will seek for things to dress up in, loin-cloths (*leba*), fine hats, stone bangles. The boys will buy for their lovers good leather 'leaves' and head-bands. They will shave their heads in the manner called (A) *gulega*, or (B) *zun kila*, or (C) *nayiga kunvogura*, or (D) *yintase*, or (E) *bonjebego*. They will buy kola-nuts and set them aside for the day of the funeral, and *kyero* (antimony)—to blacken the eyes —which they will grind and put into *kyerotoyo* (little skin flasks). They will buy red thread and black thread. Women who are old enough to wear two sets of leaves, will buy front leaves and black thread 'leaves',[1] also bangles for wrists and brass bangles for the upper arm (*ban'diba*), and iron bangles (*nyoyom base*) and rams eyes (*pera nini*)—a kind of bead—to wear round the neck. They seek for cowries to present to the singers and drummers who will, in return for these gifts, sing that So-and-so is the son of So-and-so. Where there is finery to be bought, however much it costs, they will go and buy it, fine quivers and new bows; they will seek new leathers to fasten on the bamboo bow-strings.[2] The leather-covered *kara*[3] are renewed; arrow shafts are bound with water-lizard's skin, and the owner of such things goes forth with eyes shut to any one else's manly beauty but his own; it is as if he did not know that any one else existed at all.

When the old person is dead, the body will lie for three days in the room of his senior wife, before they 'catch' the news (i.e. inform relations who live in other towns). Meanwhile, they will be doing what is required by custom. The daughters of the deceased who have married in other towns are informed. Towards night, people will hear the beating of drums and learn that some one is 'lying in a room', and the *gulu* and *luse* drums and singers will spread the news until day-break, and people will keep giving them cowries and fowls.

Next morning, the *zenore* is quite full of people and no space remains. A cow lies there with its legs sticking up. They will take down the bow and quiver of the dead man, and his soothsayer's bag, and hang them outside on the wall of his cattle-kraal. If the deceased had *tobega*, the shrine will be taken down from where it was hanging and suspended on a stick at the kitchen midden. When a cow is killed at a funeral, a new grave is always dug and the *bayase* (sextons) are given a sheep 'to dig' the grave. They dig the mouth so narrow that when one sees it, he will think that a man could not enter, yet ten people can be buried inside, for it is dug wide within like a room—like the hole of a mouse.

Next morning, the people are seen grouped in companies,[4] each company with its own war-dance (*dea*).

People from a far place who were related to the deceased and people from towns near by, also form their own companies. They dance the war-dances in the morning, and at 'the mouth' of evening, when the sun is slanting, they circle the grave. It is now that the corpse is taken

---

[1] *Vo' neŋa*, front leaves; *pore vo*, leaves worn behind; *sim vo*, black thread leaves; see pp. 331–32.   [2] See p. 333.   [3] See p. 174.

[4] *Tansugere*. Derivation *tafo sugere*, lit. separate bowmen.

to the grave. The sextons (*bayase*) come and enter the house where death has killed him. Women of the town sit beside the corpse with fans in order that a fly may not come and do a bad thing to it. The *bayase* enter the room and lift the corpse outside to the *zenzaka* (yard) and wrap it in a new mat, the red, black, and white edges of which have been first cut off, and they tie it firmly with string. While this is being done, the orphans (sons, grandsons, daughters, grand-daughters, in the classificatory sense) do a war-dance round it to hide it, so that other people may not see. When the *bayase* have finished tying it up, they take it on their left shoulders and descend (that is climb over the partition) to the cattle-kraal and run towards the entrance of the compound.

The eldest son now climbs on the wall[1] at the entrance to the *zoyo* (hut) and calls the name of the dead person loudly: 'E! E! So-and-so, if formerly, when you were alive, you were catching people and were a hot-bellied witch; you did not want people to live, and you perched on a wall, chewing people, and you used to take only a small portion of food and put it in the hand of your neighbour's child[2]—that is what is meant by being a hot-bellied witch—if it was on account of such things that *Yini* killed you, come hither quickly.'[3] The corpse with the *bayase* recedes and does not consent to come where they are calling it.

He again calls: 'Oh! if your days have "reached" and your father has called you and your *Yini* (God) has called you, then come hither quickly.'

Then the corpse, with the *bayase*, run and come to the *zenore* where the son stands and is calling. The *bayase* then run round the compound three times[4] with the body. Other *bayase* now relieve the ones who have been carrying the corpse and carry it to the grave. When they reach there, they untie all the string, while the sons and grand-sons are dancing the war-dance around the grave. They will allow the eldest son of the dead man to look into the grave before they bury the corpse.

They then take the body out of the mat, and a *baya* will enter the grave and receive the body (which is let down feet first). It is arranged nicely and laid on its left side.[5] When this is done, the junior *baya*

---

[1] In case of a female, he climbs on the flat roof of a hut.
[2] Instead of inviting it to eat out of the same dish.
[3] Compare carrying the corpse, see *Religion and Art in Ashanti*, Chapter XV.
[4] Four times, if a woman. [5] A woman on her right side; and she is buried naked.

will take the mat and burn it down in the valley, or, if it is the wet season, throw it away there, because if he were to burn it, the crops would all be spoiled wherever the smoke blew upon them. The *bayase* will now go to where there is water to bathe their bodies, while those who were in the house with the corpse wash their hands with cow dung (*bili*). After bathing, the *bayase* return to the *zenore*, and the Elders who were left sitting behind, salute them. Towards afternoon, the 'beaters of the fowls' (*nonwereba*) will climb on the flat roof and beat (to death) beasts, fowls, sheep and goats, and guinea-fowls, and give them to the one who has died.[1] Those whom the deceased called *dayose* (sons in the classificatory sense) are those who 'beat'. The dead man's eldest son will 'beat' before any one else.[2] Sometimes he will have a sheep to beat for his father. While he is beating, the *sɔbia*[3] (lit. father's child, i.e. 'half-brothers') are inside the *zenzaka* (yard). The eldest son will say, addressing the *sɔ-bia*, 'Have you answered?' One replies, 'Yes, I have answered.' The son continues, 'This, my father, who has died to-day has left me in poverty; he told me such-and-such things', and he relates all that his father had done and said. He continues, 'To-day he is dead, if indeed he has "reached" his father and great-grandfather and So-and-so and So-and-so (naming more remote ancestors), here is a sheep I am going to give him. As he is dead and has left this house, I stand confused; I do not know what I must do to keep this house safe, as he used to keep it. Receive this sheep and keep this house and join your father and grandfather in guarding it properly, for in a house where even a few still remain, they will not plant tobacco.'[4]

The sheep is 'beaten' and thrown down into the yard. Another 'son' will take his place and call the *sɔ-bia*; say (to the spirits) what is

---

[1] The sheep and goats are really killed down below by strangulation, but the fowls and guinea-fowls are killed by knocking their heads against the wall.

[2] In other cases, he who begins is generally the *kyib-kyɛma*, i.e. a 'son'—in the classificatory sense—who was already an orphan before the death of the deceased.

[3] *Sɔ-bia* means literally 'half-brothers', but the term is here used of descendants of a half-brother of the original ancestor. These relations are always in charge of the funeral celebrations, as the full 'brothers' of the deceased are expected to be too heartbroken to manage the obsequies. They (the *sɔ-bia*) get all the meat of sacrifices save what is given to the spirit of the deceased.

[4] When a man dies and leaves no 'sons' (or brothers), his compound is broken down and tobacco or corn is planted within the ruined walls, because the yard is rich in manure (having been a cattle-kraal). When a man has not any children, he is sometimes laughed at, and told 'What are you, if you were to die, they would break down your house and plant tobacco in it.'

in his heart, and 'beat' his offering. Another will take his place and speak what he likes—about their marriages, their farming, rearing of fowls; whatever each one wishes to possess and what he lies and thinks about at night.

On such a day, they will finish all the fowls and fill the yard below (with what they cast down). Some throw their offerings down into the *zenzaka* (cattle-yard) below; others throw theirs into the kitchen. All those thrown into the *zenzaka* will be taken up and are for the 'half-brothers', and those in the kitchen are for the spirit and will be cooked in the deceased's pot. When they have finished all this, those who are the right ones to do so, will gather together to take the skin of the cow which they have killed 'to rest the head of the deceased upon'.

Young people have nothing to do with that, only the Elders. They will divide it exactly, for if they do not follow the usual division, there will be quarrelling, and if they are not careful, people will be beating each other.[1]

The playing and dancing go on for three days, and meanwhile they will have consulted the soothsayers to see what the dead man says must be done next. An old man's funeral is not 'burned' quickly. They will possibly put off the second funeral for one year. The Elders will sit and discuss the matter until their 'mouths become one'. They now pour out the *kya* (corn) for the *poyablese* (every woman born in the town of which the deceased was a native, is so called) to make beer, and some for the *yi'poyaba* (i.e. the women of the same town who have become residents in it by marriage with townsmen). The *poyablese* prepare their corn outside and the *yi'poyaba* in the kitchen inside the compound, setting their pots there, while the beer-pots of the *poyablese* stand in the *zoŋo*—from which the beasts have been driven for the night. The Elders will send a boy to look after the beer which is being made in the kitchen and another boy to look after that in the *zoŋo*. On the day of pouring out the *kya*[2] (corn) the Elders have told the *sɔ-bia* (the 'half-brothers') to bring the soothsayer. They consult to find out if something had killed the deceased. Perhaps they will discover that it was nothing else than an eldest daughter's cow, or on

---

[1] The *sɔ-bia*, as already noted, are entitled to most of the meat of the birds and animals killed, and the reference to possible quarrelling is to this fact.

[2] *Kya* is prepared as follows. Corn is put in a large pot of water and allowed to soak for four or five hours; it is then taken out and spread on the kitchen floor and covered with leaves, and water sprinkled on from time to time, for three days; it is then dried on the flat roof for two hours; put in a basket for twenty-four hours, and then finally dried, when it is called *kya*.

account of the first cow bought with the proceeds of farming, which he had omitted to give his ancestors (spirits). An eldest daughter's cow is this. A girl who is an eldest daughter marries and her house-people receive a cow or cows (as *sulle*, bride-price); now one of these must be killed for the *yaba* (ancestor), and the Elders must sit together and kill it. The *yaba's* shrine is always a horn (buried in the conical earth mound of the *bagere* [1]).

'A first farming cow' is this. When a Goreŋa man farms, and after he has taken out of his crop what is required to support his household, he exchanges the remainder for a beast, perhaps first a goat, then he exchanges the young goats for a sheep, and sheep for a cow. This first cow which he comes to possess is called a '*koa nafo*' (cow bought with the proceeds of farming) and this cow should always be given to a spirit; failure to do so will cause a death in that family.

Yet another cause of death may be when a man makes a vow on a shrine, but does not keep his promise. When death kills, *that* (not fulfilling his promise) is what has really killed. Yet again, a *bagere* (shrine) may ask (through a soothsayer) for something, and yet they do not give it. When death kills, *that* is what it has killed. It is for these reasons that they consult the soothsayers on a person's death, because, before they have paid the debt due (to a spirit) they cannot hold the second funeral custom. The dead man would be chased away by his ancestor in order that he might return and receive the cow. The dead man would then return and punish those who remain, until the debt is paid, for until it is, he, the deceased, may not join his ancestor and live with him. If they persist in refusing, death will again kill in that same house. The soothsayer will say, 'It is the ancestor's eldest daughter's cow which they refused to give him, so he killed the father, and yet they did not pay the debt, so *Yaba* has chased away his son, saying that he may not "enter" with him. On account of that, he wanders about and returns and kills, so that they may hear, for the matter of the cow is "sour" to him, (the spirit). He wanders in the long grass, while they sit at home, so he kills in order that their hearts, too, may be destroyed (suffer).' They will now, if they cannot find a cow any other way, borrow one (lit. eat a debt) to pay the debt.

Sometimes, *bagere* (lit. shrine, but used of the spirit in the shrine) will ask a person for a sacrifice and that person refuse. Death will kill,

[1] That of the original founder of the whole family group is kept by the head of that group, who has now become what we call 'a section head.' It (the horn) is in this case hung up in his house by strings off the neck of sacrificed animals.

and the cause will be revealed. A *bakologo* (i.e. the spirit in a shrine which wishes to be employed, by the soothsayer, to interpret and make known the wants of other spirits) may 'follow' a person in order to be given *velego* [1] and *nwaa* ceremonies, and that person may refuse. When he dies, the cause of his death will be revealed. He has died for the lack of bringing the roots he was asked for. Among all the shrines of the Gorense, the soothsayer's shrine is the most bitter; it does not delay in death-killing.

When they have finished consulting, now comes an important thing. On that day, they tie the *dono* strings on the eldest son and eldest daughter and on the youngest son and youngest daughter and also on the wives of the sons. [2] The eldest children fasten 'black' *dono*, the remainder, the ordinary *dono*. [3] The 'black' *dono* is 'untied with a beast'. [4] The grandchildren shave their heads in the manner known as 'grandchildren's-half'. They will continue to wear the *dono* until 'the burning' of the funeral, when the *dono* is untied.

The widows, meanwhile, shave the whole head and put on widow's leaves, [5] and when it comes to the burning, will eat widow's medicine. Should a widow, before the burning of the funeral, 'make a mistake', and sleep with a man, she breaks a taboo and has what is called *'gaba'*. [6] We fear such women very much, for when a man is sick, and a woman who has *gaba* goes near to him, however sick he is he will rise up and run from that place, because she who has *gaba* is an unclean thing, and if she looks upon him, his illness will become more severe. Not until after the burning of a funeral, should widows 'do anything'.

Should a black ant bite a widow during the burning of a funeral custom, there is a reason for that. Men will go to consult the sooth-sayers about it. If the widow has not done anything wrong, then it is a spirit which is angry about something and has taken a black ant to bite the woman so that the matter may come to light.

[The remainder of the account of this funeral custom need not be given, as it resembles that held for an old woman, which is described elsewhere.]

---

[1] *Vile* is to make the preliminary small shrine which is later built up into a full-sized soothsaying shrine. *Nwaa*, lit. cutting, is a ceremony at which roots are cut, at which the soothsayer's wife rides a black goat. See Chapter XV.   [2] *Sanpoy'ba*.

[3] The string is really all the same colour; 'black' is here used in the sense of 'important'. *Dono* is a string made of a couple of strands of *bero* fibre.

[4] If too poor, then a hoe. In case of the ordinary *dono*, the fee for untying it is a guinea-fowl.

[5] Leaves of the shea butter tree. See also p. 332.   [6] See also p. 395.

XIII

FUNERAL CUSTOMS (*continued*)

The Funeral of a Middle-aged (lit. 'a middle-land') Person, and some Customs relating to Tobega

'MIDDLE-LAND' funerals are for those who have wives and children, sons and daughters, but who are not yet very old and have not yet become the heads of sections. When such an one dies, those whom he begat will do the necessary things—the *dea* (war-dance)—for their 'father', but if it is the dry season, the *yoyo* dance. On the day of burial, his children will climb on the *gosogo*, calling their kinsmen to join them (i.e. their 'half-brothers') [1], and beat a fowl to death on the roof and kill a beast for them. If the deceased was the 'owner of hands' (i.e. rich) and the children too 'want a name', they will kill a cow and place it on the midden heap. They will dig a grave 'with a sheep' (i.e. the sextons are given a sheep for digging a grave), and 'cut *nanwoo*' [2] with a goat, which is also paid to the sextons (*bayase*).

The deceased's daughters' husbands will come to mourn him and throw cowries, and bring a sheep with them to mourn for their *dema* (father-in-law), and a hoe 'to rest his head upon' (*kogele*), and many other things. Girls and boys follow each other in a long line and make a big crowd, crying aloud. All his 'daughters' who have married in other towns do the same. The son-in-law who has failed to come, and happens not to have paid up all the cows due for the *sulle* (bride-price), will have his wife taken from him.

They will arrive on the 'fresh' funeral day (*kumasere*) (the day of burial) and return again on the day on which they consult (i.e. the third day). The sons-in-law also bring beer with them which they have made. Such a corpse which is not very old, they will bury quickly without delay. Next day, after the burial, the Elders of the various sections will issue out *kya* [3] to the *poyablese* [4] and they will make beer, and the Elders will consult the soothsayers and find out the cause of death. [5]

If it is the wet season, they will wait until the dry season 'to burn' the funeral. The *dono* [6] is tied on after the body is buried [this custom

---

[1] See footnote, p. 202.　　[2] See footnote, p. 186.　　[3] See footnote, p. 197.
[4] See footnote, p. 188.　　　[5] See p. 356.　　　　　　　[6] See p. 199.

has already been fully described]. Those he calls *yisi* ('grandchildren') shave half their heads. They take a razor and set it on the middle of the head exactly, and shave one side completely, leaving one side with hairs. When they have done all that they ought to do, they will set aside the funeral custom until the time for 'burning' it. When this time comes, they will again follow up all those to whom the deceased was related in order to make the second funeral (*wue*). Every one assembles, and when they have finished eating, about the time when every one 'enters' upon sleep, the wailing and beating of drums will begin. This is the second funeral. The *seba-nso* (i.e. those who own the dead man) will call the senior *poyablega* and give the *kya* to her, and she will distribute it to the various women of the compounds and all will grind their portions separately.

The Making of Beer. They will fetch plenty of water and pour it into big *sea* pots. The flour which has already been ground (the *kya*) is mixed in it, and there it stands until morning. Some of the flour is also put in ordinary cooking-pots and heated (boiled). At the time when people have finished eating, they will pour out this hot beer into the cold beer, and when day breaks it has become *mie* (bitter). As there is so much beer, each woman has her own sieve to strain it, into yet another big *sea* pot. When it is all strained, it is poured into still larger pots and boiled properly until it gets *loko*,[1] so that those who drink may praise them (the brewers). When they have finished the second cooking, they will take the beer out of the big pots and pout it into the *sea* pots. When it becomes tepid, they will fill other pots, called *dose* pots, in order that the beer in these may 'cry out' (*kyele*) quickly, and this they will use to strengthen the beer which has not yet 'cried out'; a little is added to each pot until the beer in the big pot also begins to 'cry out'. When day breaks, all the beer is 'crying out' with a sound like *nwe-ke-kee*, and froths and bubbles while it 'cries' as if it were boiling on a fire, but it really is the strength of the beer. Next morning when the sun rises, those Elders who reached there first, and are important people, will take a *doa* pot full of beer for themselves. When those who have brewed it are carrying it out-side to them, they cover their mouths with their left hand and keep silent, because they are shy and nervous lest the beer may not be good. When they are praised they are pleased. When the *sɔ-bia* have got their beer, they will ask of the soothsayers exactly what kind of shrine (i.e. spirit) has caused the death. The soothsayer will tell them what

---

[1] See footnote, p. 175.

to do, in order that the spirit may not kill some one else. When they have finished consulting, they will present the *baga* (soothsayer) with corn and a fowl, flour-water in a calabash, and a pot of beer, and let him depart. Those who want to share these things will follow 'his bag'.

Several pots of beer are now sent out to where every one is sitting; each group[1] has its pot. Any one who 'owns his own head' will be given a pot to himself.

If the relations of the dead man are able, they will make beer separately. This beer is called *dazelebo*, which means 'beer set aside' (for the spirits). This beer is also used for the 'untying' of the *dono* strings, and also for the 'burning' of the funeral.

The *dono* is untied 'with guinea-fowls'. They will collect them and cook them and also make *sayebo* (grain foods), and both those who have the *dono* fastened upon them, and those who did the fastening, join together and eat the food; only orphans may eat of this food. After this, the *gore* 'calabash things' will be made in order that the dead man's mother's children (i.e. uterine 'brothers' and 'sisters') may dip their hands in them; among these also, any one whose 'mother's child' has not died may not touch the food. They will make grain food and set it aside till day-break for the dead, and very early in the

[1] Sections (a word which will be explained later) were originally founded by sons by different mothers, but the same father. All descendants from one father and one mother form one section; new sections were founded by *sɔ-bia*, i.e. 'father's children', i.e. half-brothers. *Sɔ-bia* is also sometimes found in the forms *ba-bia*. The following diagram illustrates this. A, is the original ancestor, who had married three wives (all of

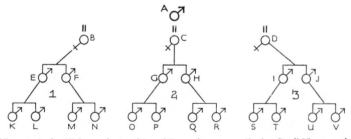

different clan). All descendants of A and B continue to swell what I call No. 1 section. All descendants of A and C, No. 2 section; and all descendants of A and D, No. 3 section. The people of Nos. 2 and 3 sections trace their descent from G and I respectively, but still regard A as their senior common ancestor, whom they share in common with section 1. Each section continues to throw off *deto* (lit. rooms) or *yi-dema*, e.g. in section 1. E and F each found a new *deo* (pl. *deto*) which becomes a sub-division in No. 1 section, and so on throughout.

morning the orphans and those who are not forbidden will assist to eat it. They will point to the food, saying, 'Look here, and here, can't you see these holes (in the food), that is the eating-place of the spirit.' Some beer is also put in a red pot called a *kare*[1] pot, but I do not know exactly what the ceremony is.

On the day of 'breaking' the funeral, they will make shea butter and cook *tuntu* seeds. (The pots and calabashes of the dead are broken at the cross-roads leading to the town of the deceased's mother.) They make *kyenkyera* cakes and share them according to custom among the *zutto-dana* (Elders). Each one has his own calabash, and even if an Elder is not present himself, some one from his compound will receive his share. The 'breaking' ceremony is performed by both men and women, but no one who is still able to bear children should attend. Young people do not go to the ceremony, lest, should they go, they might break a taboo. They do the custom in the silence of night. Young children are driven away, also any one who coughs. A mother with a baby will be chased away, because, while the ceremony is being performed, if the child cries there would be trouble; it would become ill.

The bow and quiver[2] of the dead are laid at the cross-roads and they dance round them with loud lamentations while others sing war songs and pretend to shoot arrows. All those who remain at home do not make the slightest noise. Before they begin the ceremony, a man will come running from the compound of the deceased, and the sound of his running is *gute gute*, and he stands in the cattle-yard between the two pillars at the entrance to the compound and calls out, 'Silence, silence', and goes back. Every one becomes as silent as if there was not anybody there. After this admonition to silence, if any one makes a noise, even if a man who has a cough, coughs, he will never after be cured of his cough, try every kind of medicine as he may. On account of all this, people are very afraid and keep all the rules.

When they have finished 'breaking' the funeral, next day in the morning there will be a pot of beer for 'washing the entrance' of the compound (*zanore pere*).

Tobega. If the dead man possessed *tobega*, or was one 'who knew water' (*mi kom*), then they will find some one who also possesses *tobega*, and they will give him a small red cock in order that he may remove the *tobega* and that it may return where it formerly was, because its

---

[1] Every woman has one or more *kare* pots which are only used at funerals.

[2] The arrows are removed from the quiver and stalks of grass substituted.

owner (i.e. the deceased) is no more. *Tobega* means that you have gone down into the valley with arrows and killed a man with an arrow. After the fight is over you 'boil'[1] the person you have killed. If you fail to do this you will be ill, or 'it' will kill you, or kill your house-people, or you will die suddenly without being ill. Such things will happen unless you 'set a pot' (*dogele*).[2] Therefore, when they see that *zeem* has struck a man, they will run to some one who possesses the necessary roots to get medicine to treat him. They will give this man fowls, a dog,[3] a goat; beer will be made.

I do not know the kind of roots used, and I do not know exactly how they are used, but they cook them until their water is boiling; then they take this water in a calabash and pour it over the head of him who has the *zeem*, three times, and do so for three days. On the day on which they throw the roots away, those who 'know water' (i.e. those who have killed their man) gather in their numbers, carry the roots, and take them away singing in chorus (*sakera*) as they descend into the valley, just as they had once done when men had gone to kill each other. There they cast away the roots. When they return, they take the skin of a *tobega* (a kind of squirrel) and a sheep's horn over which has been stretched the skin off the neck of a cock. Inside the *tobega* skin they put some of the powdered charcoal made out of the roots and inside the horn some more of this charcoal mixed with shea butter. These things are hung up in the *zoyo* hut.[4]

No one may now enter into the *zoyo* hut but the owner of the *tobega*. He will do so in order to sacrifice to it, giving it dogs and goats every year. When the new harvest comes, the people in that house are forbidden to eat the new crops until the *tobega* shrine has first been given some. Of these sacrifices, no one may eat (except persons who have *tobega*, i.e. who have killed some one?). A person who has *tobega* may not offer any one anything with his left hand, nor may he strike any one with his left hand. The owner of a *tobega* shrine must not drink of the new season's beer until he has first given his *tobega* some. On account of all this, every kind of new food—new early millet, new beans, new ground-nuts, new corn, new leaves of beans, or anything which is sown in the ground—must be given to

---

[1] Not literally of course, the boiling refers to the roots used.

[2] This word is always used to mean the preparation of medicine in connexion with some ceremony.

[3] The majority of these N.T. tribes consider dog a great delicacy.

[4] The room near the entrance to the *na'dene* (cattle-kraal) in which the sheep and goats and fowls are shut up for the night.

the *tobega* first before the household eat. Why? Because a man has killed by his own power (*paya*) some one who, if he had not been killed, might have been alive and gathering his own crops.[1] No one may splash cold water on a *tobega-dana* (an owner of *tobega*). If one does so, and the *tobega-dana* does not immediately do the same to you, you will get a swollen belly (*ukere*).

When an 'owner of *tobega*' dies, his son will take a red cock, and summon others who have *tobega*, and they will take the skin and horn of the deceased, and go with them in the direction of the town where the killed or murdered man used to live. When they reach the valley, they cast the shrine away, in order that 'he' (the spirit of the murdered man) may depart, because his 'owner' is no longer alive, and that he may return to his own place (*kukun*).

The burning of a funeral for 'old things' and those who are not so old is the same. Before the burning, the deceased's wife's sister will come and throw stones at people's guinea-fowls and 'ride a horse'[2] round his compound, and look into his grain-store, and take corn out of it, while one of the 'house-people' stands and throws it back, leaving only a little of what she has taken out.[3]

Widows. After the burning of a funeral, the *pogosigera*[4] will go to the widows and say, 'When something spoils, it spoils entirely; he is no longer ours; tell us with whom you will stand'. When he speaks thus, he means that they may choose new husbands. One may say, 'I like this man', but sometimes a widow refuses to choose, saying that the men themselves can do so. When a widow chooses thus, and bears children by her new husband, these children belong to her first husband (now dead), but in some other places the new husband owns them.[5] If one of the cows (the bride-price) still remains to be paid,

[1] 'A woman who delivers "two hands" (i.e. has twins) is like one who has *tobega* in so far as she must eat the first-fruits of anything which she has sown, before any one else touches them.' 'A *tobega* may sometimes demand (through the soothsayers) human flesh. If the man who killed him is a witch, he will easily be able to get this, if not, he will have to cut his own finger or toe and feed his *tobega* on this.'

[2] The horse is a stalk of guinea-corn which she straddles.

[3] The family grain-store is generally handed over to some one among the deceased's *sɔ-bia's* section, and he issues corn to the *poyablese* and others in connexion with the funeral.

[4] The messenger and witness of every legal marriage who is sent by the bridegroom (or rather, the senior male in the compound) to the bride's town, to inform the head of her section of the marriage, and thus obtain an independent witness of the contract.

[5] This is the case at Tongo, Sia, Winduri, Gorogo, Zandoo, and also among the Namnam and Kusase.

the new 'owner of the woman' will pay it to the widow's 'house-people'. The 'brothers' of the widows chosen will follow them and the new husband will kill things for them.

The Funeral Custom of a Baby. When a baby dies and has no *nyere*,[1] they consult the *baga* (soothsayer) and he tells them what kind of a thing the child who has died really was, and whether it should 'sit' or should enter the long grass. If it is to 'sit', a grave will be dug on a *loya*[2] plot in front of the entrance to the compound (i.e. at the *zenore*) and there it will be buried. When they are taking it out to bury, they carry the calabash which its mother used for giving it water and lay it down inverted, and mark out a circle, and there they begin to dig the grave. First of all they dig it straight down, and when the hole has gone down a little, they dig inwards like a room. When finished, the corpse is carried out and buried by the *baya* (sexton), and the calabash put above the grave that the spirit may come and drink out of it. When they have finished burying it, the mother of the dead baby will come out from the house and stand between the walls of the entrance leading into the *naga-dene* (cattle-yard). The *baya* who buried it will stand near facing her. The woman is standing between the two pillars (*ugese*) at the entrance (see Fig. 4) and the *baya* just outside. The woman has come with water in a calabash. This the *baya* receives from her and pours out between the two pillars. He then takes his foot and rubs where the water runs. The woman squats down and the *baya* takes his wet foot and with it smears over both breasts of the woman. Why? Because otherwise her breasts would swell. In future, the woman will wander and seek for guinea-corn-stalks which have been eaten by white ants. She will pick out the earth which the ants have deposited inside the stalks, and mash it, and smear this on her breasts. Her milk which was plenty will now disperse. In about three days, they will again consult the soothsayer; the father and mother of the dead baby will shave their heads, and the mother will put on *bayere* fibre strings round her waist, if this was her first baby to have died. When the hair has grown a little it is shaved again in a circle round the base.

The Funeral Custom of a Child which is really a Fairy. When a child has died, and they have fetched the soothsayer to come and consult, and his bag says, 'The child says he is going into the long grass to chew *kenkayera* and *sunsobera* fruit', that means that the spirit does not wish to sit with persons, and that again means that he does not

[1] See p. 8.   [2] See footnote, p. 137.

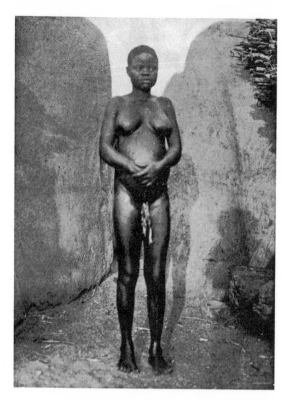

Fig. 4. 'The woman is standing between the two
pillars of the entrance'

wish to be buried at the compound or in the garden near the compound. On account of such a child, they will seek a *kyinkyinga* horn and *kyinkyinga* medicine, and wrap up the body in grass and take it where the black ants live, and dig a hole and put it there. The doctor who has brought the *kyinkyinga* horn will take it and put it on the neck of the mother. The soothsayer will reveal this thing and that thing which it (the spirit) wants, and they will seek for these things. On the day on which the body is buried, it is as if the father and mother were ill, and the doctor will give them roots to eat and some to soak in water for three days and then bathe. On the third day, the beer will be ready and they will have got together all those things which the soothsayer had revealed that the spirit wanted. In the evening the doctor will come, and they will take a pot of beer and a calabash of *tuntu* (seeds) and go and empty out the roots with which they have bathed, and take the things to the place where the black ants live and where the child is buried and place them there, and the child is told that it may go for ever and not return. On returning, the horn which had been hung around the mother's neck is taken off and the parents' heads are shaved. If all this is not done and they omit anything, when the woman again delivers, it will be the very same 'thing' which she gives birth to. Why? Because this 'fairy' has not received all the things which it asked for. It is only by following all the *baga's* instructions that they can prevent this happening again. When the parents' hair grows again, they will shave it in the manner known as *zu mure* (all round the base of the skull). When they have done so, the ceremony is finished.

The Funeral Custom of a Child who has a Nyere.[1] When a child dies who has a *nyere*, on the day he dies they will take the soothsayer's bag to consult in order to know the cause of death, for perhaps they have offended something and this has caused a spirit to kill, or it may be *Yini kum* (God's death), i.e. a natural death.

When the soothsayer comes, and they have caught hold of his wand, and if he says that a spirit was the cause of death, they will do this and that and the soothsayer may tell them to give satisfaction to the

---

[1] See p. 8. *Nyere* may not marry each other's wives, e.g. A has two brothers, B and C; B is A's *nyere*, i.e. his next eldest brother. A dies; B may not marry A's wife, but C may do so. B dies, A may not marry his wife, nor C, because C is *nyere* to B. Two female *nyere* may not marry the same man, or even marry into the same compound, unless they 'bury' a hoe at the entrance of the compound, and give a cow and that cow's *nyere* as part of the *sulle* (bride-price). Superstitions regarding *nyere* are found among many other tribes.

spirit before consulting further. When they have finished consulting, the *kya* for beer will be 'poured out' (i.e. distributed), and in the evening they will boil it for the first time and next morning boil it again and fill up the pots. On the third day, a 'half-brother's child' will again consult the soothsayer. It is our custom, when some one dies, for the son of a 'half-brother' in another section to consult and find out the thing which 'did' thus to his 'half-brother', because a full brother of the dead person is sorrowing and has 'no face' (heart) to do so. Thus they help each other.

As the corpse is a little one, no beast is killed, only a fowl 'cut' for the *nanwoo* rite.[1] The father and mother of the dead child will shave their heads, as it is 'a bad head' (something unlucky) which has befallen them. The mother's children (i.e. uterine brothers and sisters), whether they are younger or older than the deceased, will shave their bad heads away.

The second time of consulting the soothsayer is on the third day, and this is also the funeral-burning day (*kure nyoa dare*). They will prepare grain food (*sayabo*) and place it in a *gore* calabash[2] in order that the deceased's mother's children may eat. If the child was the first one whom the mother had lost, she will put on the *bayere* fibre girdle.

When the sun sets, they will burn the child's funeral according to the usual custom. The funeral of a boy who has brothers or sisters and is nearing puberty is the same as that of a girl who has brothers or sisters and is nearing puberty.

The *bayase* (sextons) are given some ground-nuts for making the grave.

The Funeral Custom for a Married Man who has not begat any Children, with Special Reference to the Remarriage of his Widows. When a man dies who has a wife but no children, or a woman dies who has a husband but no children, their funeral customs are similar.

The widow will put on widow's leaves, and widow's medicine will be given to her. If the dead man had a beast, perhaps they will kill it for him. They will consult twice and the *kya* will be poured out.

Remarriage of Widows. After they have finished burning the funeral, the kinsmen of the deceased will enter the hut of the widow and talk

---

[1] See footnote, p. 186. The fowl is killed and a leg cut off at the joint. This leg is then placed in a calabash and buried with the body.

[2] A calabash with a narrow mouth; a *wama* calabash is a gourd cut through the centre, which has a wide opening.

with her that she may choose a person who will keep her as a wife, but as this man will not own his own children whom he may have by her, he will really have all his trouble for nothing (the ghost husband claims the children the ghost's brother is responsible for them).[1]

Before Europeans (came to our land) if a Goreŋa man (in his prime) died without having any illness, that meant arrows (i e. war) unless some one was able to prevent them. Every male would go forth with his quiver to attack and shoot enemies and add a corpse to that of their dead clansman. For this reason they would keep a careful watch on the *sora* (plural of *sɔ̃ɔ̃*) relations. If they did not do so, they would see that some one had done something to himself owing to the paining of the heart. It is the duty of the *sɔ-bia* to see to this and not let 'the yard spoil'.[2]

Sometimes when a widow is a young girl, her neighbours will 'chew her ears', *obe de toba* (give her bad advice), and she will run away to marry in some town,[3] but if they (her late husband's people) had paid the cows and there were good men left in the compound, she will not run away, or if they allow her to choose the one whom she loves (among her late husband's clansmen). If, however, they force her and give her to one whom she does not want, she will 'go out'.

---

[1] Among the Nankanse, as among all these tribes, the ordinary procedure is for a brother to inherit a dead brother's wives, and this he will probably do if the widows and himself are in the same age class. Widows, however, are often allowed to choose their second husband (as described in Chap. XXII). All that such a freedom of choice implies, however, is that, instead of marrying a brother of her late husband, she is permitted to choose 'a brother' in the classificatory sense, i.e. a clansman in her late husband's town. Such a marriage implies (a) that the woman still continues to reside in the compound of her late husband; (b) that all children born to her new husband belong not to him but to the dead husband, and will sacrifice to him and not to their own father; (c) the new husband will not have to pay any *sulle* (bride-price) but will kill a goat for her brothers; (d) the children by the second marriage take the clan of the deceased. The widow really continues to be the wife of her dead husband.

[2] The bereaved often throw themselves against a wall, or stab themselves with an arrow. In the old days, war was an outlet for this feeling. Here again we have grief and anger as synonymous, as among the Ashanti.

[3] That is, a town other than that of her late husband and to a man not a 'brother', i.e. not a clansman of her late husband.

XIV

FUNERAL CUSTOMS (*continued*)

'*The Burning*' (Nyoa)[1] *of the Funeral Custom of the Head of a Section*

WHEN he died, his younger brother was the first to fetch water in a calabash and was the first to bathe the corpse. As he began with his right hand, the next one to bathe the body began with his left, the third with his right again, and so on until they had finished bathing the body. His senior wife supplied a new mat[2] from which had been cut the coloured edges, before the corpse was laid on it. The corpse was bathed in the yard and afterwards taken back into the room. Next, a goat[3] was caught and they stood in the cattle-yard and took a knife and skinned the neck of the goat—they did not kill it—and took the skin and tied it with a bit of *bea* string round the waist of the corpse and between its legs. This custom is called *nyare kum* (binding something between the legs of the corpse). When they were ready to come and take the body to be buried, they took it, wrapped in the new mat, into the *zoyo*[4] hut. Here they made an opening in the wall of the hut leading to outside the compound, and through this hole it was carried outside, when the *bayase* took it on their shoulders stepping as they did so across the half-skinned goat. The eldest son of the dead man now climbed on the wall of the *zoyo* hut, holding the tail of a cow, which had been killed, in his hand and called the name of his father loudly and said:

'If, when you were alive, there were no new children or new wives in this compound, because you were killing them (being a witch), and on account of this your father struck you down, come hither.'

The corpse stood there, not coming forward, and again he said:

'Oh, if you yourself have 'reached' your day, come hither.' The corpse now came running and beat against the *zoyo* hut. The *bayase* then ran round the compound three times with the body, and then

[1] Also sometimes called *ku'wure* (repetition of funeral).
[2] Women weave mats.
[3] A goat was the totem of the deceased, this deliberate violation of a taboo is a marked feature of many funeral customs, as will be noted later.
[4] A *Ti-dana* (head of a compound), when he becomes very old, often prefers to sleep in this hut, which is cleaned out for him and has the floor nicely beaten hard.

set off to the grave to bury it. When they returned from the grave, the goat was killed and laid down outside the *zoyo* hut; this goat was not eaten; it was buried.

When the *bayase* had returned, then fowls were 'beaten' to death to give to the dead. Some people beat fowls, others goats, others sheep, others guinea-fowls. As each one gave his offering he said what his heart wanted. On the third day, the 'half-brother'[1] skinned the cow which had been lying at the foot of the kitchen midden. This cow was killed 'to rest the corpse's head upon'.

The eldest son of 'a sister'[2] of the dead man chose the foreleg, upon which they were to begin the skinning of it. The cow was then skinned and portioned out; 'the half-brother' of the deceased took one of the hind legs, and the eldest son of a 'sister' took a foreleg; the remainder of the cow was for the *deo*[3] of the deceased.

They cut a piece of meat from the hind leg, and a piece of the liver and the stomach, and cooked it outside the compound, but did not add any salt or pepper,[4] and when cooked they placed it on a rack outside the *zoyo* hut (for the spirit). Next morning they took it and gave it to those who were orphans. The one who had been an orphan for the longest time was the first to chew the meat. The second funeral custom was now arranged for a year hence.

When this time came, a goat was killed, and a piece of its liver cut, and a piece of meat from its hind leg, and its stomach taken, and, on the day on which they commenced cooking the beer, they dug a small hole and placed this meat uncooked in it, and covered the hole over with a small round potsherd and set a big *sere* pot on top of all and left it for three days. When they uncovered it, they found that the meat in the hole was not putrefied and that nothing was wrong with it. That was a sign that no misfortune would happen; had they found the meat rotten, they would have known that death would again slay. On the day they uncovered the meat, no one was allowed to climb on the flat roof, and the women had to take off both their front and back leaves and the men their loin-cloths. The eldest daughter of the deceased then took a calabash, over which another was placed, and set out in front followed by all the rest, naked, and dancing with a movement of the hands and feet, made her way to the pond called

[1] See footnote, p. 202.
[2] Here means a woman of the deceased's clan who had married in some other town (*teya*).
[3] See p. 245.
[4] A taboo for spirits, except those which reside in *bakologo*, see Chapter. XV.

Abenpelem near Winkoŋo. When they reached there, the eldest daughter took one of the two calabashes, and placed it upside down on the surface of the water. She then took the second calabash and put it beneath the first and withdrew both—the one underneath being full of water, the uppermost one covering that beneath, in which the water splashed *du! du! du! du!* They set off homeward, the eldest daughter again leading. While they were at the pond, another daughter had remained behind grinding earth as if it were flour and waiting for them to return. The eldest son of the deceased, together with the eldest daughter of his younger brother, had gone with the others to the water. The youngest daughter of the dead man had run to catch grasshoppers and cook them for those who had gone to the water. They then took the earth, which had been ground as if it were flour, and the grasshoppers and cooked these. The grasshoppers were broken up and put on several plates, and the earth on three broken potsherds. These were handed to a 'half-brother' of the deceased, and he and the people of his 'section' made pretence to eat them, after which they took all and emptied it into the hole which they had dug for the meat. When the sun became cool and dark, they next entered a room and ate real meat of wild beasts—hare and bush-buck and 'black fish'. Guinea-fowls and grain foods were cooked. The water drawn from the pond was used for cooking the food. When they were returning with it no one spoke or even coughed, and when they reached home every one had put on their 'clothes' again.

When all were ready, the one whose duty it was to do so, stood up and ran straight towards the *zenore*, shouting out, 'Stop that noise, that noise, that I may do my father's business, my ancestor's business.' He took some of the food which I have mentioned and threw it here and there and again shouted, 'You (pl.) laugh at them Ha! ha! ha!'; then he himself fell down and laughed. While he was doing this every one remained silent. Now, he took a calabash containing some of the food that had been prepared, and pushed it along the ground to the women who were in the compound, and another calabash, and pushed it along the ground to the men who were outside the compound.

At daybreak, when the rays of the sun had climbed, they took his *loko*[1] (quiver and bow) and went out on the path leading to his *aseba's* town (mother's brother's town), and set them down. That

---

[1] Not the deceased's own bow and arrows. A rough model is made and grass stalks take the place of real arrows.

was the path leading to where his *sōō*[1] or *zeem* or *nifi* came from (i.e his blood as opposed to his clan relations). Here they cut up the quiver and bow and arrows with an axe and buried the fragments. They were not burned because it was the wet season.[2]

They had taken some flour and beer—in a red clay pot— with them to the cross-roads, and they mixed the flour and beer and broke up little pieces and put some on the back of the hand of the eldest son, and he let it fall off his hand on to the ground. This was done three times. The eldest daughter was given some in her palms and she threw it down, and, in her case, this was repeated four times. The eldest son and eldest daughter now ate what remained in the red pot and every one returned to the compound.

Some one now descended into the deceased's grain-store and took out a single stalk of corn and squeezed the grain off it and let it scatter on the ground of the cattle-yard, and orphans came and picked up the grains, weeping and crying:

'Our father to-day has gone forever,
Our father to-day has gone forever.'

The Funeral Custom of a Leper. When a leper dies, they wash the body as usual and place it on a mat, cutting off the red and black edging before doing so. The reason they do so is because living persons sleep on mats which have these coloured lines, and it is not proper that a dead person should do so. After the corpse is bathed, it is tied up in the mat by the *bayase* and taken out to bury. All those who have touched the body take cow dung and *kuenka*[3] grass and rub their hands. When the sextons (*bayase*) return from the grave, they fetch *dawa dawa* leaves and certain roots, and put these in a calabash of water and sprinkle the water on all those who have entered the house and touched the body. The reason why they do so is in order not to infect (*lomse*) themselves. They now call one of the *bayase* who buried the body and give him a goat, in order that he may bring roots. He cuts the roots up. They give him a red cock and a black hen. He sacrifices the red cock upon his *baya* medicine pot (*bayan doko*), then the black hen, and last of all the goat. He next takes the roots which he had cut up and puts them into the pot and adds water and boils them until the water bubbles, when those who were present at her[4]

---

[1] These terms will be fully examined later, see Chapter XVIII.   [2] See p. 201.

[3] The smell of this grass is also used to drive away ghosts.

[4] The account is the actual ceremony in connexion with the funeral of a leper woman called Asera.

death bathe in the water in order that they may not be infected by the sickness. Some of the roots which remain are burned, and ground, and mixed with shea butter.

They cook the things which were killed and make grain food, and the *baya* takes some and gives it as an offering to his *baya* pot of medicine, after which all those who have bathed in the water eat some of the roots, and shea butter and food. By doing so they drive away the sickness. As this leper woman had died without any one being present, her husband brought a guinea-fowl to 'set a pot' (*dogele*).[1]

[1] The following are a few additional notes on funeral customs. Both men and women are generally buried naked. The head of a male is placed towards the east, a female's head to the west. The eldest son always follows the *bayase* and looks into the grave. Nothing belonging to the deceased is ever buried in graves. Anything found in a grave is a 'soul thing' (see p. 186) belonging to a living person. The dead person's clothes, if he or she had any, are placed on the roof of the *zoŋo* and smoked with *kuenka* grass. A male's bow and quiver after death are hung up on the wall of the *zoŋo*.

XV

SHRINES

The Making of an Ancestral Shrine. An Offering of Early Millet

BAGERE[1] and *Bakologo* are both shrines of spirits, of a father, mother, father's father, mother's mother (&c.). They are similar. Some one dies and they bury him and 'burn' his funeral custom. His eldest son, who already knows 'the words and customs' of his father, he is the one to sacrifice (to his father's spirit) after they have finished burning his funeral custom. The son goes to the house of the *baga* (soothsayer) to hear 'from his bag' what the spirit of his late father has to say. The soothsayer will tell him that a spirit, perhaps that of his late father, mother, father's father, or mother's mother, says that they must pour water (*ka kom*) for it. He, the *baga* will then mention something, a hoe, an axe, a bangle, a pot, anything at all, saying that his father, mother, father's father, or mother's mother *is* that iron or pot. The thing named is sought for, set down, and sacrificed upon (*kabere*), because that thing *is* the ancestor. All those whom the spirit 'owned' are called to attend the ceremony. The one who is performing it will catch a fowl, and the son of the deceased will tell them all he has heard from the *baga* and inform them that he wishes to 'test' with a fowl (*pose noa*).

They speak as follows: (addressing the spirit) 'So-and-so, you said at the compound of the soothsayer that you have entered into a new state (*nam*[2]) and that we must give (*ka*) you an offering of water. On

---

[1] The following are briefly the main distinctions between *Bagere* and *Bakologo* shrines :

(*a*) A *Bagere* is a shrine, but is not used to 'consult'.

(*b*) A *Bakologo* is a *bagere* which has been specially consecrated by the *nwa* ceremony, after which the spirit or spirits which reside in it give their services to others than descendants, through the soothsayers. *Bakologo* means literally *Baga-kologo*, i.e. soothsayer's bag, but the word is also used for the shrine which the soothsayer consults and for the soothsayer.

(*c*) The medium, or soothsayer as I have called this person throughout these volumes, is called a *baga*, pl. *bagaba*, but he is also often called the soothsayer's bag. A clear understanding of these terms is essential, and this and the following description give us a wonderfully clear conception of the relative significance of these words.

[2] *Nam* is used also to express creation.

account of this, I have gathered all your people who are sitting here, and also the thing the soothsayer mentioned; if, indeed, you have spoken as reported, let this fowl salute the Sky-God (*noa puse Ɣini*); if the soothsayer has lied for you, then let it fall on its chest.'

The flour-water is first poured out, and made to fall on top of the thing (axe or hoe, &c.). They then cut the throat of the fowl and cast it down, and in its flutterings, when it turns its face towards God, that shows that it has been accepted and that the *baga* man has 'seen' and spoken the truth. If the fowl takes its belly and covers the ground and shows its back to God, then the soothsayer has lied. When the fowl is 'received', the water is poured out, and fowls and a beast killed on the thing which the soothsayer had indicated to be the spirit (the abode of the spirit ?). Some time will now elapse (possibly a year), when he (the son ?) will go and consult the soothsayer again. The *baga* tells him that his father, mother, grandfather, or grandmother, on account of whom he has performed the *luɲere* [1] ceremony (described above) now says he (or she) wants a *deo* (a room). He will seek for *kya* and for a beast, and for fowls and guinea-fowls. He will follow up all the relations and tell them that their spirit is saying it wants him to give it a dwelling room (*deo*). If they are sleeping well, [2] they will consent to come and give it a room. When all are ready, every one comes with something in his hand, according to what they used to bring the deceased during his (or her) lifetime. Beer will be made after the *kya* has been distributed. They will build up a mound of earth (*uka*), making a small hole underneath its foundation. That is the mouth or entrance by which the spirit will go in or out. (See Fig. 5.) The women will smooth it nicely [3] and splash on *am*. [4] On the day of offering the beer, the Elders will come to kill things and sacrifice. They will mix some beer with flour and address the spirit, saying: 'You have told us at the house of the soothsayer that we may give you a *deo*, because you have no place to enter, so we have built you a room. Here stands your beer in pots, fowls and guinea-fowls are here in

[1] *Luɲere* is the first offering of flour and water and the testing with the fowl. After this ceremony, the iron, or whatever the thing may be, was placed in a small mound of earth, outside, if the spirit supposed to be in it is a male, inside the yard, if a female spirit.

[2] Sleeping well, here means that there is no sickness of untoward event in their family at the time, which they would ascribe to the influence of the late departed.

[3] Men build a house, but women do the plastering of the walls and the beating of the mud floors.

[4] A decoction of the bark of various trees and husks of seeds of *dawa dawa* trees.

plenty. Here stands your beast. If you have, indeed, said all this, and the soothsayers have not lied for you, then accept this, your room, and do good to this compound and do not let (its occupants) lack anything and permit this fowl to salute God.'

After the fowl has been killed and been 'accepted', then they will kill all the fowls and the beast. If the first fowl is not accepted, they will go again to consult and find out what is wrong, and if they fail to find a cause, the beer will have been drunk in vain, and the fowls and the beast will not be sacrificed, until some other time they find the cause, when they will again bring the things for sacrifice. When the spirit consents to receive, they then believe that it continues to love them, and that it will enter into the thing which they have built for it, and will bring profit in their lives and do them good, and that they will get all things at the shrine. They will sacrifice there always, continuing until son's sons (i.e. for many generations), without ever forgetting. (Future) descendants will sacrifice and call it 'father' or 'mother'. Others will come to it without even knowing whose 'father', or whose 'mother' it is, but addressing it as 'father' or 'mother'. If you are a stranger, and do not know our customs, you will suppose that it is their own father or their own mother and not know that it is (a spirit) of long ago. That is what a *bagere*[1] (shrine) is.

The Making of a Soothsayer's Shrine:

A *bagere* is a dwelling-place of a spirit of a person who is dead. After he (or she) is dead and the funeral has been 'burned', he becomes a *kyima* (spirit). A son sacrifices to his father and to his mother. When they have finished burning the funeral, they build the dead a *bagere*, that is a room (*deo*) for it—a living-room for the spirit—and it enters as a living person would and lives in the same manner. They sacrifice to it and give it everything which it requires, and the belly of the spirit 'becomes washed' (contented, happy) and he thinks to do good for his child. That child now goes and consults the soothsayers in order to hear what words his spirit will say; it will perhaps want something. When he (the soothsayer) hears from the mouth of the spirit that it has entered the state of being a *bagere* (*nam bagere*), and that the son has 'tested' (with a fowl) and finished building a shrine (as already

---

[1] The eldest son is in charge of the shrine of his own parents, but the ancestral shrine is inherited by the next brother and descends to each in turn, then to the eldest son of these brothers, but not necessarily to the eldest son of the eldest brother. A man may thus find himself in possession of two shrines, one of his remote ancestor, the other of his father.

described), and that it now wants to bless its child and seek things for him, it will speak before the soothsayer, saying that it is now entered into the state of being a *bakologo* (*nam bakologo*), because it is happy with the offerings made to it, and wishes to do good to him in return and let him receive other people's things (i.e. the presents people bring when they come to consult). That is why the spirit says, 'I am *bakologo*.'

They consult a *bakologo* but do not consult a *bagere*. To (the latter) the living only give their offerings and it can only bless them (the donors) and look after them. Now, when day breaks, and a man has not slept, he goes to consult, and when going, he takes something with him in payment—cowries, a hoe, a fowl, or corn for beer (*kya*). Therefore people prefer to possess a *bakologo* shrine rather than an (ordinary) *bagere*.

This is the reason why a *bagere* turns into a *bakologo*. It does so in order to repay the one who has spent (lit. spoiled, *same*) his substance giving it offerings while it was a *bagere*.

Again, if a man is too poor to give offerings to his *bagere*, the spirit may tell him through a soothsayer saying 'I am a *bakologo*.' Then the son will build a little mound (*vule*) and cook beer and catch things that scratch (i.e. fowls and guinea-fowls) and go to the *tumsum*[1] (the more remote ancestral spirits of the younger spirit) of the spirit and give them beer and 'scratching things' and give further offerings to the *segere* of these ancestors and to other *bagere* to whom offerings should be made. They, who are about to make the new soothsaying shrine will prepare the clay, and the son will catch scratching things and they will build a clay mound (beside the original *bagere* shrine) and give their offerings upon it. That is how the *vilego* ceremony is performed. They kill a fowl there, and when it is 'received', that spirit which was formerly a *bagere* has now 'turned' into a *bakol-vilego* and does good to the person who has made it so that he may know that what the spirit (in its former state) had demanded was true. The *bakol-vilego* cannot, however, yet be used for 'consulting'. The 'good' it will do means that the person will get good crops, fowls, guinea-fowls, goats and sheep, and 'new' children. A year or more may now elapse between the *vilego* rite and the *nwaa* ceremony (the final rite which will make the new shrine into a fully consecrated soothsayer's shrine) when the owner will be able to begin acting as a soothsayer and receiving things (i.e. fees).

---

[1] A generic term embracing relations on both fathers and mothers side, i.e. both *bura* and *sõõ*.

Fig. 5. Soothsayer's shrine, showing hole by which the spirit goes in and out

Fig. 6. A soothsayer's shrine

The Nwaa *Ceremony*: He will soak *kya* for beer,[1] seek for a beast and scratching things, go to those who are in charge of the spirit of the original ancestor and ask him to come and 'cut' (*nwaa*) his *bakologo*[2] for him. They will name a day on which they will begin to make beer. That one whom the new *bakologo* is going to follow will rise up in the morning and give a pot of beer and corn to his wife to carry, and he himself will carry the scratching things, and they set off to the house of the descendants of the first ancestor. They will receive these things, and give them as an offering to those spirits which 'own the word' (i.e. the spirit of the father of the relation who is going to assist at the ceremony and the spirit of the *segere* of the original ancestor). They, in turn, will fill this pot with water—the one which had contained the beer—which is called the 'consulting pot' (*bogere kom*) and hand it back to the ones who had brought it, and they go back home. After they have gone, two or three of the *tumsum* will follow them and when they get near the compound they stop on the path and are met there with food (grain) and a cooked guinea-fowl and a pot of beer; these things are for 'buying the roots' which they have brought with them. They receive them, eat the food, drink the beer, and put the guinea-fowl in their leather bag. Then they rise up and come to the *zenore* and greet the people there, '*Zare!*' Next, the people in the compound will bring a black hen and a white hen and a third hen—it does not matter what colour it is—for painting the medicine (*tiimda*). The 'strangers' will cut the roots into small pieces and lay them down and kill the white fowl,[3] and if it is 'received' then the black one, and when that is 'received', too, all the people who have assembled call out, '*Wo!* they have whitened[4] So-and-so's *bakologo* this day.'

The senior wife of the new soothsayer now rides upon a goat as if it were a horse, while those gathered at the *zenore* sing in chorus:

> 'The soothsayer's wife sees a goat;
> She is laughing sweetly.'

She rides the goat until she arrives where the clay mound has been made, when the 'strangers' take the goat and sacrifice it and all the

---

[1] See footnote 2, p. 197.

[2] A *bakologo* shrine is not subject to the ordinary rules of inheritance for shrines, but may pass on death of its curator to any one, even to a daughter's son who lives in another town and is of another clan.

[3] Before doing so they pour out the flour-water.

[4] Cleared up, come to a full understanding in any difficult matter. To 'blacken a house' means to bless it.

fowls which have been brought. They fetch a calabash which is called *bakolwola*. While they are skinning the goat, some of the others make a fire and take the roots and put them in a big *sera* pot and set the pot on the fire. When they are burned, they take them and grind them along with pepper and salt and put them in *bakolwola* (calabash) and put some beer in it, and an old soothsayer holds it for the new soothsayer to drink from while all the people sing:

'The soothsayer is drinking, he has drank too much.'

They compel him to drink all, and soon he becomes really intoxicated, because on the day of the 'cutting' of *bakologo* he must not eat anything from morning until night, thus, when he is given to drink, the beer seizes on him quickly. Now, they hand him a stick made out of a *gotena* tree. Something has already been hidden, and they address him, saying, '*Baga*, I have stolen from you, *Baga*, I have stolen from you. If your (new) shrine is a real shrine and has eyes, then it will not be hard for it to follow and take the hidden thing.'

Into the skin of the goat which has been killed they put all the soothsayer's *yala*.[1] Some of the flesh of all the sacrifices is cooked and given to the shrine.

Next morning they catch a cock and kill it, and skin its neck and stretch the skin over a cow's horn, and put 'medicine' into the horn. This medicine is used to paint the shrine (see Fig. 6), and it is also rubbed over the head of the new soothsayer.

An ordinary shrine (*bagere*) does not eat peppers, but a *bakologo* shrine does so. *Bakologo* can look, and see, and tell; a *bagere* does not do so.

People now come with things to consult, and the owner of the shrine receives them; a *bagere* does not do so; the owner of one only takes his own things and offers them. Thus, a man who makes offerings to his own (private) spirit, receives these back again in the offerings people bring to him for his *bakologo* (in the form of fees).

(Another distinction between a *bagere* and a *bakologo* is that) a *bakologo* is (as it were) purchased with the things one gives the *tumsum*, but not so with a *bagere*; nevertheless both are spirits.[2]

---

[1] The articles of his stock-in-trade which he uses in his séances. *Yala* means literally afterbirth. See Chapter XXIX for a description of these.

[2] A spirit may become *bakologo* directly, i.e. without ever having had a shrine at all, or it may reach the *bakologo* stage by way of being first a *bagere*, as here described. In the latter case the conical mound of the original *bagere* is not removed and offerings

An Offering of the Early Millet:

Abasia, Apemi, Ayo, and Ayini brought their flour in calabashes to make their offerings at the grove to their ancestor, Anudi.

Abasia spoke, saying: 'Ancestor Anudi, I call you thus. Have you heard? The first rains fell and we brought you flour,[1] saying that the rains had fallen and asking you if we might sow, and that one calabash of seed might suffice (i.e. that after sowing the rain should not cease) and the seed die, necessitating a second sowing). The rain ceased and it spoiled and you "owned" (i.e. were the cause of) that. You ought to have climbed to God and brought rain, but you failed to do so and this caused the early millet to fail. We cannot "reach" where you are; if we could it would not be necessary to give you this water. There is not any "early millet", so what else could we give you; indeed, it would have been proper if we had refused to give you even this millet offering which we are now making, because you refused to help us. There is now no corn which a woman and a child may eat, and in consequence, they are about to go to strange places (*tun*) in search of food. You allowed the early millet to spoil. Every one is descending to Dagbono and we have seen them going, so we have brought you flour. Apemi has brought, Ayo has brought, Ayini has brought flour for you in order that you may have some care of women, children, and men. But if you fail to have them in your care, so that they have to descend in search of food, we, too, will have to follow them and then where will you obtain water.[2] So receive this flour and let women and men cease from having to go out (in search of food), and permit them to remain (where they are). Have also in your care the leaves of the early millet upon which all of us have our eyes. You failed to give us the first sowing. Try and do well for us before taking our offerings, so that when the dry season comes you will be able to receive your offering, my ancestor Anudi.'

continue to be made to it. The new shrine is built beside the old one. A *bakologo* may also be joined by other spirits—those of animals, of rivers, trees, or fairies—while a *bagere* is a single human spirit. There are also *Yini bakologo* where, as the name implies, the spirit is that of God. A soothsayer, when he wants to consult about his own affairs, will do so through a brother soothsayer rather than consult his own shrine. Women, if they wish to consult, will do so through their husbands or brothers. Among the Kasena there are women soothsayers.

[1] He refers to the ceremony which I attended in March 1928 at Winkoŋo, which is described elsewhere, see Chapter XXX.

[2] This, I am informed, was only a threat; as had they to go, they would have taken the *Yaba dono* (ancestors' horn) with them.

XVI

SPECIMENS OF NANKANSE FOLK-TALES

(1) *The Youth and his Three Lovers*[1]

(THERE was once) a youth who had (lit. caught) three lovers. All their houses were together in a line. One day he went to visit them. The first one said, 'Return the day after to-morrow and I will make beer.' The second one said, 'Return the day after to-morrow and I will make beer.' The third one also (said), 'Return the day after to-morrow and I will make beer.'

Of a truth, the youth returned on the third day. Now, as their houses were together in a line, and the three paths which led to them met together, he walked until he came to where the roads converged, when he stood, not knowing what to do. He thought to take the path leading to the first house, but returned and stood at (the junction of) the three ways because he realized (lit. thought) that if he went there first the other two would quarrel. Again, he took the path leading to the second house, but again came back and stood thinking that if he went there first the other two would quarrel, so he returned and stood. Again, he took the path leading to the third house, and again retired and stood not knowing what to do. (After that) he stood with confused mind and nothing better fell in the youth's mind than that he should kill himself. So, behold, he killed himself. The girls waited long in vain (lit. and failed). The first remembered the saying of the Yulega[2] man, that one (lit. he) should not blame his child (for having delayed) while he was still in the long grass (i.e. without being sure what had befallen him). So she rose up, thinking that perhaps she would meet him on the way. She reached the (junction of the) three paths and there was the male child lying dead. The maiden exclaimed, 'Oh! what misfortune! that is just what I said before' (about not judging him too hastily), and she said she would not leave her lover alone,

---

[1] When a story is about to be told the audience address the story-teller, saying: 'Let us make make' (*To mayese mayese*). He replies, 'Let us make believe' (*To belim balla*).

The story-teller ends his tale with, 'It was thus, I said I would open and show you; if it was a ripe shea butter nut, eat it up; if not ripe, chew it.' Compare the ending of Ashanti folk-tales. See *Akan Ashanti Folk-tales*.

[2] The Nankanse call the Kasena *Yulse* (s. *Yulega*).

lest afterwards something should come and pull out his eyes. 'I shall watch him' (she said) 'so that nothing may chew him up.' Of a truth she stood there by the youth and waited. The second (girl) waited in vain, and she, too, said that she would go to meet him to see if perhaps he was on the way, coming. Of a truth, she reached where the three paths met, and there was her lover lying dead and her neighbour sitting still in tears. This (sight) set the second (girl) on fire, so that there was nothing she could do, and behold! she died also and joined her lover. The third one also waited and also failed (to see her lover coming) and said, 'I will go to meet him and look for him.' Truly, she went out and reached (the junction of) the paths, and there was the youth lying dead, and his lover as well, (lit. added) lying dead and the other one sitting and still weeping. The maiden beat her breast *bira!* and said, 'Ah! what misfortune! It was because of such a thing that the *Yulega* man has said that he cannot upbraid his child while he is still in the long grass.' She turned back quickly and returned home swiftly to bring lumps of medicine, and she came back and blew (the medicine in the nose of) the youth, and he rose up. She blew upon the (dead) girl and she also rose or came to life. Well, I now ask you something. When he came to life, which of them should he try to love more than the other? The one who watched over him because she could not allow something to pull out his eyes, or the one who died to join him, or the one who blew medicine upon him?

(2) *The Woman and her Daughter*

There was once a woman who cooked beer for the spirits, strained it, set it aside (for the second boiling), and went to the river (to fetch water). After (she had gone) her children began to drink, and one of them, as she was going to drink, took a calabash to do so; smash went the calabash! She had broken it, and when their mother came back and saw the calabash the sight of it blinded her eyes in darkness. She set down the water-pot quickly on its stand and fetched a birch, beat the child, and drove her away saying that she must sew up the broken calabash. Because of this the girl took her way and went off to the midst of the tall grass land and sang:

'My mother cooked her spirits' beer;
  This child toddled along to get some to drink;
That child toddled along to get some to drink;
  I also hastened hastened along to fetch some to drink;
Our father's food calabash, it did break;

It must be sewn up with a leopard's skin thong, and with hyena's
    skin thong, and with you witches' veins;
There is no leopard's skin near by, near by;
    There is no hyena's skin near by, near by;
You witches' veins, there are also none, near by.'

A leopard (appeared, took the calabash and) sewed it for her. Next
she came (to a place where there was) a hyena. He also took (the
calabash) from her and sewed it and gave it back to her. She next
came to where there was an old witch-woman, and she took the veins
of witches and sewed it (the calabash) for her, and she (the witch)
said, 'This is how you must go home. When you come to clean clean
water, you must not go in that; but water which is muddy, go down
into that.' Of a truth, the girl, when she reached (the water) did as
she was told; she left the good water but descended into the bad
water and emerged with bangles and beads and with body shimmering
wagegege. When she reached home and her mother saw the child she
shook at seeing her again. Her husband's other wife (the *yenta*[1] of the
first one) also saw her thus, rose up all in a hurry *tige tige!* boiled beer,
reboiled it, set it down, and instructed her child, saying, 'You, after I
have gone out, break the food calabash belonging to your father.

She (the mother) went off to the stream. The child came and broke
the calabash and sat waiting for her (mother) to return. She came back,
reached the compound, climbed down over the wall, shouting, 'Who
broke this calabash?' She took a birch and whipped the child, *waribe!* and
drove her out of the yard. The child walked off *tuna! tuna!* not knowing
where she was going, into the middle of the long grass (and began to sing):

'My mother cooked the spirits' beer;
    This child quickly quickly came to drink;
Another child quickly quickly came to fetch and drink;
    I too came quickly to fetch and drink;
Our father's food calabash did break;
    It must be sewn with a leopard's skin thong;
Sewn with a hyena's skin thong;
    Sewn with the vein(s) of you witches;
A leopard's skin thong is not near by, near by;
    A hyena's skin thong is not near by, near by;
Veins of you witches are not near by, near by;
    My mother approach and hear, my mother.'

[1] Co-wife.

Fig. 7. A hunter with arm-quiver, and 'hunting-calabash' on head

A leopard took (the calabash) from her and sewed it. A hyena took (the calabash) from her and sewed it. Witches took (the calabash from her) and sewed it. An old woman (witch) said, 'When you reach water which is good, do not descend into the clear clear water, but the water which is bad, go down into it.'

The girl argued, saying: 'Why, when I see good water, should I go down into the mud?' So she went down into the clear water and came out again with snails on her body, *zurrr!* all sticking to her.

When she reached home her mother grew tired of picking them off, and hurt her body until it was all red.

(3) *The Chief's Daughter*

There once lived a chief's daughter. He (her father) said that he wanted all the animals to meet together and weed (his farm) until the sun became dark, and that the one who did not drink water until the sun fell, he should eat (i.e. marry) this, his daughter. Of a truth, they assembled and formed a big company for the hoeing. Now the hare [1] acted like a bad child and put water in his arm-quiver (see Fig. 7).

They hoed until the sun was overhead. Try as they could (*wode wode*) (to do without water) they failed, and they all went to drink at last, but the hare continued hoeing, hoeing; (then he said he was) going to spread his arrows in the sun to dry; (while he was pretending to do so) he emptied the water from one of the pockets of the arm-quiver and drank. He did so again and again until the sun fell. They said that all the people (animals) had drank water, only the hare had not drank, so they took the woman and gave to the hare to have as his wife, and take home (*kule*). Not many days after, the woman conceived and bore a child. One day the woman was going to the river, so she gave the child to the hare (to look after). The hare took a rattle and rattled it and began singing thus to soothe the child: 'This, my sense (made me) take water and fill my arm-quiver and I married my wife. This my sense (made me) take water and fill my arm-quiver and I married a wife. If I had not had sense, where would I have got a wife to bear me a child?' There and then the woman approached, set down the pot, and snatched the child from the hare's hands and went away to her house. The hare made haste, took a cowrie shell, fixed it in one eye, made a fire, took the charcoal and rubbed his face

---

[1] Here we have a very distinctive characteristic of Northern Territory folk-lore, i.e. the appearance of the hare in place of the spider as the hero of the story.

all over, and ran fast to pass his wife and leave her behind. He reached to where some herdsmen were, and the hare began to sing (his song as before), and they learned it. He ran on, faster than before, and came to the house of his father-in-law, and there children were sitting at the *zenore* (outside the entrance of the compound) (Here he sang his song again). Again he sang it outside the Chief's compound. They, too, learned it. Then he returned and washed the things off his face and took off the cowrie, and followed behind his wife, reached her home and saluted his parents-in-law and told what had happened. They asked the woman. She told how she had gone to the river and taken the child and given it to him, and how she had come back and found him singing that his sense had made him take water and fill his arm-quiver and thus get a wife, and how, if he had not had sense to do so, where would he have got a wife to bear him a child—and how, on account of this, she had run away home, because she had not known before that he had acted thus. They replied, 'What! a song that every one is singing?'

Bidibila la ka zabdema bata la

Bidibila n nyoyo ka zabedema bata. Ba wu yea kye taba. Dare deyema te ka kyene ta limse se. Yiyadana yele ka ydare lemna te n wam enne dam. Yiriga la me dare lemna, te n wan enne dam. Tarega la me dare lemna, te n wan enne dam. Te bidibila sere man daredema la lebera. Yea me n kye taba la soa me yebe taba. Ka kyina kyina ta pae du zea zina ena wan enne sere (seen) dekke yiyadana la yiri sore enne potere, visi lemna wa zia, soyebesa la zuo, te a san kyine bila yiya bana bayi la wan zabe. Le dekke yiriga la yiri sore yea, ta visi le wa zea. Te a san kyine bila yiya, bana bayii la wan zabe; visi wa zea. Le dekkera tarega la me yiri sore te ka kyine, visi lemna wa zea. Zina ka wa ene seen yere gam zea la potezura. Sere sonnale ka lu bidibila yeame, te ka wan ko la ka mena, sere bise ka mena ka ko me wa. Puguto la guse wu kakke; Yiyadana la ene potere te Yuliga yete: 'a kan bo a abia kono, gye te ka bona moon.' Isike te a wan tuse me bise, te a zin wan ta sekke e soren. Ta pae soyebesa la puam, te bidibi la n bela kyi ga. Pugula yete: 'Kumpiino yaa! Wana te n yelene la.' Te ena kan dekke a zaba base te sela leen kweye a nini, n wan gu e, te sela da obe e. Sere zea gura bidibila la. Te yiriga la me guse wu kone, yete: Ena me wan tuse me ta bise, te a zin bosore sina. Sere ta pae soyebesa la puam, te a zaba la kyi ga, gye te a tadana me zea la koono sekke. Yiriga, la kyine dokke e daye ba enne sere, enna me bise a

menna, a kyi me wa poe a zaba la. Tarega la me guse a me kakke.
Yete: N wan tuse bise, sere yese ta pae soyebesa la puam te bidibila n
bela bila kyi ga, te ka zabe ena la me po kyi ga, gye te ayema me zia
la kono sekke. Pugula mwe nyoo bira, yete: 'yalese yaa, wana te Yuliga
la sere yele laa, te enna kan bo a abia kono, gye te ka bona moon laa.
Ene vio, kalamm lebe yiri ta dekke musere, wa pebele bidibila la te ka
isike. Pebele pugula la te kana me isike bii voe.'
    Ehe n nyana soke, fo tese te ka n isike (voe la) kama saam te ka wan
ba bo gana ?

> Sea n gu e; te a kan vam te sela wa kweye a nini laa, bii
> Sea n kyi poe e laa bii
> Sea n pebele e la musre laa.

Poka la la ka poyoa

Poka n doye kyim dam, te zeele, gye kyine kulega. Te a koma, leen
kabesa nyura. Te ayema nyana yea, te a ta kabege nyu la wane po a
worege ya. Te ba ma la n bela para nye wanne la, la kyine fo a nini
birimm. Te a tue yore zeele kalamm dekera kafabega febi bia la,
dige ka. Te ka pon tara wane la ta pe na. Denne te pugula dekera
goo sore kyine feme la goo tena sokka ta. Nyuna: 'N ma doye a kyima
dam bi kana loye loye ta kabe nyu, bi kana loye loye ta kabege
nyu, mam me loye loye ta kabege nyu, to ba saye wane la mwa ya,
de pere la yebaa gono gye pera gbingbire gono, gye pera ya sooba
gyile. Yebaa gono la kana nyoma nyoma, gbingbiri gono la kana nyoma
nyoma, ya sooba giile la me kana nyoma nyoma.' Te yebaa toe pe bo e.
Le ta pae gbingbiri me toe pe bo e. Ta pae poyonyan soa te kana me
enne soba giile pe bo e. Te ka yele e yete: 'Enna n yea kula wa, san
ta pae ko sebo, n yelese yelese la, a da sige bomo puam, gye sebo n
ann lew la a ta sige bomo puam.' Pugula sere ta pae tu wo ba paale e
seen, ta base ko somo la gye sige ko berula puam doe la inna la base la
samise wagegegee. Ta pae yiri a ma nyana nye bia la gbera ka inna la
yeasa. A yentaa me nye bela, isike toyon la dam tigetige, koye, bise
zeele, gye kaye a bia yete, 'Fo san leen enne fo worege wane la, dena
fo so saye wane la, fo worege base ya.' La kolega a sige ya; bia me
leen sere leen worege gye zia gura e. A wa para ton sigera gye: 'Tase
anne n worege wane wa?' Dekkera kafabega la bia warebi, gye dige
ka base yina. Bia tuna tuna la goo tennasoka. 'N ma n doye a kyima
dam, bi kana loye loye ta kabege nyu, bi kana loye loye ta kabege
nyu, mam me loye loye ta kabege nyu, to ba saye wane la mwa ya,
de pere la yebaa gono, gye pera gbingbiri gono, gye pera ya sooba

gyile. Yebaa gono la kana nyoma nyoma, gbingbiri gono la me kana nyoma nyoma. Ya sooba gyile la me kana nyoma nyoma. N ma len na wa wom, n ma. 'Yebaa toe pe bo e, gbingbiri toe pe bo e, sooba toe pe bo e. Poγo nyana: 'Fo san ta pae ko sebo n yelese yelese la, fo da sige bini, sebo n ann lew la, sige bila ya. Pugula zagse, tebo, n nye la ko somo me gye sigera begero puam ? Ta sige ko somo la puam, doe la kateyegela la inna zururu, ta pae yiri te a ma gose tarege lonn, fule inna zaa gbanne.

Naba poγoa la

Naba poγoa n boi, te a yete, enna bote te go duse zaa laγese wa kwo nyulum yini, mina n ka nyu koom, gyete yini lu la a dana n dite a poγoa mea. Te ba sere laγese ta enne tan sugere katele te ba kwo. Asonna enne bibea enne koom sum kamarega puam. Ba tara kwoa tara tarala wunteena zuo tenasoka. Wole wole ta kake. Ba kyine nyu ba zaa ta tue ba zaa. Asonna kwora kwora, te enna yea te a ta dile la a peem. Ta kai koom la kamarega ka yema puam nyu. Le bona bona le ta kai ka yema le nyu. A ete la bela la yini lua. Te ba yete; Te nereba la zono nyu koom ta tue me, gyee la asoona yema n ka nyu. Te ba dekke poka bo e. Asoona tare a poγa la kule. Dabesere ka tukke poka la poore kpwiu, doγe bia. Dare de yema poka nyana yea kolega, dekke bia bo asoona. Asoona dekke baγesenyeka a mwere me wa, nyuna basa bia:

'Mam yeam wa zan koom sum kamarikan di n poγa,
Mam yeam wa zan koom sum kamarikan di n poγa.
N da po nye yeam ee, n na nye poγa la be doγe bia.'

Te poka n bela duee sige tue yore zeele laale zee bia asoona nusen la ka yiri fagamm. Asoona enne atoto dekke lagefo kpa nifo, enne bugumsana soe nenna zaa, zo sasa ta zoe a poγa base poren, ta pae te dukyima n bela, asona n nyum. Bama kokke. A le enne sasa zo ta pae a deema la yiri, te koma zia zannoren. A le nyum naba yiri zannoren la. Ba le kokke de bila me yeasa. A enne vio ta pee bono la a nennan la base, foe lagefo la me base, gye nyana taae a poγa pore yea. Ta pae puse a deema la toγese la n enne seen. Ba soke poka, ka me nae bela; Te a kyine la koɭega gye dekke bia bo e, wa pae, te a bo bini nyuna, te enna yeam wa, te a da enne koom sum kamarikan di poγa, a da san ka enne ne yeam wa, a nye ne poγa la be doγera bia. Bela te enna me bo kulena, enna ye banne te a da enne la bela. Ba yete: 'Nyune wa te ba tae nyuna de wa.'

XVII

INTRODUCTORY

I HAVE experienced some difficulty in determining the lines which the succeeding chapters of these volumes should follow. There appear to be at least two methods of approach by which the large mass of material collected in the field might be presented to the reader.

In the Northern Territories of the Gold Coast, any anthropological survey at present undertaken is still concerned with an extensive area which, theoretically, is inhabited by peoples who have hitherto not been regarded as comprising a homogeneous group or nation. This area has not even, like Ashanti in the south, ever come under the sway of a single Native ruler. Had Dagomba or Mampruse, for example, extended its overlordship to cover the whole country, and given it its name, I think I would not have had the same hesitation about presenting the total results of these investigations to my readers under a single broad general heading, ignoring any necessity for designating more minutely exact localities and tribes in which the various descriptions now presented had been obtained. I should probably have taken it for granted, unless the contrary was very much in evidence, that, when a custom or belief was observed and recorded for one district, although it might vary in detail in another, yet this difference would not be so material as to necessitate a re-examination of each custom, in each new area subjected to investigation.

A knowledge that a field of inquiry comprises a known homogeneous unit lightens the task of the investigator enormously. These were the conditions in Ashanti, where I had lived for some sixteen years before commencing intensive anthropological work there. Moreover, there was already an extensive literature dealing with that area.

It was far otherwise in this new field. I came to my task as much in the dark about local conditions as it was possible to be. Practically nothing detailed was known about the country from the anthropological standpoint. There was not at the time an official in it who had a colloquial knowledge of a single one of the diverse tongues supposed to be spoken within its boundaries. The problem before me was therefore somewhat disconcerting. This was especially the case to some one who, like myself, had always been the exponent of a special doctrine and had been the author of the *obiter dictum* that, 'the most urgent need of this science (i.e. anthropology) to-day is not for ... broad general surveys of districts or areas as for minute and exact detailed accounts of social and religious beliefs, rites, and customs.'[1] I was aware, also, that I had not the years before me for this new task, to which I had looked forward when similar work was begun in Ashanti.

The reader has by now at least become familiar with the distinctive names of nearly a score of 'languages' or dialects spoken by as many equally diversely named tribes. When I state that when I began work in the Northern Territories I passed on from tribe to tribe and from one area to another, not knowing with any certainty beforehand that each tribe and area would not represent a new language and a new culture, the uncertainty and difficulty of the task which confronted me will perhaps be appreciated.

Thus it came about that circumstances compelled me to undertake that 'broad general survey', which, in the case of the Ashanti, had been so ably undertaken by others. The only other alternative would have been for me to select a single area or tribe, for intensive investigation, leaving all the rest untouched for future examination. This method might have had something to recommend it, had there been half a dozen workers in the field all similarly employed, or had there ultimately been any prospect that I would have time to cover all the ground; but such was not the case. It was, indeed, fortunate that the former line of attack was decided upon and followed up, at the expense, it is true, of some valuable time, for by doing so, more than half of the difficulties disappeared. The language survey, which was first undertaken, proved what I had already half suspected, namely, that eighty per cent. of our arbitrary linguistic boundaries could be dispensed with, and that a great area, hitherto split up in eleven or more supposed language groups, could fairly be reckoned as a single linguistic area. A rapid anthropological survey followed—as language is often but a poor guide to determine racial and cultural affinities—and this afforded even more striking results, in the general similarity in religion and customs which was found to exist over the whole area.

A compromise of methods was thus finally attained. Having satisfied myself regarding the general similarity underlying the linguistic, social, political and religious life of all the tribes inhabiting the Northern Territories by a rapid survey of these activities, I settled down to make as far as possible a more detailed examination of the

[1] See *Ashanti*, Preface, p. 8.

same phenomena, but spread the sphere of investigation over as wide
an area as possible.

The advantage of this treatment of my subject will, I hope, be
manifest. First, instead of, as it were, a general reference being given,
e.g. a description of rites, &c., as 'Customs of the Northern Territories', which in a sense they are, chapter and verse are quoted and
each account is tabulated as a detailed record of a particular specified
tribal unit. While no one tribal area could thus be exhaustively
covered, nevertheless a general idea of the whole is obtained, and the
lacunae can the more easily be filled in, as more intensive study of
each area comes to be undertaken.

The disadvantage of grouping the sum total of the data at my disposal piecemeal under particular tribal headings is chiefly noticeable
from a literary and artistic standpoint. It leaves the final effect perhaps
a trifle ragged and disjointed. This defect I hope to mitigate in these
or a future volume by summarizing the whole. I have also, wherever
possible, drawn attention to the links which will help to bind the whole
together so as to form one composite picture of primitive life in the
Ashanti Hinterland.

XVIII

THE NANKANSE

History. *Tribal, Clan, and Sõõ Organization*

THIS tribe, which occupies the area shown on the map, is the most numerous of the tribal groups in the Northern Territories. According to the 1921 census it numbered 82,395 persons of both sexes. The members of this tribe do not, as a rule, call themselves by the name which we and others have bestowed upon them. They prefer to be known as Gurense (singular Gureŋa or Guriŋa) and their language Gureŋe. This name, as will be seen later, is, curiously enough, in most cases objected to by other tribes, as having a disparaging and derogatory significance. Gurense (*Anglice* Grunshi) is very much the equivalent of the word 'Kaffir'—unbeliever, eater of dogs—as bestowed by Mohammedans on those who do not follow the Prophet. The name Nankareŋa (plural Nankanse) was, they state, that given them by the Kasena (whom they in turn call Yulse (singular Yulega).)[1] The language is Nankane. To Europeans they are popularly known as 'Fra Fra'—from the supposed sound of the word which they use as a salutation or in thanks, i.e. *fura fura*.[2]

The tribe is divided into some twenty-six totemic clans (*bute*, plural *bura*), each of which is patrilineal and exogamous.[3]

There are three ways of inquiring of a man (if you have the temerity to do so, without good reason for your curiosity) to what clan he belongs. These are as follows:

Fo bute de la bem? What is your male kindred group?
Fo pɔte de la bem? What is your oath?[4] (*pɔ*, to swear; *pɔte*, an oath).
Fo kyisiri de la bem? What is your avoidance (taboo)?

Besides belonging to one or another of these clans, every one is also

---

[1] The Nankanse also speak of the Isala as Yulse.

[2] A war memorial at Zuaragu, testifying to their valour, has actually this verbal monstrosity perpetrated upon it.

[3] At least, up to a point, as will be noted presently.

[4] A man may swear by his father's or mother's clan. He may do the latter if he had taken an ancestor on his mother's side as his *segere*. This helps to explain why many people respect both father's and mother's totems. Some examples of oaths have already been given (see Chapter VI), but here the oath has a different origin.

a member of another kindred group which is determined by descent traced through the female line alone. This is called *sōō* or *nifu* (lit. eye), or *zeem* (blood). The *sōō* has not, so far as I could discover, any *totem*, nor does it entail any food or other avoidances. It is the inheritance of blood. Through this line alone the taint of witchcraft can be inherited. This *sōō* inherited relationship will be found again in the extreme west among the Lobi and elsewhere in a form which will explain much that is obscure among the Nankanse. Both the clan (patrilineal) and the *sōō* (matrilineal) relationships will be dealt with fully presently, but before doing so I will give such historical information about the tribe as I have been able to obtain.

The history of any of these tribes is always a composite record; it is the history of every clan of which the tribe is composed. The history of a clan is the history of the first head of that clan. This, in the Northern Territories, is seldom or never that of the Chief. In the Northern Territories, to speak of a town (i.e. a group of compounds) is still, to the Native mind, to conjure up the idea of the place of residence of a particular clan. A recognition of these simple facts would remove the main cause of confusion and misunderstandings into which we fall in dealing with tribal origins and tribal histories. We may, with some hope of accuracy, attempt to trace at least the more recent origin and migration of a clan. To seek for a common origin for what is now regarded as a tribe is a foolish waste of time; the units which comprise it may have come from every point of the compass and even consist of persons who formerly belonged to other tribes. To write the history of the origin of the Nankanse would therefore entail the study of the migrations and vicissitudes of each of the twenty-six or more clans which now constitute this tribal division. It would clearly (in the scope of these volumes) be impossible to do so, and would serve little purpose. One example must therefore suffice.

History of Winkoyo, the Head Settlement of the We'ba Clan (We'ba, lit. bush-dog, i.e. the leopard). 'Before the Dagomba came, and before the Europeans came, the *Ten'dana,* Anvenyo, was head *Ten'dana* of all the *weba kyiseba* (lit. those who taboo the leopard). The clan is divided into three (main) *yi-zuto* (singular *yi-zuo*) (lit. chief or head compounds[1]), each tracing descent from one of three "half-brothers" by the same "father" but by different mothers. This common

---

[1] These terms will be fully explained later when dealing with the composition of what we now call a 'section'.

"father" was called Abonposogo[1] (lit. Rotten Thing). He was the "father" of the leopard clan, and the first of that clan. It came about thus: He had become blind, when a leopard came and licked his eyes, which then opened. He thereupon took an oath that neither he nor any of his children would ever eat or kill a leopard again. After regaining his sight, he married and begat Atonaba. Atonaba, when still an infant, was saved from being burned to death by a hen which gave the alarm when the hut in which the infant was asleep caught fire. Abonposogo then took another oath, that no first-born (*bi-kyeŋa*) of his should ever eat a fowl.[2] Atonaba begat Avila (alias Akungue ?). Avila begat Anude. The clan became known as *we'ba*[3] *la noa kyiseba* (they who taboo leopard and fowl). When an old man of the clan falls ill, and is about to die, we see a leopard among the compounds, and, on death, he "rises up" a leopard.'

Violation of the Totem. On the death of a clansman, a fowl is killed, and one leg placed on the mat beside the corpse, and this is later buried with it, the following words being spoken: 'Receive this, your fowl, to-day, because you are departing.'[4] [This ceremony is called *nanwoo*, the marking of a bird with the owner's mark; see Chapter XI, footnote[3].]

'Women of the clan do not turn into leopards,[5] nor do young children who die before they have begun to keep the taboos, nor children who die before their mother has given birth to another child,[6] because no proper funeral custom is held for such and they are not full and proper members of the clan.

'If a clansman sees a dead leopard he will touch it with his finger and then touch his own head, and will dig a hole and bury it. If some one kills a leopard, and you have power over him, you will take it from him and bury it and afterwards bathe. No second funeral custom is made because the leopard is my ancestor who has already died and for whom a second funeral has already been held.' [This was in answer to my question.] 'A full-grown man who dies will turn into a leopard, but not a person who has not had a (proper) funeral

---

[1] His 'father' is stated to have been called Agunwa and to have come from the locality now known as Mampruse.

[2] See p. 179.

[3] *We'ba* is sometimes pronounced *Ye'ba*.

[4] A year after this information was recorded, another informant stated: 'The leg is cut off with an axe. The fowl must not be a cock, but its colour does not matter. The *baya* will take the remainder of the fowl.'

[5] Other informants state that they do so.   [6] *Nyere*; see p. 8.

custom. We (leopards) do not eat people unless they owe us a debt. When this happens, we (the living) consult a soothsayer and find out the reason why a leopard has killed some one, and make satisfaction. Clansmen cannot become leopards while alive, but when a man is about to die a leopard will come to the compound. When a clansman meets a leopard, he will salute it by slapping his thigh or clapping his hands. If a leopard begins to kill the live stock, it is liable to be killed, but later an offering will be made at the sacred grove (*tingane*) and a report made—that "your (i.e. the ancestor's) child was a thief and was punished".

'The original ancestor of the clan came from the country of Mampurugu (Mampruse); from there to Kurugu; from Kurugu to Tɔngo. The clan at first practised circumcision, but when it reached its present home it gave up the practice, as the local women did not like the custom and named us "the *Sampana*", i.e. "spoil penis".'

Such is briefly the history of a single clan among the Nankanse. The explanation as to how this clan became possessed of its totem animal finds its parallel among every tribe, which by some similar explanation accounts for the respect it now pays to some animal, bird, inanimate object, &c. The story of the fowl explains how sub-totems and associated totems may arise. Sub-totems may here be found in the making almost under our eyes, as will be seen later on in this volume.

I have stated above that among the Nankanse and elsewhere, to mention a 'town' [1] is almost the equivalent to all the local people of the mention of a particular clan. We are later going to find this idea further developed elsewhere; so much so, that the prominence always given to the totemic side of clan exogamy will be found here to be open to question.

Of the remaining clans, which to-day form what may be called 'the Nankanse Tribe', the following are a fairly representative list. The town in which a particular clan resides is given where known. The tendency, of course—and it is one which is spreading with extraordinary rapidity with the opening up of communications—is for these

---

[1] There is hardly such a thing as a 'town', in the ordinary accepted sense of the word, in the Northern Territories. *Teŋa*, the word used by the Natives of the country, means literally 'land'. The settlement of a clan is the 'land' over which the clan are scattered in more or less isolated compounds, built a hundred or more yards apart. This is essentially the case among the Nankanse. Exceptions to the above rule will be noted when they occur.

clan reserves, as one might term them, to become more and more cosmopolitan. Until a few years ago, except in those areas which had been turned inside out by Kazare, Babatu, Isaka, Ali Mori, Baheri Bisibisi, and other famous slave-raiders, practically the only non-clansmen resident in a particular town were the women-folk, who were the wives of the clansmen.

Clan.	English.	Locality and Remarks.
1. Wobogo.	Elephant.	Bulugu.
2. Ebega or Bantaŋ.	Crocodile.	The clan of the *Ten'nama* (*Ten'dama*) including those known as the 'Black' and 'East side' *Ten'dama*, and also the clan of the blacksmiths, is also an Isala clan, &c.
3. Mɛŋa.	Water-tortoise.	Sia, Gorogo, Winduri; of Builsa, Kasena, and Talanse origins.
4. We'ba la noa.	Leopard and fowl.	Winkoŋo. See above account of origin. Leopard clan also found among Isala, &c.
5. Dulugu.	Giant hornbill.	Serego.
6. Gwegene.	Lion.	Kologo (Anglice Palago on map), Orogo, Bisigo. Said to have come from locality now called Dagomba and to be of mixed Dagomba, Nankanse, and Talense origin.
7. Bugum-nwabiliga.	Crown-bird.	? This clan is also found among Isala and elsewhere.
8. Tenanboŋa.	Lit. Earth-donkey, Ant-eater ?	?
9. Ene.	Hippo.	Doo. Origin said to be from Dagomba.
10. Sase.	Hyena.	Originally from Moshi.
11. Ko.	Roan.	?Also an Isala and Dagomba clan.
12. Gonafo.	Bush-cow.	?
13. Tugfo.	Eagle.	?
14. Wafo or Wa'gyifo.	Python.	Wakyia (Talense origin); members of this clan also found in Labisi section of Winkoŋo; how introduced will be seen presently in examination of village constitution; is also an Isala clan, &c., &c.
15. Woo.	Water-lizard.	Zono, near Nabare; Dagomba origin.
16. Sebega.	Hartebeest.	?
17. Puŋyoŋo.	Big crocodile.	Saba.
18. Tuneŋa.	A kind of fish.	Namose (Talense origin).

Clan.	English.	Locality and Remarks.
19. Yowa zifu.	Yowa fish.	Yowa, a river near Paga; Gambebebu.
20. Yiu.	Iguana?	?
21. Nwana.	Monkey.	Zuaragu.
22. Kyia.	Janet.	Kalebio (also an Isala clan).
23. Wurega.	Canary.	Balega.
24. Sakuri.	Porcupine.	?Also an Isala clan, &c.
25. Bu.	Goat.	?Also an Isala clan; entails violation of totem on death; also found among Isala; rite to be described later.
26. Pesego.	Sheep.	?Also an Isala clan.

I have stated above that a clansman may not marry a clanswoman, but this statement requires qualification, in so far as this prohibition would not apply were the relationship so remote that it could not be traced. This latitude is not, however, generally allowed in the case of *sōō* relationship, which will be discussed presently.

In the earlier chapters of this volume it has been described how an infant may have some ancestral spirit as its guardian spirit (*segere*). This spirit may be, and more often than not is, one on the mother's side. A person who is watched over by such a spirit must respect the totem of that spirit. We have thus many cases of persons who may state that they belong to both their father's and their mother's clan. This is confusing, and might easily cause misunderstanding unless we know the reason for the observance. Such a *segere's* clan is not, however, transferred by the male to his children, unless one of these happens also to be adopted by the same guardian spirit.

Neither the husband of women of other clans, nor his children, are otherwise concerned with the wives' or mothers' totems respectively, although they will not wilfully violate them.

On marriage, once the *sandono*[1] has been made, and quite irrespectively of whether the *sulle* (bride-price) has been fully paid or not, the children are considered at least as potential initiates into the clan of their father.

Before leaving the subject of Nankanse clans, the following notes, translated from accounts taken down in the vernacular, will throw further light on the subject. *Kyima isige* (with the verbal noun *kyisigo*) means 'the rising up of an ancestor' after death. The word *lebege* is also used, meaning to 'turn into'. *M'sɔ n'kyi isege ye'ba* ('My father died and became a leopard'). Again: *Neda wo sen kyi, ena isigire la a bute nde seba la* ('Every one when he dies rises up his clan totem').

'If a stranger asked me what my clan was, I would never tell him, because he would thereby "whiten" me (*a pelege mam*) [1] and would also, if he were to quarrel with me, tell me I am only a common leopard, saying, *Ita te n'yel fo, fo da yel mam bantaŋ isigera wa ye'ba isigera wa* ("Let me tell you, you have said I am a crocodile-rising man, you, you leopard-rising fellow"). *Da pelege mam* ('Don't whiten me'). A man whitens his neighbour and he will die; a man whitens another by making known his avoidance, taboo (*kyisiri*). When some one abuses you thus, you will not turn into your animal when you die. In olden times we would have killed any one abusing or laughing at our *kyiseri* (taboo, totem).'

Again: 'It is our father's custom to rise up (after death) as a leopard, but we know that our real father is in the axe we sacrifice to on the *bagere*.[2] The leopard too knows that it is my ancestor. The rising is *ɲalse* (magic ?)'

When a child is old enough, he will be told the clan secrets by his father, in the night. He (the father) will say: 'My son, come hither and sit down here. Have you not got hairs in front? Do you not see that I have (something) to tell you? Know that my *kyisiri* (avoidance, totem) is a leopard. Some day, when you go into the long grass, and see a leopard, do not kill it. If you kill it, you have killed me, myself who am sitting here. If, on some to-morrow, I am about to die (lit. I want death), I will turn into a leopard, and come here, and you will see it (*ka*, the class pronoun, is used in the original). Now, this is my most important avoidance (lit. my black avoidance).[3] If, some to-morrow, you see this leopard in the house, do not kill it, it is just me. On account of this I tell you beforehand, lest some to-morrow you will see one and kill it. You will remember when I die some day, that they will "have" me and take me to bury. You follow. When they have finished burying, the *bayase* (sextons) will descend into the stream to bathe their bodies. When they have reached the bathing-place, you too will bathe there, you will not "remove your share of the bathing" to wash elsewhere. When you (plural) have thus finished bathing, I will rise up a leopard. When I have finished rising up a leopard, I shall return to circle the compound and "see". When I come and reach it, I will climb on the flat roof, and descend into the courtyard. Do not sleep on that night. When I see you are not asleep, I shall say, "O! O! it is a clever boy." Next I jump and mount

---

[1] See footnote 5, p. 145. [2] See p. 215.

[3] *Ned'sabele* (lit. a black man) means in Nankane a rich, powerful man.

the wall and pass outside. I then enter the long grass. If you remember and follow this advice, you also, on some to-morrow, will rise up a leopard. I shall not tell my daughter about all this. She will go some day to some man's house. Nor do I tell my wife, lest some to-morrow we quarrel. Even if she entreats me with her vagina, I shall not tell, she can keep it. She could kill me some day, if she knew. She would say, "You rascal, you rise up a leopard." As soon as she says so, you will fall sick and surely die; your ancestor will be angry and they will have whitened you.'

Another informant stated: 'If I find a dead leopard, I will bury it and say, "Ancestor, I didn't kill you, I found you here, and as I can't take you and throw you away I will bury you." I will touch the leopard between its toes and then touch my head. After burying it, I may either kill a bird with a stick, or one may fall dead, killed by an eagle. That bird is for the dead leopard's *naywoo* (foot-cutting ceremony). If my wife were to eat leopard's flesh when *enceinte*, my child would die. All that I tell her, however, is not to bring such and such food inside the compound.'

A wife keeps both her own and her husband's taboos, and a husband respects his wife's taboo, in so far as he does not eat it in her compound, and if he does so elsewhere, he washes his hands.

The word used for violating a taboo is *galem*. *Ba galem la n' kyisiri* ('They have violated my taboo'). *Tue galem* is to break a taboo unintentionally. 'If you do so, you will fall ill, then you will bathe in the river where the mourners bathe.'

Intentional violation of a taboo is *mina gye galem*. 'We will tell such an one that if he does so again, he will certainly be caught by a leopard. We will catch him by the ear, twist it, and say, "Don't do so, do not those two ears of yours hear?" ' [1]

Sŏŏ Relationship. We have now seen that the Nankanse possess totemic clans which are based on lines familiar to all anthropologists and apparently follow most of the orthodox conceptions of totemic institutions with which we are familiar in other parts of the world. Descent in these clans is patrilineal. Females, equally with males, fall into clans, taking as they do that of the father, but they are unable to transmit their clan to their children, who inherit, or rather perhaps *are initiated or adopted into*, that of the male parent. All this seems very much what we have been familiar with in Ashanti, except that there these clans appear to be matrilineal, the child belonging to the

---

[1] Taboos are, however, sometimes violated ceremonially.

clan of its mother, or, looking at it from another standpoint (the particular significance of which will be seen later), to the clan of its mother's brother—the maternal uncle. It is he who has all the customary authority over his nephew which we would expect to be wielded by the natural parent. The female in Ashanti transmits her blood to her children which thus seems synonymous with clan. An Ashanti child takes from his father some spiritual element called *ntoro* or *ntoŋ*. These recent researches in the north, among a really primitive people, have shed some new light on these and other general problems concerning totemism and exogamy, which will be discussed again in later chapters. In the meantime, however, I shall continue to confine my remarks to that particular tribe whose clan system is being examined.

The Sōō. Besides the *Bute*, or patrilineal exogamous totemic clan, to one or another of which every Nankareŋa belongs, each individual has *from birth* an element which he or she inherits from and through the mother. This is called *sōō*, with alternative expressions, *Nifu* (eye), and *zeem* (blood). *To dela nifu* means: 'We are descended through the female line from a common ancestress.' A person's *sōō* consist of that individual's:

(*a*) Mother, grandmother, and all female ascendants.
(*b*) Mother's brothers (*aseba*, maternal uncles) who are also the same clan (*bute*) as the mother.
(*c*) Mother's sisters.
(*d*) Sister's children, grandchildren, and so on down the female line only.

Sōō is thus the exact equivalent of the Ashanti *mogya* (blood) in this physiological sense.

'*Sōō* or *nifu* you inherit through your mother. When a child is born, its navel is cut; the next one is cut, and so on; the *zeem* (blood) is the same.' 'My blood is my mother's blood.' *Mam la ena de la nifo* ('I and he have one mother'). 'You cannot take the eye of your father.'

There is one inherited characteristic, the 'taint of blood', which seems almost invariably associated with the *sōō*. Witchcraft can only be inherited from and transmitted down the female line. 'If your mother is a witch, then, when the *lu pema* (ordeal by arrows) is about to be used to find out who else in the family are witches, descendants of her brothers have not to undergo this ordeal, but those of her sisters must do so.'[1] The word *nifu* (eye), as an alternative for *sõõ*, is possibly used in this context, as in the phrase *a tara nifu*. 'She has an eye' and 'She can see' are employed euphemistically to express: 'She is a witch.' The word for witch in Nankanse is *sõa*, which might appear to have some etymological relationship to *sõõ*, although I am informed this is not the case. This contention seems borne out by the fact that *sõõ* (blood relationship) is popularly divided into groups, one of which is known to be tainted with witchcraft, and one that is not; the latter is sometimes called 'white *sõõ*'. This is, however, more in the nature of a popular division than a recognized social grouping. Thus far it will be observed that up to a point the *sõõ* possesses the identical characteristics of the 'blood' (*mogya*) in Ashanti.[2] It is inherited through the female line and can only be transmitted down the female line. *Sõõ* relationship is also an absolute bar to legal marriage, and, in theory, even to sexual intercourse. It thus forms to all intents and purposes a matrilineal exogamous division, in contrast to the *bura*, the patrilineal exogamous division with its totemic associations. To sum up the data now presented: Among the Nankanse, every man and woman knows to what clan he or she belongs. These clans are classified and, as it were, labelled with distinctive appellations, the most popular classification being under the name of the particular object which forms the main *kyisiri* (avoidance or taboo) of the clan. The *sõõ*, on the other hand, has not any totem or taboos nor any apparent divisions marked by special names. Yet *sõõ* divisions do exist, anonymously, so to speak. They consist of kindred groups, each well known to those concerned, in which descent is traced through a common ancestress. Each group is exogamous.

The more dramatic conception of the patrilineal exogamous division[3] as a totemic group tends to obscure the fact that it was originally just such a kindred group as the *sõõ*, but tracing descent from a common male ancestor down the male line alone; this *totemic* characteristic, I cannot help thinking, we are apt to stress unduly. Clan descent (and inheritance, as will be seen presently) are traced through the male among the Nankanse. The only effect therefore of the *sõõ*

[1] This is very reminiscent of the Ashanti saying, 'However fierce a witch's mouth may be, she eats on her own side of the stream, but cannot cross the water.' See *Religion and Art in Ashanti*, p. 28, where it is stated, 'a witch is powerless to use her enchantment over any one outside the witch's clan' (*abusua*).

[2] The one outstanding difference would appear to be that 'blood' (*mogya*) and *abusua* clan, are apparently synonymous.

[3] The popularly named Totemic Clans so stressed by the anthropologist.

relationship that at present remains in this tribe is that it is a bar (and a stricter bar than clan (*bute*) relationship to unions of the sexes), and that it alone carries the taint of blood.

Later on in these volumes I shall return to this subject, when accumulated evidence, derived from an examination of other tribes, will enable us to come to some important conclusions.

Before I pass on to describe other features of the Nankanse social and political organization, I append an answer to a question as to which was considered the more important, the *bute* or *sōō* kinship. The reply was as follows: '*Bute*,' said my informant, 'because your own son will do everything for you, while your sister's son will trouble himself for some one else. Suppose I get some new medicine, do you think I am going to eat this medicine with my son or eat it with my sister's son? I am going to eat it with my son. The reason I say so, is that my son will sacrifice to his father, my sister's son will sacrifice to his own father.'

XIX

THE NANKANSE (*continued*)

The Clan Settlement or 'Town' (Teŋa)

THE 'town' (*teŋa*) of Winkoŋo, the settlement of the Leopard and Fowl clan, will now be examined in more detail.

We have seen in the previous chapter that the *Yaba*, or first ancestor, was a man called Abonposogo, who after various wanderings settled at the spot where his descendants are now found.

Abonposogo had three 'sons' (this word being here used in the classificatory sense), Atonaba (or Anaba), who in his infancy had the adventure with the fowl, Akungue, alias Avila, and Anudi. They were 'half-brothers' or *sɔ-bisi*, lit. 'father's children'. These three 'sons' were the founders of three kindred groups, the members of which trace descent from one or other of them, while all three groups equally acknowledge the 'father', Abonposogo, as their common great ancestor.

Atonaba, Akungue, and Anudi have been referred to as 'sons' of a common remote ancestor, but this relationship is such only in the classificatory sense. The exact tie between them is not easy to trace, and perhaps is not actually known. Anudi is said to have been a son of Akungue who was the son of Atonaba, who was the son of Abonposogo. If this is the correct genealogy, then Anudi was the great-grandson of the first ancestor, and the 'half-brother' relationship between the three 'sons' is also not meant literally, though to the Native mind there is nothing incongruous in such a description, as all were 'sons' of one 'father' by different 'mothers'. Abonposogo also had a daughter, called Amaleba, who had married a man from Wachia of the python clan and borne him children. Later, she was accused of being a witch and was driven away and returned to Winkoŋo, taking her young 'python children' with her. This accounts for the presence of this totem in the leopard clan settlement.

The woman, Amaleba, thereafter stayed at home and mated with a clansman,[1] and her descendants founded yet another kindred group, named after her eldest 'son', Ala.[2] The descendants of these individual

---

[1] See p. 161.

[2] Derivation *la*, an earthenware plate.

ancestors each constitute a group of persons who are known as 'the children of So-and-so'; thus we have:

(1) *Anaba-bisi.*
(2) *Akungue* (alias *Avila*) *-bisi.*
(3) *Anudi-bisi.*[1]
(4) *Ala-bisi.*

The groupings, as apart from the individuals they contain, are known as *yi-zuto* (singular *yi-zuo*), which means lit. 'head-houses', or 'important houses', and each forms what we term a 'section'. These four sections constitute the *teŋa* ('town', or rather settlement, of Winkoŋo, under a Head called *Ten'dana* (the one who possesses the 'town' or settlement). Each separate section is under the senior member of that group, whose title is *yi-zuo-kyɛma,*[2] i.e. senior of an important house[3] (Section-head).

The *yi-zuo* (section) for administrative purposes is again subdivided into a number of *detto,* singular *deo,* each under an Elder known as *deo-kyɛma*[4] (senior of a *deo*). (The word *deo* is here used in exactly the same wide sense in which *yiri,* in the word *yi-zuo* (section), is employed.) These *detto,* which naturally vary in number in different 'sections', are lesser kindred groups within the greater group, which have been founded by 'sons', by the same mother, of the original *yi-zuo* ancestor. For example: Taking one section (*yi-zuo*), that of Anudi, we have (*a*) the section under its *yi-zuo-kyɛma* (head of section) divided into (*b*) four *detto,* known as:

(*a*) *Agwobega deo,*[5] lit. Agwobega's room, &c., &c.
(*b*) *Akumie deo.*[6]
(*c*) *Abame deo.*
(*d*) *Atia deo.*

---

[1] These three sections are often spoken of as *Anaba-bisi,* the tendency being to forget the older ancestor and ever to substitute one less and less remote.

[2] Also *Kyeŋovara.*

[3] 'House' here being a collective noun, comprising possibly many hundreds of actual dwellings.

[4] *Deo-dana* (owner of the *deo*), as will be noted presently, has quite a different significance. The word *deo* means literally, a suite of rooms as occupied by a man and wife in the larger compound, which may contain several such *detto.* See Chapter XX.

[5] A, B, and C are also known as *Awo-bisi,* children of Awo. Awo was a wife of Anudi, the ancestor of the Section. Atia *deo* is composed of descendants of Abame by a wife, Atia.

[6] The compounds of members of this *deo* are plastered with a dull red clay (*zinzag-mologo*). The story goes that there were two brothers, Akumie and Ayiriyea, each of

Each is under an Elder (*deo-kyɛma*), who in turn is under the *yi-zuo-kyɛma* (Section-head). The process of subdivision is not yet, however, ended. The *detto* are split up into other lesser groups, e.g. *Agwobega deo* consists of three small family groups known as:

(a) *Atada-bisi* (Atada's children, &c., &c.).
(b) *Akyemba-bisi*.
(c) *Ayiriyea-bisi*.

Each group having a less and less remote ancestor with whose spirit it is chiefly concerned. By this process we finally arrive at the single compound (*yiri*) ruled by its own *Yi-dana* (master, or owner of the compound) and a *deo-dana* mistress of the *detto*, his senior wife or mother. Even here the process of division and subdivision is not at an end. The plan and a detailed description of a compound (*yiri*) will be given in the next chapter, but here the following brief reference is necessary to explain the terminology employed to describe section and sub-section.

Every *yiri* (compound) contains a certain number of *detto* (suites of rooms, or self-contained 'flats', to use a term which will convey something of the meaning to my readers). Each *deo* is inhabited by a member of the family, a brother, son, &c., of the *Yi-dana*. Each *deo* contains so many *bɔɔ* (rooms). It is on this analogy that the word *deo* has been borrowed to signify a lesser group of compounds, within the greater group, which on the same analogy becomes simply *yiri* (compound) though now it may contain hundreds of houses and thousands of *detto*. The terminology, as expansion took place, has always been based on the family unit. Besides these sections now enumerated, there is a modern one, known as *Gorogo* (derivation *go*, to wander), composed of strangers. This is under its own head-man, and is a modern innovation.

To recapitulate: The *teŋa* (town), or rather settlement, of the leopard clan consists of: (a) *yi-zuto*, sections, each under its own head (*yi-zuo-kyɛma*). Each section is subdivided for administrative purposes into numbers of *detto*, each under its Elder. Each *deo* is

whom had wives. One day Ayiriyea's wife was plastering the walls of the compound with red clay. People praised her work and she died. The praise had killed her (that praise can cause harm is a generally common belief, and many people have a charm (*noa doko*), a mouth pot, against it). The woman's husband, Ayiyea or Ayiriyea, thereupon swore an oath, that none of his descendants would ever use red clay again. The wife of the other brother said she would not agree to give up using red clay and the descendants of this brother continue to do so to this day.

re-subdivided into lesser *detto*. The whole consists of hundreds of *yia* or single compounds each under its compound master (*Yi-dana*) and its mistress (*deo-dana*), and itself the home of other families, for whom the *yi-dana* is responsible.

The whole is, or rather was, under an elected head, called the *Ten'dana* (he who possesses or owns or is responsible for the *teya*), the 'town', which is in this case a settlement of widely dispersed compounds spreading over many square miles of country, which is regarded as the land (*teya*) of the clan. The position of the *Na* (Chief) —in the more modern territorial sense—in this organization will be fully discussed later.

Each section has its sacred grove, *tingana* (pl. *tingane*). This word is probably derived from two words, and means surpassing all trees. This grove, or a spot in it, is regarded as the potential habitat of a human spirit which is supposed to be that of the ancestor [1] after which the section takes its name. These groves are variously known as *yaba tingane* or *yaba tisi* (i.e. ancestors' sacred groves or ancestors' trees, or, when more particularly designated, as Anaba's, Avila's, Anude's, and Abonposogo's trees. A ceremony I attended at one of these groves will be recorded later,[2] when this and other religious activities of the clan are discussed.

The head of each section (*yi-zuo-kyɛma*) is in charge of, and officiates at all ceremonies connected with his sacred grove, never the *Ten'dana*, unless the latter also happens to be a section-head, when he will do so in that capacity.

Before I pass on to describe the position and functions of the *Na* (Territorial Chief), *Ten'dana* (Priest-King), Elders, *yi-zuto-kyɛmdema*, and *yi-dana*, head of the simple family group, all of whom have been briefly mentioned above, I propose to digress for a little to describe in the next chapter a typical compound or family residence, an aggregate of which comprises the township, the political and social organization of which has now been partly described.

---

[1] And often also some of kindred, e.g. a mother, as in the case of Aundi's grove.
[2] See also Chapter XXX.

Fig. 9. Grain-stores

Fig. 8. Showing exterior of compound wall

XX

THE NANKANSE (*continued*)

The Family Compound (Yiri)

THE following is a description of a typical *yiri* or compound, an aggregate of which form a sub- *deo*, a larger aggregate a *deo*, and a still greater aggregate a *yi-zuo* (section), while an aggregate of sections form a *teya* or 'town', the settlement of a clan.

The whole building is called a *yiri*. The particular *yiri* which is here described in detail consists of five *detto*, or living quarters, of various members of the family.

No. 1 *deo* is that of the *Yi-dana* or head of the compound, but he calls it *m'paya deo* (my wife's quarters).[1]

No. 2 *deo* is that of the *Yi-dana's* younger brother, and this is known accordingly as *m'yebega paya deo* (the quarters of my younger brother's wife).

No. 3 *deo* is called *m'ma deo*, my mother's quarters, although the mother in this case is already dead.

Nos. 4 and 5 *detto*, as 2 above, are those of younger brothers.

These five *detto* are built more or less in the form of a rough circle, and surrounded by a wall (*lalega*), which is the height of (or sometimes lower) than the house-walls, the outside of which themselves constitute most of the circumference of the outside wall (see Fig. 8). In the centre, round which these five *detto* are built, is a yard called *na-deye*, which means literally 'belonging to the cattle', and is, as the name implies, a cattle-kraal.

There is one entrance to the compound leading immediately into this yard and facing west.[2] This is called *yiri nore* (the mouth of the compound). The space immediately outside this main (and in this case only) entrance is known as the *zenore*. This belongs essentially to the males, the women folk in turn being regarded as supreme within the compound. Scattered about inside the cattle-yard, are six corn-bins. There is also a hollow clay mound, called *uka*, for fowls. The yard also contains a wooden peg driven into the ground, called *cha-paga* (pl. *cha-pase*) to which may be tethered a cow or horse (by the foreleg). On the right hand of the entrance, against the wall

---

[1] See footnote, p. 143.

[2] Many compounds have two entrances for reasons to be explained.

between *detto* 3 and 4, is a rack (*veo*) for drying beans. In one corner of the yard stands a large heap of manure (*buglugo*), to be used on the farm. Fig. 10 illustrates roughly the ground plan of what has now been described.

A. The whole constitutes a compound (*yiri*). 1, 2, 3, 4, and 5 are *detto* (s. *deo*) or separate self-contained living-quarters for a man and

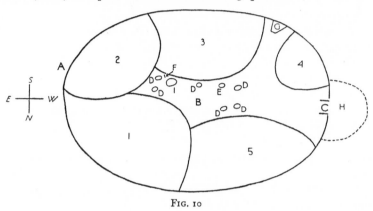

FIG. 10

wife and young family. One of these *detto* will be described presently in detail.

B. Is the cattle-yard (*na-deye*).

C. The entrance to the compound (*yi-nore*) facing west.

D &c. are six *ba* (pl. *bare*), grain stores or bins. See Fig. 9.

E. A place for fowls.

F. A wooden peg.

G. A wooden rack for drying beans, &c.

H. The hard bare open space at the entrance, called *zenore*, where the males foregather.

I. A heap of manure.

The *detto*: A detailed description of *deo* No. 3, that of the *yi-dana*, or head of the compound, will now be given, and this will be followed by another detailed account of the rooms (*bɔɔ*) which go to make up a *deo*. Each *deo* is shut off from the central yard, B, i.e. from the cattle-kraal by a low irregular wall called, like the outside wall, *lalega*. A log of wood cut into steps leads up to a dip, called *gyasiŋa*, in this wall. This is called *dodogo* (a step ladder). Broken potsherds (*chewia*) are let into the top of the wall where the ladder leans against it to reinforce

Fig. 12. Showing dry-season kitchen; corn-bins in foreground

Fig. 11. Showing dry-season kitchen, and exterior of wet-season kitchen: note buttress foundation of latter, called *tatere*

FIG. 13. Showing entrance to the *de'-kyeyo*

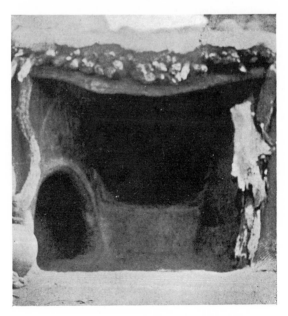

FIG. 14. Showing raised platform where the *Yi-dana* may sleep

the mud surface. At the foot of the ladder is a round stone (*kugere*), to place the foot upon when descending from the ladder. To the right of this ladder there is a hole (*nore*) (lit. mouth) in the wall to let the fowls in and out. To the right of the ladder, the wall is carried on inside to form a small room for goats (*bu'zonko*).

On climbing over this wall, one steps down into a courtyard called *zinzaka*. The most striking objects in this yard are the shrines seen in Figs. 17 and 18. These will be described in detail presently. The yard also contains a small basket-woven corn-bin called *kuyoko* or *kuyonko*.

The whole *deo* consists of five separate huts or lesser *deo*. From left to right these are:

No. 1. The hut of the *Yi-dana's* son and his wife. This is grass roofed, in contrast to the remainder, which have flat mud roofs. Such a hut, which is found in most compounds, is called after its construction *de'tene* (grass *deo*). On top of the thatch is a broken pot to keep the rain out. This hut is detached from the next, except for the compound wall which links it with No. 2. This (No. 2) is a dry season kitchen and has not a proper roof, only some guinea-corn stalks laid across. The entrance is only a dip in the wall (see Figs. 11 and 12). Such a kitchen is called *daaya* in Nankane (*guluŋo* in Kasen'). The back of this kitchen forms part of the outside wall of the compound.

A few feet of outside wall again links up this hut with the next, No. 3, which is really a room (*bɔɔ*) leading off No. 4, and part of the same hut. This room (No. 3) is the wet season kitchen, the interior of which will be described presently. This hut is called *serega* or *sera*. The buttress foundation, so common in all these buildings is called *tatere* and may be seen in Fig. 11. No. 4, is the hut of the wife of the *Yi-dana*. Her title is *deo-dana*, and she is, theoretically, in charge of the whole of the five *detto* in the compound. This hut, which includes the kitchen leading off it, which is entered from the inside room, is known as *de'nyaŋa* or *de'kyeŋo* (i.e. the female room or the big room). It is entered by a doorway (*di'nore*), lit. the mouth of the *deo*, seen in Fig. 13.

The hole in the flat roof through which the calabash was thrust, as described in the ceremony recorded on page 177, is called *sulega*. This hole ventilates the room below and lets out some of the smoke. It is covered with a potsherd. The flat roof of a hut is called *gɔsogo*; there is a gap in the raised edging round the flat roof for the rain-water to run off, called *santeko* (*seteko* in Kasen').

No. 5 is the hut of the *Yi-dana*. It is called *bogo*. Outside, and near the doorway, is a raised platform made of beaten earth with a porch or sloping roof (see Fig. 14). Here the *Yi-dana* rests or sleeps when it is very hot.

Fig. 15 shows a rough plan in elevation of the *deo* which has now been described. This and the photographs will, I trust, convey to my readers some idea of the homes in which the people dwell whose lives

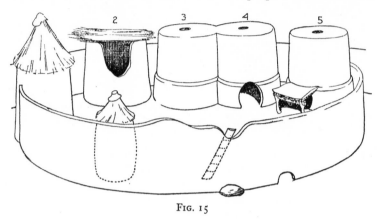

FIG. 15

I am attempting to depict. Fig. 16 shows the exterior of such a compound with a typical baobab tree in the foreground.

Before describing the interior of one of the huts, the following description of the shrines already mentioned which stand in the *zenzaka* yard just outside the *Yi-dana's* hut, may be given.

As will be seen from the photograph and diagram Figs. 17 and 18, there are one large and three small shrines. The whole is known as a *bagere* (shrine):

(*a*) was described by the *Yi-dana* as *m'meŋa ma* that of 'my own mother'.

(*b*) *M'sɔ* or *m'cho*, i.e. my father.

(*c* and *d*) the wives of the *Yi-dana's* grandfather, who were two sisters.

The X on the mounds marks the position of small stones, *kugri*, which are the actual habitats of the spirits, the earth mounds being regarded merely as 'rooms'. On the largest mound, there is a hoe, E, 'for use in the *kye-teŋa*', land of spirits. A broken pot, F, is lying on top of the big shrine to keep fowls &c. from pecking at any offering

Fig. 16. A compound (*yiri*)

Fig. 17. Ancestral shrines

laid upon it. The particular shape of these *bagere* vary; B is known sometimes as *yi-kyeɲe*, the big compound.

We will now enter one of the huts. Crawling through the beehive doorway seen in Fig. 13, we are confronted with a partition or clay wall completely encircling the entrance. This is called *za-no-kwaka* (see Fig. 19). This partition is to keep out draughts and rain water.[1]

The flat roof overhead is supported by cross beams or poles *nyusi*

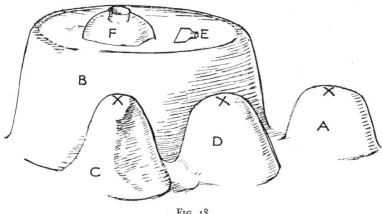

FIG. 18

(s. *nyuɲa*) resting on forked supports close up against the wall. The ceiling is made of cross sticks *da* (pl. *dase*) on which are placed crosswise other sticks called *setto* (s. *sedogo*).

Running all round the edge of the circular room is a raised projecting ledge called *kukɔra* (see Figs. 19 and 21)' Hanging above the doorway is a calabash suspended from a wooden peg by a string. This is a love charm called *zu-soɲo-tim*[2] (sweet-head-medicine). The feathers of the fowls which have been sacrificed upon it are plaited into the string (see Fig. 19). Opposite the entrance and against the wall is the place for grinding corn (*nere*) (see Figs. 20 and 22).

The foundation is a roughly semicircular platform, with a raised edging, made of mud. The top of this, which cannot be seen in the photograph but is illustrated in the diagram, contains, A and B, cups or deep hollows in the flat surface forming receptacles for the flour to fall into as it is ground, when it is swept into them out of the way.

[1] But see p. ix, *Natives of the Northern Territories*, A. W. Cardinall.

[2] The more common name for such charms is *pɔyɔletia*, which will be described elsewhere.

These holes are called *nere boko* (the grinding platform holes). Between these holes, and the edge, the surface of the platform has a slight concave depression. On the right and left hand of this hollow and directly in front of the *nere boko*, two flat granite slabs, (C) and (D), are let into the surface; these are the nether grindstones. That on the

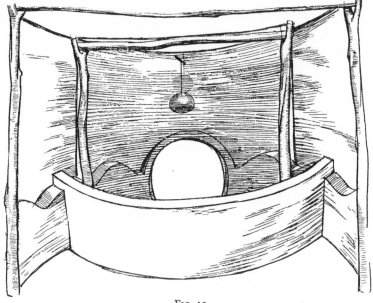

FIG. 19

right (D) is called *ebere-ga*, that on the left, (C) *bagere-ga*, and they are used respectively for the first rough grinding, and the second and final grinding. Upon these slabs are lying two round stones, (E) and (F), the upper grindstones, called *nan-biya*. At the right-hand top corner is a small conical stone (G) for resting a calabash against to prevent it toppling over. On the left is a small rough granite stone (H), used for denting the surface of the nether grindstones when they become too smooth. A neatly made grass brush (I), for brushing the flour off the surface, completes the equipment. The lady in the leaves came in while I was making these notes to say she wished to work. While she did so, she extemporized a little song to the effect that Europeans had made her land good to live in; she went on to sing that from olden times she had never possessed any clothes, but now she knew she would soon have a cloth. A dream which, needless to state, came true.

The sunlight, streaming for a minute through the open *sulega*, by great good fortune bathed her and her grinding place in transitory sunlight and enabled the photograph (Fig. 22) to be taken, before it passed over, and left the room in its former gloom. A bunch of guinea-grain may be seen hanging above her head ready to be ground.

On the left side of the room, the low ledge already noted, was

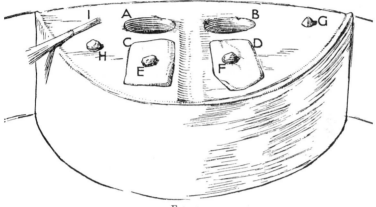

FIG. 20

continued with a serrated edge effect, on this were piled pots in the manner shown. See Fig. 21.

On this side was also the doorway, A, leading into the 'wet weather kitchen' already mentioned, and the outside of which is seen in Fig. 21. Inside this kitchen were arranged dozens of pots of all sizes, fire-wood neatly stacked, and on the floor were the usual three hearth stones, immediately above which, on the ceiling, was a round hole (*sulega*).

Returning to the first room, on the right side as one entered, were two large sealed pots which I was told contained *bondero*, i.e. provisions; in this case, I believe, ground-nuts. Hanging up on the wall, in a string net (*zaleŋa*), were layer upon layer of calabashes culminating in the *kumpio*[1] which contained the *sia* (soul) of its owner (see Fig. 2). From the ceiling (suspended by ropes) were sticks on which rested *sono* (s. *soŋo*) sleeping mats.

The head of a compound and his wife (or wives) live in the *de'kyeŋo* (the big house). When the man dies, his wife will continue to live there until she dies. The position of the eldest son is peculiar. When

[1] See Chapter VIII.

he grows up and takes a wife, he may continue to reside in his father's compound or he may 'go out' and build himself a new one. In the former case, he must make a new entrance to the compound, which is known as *bure zan-nore* (show your back entrance). It is a taboo for an eldest son after marriage to continue to use the same entrance as

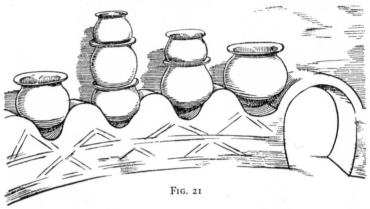

FIG. 21

his father. In the latter case, i.e. when the son decides to 'go out' (*yese*), he will be assisted to build his new home by his brothers and their wives, his friends and their wives, his in-laws, i.e. his wife's sisters and their brothers.

After his father's death (assuming that the father has no brother alive) he has the option of (*a*) returning to take over his father's compound, or (*b*) allowing his younger brother and brother's wife—whose duty it is to look after the old folk until their death—to occupy the 'big house', while he continues to live in his new compound and supervise the old home and its inmates from the new home which he has founded.

The duties and status of members in a family group will be examined in the next chapter.

FIG. 22. Grinding corn

XXI

THE NANKANSE (*continued*)

The Ten'dana. *The* Na (*the Territorial Ruler*). *The Section-head* (Yi-zuo-kyɛma). *The Family Head* (Yi-dana), *and other Members of the Undivided Household*

THE *Ten'dana*: I have purposely delayed the investigation of the position, rights, and obligations of this important official until the real significance of the word from which he derives his title had been subjected to a minute examination. As has been pointed out elsewhere,[1] more than one-half of our misunderstandings concerning African customs and beliefs arises from misconceptions due to careless or faulty interpretation of the real meaning of certain terms which the African himself uses. *Ten'dana* is derived from two words, *teya* and *dana*. *Dana* is a suffix, having the meaning of 'owner of' 'possessor of', in the sense of 'being responsible', 'being trustee' for what one owns. *Teya*, which may, in some contexts, be loosely translated by 'land', embraces, as we have now seen, more than this; it is the clan settlement which includes the land, with all the divisions from section right down to the basic unit, the single compound, inhabited by the undivided household. This is what the word *teya* conveys to the mind of a Native of the country who has not come in contact with Europeans and become confused by the loose terminology they employ to translate certain rather complicated ideas expressed in the vernacular by one word, for which there is no exact single equivalent in our language.

Ten'dana thus means he who is in charge of and responsible for the *teya*—the settlement of the clan. As nothing happens in the life of the individual or of the clan, which is not ordained by some spiritual agency, this responsibility resolves itself into one governing their spiritual well-being. The *Ten'dana* thus becomes the Chief-Priest, or Priest-King of his group.

(I) 'The *Ten'dana* of the Leopard clan was chosen by the four section-heads after consultation with the soothsayers. A good man, who had no brothers (in the literal sense) was chosen, one who could look after (lit. 'have') the people.' The Elders met and discussed the

---

[1] See *Ashanti*, Chapter IV.

possible candidates, and having decided upon one, he was sent for[1] and put in a room by himself. When the discussion was over, he was told to come out, and no sooner did he do so, than he was seized and stripped—if he happened to have any clothes—even down to his loin-cloth, and a new sheep, or calf, or antelope skin put around him (*ten'dan goŋo*); a new string hat (*ten'dan zuvokka*) was put on his head and a stalk of grain placed in his hand, and every one shouted out:

'*Abono m' bobe ten'dono.*'
                  ”   ”   ”
(So-and-so has been 'tied' with the Ten'danaship.)
            ”   ”   ”   ”   ”

After this, he was escorted back to his compound. The *teŋa* was now in his hands. When he arrived back home, he made a report to his own *yaba* (ancestral spirit), saying: 'Receive water, because they have given the "*teŋa*" to me, let it prosper and let there be good crops and marriages.' The house-people who escorted him home gave the Elders ground-nuts and flour-water to drink, and then they returned home. The women-folk sounded the *kyenkyelese* (shrill cry).

When the *teŋa* is not found to prosper under a *Ten'dana*, the hat and skin may be taken from him and given to another. Figs. 23–26 are portraits of various *Ten'dama*.

The *Ten'dana* sacrifices at the *Ten'kuga*, but not at the various section *Tingana*.[2] *Ten'kuga* means 'land stones', and there are seven of these at Winkoŋo. Their names are: *Aburuwa, Ayenguma, Anagabea, Asimbole, Atanpinpelego, Asakana,* and *Aponaba*. These 'land stones' are in groves and contain spirits of the land, and not human spirits.

After the second harvest, the *Ten'dana* and a representative from each section[3] and 'those who know how to drink' take fowls and guinea-fowls, flour and a pot of beer and go first to *Aburuwa* (which is a rock about three feet high). The *Ten'dana* picks up a stone and knocks *Aburuwa* three times, saying, 'The whole of Winkoŋo has cooked beer; fowls and guinea-fowls and flour are here. As you are receiving them, prevent headache and belly-ache; let the women bear children and let there be marriages and good farming, and in the dry season let

---

[1] After the advent of Chiefs, I was informed, this ceremony took place in the Chief's compound.

[2] See Chapter XXXII; these 'land stones' are also in groves, and are often also referred to as *tengana*, or *tingana*, but are quite distinct from those *tengana* which are the abode of the ancestors of the various kindred groups.

[3] And, after the advent of Chiefs, one also from the Chief's compound, a fuller account of this ceremony will be found in Chapter XXX.

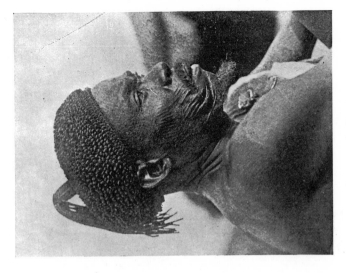

Fig. 24. A Ten'dana

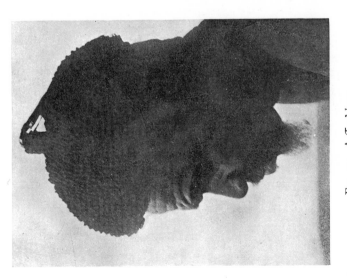

Fig. 23. A Ten'dana

Fig. 25. A *Ten'dana*

hunters kill wild animals. Rise up and go and reach the other *ten'kuga*.' After all has been given, they (the *ten'kuga*) will consult together and 'reach' *Yini* (the Sky-god) and get water for our sowing. The same sacrifice is made and the same words are spoken on each 'land stone'. We then return and go to the house of the Chief (*Na*) and enter the cattle-kraal in silence. As we are coming, no one may greet us or speak with us. Flour and beer are served out. The *Ten'dana* is sitting down, and a man kneels before him and offers him a calabash of beer, but withdraws it before he can take it, doing so twice and the third time letting him have it. He drinks it and every one eats flour prepared by the Chief. It is now dark. After this, they (the Chief's household) will give us *fura* (salutations) and we return home. We had set out at dawn. After each sacrifice, we roasted the fowls, placing a piece of flesh from the leg of each, and a piece of liver on the *ten'kugri*.' This ceremony is performed once a year. The names of six *Ten'dama* only are preserved; '*Ten'dama* live to a great age', said my informant. These six are: Anwenyoo, Adono, Amolega, Aganbiri (lit. young chameleon), Agonodono, and Adegere (the present *Ten'dama*).

The duties of the *Ten'dana* were as follows:

(*a*) To sacrifice to the land-stones (*kabere teŋa*).

(*b*) To purify the land when defiled by blood or other violation (*sale teŋa*).

(*c*) To prevent war by casting down his skin (*biŋe Ten'dana goŋo*) between the combatants.

(*d*) To allocate land to a stranger.

(*e*) To sit with Elders, to settle important disputes.

The privileges of a *Ten'dana* included:

(*a*) A *Ten'dana* does not own any man's farm, but he was entitled to anything found on it (strayed live stock), or in the ground (metal, bangles, beads, &c.).

(*b*) Meat of an animal which had been shot at, had escaped, and afterwards died.

(*c*) After harvest every year, each section used to collect corn and make beer, and give to the *Ten'dana* to give to the land.

(*d*) Skin and head of 'beast' killed at funeral custom.

Besides the insignia already mentioned, the *Ten'dana* has a cow hide or antelope hide upon which he sits. His soft calf-skin dress which he generally wears hanging down in front is called *lebere* (the same word is used for a loin-cloth). He also generally carries a string bag (*mise tapɔ*) which contains a *wula* (small calabash), a knife (*sua*), and a small leather bag (*talaŋa*).

'If a stranger came and wanted a piece of land to farm upon, he would first go to the *Ten'dana*, who would then send him to the *kusoo-dana* (the person who was using the land). If a *kusoodana* gave land to a stranger without first letting the *Ten'dana* know, the *Ten'dana* would be angry and tell him, '*Va fo kusoo*' (be off with your plot). As one cannot take land away, he cannot do so, and if he remains and continues to farm, he will be bitten by a snake, or will die, or the crops will fail.'

'New-comers to a new country will find some man already there. He is the *Ten'dana*. When people from *Tchana* (Builsa) first arrived at Gorogo, they found the Kare people already there. Thus, to this day, if the people of Gorogo find anything on the land, it belongs to Kare.'

If any one does anything which the *Ten'dana* does not wish, he will say '*Fo saane m'teŋa*' (You are spoiling my *teŋa*). In purifying the land, the blood of the sacrifice is allowed to flow into a hole in the ground; this rite is called *teŋa salego* (lit. smoothing the land). *Teŋa de la bun too, a base fo yiri*, the land is a bitter thing, it will cast out, finish, your house (if you refuse to purify it).'

The shedding of human blood seems specially abhorrent to the land and always entails purification, but exception appears to be made in the case of blood from the nose, even when resulting from two men quarrelling, *nyo sea mpusege*, and menstrual blood (*teŋa ka kyisi bala*), and blood shed in tattooing and in the incision ceremonies for girls.

To raise the war cry (*zabere kasega*) necessitates purification, even when fighting has not followed, and no one has been killed, 'but the family which raised it may not think it necessary to do so until some misfortune overtakes that family'.

A matter which is no concern of the *Ten'dana* is said to be 'neither a blood matter or a land matter' (*de daye ziim yele, di le dayena teŋa yele*). Such matters were settled by the section-head (*yi-zuo-kyema*) whose position will be discussed presently.

The *Ten'dana* would offer sacrifice to the land in case of famine or sickness. 'When a *Ten'dana* performs sacrifices, the land ascends to *Yini*, the Sky-God, and begs things (*suse bono*) from him and every one prospers.'

Not every tribe, or even clan, selected *Ten'dama* in the manner described. In many places he was selected by the soothsayers from among certain kindred groups to which the selection was wholly con-

FIG. 26. Three *Ten'dama*

fined. For example, at Bolega, there were three such groups known as the *Ten'an sabelse, molse and seba* (the Black, Red, and Blacksmith *Ten'dama*). The *Ten'dana*, under the various names by which this person is known among different tribes, will be met again and again throughout the pages of this volume, and it must be from the sum total of these data that we form our final conception as to his exact status.

(II) *The Territorial Ruler, the* Na:

The Leopard clan among the Nankanse falls into the second category mentioned in my preface, being possessed of Territorial Rulers long before the advent of the white man. Its constitution has thus passed through three stages:

(*a*) The time when the Territorial Ruler (the *Na*) was unknown, and the *Ten'dana* was the Head of the Clan.

(*b*) The period, after the Territorial Ruler had made his appearance, but before the arrival of Europeans, when he (the Chief) worked with the older constitutional rulers, fully recognizing the position of the *Ten'dana*.

(*c*) The position to-day, when the *Ten'dana* is completely ignored by the *Na* (Chief) as are, to a lesser extent, even the *Yi-zuto* (section) elders; the position of the latter has been usurped by the minor officials known as *Kambonaba*.

The first of these three phases has been discussed in the description given of the status, privileges, and obligations, of the *Ten'dana*; the second will now be briefly examined. The Head of the Mampruse who resides at Mampurugu—from which the name Mampruse is derived—had, long before the European came on the scene, appointed a 'son' territorial ruler over Kurugu. Kurugu in turn created *Na*-ships at Bino, Nangode, and Tongo. These minor Chieftainships were, and still are, bought and sold. Applicants give so many cows to the greater Chief who has *Na*-ships under his patronage. It was thus the *We ba* clan came to have a *Na*.

The position of these Chiefs in olden times is stated to have been as follows:

(*a*) People assembled at his house to dance (*yoyo* dance).

(*b*) He wore a red cap, and people saluted him '*Na, Na*'.

(*c*) When 'it was red', the Chief ran to the *Ten'dana* who had the power. He, the *Ten'dana* had only to lay down leaves, a thistle, and a corn-stalk at the entrance to a compound to cause every one in it to flee.

(d) 'The land of the tribe never belonged to the Chief.'

(e) 'No Chief could fine any man one penny' or seize his fowls or compel any man to farm for him. 'Men would have seized their quivers had he attempted to do so.'

(f) '*Nam* (Chieftainship) is like a man's wife' (This refers to the custom of bidding for it with cows.)

(g) A Chief's profit in olden days lay in his right to seize and sell strangers (slave dealing).[1]

(h) It was forbidden for a Chief to sacrifice.[2] (The *Ten'dana* and Elders did so.) It has already been described how, after certain sacrifices have been made, those who participated in the ceremony met at the Chief's compound where he had to dispense a certain amount of hospitality. When appointed for the first time, the investiture of the *Ten'dana* was also carried out at the compound of the Territorial Ruler.

The position at the present day is very different from the above picture. The territorial Ruler, the only Chief recognized by our Government, in this instance, ignores the *Ten'dana*. I found this old man living alone in a hovel and bitterly lamenting the fate which had befallen him. The functions, too, of the old section leaders was gradually but surely being usurped by men who, like the Chief, had bought their positions as head-men in the various sections. Any man who can raise the money can become a *Kambonaba* (Chief of the gun-men) as they are called. This system is a pernicious one. A man, having bought the post, proceeds to make what he can out of it to recoup himself for his initial outlay.

One informant stated, 'They, the Chiefs and their sons, prefer rascals for these minor posts and keep on changing them to get the presents, which each new candidate must bring before he is installed.'

Allowing for a certain natural bitterness on the part of some of my informants, the above account is a fairly accurate statement of facts. Here, as elsewhere, there is a growing disregard for former constitutional methods. Positions of authority are tending to fall into the hands of ambitious and unscrupulous individuals who have taken full advantage of our lamentable ignorance of the conditions under which the Native administration functioned prior to our advent.

---

[1] As we shall see later, this practice was another taboo of the land.
[2] Except of course, to his own ancestors.

(III) *The Heads of Sections*:

Their duty was, and in some cases still is:

(*a*) To offer sacrifices for the ancestor from which the section takes its name. (See page 246.)

(*b*) To decide disputes in their particular section.

(*c*) To decide the time for sowing.

(*d*) To receive reports from any one going on a journey.

(*e*) To act as witness in marriage ceremony. (See page 282).

(*f*) To report to spirits of ancestors when a new farm is about to be made, after first reporting to the *Ten'dana*.

IV. *The* Yi-dana *and other Members of the Undivided Household.*

The *Yi-dana*, as his name implies, is in charge of, and thus responsible for, the whole of the inmates in the compound, the construction of which has now been described. The inmates of such a household may consist of:

(*a*) The *Yi-dana* and his senior wife (*pɔyɔ-kyɛma*), also known as *deo-dana*, and possibly a second or third wife.

(*b*) Younger brothers of the *Yi-dana* and their wives.

(*c*) Married sons of the above (*a* and *b*) and their wives.

(*d*) Children of the above (*c*), sons, and unmarried daughters, grandsons and granddaughters.

(*e*) Possibly a grown-up daughter of the *Yi-dana* who has 'stayed at home' to bear children. (See p. 161.)

(*f*) Pawns (*talema*).

(*g*) Slaves (*daba, yamse*).

(*h*) Live stock. *Bunkobogo* (lit. hairy things).

The *Yi-dana* is responsible for:

(*a*) Religious services in the family group.

(*b*) *Pɔyɔdire*, the finding of wives for every male inmate of the compound, and paying the *sulle* (bride-price).[1]

(*c*) Settling all family quarrels (*zabere*).

(*d*) All debts.

His privileges are:

(*a*) He is entitled to the residue of all sacrifices including first fruits.

---

[1] In some cases as will be noted presently, the maternal uncle accepts this responsibility.

(*b*) He receives the cattle paid as *sulle* (bride-price) for all his 'daughters'.

(*c*) He receives all small game killed by members of the household in hunting (large animals killed have to be given to his section-head).

(*d*) He has power to punish, sell or drive out (*dige* or *solem base yeŋa*) an unruly member of the household.

(*e*) He has the right to claim assistance of all members of his establishment for work on his *samane* and *vaam* farms.[1]

(*f*) He has the right to a pot of shea butter once a year, known as *bagere kam* (butter for the shrine).

(*g*) He has the right to a ball of tobacco once a year.

(*h*) He has the right to one guinea-fowl from each new brood at the beginning of every wet season.

The *Yi-dana's* senior wife has also certain privileges which include:

(*a*) A hind leg of all sacrifices, which it is her right to cook.

(*b*) She receives all the preliminary gifts which the suitors bring when courting the girls in the compound (*pɔyɔ bɔre-bono*).[2]

(*c*) She is in charge of all the women in the compound and nominally in charge of the whole of the inside of the compound, in which capacity she is called *deo-dana*.[3]

(*d*) Her quarters are called *de-kyeyo*; there her husband keeps his bow, arrows and quiver, and his leather bag.

When a *Yi-dana* marries a second wife (*pɔ-saraya*), she will have a room (*bɔɔ*) in the *de-kyeyo* until her husband builds her her own separate quarters. Quarrels between the two women will hasten, and are generally the cause of, this being done.

The position of the eldest son has already been discussed. (See Chapter XX, p. 254.) When he marries, he may continue living in the paternal compound, after making a new entrance. He will eventually leave it and build himself a new house; this action, again, is often precipitated owing to friction between the women-folk. He, the eldest son, will consult the soothsayers before moving out. The wife of the first son to marry, cooks for her parents-in-law, assisted by any unmarried girls in the compound. When a second (younger) son marries, his wife will take over these duties, and so they pass on from son to son, until finally the youngest son and his wife are looking after the aged parents of the former. Unmarried sons live in their father's *deo*, as do unmarried

---

[1] See footnote, p. 137.
[2] She will share these out later. See Chapter VI.   [3] See footnote, p. 143.

daughters. About the age of six to eight, the latter are given their own sleeping mats, or if sufficient space is available, a separate room. They will continue to live with their parents until marriage. The only form of matrilocal marriage known is that described in Chapter III, and again referred to later, but the fact that it is 'a black taboo' for a married girl ever to have sexual intercourse, even with her own husband, in her parents-in-law's compound, may perhaps be taken as an indication that this form of marriage was once the vogue.

Grand-children: Grand-parents are entitled to the services of the first-born son and daughter of their eldest son. These children will leave the home of their parents (supposing the eldest son to have 'gone out' and built his own compound) as soon as they can walk, and go to live with their grand-parents, until they marry. They will, however, visit their own parents from time to time.

Among the Nankanse, as also among many other tribes, it is forbidden for the first born (male and female) to make use of any personal property belonging to the parents, e.g. to touch a father's weapons, put on his cap or skin covering, to look into his grain store, or into his *tapɔ*, leather bag, or in case of the female, to pry into her mother's *kumpio*. 'Parents do not like their first-born and it is unlucky to live with them.' I think the idea is that they are waiting, as we would say, 'to step into the dead man's shoes'.

Pawns (talama): the following is a translation from the vernacular: 'Suppose I am a poor man, and have not been able to pay the cows (*sulle*, bride-price) for my wife, I will take one of my children,[1] a girl, to some man in the same town and say, 'I am poor, and they wish to take my wife away, accept my child and give me a cow.' I will ask some one to be my witness, and the man who takes my child will have his witness. My child will continue to live with me, but when she grows up, the man who gave me a cow will take the cows which I should receive for the *sulle* (bride-price) of my daughter and my debt will thus be paid off. I would not pawn my child in another town (i.e. in another clan), that would be selling her.'

The debtor is called *sandan*; the creditor *bondan*. If the pawn dies, the debt is not liquidated.

Slaves (dabere, pl. daba; yamsega, pl. yamsɛ): The Earth Goddess did not favour the buying and selling of human beings, and I believe the institution of slavery only became the practice among the more or

[1] It has to be remembered that the bride-price may be paid years, even a generation, after the marriage.

less autochthonous inhabitants after the arrival of the foreign elements in the population which gave them Chiefs.

'There is not any funeral custom for a slave. Some people did not allow male slaves to marry a free woman, as she would deliver 'small slaves'. A slave could not sacrifice. A slave lived with and fed with the family, but not with the *Yi-dana*.' [1]

The bar sinister was never forgotten, but the slaves' origin was never wantonly alluded to, and a slave might only know his real status from some one outside the family circle; only in the event of some grave offence was his low origin cast up against him.

A free man might marry a slave woman (*da, yam-pɔka*) and the children would be free. The husband would *lu sandono* (tie the *sandono* —the tobacco and the dead guinea-fowl—to the person from whom he bought the slave, and the live cock to the *yi-zuo-kyɛma* of another section, who thus became witness of the marriage).

The following is from an account taken down in the vernacular:

'Among some Nankanse, it is taboo to give a wife to a slave, Others, however, only refuse to do so because they have "hot bellies", i.e. are unkind and do not wish to have to pay four cows and four hoes and all the small presents in addition. It is not as if the slave were a man's own son; perhaps to-morrow he will run away, and his master thus have "a double fall". A master will not tell his slave openly that he will not get a wife for him, lest if he tell him so, the slave will "put out young leaves in his belly" and deliberately bungle his work or even run away. When a male slave sees some woman and loves her and she, too, loves the slave, and the slave's master sees what is happening, he, the master, will go to the woman and influence her cunningly against the slave. Some other masters, when the work days approach, make a great ado about finding a wife for their slave, and when the slave sees this, "he has his belly washed" and works cheerfully. He does not know that his master is deceiving him. The master will go and visit the woman whom he is pretending to find as a wife for his slave and tell her and her house-folk that when the slave brings them gifts they must receive them and treat the slave well, but they will warn the girl saying "if you marry him and bear children, they are of the slave's clan and 'Chief's children'" (this in derision). This fear that she will bear "small slaves" is a "barrier" to her, and even if she loves the slave, the thought is like a thorn to her (*gose ka zia*).'

---

[1] A *Yi-dana* eats alone with his small grandson or with his youngest son, never with his eldest son. Men and women do not eat together.

'There are others, such as the *Ten'dama*, whose great taboo it is to give a wife to a slave.'

Live Stock: Goats, fowls, and guinea-fowls may become the personal private property of the individual, e.g. of a younger brother, son, daughter. When a daughter marries, she will generally leave them behind her, but her son may come some day and ask for them, but he cannot claim them as of right. If the woman takes live stock with her to her husband's home, it belongs to her, and if he takes any of it, he incurs a debt. (The proceeds of a wife's joint work, however, goes to her husband who is responsible for his wife's debts.)

All cows and sheep belong to the *Yi-dana*, including those acquired by younger brothers, sons, younger brothers' sons. It must always be remembered that the *Yi-dana* is responsible for paying the bride-price (*sulle*) for every unmarried male in the compound, and is also responsible for the debts of all, and these obligations are met out of the family pool. The position of a daughter of a *Yi-dana*, who has remained at home to raise 'male seed' to her house has already been noted in a previous chapter.[1] The status of this woman in her father's compound is not a very enviable one. She is liable to be laughed at and told, 'You are like a stalk of guinea-corn squatting there'; 'You are like a dry leaf blown about by the wind'. The children, too, have not the same status as the 'legitimate sons' of the *Yi-dana*, e.g. they may never become the heads of sections.

[1] See p. 51.

XXII

THE NANKANSE (*continued*)

Property and Inheritance

A MAN'S property may consist of the following:

1. Wives and children.

2. Live stock: cattle, sheep, goats, donkeys, fowls, ducks, guinea-fowls, dogs.

3. Personal belongings: A cloth, a head cover, a waist cloth or skin, bows, arrows, and quiver, a leather bag, sandals, cowries, axe, hoe, knife, flint and steel (*chibere*), mats (*sono*), pots, water-pots, calabashes, earthen plates, a big pot for making shea butter, a stirring stick.

4. Land: The farm near the compound (*samane*) and in the bush (*vaam*). Standing crops, and the grain in the corn-bins.

5. Shrines: These may include *Yaba, Sɔ la ma, Yini* and *tiim baga, bakologo, segere,* &c., &c.

6. Pawns.

7. Slaves.

The whole of the above, in theory, form a man's estate, but in practice, everything falls into one or other of two divisions:

1. Private or personal property.

2. Family or family ancestral property.

1. *Private Property*:

There are various names by which this is distinguished from family property, e.g. *fo meya muregere bono,* your own sweat things; *fo koa bono,* your own cultivation things, i.e. anything bought or bartered in exchange for some farm-produce out of a man's own farm; *kutɔnko bono,* lit. ant (eating) things, i.e. hens, guinea-fowls, &c., or anything derived from the sale or barter of such.

In a different context, which will be explained presently, a man's private personal belongings are also classified under the heading of *degero bono* (unclean belongings).

2. *Family and Family Ancestral Property*:

These are known as *fare bono* (things for which one is responsible to others). These two kinds of property (family and personal) devolve upon two distinct classes of heirs, (*a*) the brother, (*b*) the eldest son of the deceased.

Family Property (*fare bono*): Wives and children of the deceased are considered as *fare bono*, because a wife is paid for out of the family property. Therefore, when a man dies, his 'brother' inherits (*vai*) them. He may himself 'marry' the widows or give them in marriage to whom he wishes. In either case, any children born to the second husband are regarded as belonging to the late husband. They are the children of the ghost. The heir may give his late brother's widow to his younger brother—but not to one who is his *nyere* (immediate next in age), or he may give her to a fellow clansman, or to the son of a woman of the *teŋa* of the deceased (an *isiga*). No further *sulle* (bride-price) is demanded or is necessary, and in no case does the widow leave the compound of the heir, even if her new husband lives in another *teŋa*. In every case also, any children from the second marriage become members of the deceased's clan, and, in the case of males, will, when the time comes for them to do so, sacrifice to their mother's first husband's spirit and not to their natural father. The latter, in fact, does not claim any authority over them. Such unions are called *pokuredia* or *pokure-tarega*. A widow may refuse to marry the heir, or the person to whom the heir wishes to give her, and she may go back to her own *teŋa*. Even there, however, if she bears any children, she will bring them to the heir, or, if this is not insisted upon, they are brought up to observe her late husband's taboos. If a widow is very young, and has not borne any children, the cows originally paid for her may be returned to the heir. The young widow is then free to marry whom she will, and any children born of the union belong to her second husband in the ordinary way. When a widow is very old and past child-bearing, the heir has no option but to support her as long as she lives. She becomes a *kyima pɔka* (wife of a ghost).

Children of the deceased belong to the heir, and may not be taken away by the mother, provided the late husband had performed the *sandono* ceremony. Even when the *sulle* (cows) have been paid, but the *sandono* rite not performed, the widow can claim the children.

Live-stock (*dunse*): All cows, horses, donkeys, and sheep, even those acquired by his own 'sweat', devolve upon the heir, and are considered family property. Goats, fowls, guinea-fowls, dogs, ducks, if acquired by the individual efforts of the 'owner', are, on the other hand, considered as his personal private property, and devolve upon the eldest son, not the brother of the deceased.

Personal Effects: The eldest son takes these as by right. They are the *degero bono, par excellence*, and the brother may not touch them. They have the 'dirt' of the dead man upon them, and as the son, not the brother, takes the spirit of the dead, it is fitting that the former should have his father's things. These 'dirty things' include his father's *tapɔ* (leather bag), into which the eldest son may never look during the lifetime of his father; his *loko*, which include bow, arrows, quiver, and arm-guard (*polle*); his cap (*zu-vokka*), loin-cloth (*lebere*); cloth (*fuo*); sandals (*tagera*); axe (*lia*).

Farm-produce: This, whether in the grain-stores or as standing crops in the farms (both the *samane* and *vaam* farms), goes to the eldest son.

Land: The brother of the dead man has a right to the farms (*yaba samane, yaba daboo*) of the deceased, but 'if he is a good man, he will give some to the eldest son'. A new farm made by the dead man will pass, in any case, to the son.

Shrines: There is a clear-cut distinction between those spirits, human and otherwise, which the dead man had personally acquired and served personally, and the spirits to which he ministered in his capacity as head of the family. The latter pass to the heir, i.e. to the one who assumes the family responsibilities; the former go to the eldest son, who will eventually take in his charge the spirit of his dead father. A son thus eventually acquires the shrines known as *sɔ la ma* (his father and mother), his father's personal *Yini* shrine (not an ancestral *Yini*), his own father's *tiim baga* (medicine shrines) and all charms, amulets, fetishes, which his father had acquired personally, and used for his personal benefit. The dead man himself might have inherited, from his father, an exactly similar array of shrines, but these on his death devolve upon the heir along with the family property of which they form a part.

Pawns and Slaves: These are family property, but are generally not taken away by the heir from the compound where they have hitherto lived. 'A good heir will not even take away all the cows, but will leave some in the son's compound so that he can have their dung for manure for his farm.' The procedure is often for the heir to drive them all off to his compound for a few days, just to demonstrate his right to them, after which he will return several to the son of the deceased, who will herd them and thus feel that he has at least a part-proprietary interest in them. The heir will draw on them to meet family needs when necessity arises.

Order of Succession to Family Ancestral Property:[1]

(1) *Brothers and Half-brothers*, i.e. by the same father but different mothers; the eldest succeeds, irrespective of whether full- or half-brother.

(2) *'Sons'*: The eldest 'son' in the classificatory sense. This means that all the sons of the deceased's brothers are, for purposes of inheritance, equally considered 'sons' of the deceased, and that the eldest of these succeeds, irrespective of the seniority of the 'father'. Thus, a son of the youngest of the brothers, if older than the eldest son of the oldest brother, will succeed to the family property. Nothing could demonstrate more clearly the Native outlook, whereby a man regards all his nephews (sons of his brothers) as his own 'sons'.

(3) *'Grandsons'*: The eldest, irrespective of the seniority of the 'father, 'father' again being used in the classificatory sense. In cases where the 'grandson' is an infant, the section-head will administer the property until the heir grows up, or perhaps a 'sister's' son will do so, if there is such in the compound.

(4) *'Sister's Son'*, but in a limited, special sense. The reference is to a sister who has 'stayed at home' to raise seed for her father's house. He, however, may only sacrifice indirectly to the deceased by giving offerings to his mother's father and mother's mother, who will then ask the spirit of the deceased, that is of the maternal uncle, to 'dine' with them. A 'sister's son' is barred, however senior, so long as there are 'legitimate' descendants.

'When your mother's father is alive, and you go to visit him, you will take him a present; so it is when he is dead. His own son is your *aseba* (maternal uncle) and calls him (your uncle) his father, but you do not do so. So you find a way to continue these gifts after he (your mother's father) is dead. He may become *segere* to your children and *Yini* to you, and you will keep his clan taboos as well as your own.'

Succession to Private Property (degero bono):

(1) Eldest son, in literal, not classificatory sense.
(2) Grandson (in literal sense).
(3) Grandson (i.e. 'sister's son'), i.e. a sister who 'stayed at home'.
(4) Brother.

In the last case, if the deceased had any wives remaining on in the late husband's compound, the *degero bono* (clothes, quiver, &c.) must

[1] Before an heir may take over the property, the full funeral rites must be carried out.

not be removed, as they are still considered as being used by the spirit.

'Even if an heir is a bad man he may not be passed over, because he is in charge of the ancestral spirits. The remainder of the family will advise him. Although the eldest takes all, the junior members of the family have a claim on everything; the heir has to find them wives and pay their debts.'

The rules of inheritance are largely, I believe, governed by spiritual considerations. It may thus not be out of place here to examine the spiritual obligations and disabilities of various members of the family group.

A man may not make offering to, that is, is not directly concerned with, the following spirits:

(1) That of a brother or sister. (His or her eldest son will see to that; if no son, these spirits may become *Ɣini* to a daughter's son, and thus receive offerings indirectly; otherwise they will have to take their chance of getting what is known as *akadana kom*, 'the water for those whom no person owns'.)

(2) Father's brothers and father's sisters. (Their sons will see to them. If none, they will have to rely on *akadana kom*.)

(3) A son or daughter; *kom ka zote tuntula* (i.e. water does not flow backwards). Their own sons will see to them.

(4) A mother's father ('unless he becomes *Ɣini* or *bakologo* to you').

(5) Mother's brother or sister.

(6) A wife.

The expression recorded above, i.e. 'unless he becomes *Ɣini* or *bakologo* to you', was explained to me as follows:

'Sometimes, when a man is hunting, he will kill a beast, take it home, and when the meat has all been eaten and the head become a bone, a soothsayer will tell him that that head is his mother's father. It then becomes a *Ɣini* shrine or a soothsaying shrine for that man. Your mother's brother who sacrifices to the same spirit as his *sɔ* (father) will come and show you what to do, i.e. how to consecrate the new shrine).

'If you have no son, you cannot get "water" to drink (directly); you may get *akadana kom*, but that is only given in pity.'

A man is principally and directly concerned with the spirits of

(1) *Sɔ la ma*, father and mother (as a son).

(2) *Ɣaba* (ancestor), paternal 'grandfather' and 'grandmother' (i.e. mother's mother) and all family ancestral spirits (as head of a house).

Succession to Property of a Married Woman:

A married woman may own property independently of her husband. Everything which she brings with her to her husband's home on marriage remains her own. If she makes pots, or baskets, and makes a profit on them, this belongs to her, 'but she will give some to her husband for his spirits'. On her death without issue, all this private property goes back to her own family. If she has children, her beads and all things pertaining to women go to her daughter, but her *kumpio* is returned to her father's compound in order that they may make her funeral custom. Any live stock she possesses may go to her son, never to her husband, or her family (parents) may claim it.

XXIII

THE NANKANSE (*continued*)

The Particular Significance of Certain other Relationships

FATHER'S sister (*pugera*): 'She is your "father" and came from the same navel string as your father. Her husband also, out of respect, is addressed as "father"; he is not to be treated lightly.' Marriage with a father's sister's child, as will be noted presently, is prohibited. 'If a man marries his *pugera bia* (paternal aunt's child) and has children, they will die, and when this happens the couple will have to break the calabash.[1] A father's sister's child is addressed as 'sister'; she is only spoken of as *pugera bia* to strangers.[2] A *pugera* may be head of a *yiri* (compound) if all her brothers are dead, but in this case one of her brothers' sons will perform the family sacrifices. A *pugera* may not inherit the family property when all her brothers are dead, but she may become nominal head of the house and formally hand over the property of her late brother to her brother's son.

'When a man dies, his *pugera* will take charge of the funeral custom, even if her brothers are alive. She knows all the rules of a funeral custom, and becomes *kure kyɛma* (senior of the funeral custom).'

A *pugera* may be asked to take back a curse spoken by her brother and not revoked before his death, or the death of all his brothers. (Examples of oaths will be given in another chapter.)

A woman may not herself go to consult the soothsayers, but a paternal aunt (and indeed any woman whose husband is dead) may *kaa*, i.e. offer up a prayer.

'When your *pugera* dies (being married and living in another clan settlement) her *kumpio* will be carried to her parents' home by her eldest daughter.'

Mother's Brother (*aseba*): The position of this individual *vis-à-vis* the nephew, is particularly interesting. As we are aware, the Nankanse now take their father's clan, and inheritance is through the male line, first brothers, then sons, a sister's son only succeeding to the family

---

[1] See p. 177.

[2] *Pugera* in the above context refers to an aunt who has been kept at home to raise seed for her father's house. In the case of a paternal aunt who has married 'outside' and borne children, these are *isiga* with reciprocal *aseba dayoa* (or *poyoa*) or simply *aseba*, which term is also used for maternal uncle.

property under the very special circumstances already described. All this seems the very antithesis of the Ashanti system of matrilineal descent with inheritance traced through the sister's son, to the entire exclusion of a man's own son. To all outward appearances, therefore, the father among the Nankanse takes the place of the uncle among such tribes as the Ashanti. The change-over from the so-called 'matrilineal' to a 'patrilineal' way of reckoning has been so comparatively recent, however, as to leave extraordinarily interesting survivals of the older institution, not so far below the surface but that they may still be traced.

'If a youth's father is so poor that he cannot find the cows for *sulle* for a wife for his son, the latter may go to his mother's brother and ask for them, or even take them without asking.' The uncle thus accepts the obligations and asserts the right of a father, in that he in turn, or his descendants, will in the future claim the cows, which, in later years, will be demanded for his nephew's as yet unborn daughter. In such a case any children born to the nephew for whom the uncle has found a wife, will have guardian spirits (*sega*) drawn from the mother's, i.e. the uncle's, side of the family. This implies the observance of the uncle's clan (totemic) taboos. In other words these children become, as it were, honorary clansmen of the uncle's totemic group.

It is not uncommon for Nankanse children to be brought up in the maternal uncle's compound, with the full consent of the natural parents. 'Your mother's mother often loves you more than your mother. You may take anything you like at your uncle's compound and be familiar with his mother, calling her "old grey hairs". A child may continue to live at his uncle's house until he grows up, and may marry and continue to live with his uncle after marriage.

Again: 'A man does not inherit from his uncle, but he cannot "steal" from him; that is, he may help himself to his uncle's things and, with regard to such things as fowls and guinea-fowls, this licence extends to the whole of the uncle's *teŋa*' (clan settlement).[1]

Nephews and nieces have to assist uncles with work on their farms. 'You attend an uncle's funeral taking a sheep, some beer, and corn.[2] Nephews have no concern, however, with an uncle's spirit. When he dies, his son is in charge of that.' *Isiga dela siliga*, nephews are like hawks, is a saying which has its exact equivalent in Isal, *Niara na sangon*, referring to a nephew's privilege to 'take' an uncle's belongings.

---

[1] Among the Isala this licence extends even to sheep and goats.

[2] Among the Isala the nephew has also to supply a gown for the corpse.

The following account of the funeral of a maternal uncle is a translation from the vernacular:

'The house where your mother comes from you call your *aseba yiri*;
they call yours *isiga yiri* (uncle's compound, nephew's compound).
When your own mother dies, the people in your uncle's compound
will come to receive her *kumpio*.

'When your *aseba* (maternal uncle) dies,[1] you, whom he always calls
his "son" (*Isiga* is only used to strangers), will go to his house with a
fowl and a goat and corn, carried by your wife. When you reach the
compound you will climb on the roof of the *zoŋo* hut and say: "My
aseba is dead, and I have a fowl, and have brought grain, and have let
my wife carry it, and when she reached here my wife walked straight
into the house, but I climbed on top of the *zoŋo*. I have my fowl with
me. I called some one and he answered, and I said, 'If my *aseba* is dead
and has "reached" his father and mother and ancestors, let him receive
this fowl, and may they allow me to marry and beget children, have
fowls to feed and four-footed animals to rear, corn to harvest, and let
me build (found) a house'."

'You will kill the fowl and throw it down to the people below, saying
as you do so, "and if I get these things I will know he is really dead"
(*Ti n'sere baŋe te a kyia*).

'An *aseba* may say to his "son" (i.e. nephew), "Look here, my own
children are very young, if I die look after them for me"; that is, if
he has no brothers.'

Other equally significant customs among other tribes will be noted
from time to time throughout these volumes.

Parents-in-law: The fear and respect in which parents-in-law are
held among this and other tribes in the Northern Territories has, I
believe, not a little to do with the power which these relations have to
take away their daughters when the *sulle* (bride-price) has not been
paid, or to influence them to leave the men whom they have married.
It must be realized that, in speaking of parents-in-law, Natives of this
country (the Northern Territories) are visualizing groups other than
their own, who reside in a strange *teŋa*, which, apart from the bond of
marriage, was until very recently as often as not hostile to their own
group. 'Parents-in-law are like lions' is a Nankane saying.

In contrast to this, a man regards his mother's 'town' very much as
he does his own. 'All the women in my mother's town, of my mother's

---

[1] A nephew sometimes 'marries' his late uncle's widow; any children resulting from
the union belong, however, to the clan of the deceased.

age, are my "mothers"; all the males of her generation are my "uncles"; all the girls of my age are my "sisters", and the men of my age my "brothers". A man may behave in his mother's town as if it were his own.' (The above has also a direct bearing on the subject discussed under the previous heading.)

'In a wife's village, all those whom she calls "father" and "mother" are *demdema* (s. *dema*) to you, and those she calls "brother" and "sister" are your *dekya*. When you go to her village you behave as a stranger should. You must be careful how you speak or act; you must eat sparingly; you must not laugh too much; you must wait to be shown a sitting-place; you must not play about the flat roofs.'

It is a strict taboo among the Nankanse for a man to have sexual intercourse with any woman, even his own wife, at the 'town' of his parents-in-law. 'If you do so, your wife will be taken from you and also your children, and nothing will be given back to you, for it would cause death to the people in that compound.' *A saam la deo*, he has destroyed the *deo*, is the expression used. For this reason, a husband and wife seldom visit the latter's town in each other's company.[1] It is even forbidden for a man to meet his wife on the path leading from her 'town' to his 'town' on the day when she is returning home from a visit to the former.[2]

The following are some well-known mother-in-law (*dem pɔka*) avoidances.

(a) You may not eat with her.

(b) You may not sit on the same mat with her.

(c) You must not abuse any one in her or her husband's presence (to do so would be a veiled way of abusing them; compare the Ashanti).[3]

(d) A mother-in-law may not cook in her son-in-law's compound.

(e) She, too, has to behave like a stranger when visiting her son-in-law's compound.

(f) She must not appear to be greedy about food, even if hungry.

(g) A mother-in-law is given presents out of each new crop; i.e. two baskets of early millet, new potatoes, &c.

(h) After a big harvest, she will be presented with guinea-fowls and tobacco.

---

[1] Among the Isala, this prohibition applies only before marriage, after marriage, it applies only to other women in the wife's town, not to the man's own wife.

[2] The first visit (*limsego*) after marriage lasts three days; the second visit lasts a month and is known as *basega*.   [3] See *Akan-Ashanti Folk Tales*, preface.

(*i*) On birth of the first son, the mother-in-law is presented with a cock and a stick; in case of a female child, a hen. *Deŋ'teŋa tara vi* (We are careful not to offend in mother-in-law land).

(*j*) On no account must a son-in-law have sexual intercourse with any woman, even with his own wife, in the house of his parents-in-law.

(*k*) A son-in-law may not eat out of the same dish as his father-in-law; 'if your nail were to scratch him, you would have to give him a ram and a hoe'.

(*l*) 'You have to respect your parents-in-law, because it is from them that you found a house.'

(*m*) A son-in-law, on the death of his mother-in-law, has to make beer, and take a ram and a hoe 'to rest her head upon' (*kozele*).

Again: 'You cannot, it is true, take an arrow and shoot at your wife's father and mother, but you would make war on other people in her section. Your parents-in-law, too, would not mind killing you; your *dema* relationship is not a close friendly thing; you do not tell your secrets to them or trust them, whereas your *pugera* (paternal aunt) and *aseba* (maternal uncle) are close to you.'

Sisters and Brothers-in-law: *A*, a male, marries *B*, a female. *B*'s brothers (and father) have a certain power over *A* and over *A*'s father, because they may take *A*'s wife away and because they can command *A*'s services. 'Later on, after your wife has borne several children, you may become more familiar with your brothers-in-law.[1]

The position of a man in respect to his wife's sister varies among the different tribes. Among the Nankanse, a man may marry his wife's sister if she is not a *nyere*,[2] and if she is not married, he may have intercourse with her when she comes to visit her married sister. 'She will be angry with you if you do not do so.'

Sons-in-law: 'It is very shameful for a man to go and stay with his sons-in-law', said an informant to me, when I asked why his grand-father's spirit could not go along with his wife's spirit to 'eat' at his daughter's husband's compound. The etiquette enjoined on the living extends to the world of spirits.

Position of the Wife: Many Gurense will say that they have 'bought their wives'. In a sense, this is so. If the *sulle* (bride-price) has been paid, the husband has certain rights over his wife. He can even claim her body on death. On the other hand, let a husband have the

---

[1] The familiarity of a brother-in-law *vis-à-vis* the man who has married his sister is not reciprocal, it does not apply to the man who has married that man's sister.

[2] See p. 8.

temerity to boast that his wife is little better than a slave whom he has 'bought', and she will almost certainly run away and return to her parents. The fear in which parents-in-law are held, and the respect accorded to them by their sons-in-law, negative any assumption that wives are chattels in a literal sense. A wife's property is her own. The first wife has also a position of great authority in the household, and, among the Nankanse, even receives a hind leg of certain sacrifices. Among the Isala, a wife would refuse to give her favours to a husband who also kept a concubine.

XXIV

THE NANKANSE (*continued*)

Marriages Prohibited and Allowed. Marriage Customs [1]

THE two broad divisions into which a person may not marry are their own *bute* (totemic clan) and *sōō* (blood group). Relationship in the former is traced through the male, in the latter is inherited through the female. Of the two prohibitions, the *sōō* relationship is the stricter; it is a *kyis too* (a bitter taboo). Clan kinship, if so remote as to be impossible to trace, is sometimes ignored, e.g. where the same clan is found in two widely separated areas, among two distinct tribes.[2] In addition to the women whom a man may not marry owing to *bute* or *sōō* kinship tie, he is also forbidden to marry, or have intercourse with, any of the following persons:

(*a*) The wife or widow of his son.
(*b*) Wife's sister's daughter.
(*c*) Wife's next younger sister, if *nyere*.
(*d*) Father's sister's daughter with reciprocal.
(*e*) Mother's brother's daughter.
(*f*) Wife's elder sister.
(*g*) Any woman from the section from which his mother came.
(*h*) Any woman in his own section.
(*i*) Grandchildren.

A man may marry (among others):

(*a*) His father's widow (other than his own mother).
(*b*) His wife's sister, who is neither older than nor *nyere* to his wife.

Before proceeding to examine these prohibited and permitted marriages in greater detail, the following peculiarities of the classificatory system should be noted:

'In my own section' said my informant, 'every person is either my "father", my 'mother", my *pugera* (paternal aunt), my "elder" or "younger brother", my "son" or "daughter", or my "wife".' In each class each person has to some extent the same privileges or obligations

[1] See also Chapters VI and X.

[2] Another exception is in the curious *zaba* (lover) unions permitted between a clansman and clanswoman in order to 'raise seed' to a family which has no son.

vis-à-vis these neighbours, as he or she would have were the actual relationship which the term employed suggests really in existence. This does not apply literally to 'wives', but, 'if the wife of some one of your own age is cooking for her husband (a clansman), and you arrive, you are entitled to eat his food.'

Again: 'In the section from which your own mother came, every woman is your "mother" and every man your *aseba* (maternal uncle). In the section into which your "sister" (which includes every clans-woman) marries, every male of the age of her husband is your *dakya* (brother-in-law). In the section into which you marry, every woman of your wife's age is your "wife" [1] (with the exception of your wife's *nyere*, or elder sister). All the women of the same age as your wife's mother or her father are *dema*. All the men of the age of your wife are *dakya* except the sons of the last wives of the old men, whom you call "father".' (I do not quite understand the latter part of this statement, but see p. 346).

Reverting to the above-mentioned prohibitions, the following are some further explanations to account for these avoidances.

(*a*) *The Wife or Widow of a Son*: In this context, I would again refer my reader to the curious nomenclature employed to designate the relationship between a man and his son's wife (see p. 6), and the particular abhorrence associated with the idea of sexual intercourse between these relatives.

(*b*) *Wife's Sister's Daughter*: The following is the explanation given for this avoidance. 'There may be five sisters, one of whom bears a child. The other four, equally with the real mother, will declare "I bore that child". If a man who had married one of the five sisters, other than the mother of this child, were to marry that woman's daughter, his wife would say, "You have married my daughter", because this child has your wife's *sōō*. A man may, however, marry his wife's brother's daughter, who is not her *sōō*'.

(*c*) *Wife's Sister, if not* nyere. This has already been discussed.

(*d*) and (*e*) *Father's Sister's Daughter, with Reciprocal*: [2] 'If you marry such and beget children, they will die.' 'Your uncle will be angry because he begat you and begat (*doye*) another child and these children have married.' The names in the classificatory system may account for this otherwise curious statement. A man's father's sister

---

[1] Also sometimes *dekya*.

[2] See Chapter XXXV for explanation of this avoidance among the Talense.

is often called 'father', and we have already seen that brothers' sons are all equally 'sons' to the speaker, even to the extent of excluding the latter's natural son from inheritance of family property. It is a curious fact that among those tribes where clan descent is what is called 'matrilineal', cross-cousin marriages are the vogue, while among those with the patrilineal way of reckoning such unions are prohibited.

(*f*) *Wife's Elder Sister*: 'If you marry a woman, and later marry that woman's elder "sister", the latter would be "junior" to her sister in your home, though "senior" to her in her own village. Quarrelling would result'.

(*g*) *Any Woman from the Section from which the Mother came*: A man may, however, marry a woman from the same clan as his mother, but from another kindred-group of that clan, i.e. from another section of his mother's clan.

(*h*) *Any Woman in his own Section*: This prohibition is explained by the relationship terms used to designate females in this section; see above.

(*i*) *Grand-children*: 'Because all these are compelled to attend your funeral custom' is the reason given for this avoidance.

Marriages Allowed:

(*a*) *A Father's Widow*, i.e. what we should term a stepmother. An eldest son may not do so, because he sacrifices to his father's spirit. A younger son who marries his father's widow (a stepmother) may not even eat of any sacrifice made to his father.

(*b*) *A Wife's Sister who is neither older nor* nyere *to the Wife*. This has already been discussed above.

Marriage Customs:

The following additional notes (translations from the vernacular) will amplify the accounts given in previous Chapters.

'When a male child has reached a certain age and learned a man's work, he will visit other compounds with his companions and converse with young girls. He will twist grass bangles (*petima*) and *valse* bangles for the girl he likes, and she in return will give him *kenkase* grass bangles. He gives tobacco and guinea-fowls to the maiden's father and mother and will do work for them for the sake of his *zaba* (sweetheart). He will make a ground-nut garden for her and she will come and sleep at his compound. He will sleep with her on the same mat, but will not have intercourse with her. If he tried to do so the girl would never marry him.

'When the ground-nuts are ripe, she will come again and collect them. His (i.e. her future husband's) mother will cook yams and potatoes and sweet potatoes and give them to her. Two baskets of ground-nuts are added to those gathered from the garden. A long line of people will carry these things back to the girl's compound. The reason that the man does all this, is in order that the owner of the girl may wash his belly (i.e. be pleased with him). Three days later, he will send some one to inquire how she has slept, and some days later will go himself, taking tobacco and guinea-fowls, and give some tobacco to the *deo-dana* and to those whom it is customary to salute.

'After some time another man will take his place on these visits—a brother, or 'small father'—and go with fowls, guinea-fowls, and tobacco. If the girl's people accept these presents, hoes are next sent, and if the girl's mother receives them, and if they know that he (the suitor) will not fail to give the cows, the girl's father will tell "him who owns his daughter" (i.e. *his* father or an elder brother) all that the suitor has done, and when they have talked the matter over and agreed, the *Ɣi-dana* of the girl's compound will go to the *Ɣi-dana* of the suitor's compound, and say: "Look! you have whitened us. I was purposely delaying matters to make you tired of coming, but I did not succeed. When one is telling lie after lie, and comes up against a wall, one does not know where to go. If there is water, let us pour it out (i.e. sacrifice). After all, a person is not a fowl that one should catch and give it straight away (that is why I procrastinated)."

'If the girl is their first-born, they will "tie a beast", take two fowls, a hen and a cock, a guinea-fowl, and a bag full of corn for making beer. On the day of the sacrifice, they will all assemble for a big beer feast in honour of So-and-so's daughter's[1] shrine (i.e. her *segere*, guardian spirit). The sacrifice at this shrine is made in the day-time. When evening comes they eat, sacrifice again, i.e. offer the cooked food, and the girl goes off to the bridegroom's "town". Next day, the towns-people come and salute her, and the head of the husband's compound will report to his ancestral spirits, and also to the bridegroom's *segere*, that a "stranger" has entered, and he will ask for their protection and that the couple should not have headache or belly-ache and that the bride may stumble well (i.e. conceive) and become a good house-

---

[1] This ceremony is held at the compound of the girl's father, if he is the head of the house, otherwise at the compound of him who 'owns her'. The bridegroom is not present.

louse.[1] These sacrifices are made before the townsfolk hear the news of the bride's arrival, because, if people see her first before the spirits have been informed, the spirits might be angry.'

The *sandono* ceremony, already described, makes the union a legal one; the cows (*sulle bono*) may possibly not be paid for many years (see below).

Marriage by Capture (*Nyokere*): 'If the owner of a woman (i.e. her father, her father's elder brother, or her grandfather) does not agree to give the woman you want, then you will take her, for to sit and scratch your head is not any return for having dressed yourself up.'

This capture is, however, in practice generally a very tame affair; it is carried out with the connivance[2] of the girl, and the *sulle* and other formalities will be seen to later after the parents have been pacified by a small gift.

'In our country the possessor of only one wife is called *dakore* (a bachelor). They laugh at him, and he is not respected. He is only "a what sort of thing", squatting there with one wife, on the day "when it does her" (i.e. when she has her menses). Another reason why men marry plenty of wives is because of work, that is, sowing. The male goes out and makes the holes (*sebera*) (see Fig. 27) for the grain, and he wishes the sowing to be done quickly. Now, a woman can only sow a little without getting tired. That means grumbling, and your wife will tell you to get another wife. Sometimes she will go herself to her relations (*tumsum*) and find another wife for her husband, possibly a sister. Such a wife is called *pɔg sõõ*.[3]

'When a man takes a wife, the first thing that happens is that her "brothers" will come and things must be killed for them. This expense makes it difficult for a man to get many wives. There are also the cows. After a man has married and his wife's brothers have come to get "the things" which he has had to kill for them, they will find a man who is known as *isiga*, and give him "a male fowl", a dead guinea-fowl, and tobacco, and he will go to the woman's "town" to the head of one of the sections who is *sɔ-bia*, "half-brother", to the bride's people. The *isiga* will greet him and say, "I have come to strike the hand of my mother", and he will take some of the tobacco and the cock and give them to this Elder. The *isiga* then goes to the

---

[1] Which is 'always at home and does not wander outside.'　　　　[2] *Dekere*.

[3] *Farm work*: Women do not clear the bush or hoe (except widows). This work is done by men, who also make the holes for the seed with a long stick. Women put in the seeds (*burega*) and cover them up (*pi*).

Fɪɢ. 27. 'The male goes out and makes the holes'

compound of the bride's father and greets the *deo-dana* and gives her the guinea-fowl and some of the tobacco; the remainder of the tobacco he gives to the *Ti-dana*, again saying that he has come to beat his mother's hand. The *deo-dana* will cook him some food. He then returns and reports that he has been well received. If, however, the bride's family are in debt and require the cows to be paid at once, they will tell the *isiga* so, and he will later return with them—three cows and one bull.[1] In some cases even, the bride's people may ask for the cattle before the woman "goes out", but a good man will wait until all the preliminaries have been completed before he will ask for the cows.

'After they have "beaten the hand", the bridegroom will go himself to salute his parents-in-law, taking guinea-fowls and tobacco. If his mother-in-law likes him she will detain him three days at her compound, and on the day he returns she will make him good food and put what he does not eat in his leather bag for the people at his home.

'If the bride is the eldest daughter (*pɔka-bi-kyɛma*) by her father's senior wife, then, after they have "beaten the hand", the bride's father and mother may not eat any food belonging to their son-in-law. If she were an eldest daughter by a second wife, then only the mother-in-law is debarred from eating the food, but after the ceremony called *nyusego* has been performed, then both parents-in-law may eat their son-in-law's food.'

The Nyusego *Ceremony* (lit. the drinking): 'To marry the eldest daughter of a Gureŋa is a bitter thing. The bridegroom will go to sacrifice to the bride's *segere* with a big ram and *dam* (beer). He will search for *kya* (corn prepared as already described) for brewing beer. When the *kya* is ready, they will send to inform the bride's relations that they (the bridegroom's people) are coming there "to give drink to them". The one who takes this message is the *isiga* (also known as *pɔyɔ 'sigera*), he who went and "beat the hand" (i.e. was commissioned to carry out the *sandono* ceremony). When all is ready, they set out for the bride's "town", taking fowls and guinea-fowls which have already been killed, also the beer, and driving a sheep before them. The *pɔyɔ'sigera* and a brother of the bridegroom are among the party, but not the bridegroom. When they arrive at her town they first go to the head of the section, and he will select a pot of beer, a fowl, and a guinea-fowl, and give them a messenger to

[1] Six to eight sheep may be accepted in place of one cow.

lead them to the bride's parents' compound. There the beer-pots are set down. One pot of this beer is known as *zem yure* (the pot of the ashes). *Zem* is grass with which salt is made, which the women have descended into the hollows to cut with knives. The grass is burned until it becomes ashes. This pot of beer is for the women who have prepared this "salt".

'The *Yi-dana* now sends to call all the people to come and see the gifts which the "strangers" have brought. When the time to hand round the beer arrives, one man will pour out some of the beer from one of the pots into a calabash, add a little flour, mix it and give it to the *Yi-dana* who is the first to drink. Next the *deo-dana* (in this case the mother of the bride) drinks. This is the *nyusego* ceremony. The restriction against the parents-in-law of the bridegroom eating the bridegroom's food is now removed. This beer, with the flour mixed in it, may not be touched by any man who has an eldest daughter as yet unmarried. Such persons may only drink the plain beer.'

The Time which may elapse before the Sulle (*Bride-price*) *is claimed*: This period varies according to special circumstances. It may be claimed:

(*a*) Before the daughter is permitted to go away from her parents' home to the man's 'town'. This has the special name of *lekka*.

(*b*) After she has done so, but before she has conceived.

(*c*) After the birth of her first child.

(*d*) After the birth of several children.

(*e*) After the daughter's death.

Payment of *sulle* (the cows), without the performance of the *sandono* or *nwe nuo* (beating of hands) ceremony, does not constitute a legal marriage, in that it does not give the husband a legal claim to the children. The performance of the *sandono* ceremony, quite apart from the payment of the cows, entitles a man to keep the children even when a wife's parents have taken her away because of failure to receive the cows. This is perhaps the most important point to note in connexion with marriage customs.

'When a *Yi-dana* asks for the cattle (*sulle*) for his "daughter", but fails to get them, such a marriage is spoiled. They will take their daughter back. If the "beating of hands" has been performed, he, the husband, is entitled to keep the children. The parents who have taken their daughter away from her husband for this cause, may give her to another man. When the latter carries out the *sandono* ceremony and pays the cows, then the woman has 'got her compound'. A wife who is thus taken away by her parents from her first husband, may love him and run back to him, and he may then be able to pay the cows and keep his wife.'

The long-deferred payment of the bride-price, the claiming of which depends more or less on the caprice of a man's parents-in-law, accounts largely, I believe, for the deference and respect paid to the latter by the son-in-law.

Failure to have Children another Ground for Divorce: 'Males sell (*dara*) [1] female children for four cows and four hoes. This is the *sulle* (bride-price). When they (the parents) fail to receive it, it becomes a subject for quarrelling. They may come to blows about it, and the brothers-in-law will beat each other, and pull each other before the heads of their sections. When this happens and the husband fails (to give the *sulle*), he will lose his wife.

'Now, a man goes to the market for the sake of profit. If he knows he will get no profit, he will not go. Therefore, when he marries and does not have any children, his wife will surely "go away". Even if a man becomes rich, and has cows without number, sheep and goats without number, cowries, and many winged creatures, he prefers children to all these. When there are no children a husband and wife are always quarrelling. If the wife is not very careful, the husband will watch her in small things, and send her back to her parents. Another man may have more sense and take another wife, keeping the childless one if her behaviour is otherwise good.

'Another man will say, "The Sky-God did not give me, it is necessary to be silent", but other people may chew the wife's ears [2] (give her bad advice), and she too, will begin to be bitter, and try always to pick quarrels with her husband and show by her actions that she wishes "to go out". One day her husband will say something, and she will carry this to her parents and add more lies to it, and they will ask the husband about it, and believe all, even if he had not opened his mouth.'

The Marriage Bond strengthened by Children: 'When a woman marries and stumbles with a good foot, i.e. conceives soon after marriage, and bears a child, and later again bears a second child, this woman respects and fears her husband and the whole of his household and works well. She does so because of the children. There are other women, however, who have not even the smallest sense, who bear children and thus

---

[1] When a man is quarreling violently with his wife he may say, *Me da fome* (I bought you), but see p. 277.   [2] *Obe toba*: to give advice, good or bad.

ought to know that they are intended for that compound. These women, however, take advantage of the fact that they have borne their husband children, and begin to act as if they cannot be sent away. They use "uncooked words" and behave foolishly, but they should have thought twice, for if they do not take care, their husbands will refuse to "accept less than half" and drive them off home. In some such cases, hardly has the *posigera* returned after leading the woman back home to her parents, than she is back at her husband's home again, saying that if he wants to send her away he may give her the children. This may go on until the husband becomes tired of sending her away, and he lets her remain, however foolish her behaviour; but she may simmer down (*sirisi*) and become cool.'

Exchange of Wives: There is a curious dislike of the idea of one woman being exchanged for another between two families or sections or clans.

'A man's sister from one section of a *teŋa* (town) goes away and marries into a section of another *teŋa*. Once her *sulle* (bride-price) has been paid, there is no objection to her "brothers" finding a wife from that "town" or even that section, but not from the same *yiri* (compound), as that would lead to the private affairs of each family becoming known. Until, however, the *sulle* had been paid, the "brothers" of the girls would not be permitted to take wives from the town where their "sister" had married, as that might lead to the marriage contract becoming a matter of exchange of the women.'

Adultery: If the adulterer is from the same section as the husband, he will make beer and seek for a fowl and will go before the head of the section, who will sacrifice these on a shrine called *pɔgɔ-bose-bagere* (a pile of stones). The word means 'sins of women'. He says the following words:

'I take a fowl and guinea-fowl for the woman who has confessed to take the sin (*buŋa*) away.'

If the woman did not confess, and were this sacrifice not made, it is thought that her children would die. Among all these tribes it is a common idea that confession saves a person from the punishment (spiritual) which would follow an unconfessed sin.

Among the Nankanse, if a man's wife is unfaithful to him, and she loves her husband and is ashamed to confess, she will run away and 'marry' the man with whom she has committed adultery. Having lived with him for a short time, she will run away from him and return to her original husband, and no longer feel that her conscience compels

her to disclose the original adultery. This curious atonement is sometimes carried even further. If the adultery is with some one who was
in a prohibited degree of relationship to the wife, so that she may not
marry him, she will marry some other man, live with him for a while,
and then run back to her first husband.

If the adulterer belongs to a different section, he must pay a sheep.
'If he is a "stranger", you will kill him, or find some one who is *isiga*
in the adulterer's town and send him with the same number of grass
stalks as you wish to claim cows. If the cows are not brought, you will
"descend into the valley" (i.e. attack the compound of the adulterer).'

Baserego: This is a pile of stones marking the spot where a man and
woman have had sexual intercourse in the bush. Everyone who sees
this must add a stone to it. The Isala sacrifice a cow, sheep or fowl
on the spot, 'or the land would be spoiled'. (Compare the Ashanti
custom.)

There is a custom known as *galase* or *tu*, whereby a man who cannot
beget children allows his friend to have access to his wife. The children belong to the husband.

Death of Wife before Birth of Children: the family of the woman need
not replace the wife, nor are the cows paid for her reclaimable.
Among the Awuna and Isala, but not as of right, the family may give
another daughter for half the usual bride-price.

XXV

THE NANKANSE (*continued*)

Rites de Passage

BIRTH, puberty, marriage, and funeral customs among the Nankanse have all been so fully dealt with in the earlier chapters of this volume as to leave but little to add from the fund of my available information. We have seen that the spiritual influences which follow men and women through their whole lives began even before birth. In some vague, undefined manner, those born into this world are supposed to have had audience before birth with God (*Yini*), and there to have chosen their fate and settled their future conduct upon earth—poverty or riches, to remain celibate, not to have a brother or sister, not to be born at all.[1] Such, and many others, may have been the wishes expressed before the spirit set forth to enter the human body. These pre-natal events are revealed by the soothsayer, who is the medium through which a spirit makes such things known to man. The next stage is an attempt to control and placate, or thank, this divine spirit (or some emanation thereof) to whom the unborn soul had made these vows—wise or foolish—before being launched into the world. The result of this endeavour is seen in the innumerable shrines, called simply *Yini* (God), one of which almost every man possesses. This *Yini* shrine may apparently be almost anything: a tree, a stone, a pot, the horns or head of an animal, a wild animal, a domestic animal, cow, sheep, goat; a fish, a water lizard, an eagle, a wooden whistle, a *kolego* (a two-stringed musical instrument). The soothsayer will reveal to you what it is, and having obtained it, you will, if your fortune is good, thank it for that good fortune; if bad, ask it to release you from the foolish words spoken before birth, which are marring all chance of happiness on earth.

The ceremonies and superstitions in connexion with conception and birth have already been described, and the following additional notes are all I have to add on the subject.

It is considered a disgrace for a woman to have another child before the previous one is weaned and old enough to walk (about three years).

---

[1] Shown by dying at birth.

Should such an event happen, however, the infant, which is known as *Nyia*, is given medicine called *nyia tiim* (*nyia* medicine), is handed over to a girl for safe keeping, and reared on cow's milk instead of being suckled. The parents are ridiculed by all their friends, and quarrel in consequence, each upbraiding the other for what has happened.

Twins. Twins are known as *liiba* or *nsusi siyi* (lit. two hands). The one to be born first is called *Ayini* or *Awene* (the Sky-God); the second, *Ateya* (the land). No sooner has a woman given birth to twins than a doctor is called in. He is known as *liiba tiba*. He brings roots, and sacrifices a fowl and a guinea-fowl over a calabash, saying: 'Here are your persons; receive these offerings and guard the children and let them sleep well.' The roots are placed in the calabash, which is hung up in one of the huts which has a grass roof (*mopille* or *de'tene*). This calabash is known as the *liiba kyia*. It is always kept in the father's compound, and even after the twins are grown up and married they must return each new harvest to be present at the ceremony of offering this shrine a selection of the first fruits. These are given to the calabash with the words: 'Rise up and receive your Two Hands' things so that we may eat without having headache and belly-ache.' Only after this ceremony may the family crops be harvested. Each twin has its own breast (while being suckled). Everything is shared equally between twins. Parents of twins are not supposed to weep lest the twins die, and for this reason they do not attend distant funerals. If one twin dies, the name of the survivor is changed from *Ayini* or *Ateya* to *Azure* (tail) or *Abane* (bangle). Female twins are considered as *nyere*, and may not marry the same man, but on the marriage of one, the other sister follows the bride to her husband's home, only to be sent back with presents. A twin must never be abused or called *Kyinkyiriga* (Fairy), or even told, 'You are a twin', or it will die.

Atule. A child born feet first is called *Atule*; it is considered unlucky (perhaps because so dangerous), and its parents may never again eat of the second bean crop. Both mother and child have to be treated with medicine.

Child Born at Mother-in-law's Teya (*Town*). Among the Nankanse, if a child happens to be born in its father's mother-in-law's village, the father of the child has to give his wife's people certain presents—a hoe, beer, guinea-fowls—to 'take away the blood' (*va zem*). As we shall see later, among other tribes such an infant is 'stolen' by its natural father and carried back from the village of the maternal uncle to its own father's clan settlement.[1]

Puberty Rites, as exemplified in the incision ceremony, have been fully described. This operation is performed among the majority of the tribes, including Kusase, Moshi, Kasena, Isala, Lobi, Dagari, Builsa, Konkomba, Bimoba, but not always at puberty. The 'cutting' is often done shortly after birth. Such details will be noted when a particular tribe comes up for investigation. The Nankanse, as we have seen, do not now circumcise, although there is the tradition of some at least of the clans having once done so (see p. 235).

The account, already given, of a father telling his son about the clan totem,[2] although an event apparently unaccompanied by any special ceremonial, is almost certainly of the nature of an initiation rite. Membership of a clan is thus acquired, I believe, by an artificial rather than a natural process depending upon parentage, as is the acquisition of the *sōō* kinship. To speak of a child 'inheriting' its clan from its father or from its mother is confusing and leads us to form wrong conclusions. I shall refer to this subject again later.

Marriage. This has been dealt with in the preceding chapter and in the early pages of this volume.

Funeral Customs. Chapters XI–XIV have dealt with this last *rite de passage*. The following notes amplify what has already been written on this subject. The funeral custom of a leper has been described. In the case of a person dying of smallpox, the body is buried without any ceremony in the kitchen midden (see Fig. 28). 'A person who dies of smallpox has disgraced his family.' A shrine may not be made for him, nor any sacrifice, after death; the spirit may not even become any one's *segere* (guardian spirit).

A man who has been killed by an arrow does not have a shrine built for him, but he may become *Yini*[3] to his son, in which case the shrine, whatever form it takes, is kept on the flat roof. Such a spirit cannot become *segere* to any child. A person killed by a snake-bite, a suicide who has used an arrow to kill himself, a witch who has died after undergoing an ordeal, is taken naked to the grave and there is no public mourning.

Funeral Contributions: these are shared out among those attending

---

[1] See p. 418. [2] See p. 238.

[3] I do not know, and have not been able to find out, if *Yini* in such a case, where the spirit would appear to be a human one, is the same as the *Yini* shrines already described. See p. 270.

FIG. 28. The kitchen midden at Paga

FIG. 29. The entrance to the grave is by a bottle-neck
circular hole

the funeral. They consist of cowries, sheep, goats, fowls, &c. Sons-in-law who fail to bring the necessary contributions (*dem-kure-bono*) to a parent-in-law's funeral for the deceased 'to rest the head upon', would be liable to lose their wives, 'who would not return again after the funeral to their husband's compounds'.

The Kumpio *in Funeral Customs*: the *kumpio* is the special calabash in which a woman keeps her valuables, beads, &c., and certain things to be used at her funeral custom. It is also considered as the shrine of the *sia*, the soul of its owner, during her lifetime. An eldest daughter must never on any account look into her mother's *kumpio* as long as her mother is alive. She will do so after her mother's death, as will also the eldest son. This custom has its counterpart in the case of the male parent, after whose death his eldest son and daughter ceremonially look into his grain-store. The male's soul is considered, during his lifetime, as frequenting this, as also his *tapɔ* (leather bag) into which it is also forbidden for the eldest child of either sex to pry.

When a woman dies, the private property found in her *kumpio* is shared among her daughters and her sons' wives. Inside the string net, *zaleŋa*, in which the *kumpio* is kept, are also a *wula*, calabash, and a *kaleŋa*, pot. The former is a specially made small calabash used as a cover for the *kumpio* and not for eating or drinking out of. Other calabashes for ordinary use are piled on top, white ones for drinking from, red ones for eating out of. A *kaleŋa* is a red pot, not used except at its owner's funeral custom, as described presently.

The *kumpio*, *wula*, and *kaleŋa* are carried by the deceased's eldest daughter to her late mother's home. When taking them thither the daughter may not speak or allow the things to shake about. She carries them on her head, resting on a new *tesunko* (grass-woven head-rest). The husband of the dead woman will kill a sheep or goat and send the meat to his parents-in-law. They then make beer (a three-days' process), and the third night at midnight, and in complete silence, save for weeping, the *kumpio*, *wula*, and *kaleŋa* are carried by the eldest daughter to the cross-roads. Here a branch of a shea butter tree with three forks at the end is set down exactly where the paths converge. The *kumpio* is set upon this branch and smashed, then the *wula* is broken up, and last of all the *kaleŋa* pot, and the fragments are heaped together and left there.

A point that has not hitherto been noted is the breaking down of the mud shrine—which was the 'room' of a spirit—after the death of the person who owned that shrine. This is done after the final funeral custom has been held. During the interval between the death of the man who owned the shrine and the final obsequies, the spirit in the shrine may not be consulted.

'When a man has a *bakologo* (a soothsaying shrine) and dies, his successor will break down the old shrine after the funeral custom is over. The hands of his father have departed, therefore he must begin with his own hands and build up a new one, beginning only with a very small mound which replaces the old one, on the very day that the latter is broken down.'

Before the old shrine is demolished, the following words are addressed to the spirit of the late owner:

'My father, receive this water, depart with your bad hands, that I again may set up my own clay mound.' The clay of the old mound is used to remodel the new one.

Ordinary *bagere* (shrines) are broken down in a similar manner and rebuilt.

'A *Yini* shrine is not broken down.' This is because its composition does not lend itself to such usage. The clay mound, which is the striking feature of most shrines, but is really only the room, as it were, for the spirit which is really in the axe or bangle, is not a feature of the *Yini bagere*, perhaps because God does not, like a human spirit, need a room.

Graves: a grave is euphemistically known as a man's *deo* (rooms, dwelling-quarters). The Nankanse do not bury their dead inside the compound walls, as do so many of these tribes.

'The burial-ground is where the first ancestor had his compound.'

The entrance to the grave is by a bottle-neck circular hole (see Fig. 29), after which the grave widens out, the whole being not unlike a decanter. The entrance is closed up with a pot which is then covered over with clay. A grave may be opened from time to time to permit other bodies to be interred.

'When a man is old enough to have a cow killed for him at his funeral custom, he will have a new grave dug for him; otherwise he will be buried in an old grave with others.'